HELMETS AND BODY ARMOR IN
MODERN WARFARE

British Standard

British (Variant)

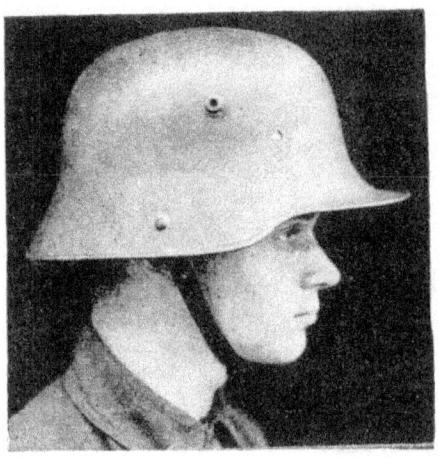
German Standard

American Model, No. 5A

American Model, No. 2A

Belgian, Visored

HELMETS, 1916-1918. STANDARD

French Standard

American Model, No. 4

American Model, No. 10

American Model, "Liberty Bell"

American Model, No. 8

French Dunand Model

AND EXPERIMENTAL MODELS

THE METROPOLITAN MUSEUM OF ART

HELMETS AND BODY ARMOR IN MODERN WARFARE

BY

BASHFORD DEAN, Ph.D.

CURATOR OF ARMOR, METROPOLITAN MUSEUM OF ART
FORMERLY MAJOR OF ORDNANCE, U. S. A., IN CHARGE OF ARMOR UNIT,
EQUIPMENT SECTION, ENGINEERING DIVISION, WASHINGTON
FORMERLY CHAIRMAN OF THE COMMITTEE ON HELMETS AND BODY ARMOR,
ENGINEERING DIVISION OF THE NATIONAL RESEARCH COUNCIL

"Effort should be continued towards the development of a satisfactory form of personal body armor."—General Pershing, 1917.

The Naval & Military Press Ltd

Published by

The Naval & Military Press Ltd
Unit 5 Riverside, Brambleside
Bellbrook Industrial Estate
Uckfield, East Sussex
TN22 1QQ England

Tel: +44 (0)1825 749494

www.naval-military-press.com
www.nmarchive.com

In reprinting in facsimile from the original, any imperfections are inevitably reproduced and the quality may fall short of modern type and cartographic standards.

PREFACE

THE present book aims to consider the virtues and failings of helmets and body armor in modern warfare. To this end it brings together materials collected from all accessible sources; it shows the kinds of armor which each nation has been using in the Great War, what practical tests they will resist, of what materials they are made, and what they have done in saving life and limb. As an introduction to these headings there has now been added a section which deals with ancient armor; this enables us to contrast the old with the new and to indicate, in clearer perspective, what degree of success the latest armor may achieve in its special field.

The results of our inquiry will show:

(1) That the helmet has been adopted as part of the regular military equipment of many nations.

(2) That helmets and body armor have been found, in broad averages, of distinct advantage to the wearers.

(3) That body armor, in spite of the protection which it affords, finds little favor with the soldier. For numerous reasons, he would rather take his chances of injury.

(4) That effort should be made, none the less, to demonstrate more clearly the protective value of body armor, to improve its material and design, and to reduce to a minimum the discomfort which will always be experienced by its wearer,—in a word, to meet the objections to the use of armor which have been brought up on the sides both of theory and of practice.

In preparing the following pages I have sought and secured aid from many sources. I am most of all indebted to the Department of War of the United States, for access to documents and materials as well as for permission to make use of them in publication. The theme of the present studies touched matters of no little practical importance; the Secretary of War, Mr. Baker, as well as his colleagues, Secretaries Crowell and Keppel, were pleased to show a personal interest in them; as did also General

Pershing, who examined critically a number of models of helmets and body armor which were submitted to him. My former chiefs, Generals C. C. Williams, E. T. Babbit and J. H. Rice, considered the problems of personal armor attentively and I owe them my thanks for their sympathetic support. For help in many directions I am indebted to other members of the Department: to Colonel Perry Osborn, of the General Staff; to my colleagues in the Ordnance, Colonels Schimelfenig, McGregor and Askew; to Captains Simonds, Mainzinger and Peebles and to Lieutenant Kienbusch. Especially I record the valuable contributions to the subject by Professor Henry M. Howe and our fellow-members of the helmet committee of the Council of National Research (page 211). Nor have I called in vain upon steel and manufacturing experts, among whom I mention Mr. A. Aigeltinger, Dr. G. W. Sargent, Mr. H. W. Baker of the Universal Rolling Mills, the Messrs. Ford and Mr. William Smith of the Ford Motor Company and Sir Robert Hadfield.

During my studies on the armor problem abroad (1917-1918) I received suggestions and critical help from the members of the general staffs of British and French armies; through their friendly care I had the opportunity of meeting armor specialists and of securing data on experimental work and production. Among those officers to whom I am especially indebted are: in Paris, Intendant-General Adrian, Commandants Le Maistre and Polack of the Bureau of Inventions; in London, Captain C. H. Ley of the Ministry of Munitions, together with Captain I. St. C. Rose and Captain Leeming of the Trench Warfare Division; also to Mr. John McIntosh, director general of the Munitions Equipment, and to Mr. W. A. Taylor in the Experimental Division of the Munitions Ministry to whose work I refer frequently in the following pages.

The present introduction would be seriously incomplete if I failed to bear witness to the more than generous cooperation in this field shown by the Metropolitan Museum of Art, from its Trustees, its President, Mr. Robert W. de Forest, and its Director, Mr. Edward Robinson, down the line. To the members of the Committee on Educational Work, to Dr. Henry S. Pritchett and Mr. Charles W. Gould, I owe my thanks for their interest in the present work. Among my associates in the Museum to whom I am indebted I should name especially Mr. Alexander McMillan Welch and Miss V. Isabel Miller and those who labored early and late in the Armor Workshop, Messrs. Tachaux, Bartel, Tinsley and Merkert.

In fact, it should be recorded that when the matter of helmets was taken up by the United States shortly after the war began and when collections of ancient armor became of especial value to the Government's experts, who were seeking to examine distinctive models, the Metropolitan Museum placed at the disposal of the War Department not only its collection of armor (which, thanks to the Riggs Benefaction, has become one of the most important extant), but also its staff of armor specialists and its armor repair shop to aid in developing and making whatever models were needed. Thus it came about that within the museum numerous types of helmets and body armor were prepared which, copied in proof metal, were later sent to the front. Hence the present volume bears, in a degree, upon the Museum's activities.

That such a work, moreover, can appear today as a publication of a museum of art is an evidence of the wide-reaching field of activity covered by a modern institution. For, at an earlier time, a museum would have considered armor only as objects of artistic value. Nevertheless, in any phase of the study of armor it becomes often difficult to distinguish between the aesthetic and the practical.* In olden times there is no question that the beauty of his armor helped the soldier to bear the burden. And in modern warfare it is more than probable that no armor would have been accepted widely had it not possessed certain aesthetic elements. The helmet, for example, worn by the French in the present war would never have gained its extraordinary success had it not been attractive in its lines,—designed, by the way, by no less a personage than Edouard Detaille, whose pictures of *beaux soldats* have for generations been familiar to all. Nor would the

---

* Classification of the two principal lines in which armor may be studied objectively.
    Utility
        Ballistic Value
            Metal
            Construction
        Weight
        Comfort in wearing
            Security in support.
    Beauty
        Form
        Surfaces, with shades and shadows
        Colors,—given by heat, "pickling" processes, paints or varnishes, overlays of various metals
        Ornament
            Etched, engraved, embossed, applied, punched, nielloed, damascened.

extremely simple British helmet have been accepted generally and promptly had it not an especial set and swing of its own.

BASHFORD DEAN.

Metropolitan Museum of Art,
July 20, 1919.

TABLE OF CONTENTS

	PAGE
Introduction: Including an Outline of the Earlier Use of Armor	25
I. The Early Use of Armor in the Present War	64
II. Armor as a Protection against Missiles of Low and Middle Velocity	68
(a) Statistics which Demonstrate the Usefulness of Modern Armor, Notably the Helmet. The Medical Viewpoint	69
(b) Frequency in the Location of Wounds and Its Bearing upon the Armor Problem	70
III. Foreign Types of Modern Helmets and Body Armor. Their Origin and Fate	74
(A) French	74
(B) English	110
(C) German (and Austrian)	133
(D) Italian	148
(E) Belgian	156
(F) Portuguese	160
(G) Slavic	161
(H) Swiss	163
(I) Spanish	171
(J) Japanese	172
IV. Shields and Their Use during the Present War	178
V. American Helmets and Body Armor	193
VI. Steel Used in Making Modern Armor. Can Other Metal than Steel Be Used for this Purpose, *e.g.*, Aluminum Alloys?	270
VII. Soft Armor (*i.e.*, Armor of Textiles), Its Beginning, Development and Possible Value	282
VIII. Concerning Tests of Modern Armor	294
IX. What Should Be Done to Improve Helmets and Body Armor at the Present Time? Summary and Conclusions	313
Index	319

LIST OF FIGURES

FIGURE		PAGE
Frontispiece	A dozen types of modern helmets	
1	European armor and its development during a period of a thousand years	28
2	Complete armor for man and horse, 1508, prepared for the Emperor Maximilian I	29
3	Model wearing costume worn under chain mail shirt and cap (coiffe)	31
3A	Model wearing chain mail of the fourteenth century (Mail in Metropolitan Museum of Art)	31
4	Half-armor, tested by musket ball, worn by the Duc de Guise († 1583). Weight 94 pounds. Artillery Museum, Paris	32
5	Armor of Pedro II of Portugal. About 1700. Weight 43 pounds. Shows marks of testing bullets on reinforcing plate for corselet. Specimen in Metropolitan Museum of Art	33
6	Three-quarters suit of armor of "proof," showing mark of testing bullet (near right shoulder plate). Weight 84 pounds. About 1620; believed to have been worn by the Marquis de Bassompièrre. Riggs Collection, Metropolitan Museum of Art	35
6A	Rear view of same armor; backplate showing testing mark	35
7	Stages in making a helmet after the ancient fashion	37
7A	Casque dated 1543 and signed by the Milanese artist, Philip de Negroli	39
8	The various kinds of helmets and their developmental sequence	47
9	Model showing costume worn about 1510 under fluted (Maximilian) armor; note laces or "points" used for supporting the defenses of the arm and leg	49
9A	Fluted armor of 1510. Suit weighing 56 pounds, exhibited in Metropolitan Museum of Art	49
10	Half-armor worn about 1760 by Jeffrey Lord Amherst; after painting by Sir Joshua Reynolds	53
11	Gorget of Captain Fanning, American Revolution. About half actual size	54

FIGURE		PAGE
12	Gorget, as last piece of armor worn; appearing in the Dickinson portrait of Washington, about 1772	55
13	Sapper's leathern helmet, eighteenth-nineteenth century. Specimen in Tower of London	56
14	Sapper's helmet, middle of nineteenth century. Specimen in Tower of London	56
15	Body armor used in American Civil War, 1862-1864; specimen preserved in Museum Military Institute, Richmond, Va.	57
16	French breast defense (jazeran) used during the war of 1870	59
17	Rifle-proof armor worn by the Australian bandit, Ned Kelly, 1894	61
18	Steel calotte used as cap-lining—French (Adrian) model, 1915	65
19	French steel helmet-lining (calotte), shown in position	66
20	Standard French helmet, 1916, shown in profile	75
21	Standard helmet shown in profile (in dotted lines) over French fireman's helmet	75
22	Standard helmet shown in profile (in dotted lines) over French dragoon's helmet	75
23	Lining of standard French helmet	76
24	Standard French helmet, Adrian model, 1916, showing steps in manufacture	77
25	French helmet, experimental, with concentric flutings on crown	83
26	British standard helmet, experimental model, having bosses stamped on crown	84
27	Revised model of French helmet, experimental handmade model (A)	85
28	Revised model of French helmet, experimental handmade model (B)	86
29	Revised model of French helmet, experimental handmade model (C)	87
30	Revised model of French helmet, experimental handmade model (D)	87
31	Siege helmet, French, 1916-1917	88
32	Experimental design for sentinel's heavy helmet. Model by MM. Dunand	88
33	French experimental visor, Polack model	88
34	French standard helmet with experimental visor. Early Polack model	88
35	Polack visor. Early experimental form arranged to	

FIGURE		PAGE
	be attached by elastic band to side of standard French helmet	89
36	Polack visor. Early experimental form. Attaches to standard helmet and rotates into position . .	89
37	Polack visor. Early experimental form, arranged to be slipped over brim of standard helmet . .	90
38	Polack visor adapted to experimental headpiece of similar type to one shown in Fig. 28 . . .	90
39	Polack visor, experimental model, adapted to brim of standard French helmet. Shown also in rotated position, when not in use	90
40	Experimental form of Polack visor, arranged for fitting head below or above brim of standard French helmet	91
41	Polack visor arranged with standard French helmet (1917-1918)	92
42	Polack visor arranged with new experimental model French helmet (1917-1918)	93
43	Polack visor arranged with new experimental model French helmet (1917-1918)	94, 95
44	Dunand helmet, hand-made model, 1916-1917 .	97
45	Dunand revised model, 1917-1918. Hand-made .	99
46	Dunand helmet model, 1918, in ballistic metal .	100
47	Helm of Sir Giles Capel, 1514 (Metropolitan Museum of Art), showing visor to which Dunand design is similar	101
48	Dunand helmet, showing result of tests . .	101
49	Early model of Dunand visor, attachable to brim of standard helmet	102
50-59	Various types of experimental visors designed by the MM. Dunand, 1916-1917	103
60	Standard French helmet to which is adjusted an early model of folding visor	104
61	Studies of perforations of visor: the large dotted circle represents the pupil of the eye	105
62	Section of Polack visor showing the arrangement of planes of the eye-plates	105
63	Sentinel's heavy face-guard	105
64	Abdominal defense—French, Adrian model, 1916 .	107
65	Abdominal defense with tassets and sporran plate. French, Adrian model, 1916-1917 . . .	107
66	Leg defenses, French, 1916-1917	109
67	British necklet lined with silk and covered in khaki. Wire frame support for collar, 1915-1916 . .	111

FIGURE		PAGE
68	British "Chemico" body shield, 1916-1917	112
69	Berkeley experimental jazeran, 1916-1917	113
70	"Franco-British cuirass," 1916-1917	114
71	"Wilkinson Safety Service Jacket." Detail indicates result of test	115
72	British "Dayfield body shield," heavy model, 1916	115
73	Dayfield body shield, 1916-1917 model; here also appears the silk-lined neck defense	116
74	Dayfield body shield, simple model	116
75	Metal foundation of simpler type of Dayfield body shield, 1917	117
76	British "Featherweight" shield. A shoulder defense appears as a detached piece	118
77	British "Best" body shield, showing front, lining of front and backplate	119
78	British body armor. "B. E. F." model, 1917-1918	120
79	British "Portobank" armored waistcoat	121
80	British Portobank body shield. 80B gives detail of construction	122
81	"Star" body shield	123
82	British standard model body armor, 1917-1918. The detached piece represents the metal foundation of the breastplate	124
83	British breastplate, standard model, 1918	125
84	"Corelli" body shield	126
85	"Roneo-Miris" body shield	127
86	British standard helmet showing indentation caused by glancing machine gun bullet	129
87	British helmet viewed from below, showing chin-strap and lining	130
88	Early experimental model of face defense. British, 1915-1916	131
89	British helmet provided with chain mail visor, 1917	132
90	German helmet showing sniper's frontal plate in position	135
91	Frontal plate detached	135
92	Lining of German helmet	136
93	Buckle and chin-strap metal fastener of German helmet	137
94	Siege or sentinel's helmet. German, 1917 model	139
95	German sniper's head shield, 1916-1917	140
96	German helmet, 1918 model (variant?)	141
97	German helmet, 1918 model, as used by sniper. Camouflaged green, buff and white	142

FIGURE		PAGE
98	German heavy breastplate, viewed from without and from within	143
99	German breastplate. Improvements suggested, 1917	146
100	German machine gun squad armed with new model helmet and heavy body armor, 1918	147
101	Italian helmet, also body shield, Ansaldo model, 1918	148
102	Italian helmet, heavy model, 1917	149
103	Italian body armor. Weights represented, 1918	150
104	Italian helmet and body armor, Ansaldo model	150
105	Italian body armor shown dismounted and used as rifle shield. Ansaldo model	151
106	Italian body armor, 1917 model	152
107	Italian body armor, Ansaldo model, shown carried on back of soldier. Note also Italian helmet in rear view	153
108	Italian body armor. Inner view	154
109	Italian body armor. Shown in use as rifle shield	154
110	"Fariselli" armored waistcoat, 1917	154
111	Italian body armor—"Gorgeno-Collaye" model, 1916-1917	154
112	Italo-British "Military" body armor	155
113	Italian trench shield used as body armor	157
114	Italian shoulder defense	157
115	Belgian helmet. Experimental model, 1917	158
116	Belgian helmet. Result of tests	159
117	Portuguese helmet	161
118	Slavic helmet (Polish), 1917	162
119	Russian breastplate. The section shows (in black) a core of ballistic steel: the covering and lining are of heavy silk matting	163
120	Experimental Swiss helmet. LePlatenier model, 1917	164
121	Similar model with shallower visor, 1918	164
122	Experimental Swiss helmet. LePlatenier model, 1917-1918	165
123	Experimental visor in place (Swiss)	166
124	Swiss helmet. Standard model, 1918	169
125	Swiss helmet compared with American helmet model No. 5—the latter represented in dotted lines	169
126	Swiss standard helmet in process of manufacture	170
127	Standard Swiss helmet shown in use by machine gunners who are wearing their gas masks	171
128	Helmet suggested for the Spanish army	173
129	Japanese breastplate showing marks of seven testing bullets, eighteenth century	174

FIGURE		PAGE
130	Japanese breast defense of triple-linked chain mail	175
130A, 130B	Body defense: Chiba model, 1905	177
130C	Portable shield: Chiba model, 1908	177
130D	Mantlet mounted on wheels: Chiba model, 1915	177
131	French (Daigre) shield and body armor. Model 1917	179
132	Sapper's mantlet, nineteenth century. In Tower of London	181
133	German trench shield, 1916. (Similar shields were manufactured in England, France and the United States)	182
134	German trench shield, 1916-1917 model	183
135	German trench shield, 1917-1918 model	184
136	Belgian trench shield. American manufacture	184
137	Russian trench shield. American manufacture	185
138	Mobile shields. French. One-man type. Used in wire cutting, 1917	188
139	Mobile shield, or one-man tank. Used in wire cutting. English model, 1917	188
140	Mobile shield for five riflemen. British experimental model, 1917	189
141	Mobile shield for nine riflemen. American experimental model	191
142	Mobile shield or "pedrail" for machine gunner and riflemen. British model, experimental, 1917	191
143	British-American helmet. Completed shell with attached rim and chin-strap loops, in condition in which it leaves the manufacturer's plant	197
144	British-American helmet in process of manufacture, shown in background at the right. The double-action press stamps out the helmet in a single "draw." Budd Mfg. Co., Philadelphia	198
145	British-American helmet in process of manufacture. The plate is being "blanked out" so as to form the helmet rim; in another part of the picture the thin separate metal rims are being spot-welded in place. Budd Mfg. Co., Philadelphia	199
146	British-American helmet in process of manufacture. Helmet shell, metal rim, chin-strap loops and rivets ready to be put together	200
147-148	Test of a plate of helmet steel. The corner of the plate is given a punch-mark; if the metal cracks, the plate is rejected	200
149	Diagram showing the mode of tightening the new chin-strap; also the new buckle-hook is pictured, by

FIGURE		PAGE
	means of which the chin-strap can be "broken" when it is passed under the tube of the gas mask	201
150, 151A, 151B, 151C	Cartridges and bullets used in testing British-American helmets	202
152	British-American helmet. Assembling. The helmets are shown arranged in rows on metal racks, front and back, ready to be immersed in the paint trough shown in right of picture. Ford Mfg. Co., Philadelphia	203
153	British-American helmet. Assembling. Freshly painted helmets being passed along over drip-boards	203
154	British-American helmet. Assembling. Freshly painted helmets about to be given a coating of sawdust in the sprinkling box shown in the foreground	205
155	British-American helmet. Assembling. Freshly painted helmets being given a coating of sawdust	205
156	British-American helmet. Assembling. Shells arranged on racks about to be passed into the heated drying chamber	206
157	British-American helmet. Assembling. Helmet shells being passed down an inclined plane to tables where linings and chin-straps are put in place	206
158	Lining of British-American helmet. From below	207
159	British-American helmets being packed for shipment	208
160	Cases of British-American helmets passed along a track for storage and shipment	209
160A	Cases of British-American helmets ready for shipment	209
161	Helmet model No. 2 "deep salade." This helmet protects the head more completely than any modern model hitherto manufactured	211
162	American experimental helmet model No. 5	213
163	Lining of preceding helmet	214
164	Improved lining of experimental helmet model No. 5. A sweat-band of light steel replaces one of cowhide	215
165	Helmet model No. 5. Stages in manufacture	216
166	Experimental helmet model No. 6	217
167	American experimental helmet model No. 8	219
168	Earlier model of helmet No. 8	220
169	Experimental helmet model No. 8. Result of test by pistol bullet at 800 foot seconds. Outline of head within helmet is shown by dotted line. Present helmet bears marks of six testing bullets	221
170	Light steel frame for carrying lining of helmet No. 8	221

20 HELMETS AND BODY ARMOR

FIGURE		PAGE
171	Carrier of helmet model No. 8, showing lining pads or tabs	222
172	Section of lining-carrier showing arrangement of tabs for head sizes 7 and under, or 7⅛ and over	222
173	American sentinel's or machine gunner's helmet. Experimental model No. 7, 1918	223
174	American sentinel's or machine gunner's helmet. Experimental model No. 9, 1918	223
175	American experimental helmet model No. 10	225
176	Experimental helmet model for American tank operator, shown with and without detachable padded-silk curtain and visor, guarding against lead splash	226
177	Thin steel scales arranged as substitute for the silk curtain of tank operator's experimental helmet	227
178	American helmet. Aviator's model, No. 14, 1918	229
179	American helmet. Aviator's model, No. 14A, 1918	230
180	American helmet. Aviator's model, No. 15, 1918	231
181	Liberty Bell helmet. Fall, 1918. Shown over profile (in dotted line) of American experimental helmet model No. 4	232
182	Splinter goggles and face defense. British, 1917	235
183	Splinter goggles, American. Reproduction of French design, 1918	235
184	Splinter goggles. Variation of model shown in 183. Manufactured through Arthur Dunn of Quincy, Ill.	235
185	Splinter goggles having single visual slit. Model by Thomas C. Harris, Washington, D. C.	235
186	Eye-shield. Wilmer model, adaptable to British-American helmet	236
187	Wilmer model eye defense. The latter figure showing a marginal supporting cushion of sponge rubber	236
188	Face defense or bavière. American experimental model, 1918	237
188A	Result of test on foregoing face-guard, with pistol bullet at 850 foot seconds	237
188B	Inner view of face-guard	238
189	Defense for neck and shoulders. Experimental, 1918	239
189A	Inner view of same defense showing cushion of sponge rubber	240
190	Similar necklet, showing result of pistol bullet at 850 foot seconds	240
191	Shoulder defense, American experimental model, 1918	241
192	Brewster body armor, 1917-1918	243

FIGURE		PAGE
193	American experimental model of sentinel's heavy armor	245
194	American sentinel's armor showing cushions of sponge rubber	246
195	American sentinel's armor shown with sentinel's heavy helmet, 1917-1918	247
196	American light body armor, 1917-1918. Experimental model. Also arm defenses and British-American helmet or American helmet model No. 5	248, 249
197	Light body armor. Inner view of laminated breastplate. A heavy cushion of sponge rubber lines the uppermost plate	250
198	Light body armor. Laminated backplate of experimental model, 1918	251
199	Light body armor. Experimental backplate. American model, pressed in single piece	252
200	Inner view of light body armor, 1918, showing cushions of sponge rubber	253
201	Haversack or box respirator of gas mask, the back of which is reinforced by plates of steel. American model. Fall, 1918	254
202	Drawing provided by British Trench Warfare Division (Captain Rose), showing area protected by armored respirator of gas mask. Fall, 1918	254
203	Drawing provided by British Trench Warfare Division (Captain Rose), showing armored back of box respirator of gas mask. Fall, 1918	254
204	Body defense or jazeran made up of overlapping scales of manganese steel. Above in middle of picture a separate scale is shown which has resisted the impact of automatic bullet at 850 foot seconds	255
205	Scaled body defense. As actually worn	256
206	Body defense formed of overlapping plates of manganese steel combined with scales as in Fig. 205. The plates of the breast defense slide together, making possible free movements of shoulders. A jazeran of this type is pictured in 206C, which has been tested by automatic bullet at 850 foot seconds. While in this test scales became detached, no bullet succeeded in penetrating	257
207	Body defense of small plates and links. Model of Columbia Steel Tank Co., Kansas City	259
208	Experimental defense—Fraser collapsible breast shield, 1918	261

FIGURE		PAGE
209	Shin-guards. American experimental model, 1917	263
210	Complete leg defenses—American experimental model, 1917	264
211	Arm defenses, American experimental model, 1918	265
212	Armored aeroplane. Armored areas represented by diagonal dotted lines. German model, 1918	267
213	Aviator's armored chair. Experimental model, American, 1918	269
214	Sections of dies for pressing British-American helmet model. Faulty model shown in 214A	277
215	Armor of cocoa fiber. Gilbert Islands. Early nineteenth century. American Museum of Natural History	283
216	Lining for helmet (or for chain mail hood). Swiss, fifteenth century. From Civic Armory in Lucerne. Riggs Collection, Metropolitan Museum of Art	284
217-219	Arm defenses, woven and tufted, sixteenth century. German 217 from altar painting in Stuttgart by Elinger 218 from painting in Munich by Anton von Worms 219 from sculpture by Veit Stoss, 1500, Nuremberg	285
220	Armor of woven material, stuffed and quilted. Russian. About 1560	286
221-222	Detail of armor ("buttonhole" jacks) of woven material, sixteenth century	287
223-224	Fibrous materials of various types arranged between bands of tissue for testing purposes	288
225	Silk-lined body defense. Taylor model, 1916-1917	289
226	Ballistic proof silken cloth or matting, Zeglin pattern, 1917	290
227	Zeglin silken matting (bullet proof) in process of being woven at the Crompton-Knowles loom, Cleveland, Ohio	291
228	Zeglin silken body defense	293
229	Similar defense arranged with reinforcing plate of ballistic alloy	293
230-232	Three breastplate models in which similar curvatures of surface are indicated by similar types of shading 230 Breastplate of 1540 231 Experimental heavy breastplate for sentinel, American 232 German heavy body armor	303
233	Cylindrical shield (white central circle) balanced on	

FIGURE		PAGE
	ball bearings. The line A B represents the course of bullet	306
234	A spring slip or plate to the end of which a bit of steel is fastened, and a section (A) showing a series of such spring plates arranged one behind the other. The course of a bullet is shown in the line A B	306
235	Shield formed of bent-over metallic plates. Joubert model, 1915-1916	307
236	Soldiers, one with and one without camouflaged body gear	309
237-239	Anatomical diagrams furnished by Trench Warfare Section, London (Captain Rose); these indicate "areas of danger" and tabulate "entry wounds" in chest and abdomen, 1918	315

INTRODUCTION

HELMETS and body armor are usually considered as objects beautiful, rather than useful. They are exhibited in museums, in halls hung with tapestries, beside faience, ivories and enamels of olden times. Some of them were designed by artists whose names are highest of all in the history of art,—Raphael, Leonardo, Donatello, Holbein, Michael Angelo—and those who actually made and decorated the armor were masters hardly less distinguished. Certainly in their day they were paid the highest honors. Serafino di Brescia, armorer of Francis I, was received at court on the same footing with Titian: the Milanese Missaglia lived in princely splendor, and Seusenhofer, the helmsmith, was one of the intimates of the knightly Maximilian.

It is, then, from the viewpoint of artistic excellence that armor has largely been treated, especially as to its decoration and its various forms. Its technical side is little known, and few there are, even among specialists, who have considered how difficult armor was to make, and how time consuming,—for a suit of armor of high quality might cost its maker years of labor. And, particularly, little is known as to its usefulness in combat, which, none the less, was the main if not the only reason for its existence.

Armor, in a word, has been studied as a dead language or, better perhaps, as the bones of a fossil animal, which the anatomist examines attentively and from which he is led to explain the habits and capabilities of the animal itself. Nevertheless, there are clearly other paths leading to a knowledge of armor which deserve to be more carefully followed, and two of these, especially, guide us in practical directions. One of them points the way to early references, which at the best are scanty and difficult of access, but which tell quite accurately what armor could do and how the early masters gained their results,—a path opened up delightfully for us by M. Ch. Buttin* in his studies of early armor of proof. Following the second path we can actually test pieces of ancient armor and then compare the results with ballistic studies on modern "armor plate": continuing this

* "*Notes sur les armures à l'épreuve.*" Annecy, 1901, 100 pp.

comparison we can then submit the old material to metallurgical examination, chemical and physical (including microscopical), and thereby gain definite information as to how the ancient steel was produced. (See hereafter, page 270.)

From early records we can clearly show that armor yielded excellent results in its day, and that during many centuries it was sought eagerly by soldiers of all classes. We learn that the prince, no less than the peasant, was quite willing to bear the discomfort of wearing it, under all conditions, even in the heat of Palestine. Indirectly we know that had it not been useful it would not have appeared in numbers in every European field of battle from early times until the epoch of Napoleon. Moreover, we discover that it was used not by adults merely, but by young as well, for many suits of armor are preserved which were made for children.* So important, indeed, was armor in the history of from 1400 to 1700 that by its means we could still give a convincing summary of the cultural and artistic changes which took place in European civilization if all other sources of human knowledge were wiped away.†

The reason for the present lack of information as to the practical nature of armor is not far to seek. Little was written systematically upon this theme in olden times, and later, when armor disappeared from general use, little was remembered about it. That it would again appear as part of the regular equipment of a soldier seemed to nearly everyone a possibility infinitely remote; for, it was reasoned, if armor were discarded even in the seventeenth century, in days of primitive gunpowder, how could any form

---

* See also Ch. ffoulkes, "The Armorer and his Craft." Methuen, London, 1912.

† That this statement may be given more definitely we point out that arms and armor unquestionably furnish the best expression of the art and the science of the metal worker of the Middle Ages and of the Renaissance: armor includes in its decoration, gilding, silvering, tinning, damascene, niello, even jewel-setting: its ornamental designs explain to us stages in the development of religious and civil customs, including pageants and sports,—not forgetting falconry. It furnished also an important medium for the art of painting: its enriched variants copy for us types of secular apparel of each period; by means of etching it pictures the stuff of which the costumes were made; it also offered an excellent medium for ornament, with lettering and borders. In its mounting it summarizes the textile art of various periods: here appear tissues from the commonest to the most costly, including galloon and fringes, and with these are adequate materials for the study of the art of the leather worker. The size of armor gives us, finally, convincing data as to the state of physical development among the men of many nations.

of armor reappear in warfare when high explosives were used? Hence the field of the practical nature of helmets and body armor was abandoned to an occasional antiquarian. Nevertheless, as in so many other phases of the Great War, armor *did* reappear in use, and thereupon there arose at once an interest, and a very practical one, in the discarded work of the armorer. Questions were speedily raised by the general staff of every warring country as to what helmets and body armor could do in protecting the soldier, what were their best forms and how they could be most speedily prepared? It may be safely said that there was not an important collection of ancient armor in Europe which was not visited by commissions, collectively or individually, in an effort to learn from the experience of the past.

Before proceeding to the already highly developed field of modern armor, let us review briefly the work of the ancient armorer* from the viewpoint of its practical value. This aspect of the subject, as we have noted, is surprisingly little known, not merely to the student of recent armor but to the antiquarian as well. The modern expert, as I have found, has often the belief that ancient armor was but a semi-barbarous defense, serviceable only against arrows, slings and swords. The antiquarian, on the other hand, is apt to forget that its primary virtue was serviceability and that the keenest minds had studied it from this standpoint from the earliest times.

Let us now attempt to answer several questions:

(A) What kinds of armor were early used?
(B) Was armor actually an important means of saving life and limb?
(C) How was it made?
(D) How was it tested?
(E) How heavy, irksome and even dangerous was it to wear?
(F) What in summary was its use in later times but prior to the Great War?

(A) *What kinds of armor were early used?*

Let us refer to Fig. 1, which illustrates the various types of armor used in Europe during a thousand years. In early times we see a jacket of padded hide discarded in favor of a coat of scales; and this in turn give place to a garment of ring or chain mail worn over a padded costume. Chain mail more or less complete was used for centuries,—it was worn,

* For critical help in preparing this section I am greatly indebted to Mr. Charles W. Gould.

28   HELMETS AND BODY ARMOR

not uncommonly indeed, down to colonial days in America, but nearly always more or less enclosed in armor of plate. Plate armor was most elab-

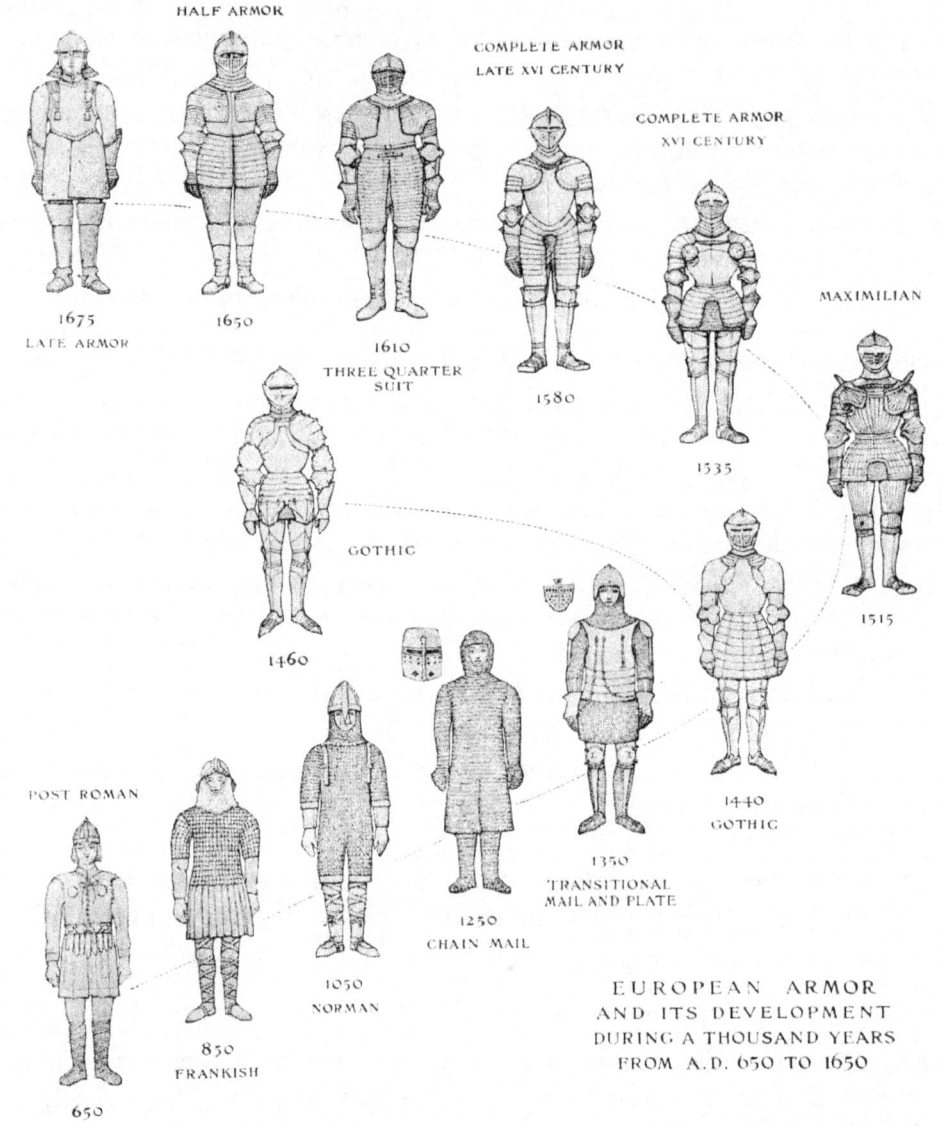

Fig. 1. European armor and its development

orately developed in the epoch of Columbus, when the knight and his horse, Fig. 2, became almost invulnerable. By Puritan times armor had become reduced to little more than corselet and headpiece. Leathern armor then reappeared in use and the soldier's leathern coat and heavy leg-gear were practically of the same defensive value as in the earliest time.

Fig. 2. Armor for man and horse, 1508

(B) *Was armor actually an important means of saving life and limb?*

Assuredly yes. Upon this point the evidence is definite. No well-made armor could have failed to preserve its wearer not merely from a very large percentage of thrusts of arrows, bolts, lances, swords and daggers, but from blows of heavy impact, given, *e.g.*, by military hammers, flails, maces, war axes; also from the firearms of the day. As token of this one may point to the evidence of ancient and formidable injuries which numerous specimens of armor exhibit today; and one may even affirm that there was scarcely a famous soldier in those days who did not owe his life, directly or indirectly, to his armor. In fact, in tilts and single combats each wearer demonstrated many times the value of his defenses; thanks to them we know that such an artist in ring-duelling (*champs clos*) as "le bon chevalier" Jacques de Lalain,* withstood the heaviest blows of a combat-axe wielded by both hands of a "fearful adversary." And we know that the blows of such an axe were trenchant indeed: its head weighed from three to five pounds; its shaft, weighing about two pounds, was over five feet long, to enable it to be swung with great effect. Can we picture, too, the thrusts which the armor of such a duellist resisted when a similar arm was used reinforced with a heavy blade or spike? Chain mail, which one rolls in his hand today, wondering how so "flimsy" a material could have been a protection, was also of the greatest value. Against sword, dagger, arrow, bolt and light lance it was unquestionably proof. Indeed, no better testimony is needed as to its merits than the fact that for at least two thousand years it was worn constantly and in large numbers, in spite of the fact that its average price of purchase appears to have been greater than that of any other type of armor.† A single instance may here be cited as evidence of the virtue of chain mail. At Tiberias (1187) when the crusaders were hemmed in by the Saracens, after two days of hard fighting, when most of the foot soldiers were killed or wounded, when hardly a horse in the army could carry its rider, the mail-clad knights are known to have suffered no serious casualties.‡ Yet

---

* Lefevre de Saint-Remy, "*Chronique de Jacques de Lalain*" [1421-1453], published in 1842, *Panthéon litteraire*.

† A shirt of mail in the collection of the Metropolitan Museum of Art contains a quarter of a million hand-made and tempered rings, each carefully formed and each separately riveted. If one estimates that a skilful armorer might make and weave together two hundred and fifty of these links in a day, it is easy to see that this mail would have cost its maker, working every day, nearly three years' work,—a low estimate, we believe, for making this particular mail. Such a shirt would therefore have cost its purchaser in round figures, at modern prices, six thousand dollars, allowing the maker six dollars a day for a thousand days!

‡ 1898, Oman, Ch., "A History of the Art of War." Methuen, London, pp. 323 et seq. "To their [the Moslems'] great surprise they found that very few of the knights

IN MODERN WARFARE

over a thousand of them exposed themselves constantly in battle. Mail, on the other hand, was not found proof to unusually heavy shocks. A stout lance or a musket ball was its bane, and the later history of mail finds it in use, as we have noted, only as a secondary defense, usually under armor of plate. Whenever it was worn it required supplemental pad-

Fig. 3. Costume worn under mail shirt and cap

Fig. 3A. Chain mail of the fourteenth century

ding to take up the shock of the blow. Ancient "documents" show what manner of quilted costume was worn under the mail, and in Fig. 3 one of these has been copied. When over this the shirt of mail is fitted (Fig. 3A), the wearer can withstand heavy blows with surprisingly little discomfort. That is to say, the mail with its padded costume becomes an elastic, springy

had been seriously hurt; their mail shirts had protected them so well from the arrow shower that few were badly wounded and hardly any slain. . . ."

complex or shield which deadens a blow with unexpected ease. Experiments made by the writer in this direction converted him to the faith that mail as a type of armor is by no means to be despised.

Fig. 4. Armor, tested by musket ball. About 1575. Weight 94 pounds. Artillery Museum, Paris

Armor of plate was a far stouter defense. Gothic armor withstood at short range the straight impact of a heavy crossbow bolt. And the ponderous armor of the late sixteenth and early seventeenth century withstood the shock of heavy bullets. Historical instances are not rare when armor saved its wearer from bullets at close range. About 1570, Strozzi, probably wearing the type of half-armor shown in Fig. 4, was hit by a musket ball at short range; he sustained no injury, his breastplate showing only the splash of molten lead; on another occasion, as he entered a breached wall, he was struck at a range so close that he was knocked down, the ball denting

Fig. 5. Armor of Pedro II of Portugal. About 1700. Weight 43 pounds. Reinforcing plate (below) shows mark of testing bullets. Specimen in Metropolitan Museum of Art, New York

his armor; again, at the siege of Rochelle (1573) he was thrice struck on the arms, and he himself relates how he came off "cheaply."* We also read

* Brantôme, "*Courronels françois*," Liv. II. Ch. I. Edit. Elzv., Vol. VII, p. 44.— In footnote p. 53, as quoted by Buttin, "voilà comme j'en eschappy à bon marché."

in Brantôme that in 1563, at the siege of Orleans, Dandelot was saved from a musket ball by the round shield which he carried; here the impact was so severe that he, too, was knocked down.

If we examine these old records we are surprised to find how often armor saved its wearer. His corselet, for example, saved Francis I "several times" at Pavia. At the siege of Rochelle mentioned above we learn that a certain Captain St. Martin remained uninjured after having been struck by musket balls no less than thirty times! So, too, the great Condé, armed probably after the style of Fig. 5 or 6, was saved many times by his armor; we have a contemporary note (1652) that at Port St. Antoine his cuirass was "full of dents." And so it goes. There is no question, therefore, that armor was useful even at a time when gunpowder was in general use. Moreover, the bullet of that period was usually of large caliber; its crushing effect must have been great, and its shock formidable.

The fact is clear that had cases not been numerous in which the soldier was saved by his armor, the armor would not have been worn. Nor was the burden too great, considered from every viewpoint, if by means of his armor a particular person could be preserved. For those were days of individualism. And the personality, courage and resourcefulness of a leader would often spell the difference between the victory and the defeat of a nation. Had Marlborough been shot, whom his soldiers followed blindly, what might have been the outcome of the battles of Malplaquet, Ramillies, or Blenheim? Or was it not of the greatest importance to the French nation that Joan of Arc should be protected by armor of best possible proof? We know indeed that she was several times saved by her armor. Fancy, too, how the history of the world might have changed had the Black Prince been killed in battle; or Cromwell, or William of Orange, or Francis I or Charles V. Yet we know that all of them exposed themselves with reckless determination, and that all of them were armored by masters. One has only to visit the royal armory in Madrid today to know what such a man as Charles V thought of the practical value of armor. He was literally a specialist in its study and he provided himself with armor for every eventuality and of every weight. He graded his armor as an optician classifies his lenses; in one instance he had at least eight reinforcing pieces for a single helmet. And for tilting he did not hesitate to wear armor which would stand a supreme shock. He was a man of modest stature and proportions, yet his tilting armor in one instance weighed no less than a hundred and twenty-five pounds and his helmet alone over forty pounds!

(C) *How was early armor made?*

The best material used by early European armorers came from special localities, where the iron occurred in natural association, probably with chromium and nickel, thus producing an alloy of great ballistic resistance.*

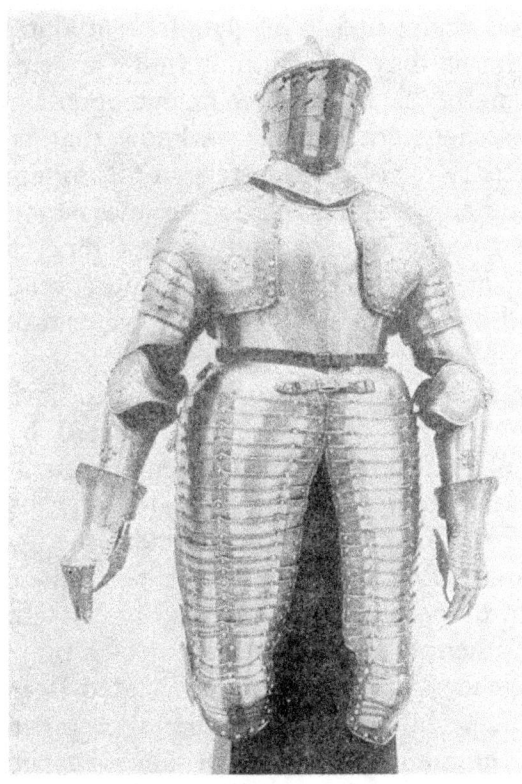 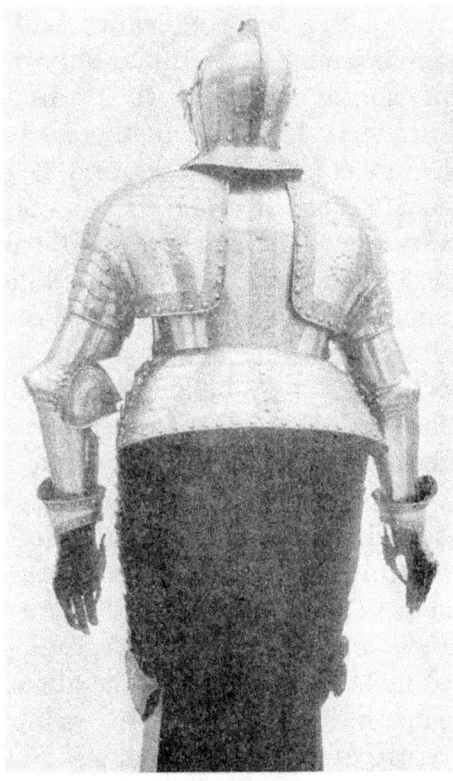

Fig. 6   Fig. 6A

Fig. 6. Armor of "proof." Weight 84 pounds. About 1620. Breast- and backplates show mark of testing bullets. Riggs Collection, Metropolitan Museum of Art

* As this is written I learn from my friend, Dr. M. Miyajima of Tokyo, this interesting point, which he in turn had from the metallurgist, Dr. O. Kochi of the Faculty of Technology of the Imperial University of Tokyo. It appears that years ago a German steel expert analyzed a part of a sword-blade made by the famous Japanese artist, Masamuné (1330 ±): and he discovered that the secret of its extraordinary hardness was that it contained the rare element molybdenum, doubtless as an impurity, in a certain proportion. This led the discoverer to determine the local source of Ma-

HELMETS AND BODY ARMOR

Cf. pages 270-272. This material, *e.g.*, from Innsbruck or Bilbao, became a staple article of commerce during the Middle Ages; it was sold in bars or in plates; the latter had been hammered out, sometimes by hand, but usually by a trip-hammer operated by water power. (See Agricola, Georgius, *De re metallica*, Basel, 1546.) In making armor the armorer worked his metal sometimes hot, sometimes cold, depending upon the kind and quality of work which had to be performed. The details in making armor need here be noted only in so far as they furnish materials for comparison or contrast with the modern methods. Thus we comment upon the extremely laborious methods of the ancient craftsman; we know that he had no stamping presses, and we have only to follow the steps in fashioning such a piece of armor as a helmet after the original method to understand why armor making was a difficult and costly task. It had, we will find, a technique of its own; and its kinds of anvils, stakes, hammers, and special apparatus may even today be counted by scores. Unfortunately we cannot illustrate helmet making from early documents; none the less we can here follow it, and I believe very accurately, for we are so fortunate as to have the various steps or stages in such a piece of work demonstrated by the armorer, D. Tachaux, of the staff of the Metropolitan Museum of Art,* who in turn had them from the Dresden armorer, Klein (1825-1882), who himself was trained in the armory of the Dukes of Saxony where the art of armor making had been handed down from the earliest centuries. These stages can now be pictured by means of numerous photographs (Fig. 7). In these one may trace the beginning of a helmet in the cutting out of a plate of metal whose diameter is about 20 inches. The plate is now heated from time to time and by countless blows of special hammers, the metal is spread centripetally and in such a way that the metal plate takes a saucer-shaped form (2); it next becomes conical (4); it then develops the beginnings of a median ridge or crest (5); its sides are produced (6); and thereafter the stages follow one another in orderly sequence. Much of the later work is done on the unheated metal, which, however, is softened (annealed) from time to time. To understand how laborious are the steps in the making of a helmet, one has only to be told that the stages between (1) and (21) as shown in our figure cost several months' assiduous work. It will be seen that

---

samuné's alloy iron: thereupon he purchased this iron in large lots, much to the surprise of the Japanese who later, when they analyzed captured German cannon, decided where a part at least of the molybdenum ore was obtained!

* See Bulletin of the Metropolitan Museum of Art, 1912, VII, 231.

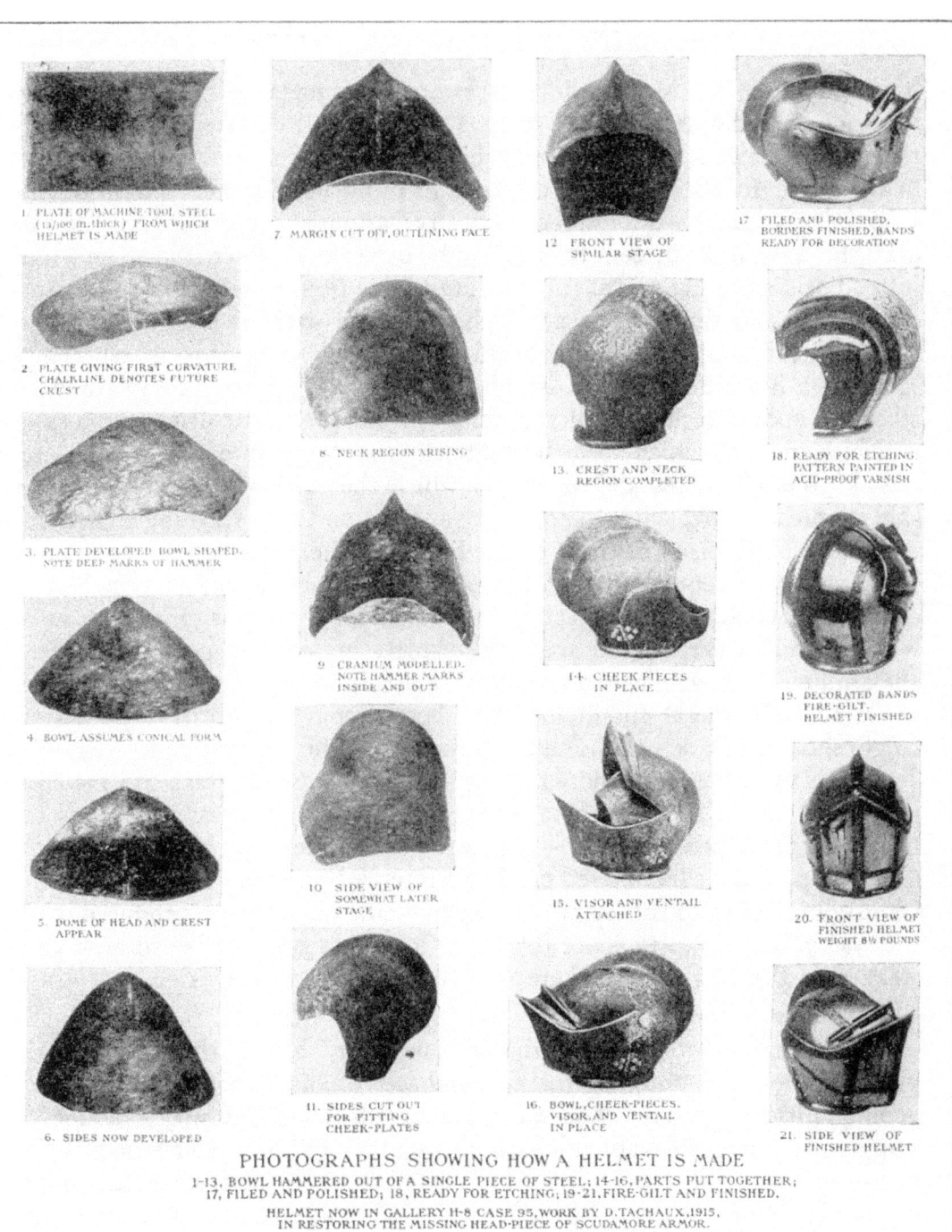

Fig. 7. Stages in making a helmet after the ancient fashion

by this mode of production the artist controls his metal with extraordinary precision. He may push it into regions where it will be later required, *e.g.*, the median crest or the forehead where the helmet is apt to encounter a heavy blow. In all cases he must keep in mind not the next phase of his work merely but the later stages. Thus the armorer could not have developed the crest in the present helmet had he begun to produce it in stage (10) instead of stage (4); and should the crest have been taller still (in ancient armor it is sometimes six inches high, embossed with such skill that it is heaviest at its top) he would probably have begun to form it at stage (2). Even then he could not have developed it successfully had he not understood the special technique of spreading his metal "elastically,"—by using special hammers (which are believed not to cut the grain of the metal) and highly polished stakes and anvils on which the "fibers" of the metal are said to spread apart, "slipping over one another and not becoming entangled or broken." Be this as it may, in the hands of the ancient armorer refractory metal was controlled with incredible skill; and a master like Philip de Negroli could work his steel into ornamental designs, Fig. 7A, in a way unexcelled even by an artist in so soft a material as gold. Moreover, the armorer, it is well worth noting, rarely forgot, even in his most ornate work, that the metal should be so embossed that the uplifted points or ridges should include not the thinnest metal but the thickest.

With this type of armor making we shall later contrast the modern method of manufacture, where by means of a single press thousands of helmets are stamped out daily—a greater number, perhaps, than the ancient armorer could have hammered out in a lifetime. But by the new method one is sadly limited as to the shape and depth of the object to be produced, and the system is also faulty, since the armor it presses is apt to be thinnest and weakest in the very region where the greatest strength is needed.

(D) *How was armor tested?*

It is not hard to conclude that the armorer, during all periods, took practical means of showing to the purchaser of his armor that it was of good quality, or "proof." And the early records when carefully examined* bring out numerous details indicating in what way and under what conditions the testing or proving of armor took place. That it was often done on standard lines there can be no doubt. And it was occasionally carried out under particularly severe conditions. In this connection let us review a number of tests.

* Cf. Ch. Buttin, *op. cit.*

The earliest one accurately recorded* occurred during the siege of Rhodes (308-304 B. C.) when Demetrius Polyorcetes, according to Plutarch (Demetrius, Section 21), received from Cyprus two heavy iron corselets (probably breastplate only), each weighing the equivalent of thirty-eight pounds Troy. Zwilos, the armorer who made them, thereupon caused them to be tested in order to show that they were of great strength and

Fig. 7A. Casque dated 1543 and signed by the Milanese artist, Philip de Negroli. J. Pierpont Morgan Collection in Metropolitan Museum of Art

* Crude tests of armor by sword, spear or arrow are doubtless as old as history itself. Here should be mentioned David's testing the armor which Saul offered him (about B. C. 1015). I Samuel, xvii, 38, 39. "And Saul armed David with his armor and he put a helmet of brass upon his head: also he armed him [by providing him] with a coat of mail. 39. And David girded [drew] his sword upon his armor and he assayed to go [to let go or strike at it]; for he had not proved it. And David said unto Saul, I cannot go with these, for I have not proved them [shown that they were not proof]. And David put them off him [put them away from him]."

It seems quite obvious that the usual translation of these verses gives no sense unless the bracketed words are suggested. The picture then becomes complete. The prompt test by the keen-witted youth warranted his rejection of the armor: add to this his shrewd decision to try light tactics in fighting, for he had probably heard (I Samuel, xvii, 5) that his adversary was woefully overweighted in his armor, "which weighed five thousand shekels of brass," or roundly 183 pounds (allowing for the heavy shekel 258 grains).

hardness; to this end they were shot at by a catapult at a range of twenty paces. The iron resisted the shock and the head of the catapult bolt merely nicked the surface "as though with a stylos." Thus the test was made under war conditions and it is noteworthy that the armor was not placed on racks or models but on living men. "One of the corselets was worn by Demetrius himself, the other by Alkinos of Epeiros."

It would be interesting to know just what this test represented in terms of modern ballistics. That it was severe goes without saying, especially since the bolt of a catapult, which represented the siege artillery of that day, had a weight which would have been hard to stop (perhaps as much as ten ounces, *i.e.*, double the weight of a heavy war-bolt of a windlass crossbow). In modern terms it is even fair to assume that had the breastplates in question been of low carbon steel, and they probably were, they would have stopped a machine gun bullet at about three hundred yards (cf. page 144).* It is surprising, therefore, that the earliest instance of a military proof of body armor recorded,—occurring some twenty-three hundred years ago,—should have given essentially modern results, but, naturally, at the cost of greater weight.

Detailed records of proving European armor do not next occur until the fourteenth century. But from this it does not follow that during the intervening time there were made no efforts to prove the armor and to standardize the tests. We incline rather to the belief that each purchaser of armor had a clear idea of the degree of resistance his shirt of mail and his iron headpiece should offer, and that even in his tests he did not fail to make use of crossbow, lance and sword. Unfortunately we do not know from actual experiment, ancient or modern, what a good shirt of mail (weighing, say twenty pounds) will resist, when each link is riveted and hardened, but it was evidently of greater strength than modern shirts of mail unriveted, which, of about equal weight, are claimed by their makers to resist service-revolver ammunition at less than fifty yards. (See page 62.) In general we know that early armor of this type was often tried out by the chopping cut (*estramaçon*) of a sword, and that a similar test was used throughout Europe down to the seventeenth century. (*Fide* Gaya, 1623.) The thrust of a heavy poignard was also a severe test. In this connection I recall in Paris many years ago discussing the proof of fifteenth-century

* A well-made modern breastplate of alloy steel weighing twenty pounds will stop a machine gun bullet at 200 to 300 yards. In the conclusion noted above we assume that carbon steel offers about half the resistance of alloy steel. See, however, p. 81.

Italian armor with M. V. R. Bachereau, the well-known antiquary of ancient arms: "That armor is indestructible," declared M. Bachereau, and "it would surprise you to know how flinty hard its surface is." He told me he had taken from a vitrine a headpiece hall-marked by the great Milanese maker, Antonio di Missaglia, and placed it on a block. He had then struck it with all his strength with a heavy-bladed dagger; the headpiece hardly showed where the point had struck. This incident I mention since it is the only one in which I have known an early helmet to be given a practical test. Perhaps it is not to be wondered at, for museums and collectors can hardly be expected to permit some of their most valuable specimens to be used in ballistic or similar tests!

As early as 1340 we have records that armor of two degrees of strength was in use, known respectively as "proof" and the "half proof." The former would withstand the bolt of a heavy crossbow, which was set with a windlass, the latter only the arrow of the war-bow and the bolt of the small crossbow. Two expressions to distinguish the strength of armor date also from this time (Italy and Savoy*), armor "proof to every thrust" (*de toute botte*), applying apparently to plate armor, and "to thrust broken" (*botte cassée*) in the sense that the armor yielded and thus broke the thrust. The latter armor, including apparently chain mail and armor of small plates or scales (jazerans, from Spanish *Jazerino* = Algerian) was apparently the more highly prized; and it was more costly (one fifth or more).

Records of proving armor become frequent during the fifteenth century. And by this time measures appear to have been taken to standardize the test. Many cities had their stamps (*poinçons*) and made use of them in certifying to the excellence of their armor. Thus numerous helmets and breastplates in our museums bear the proof mark of Nuremberg (demi-eagle and fesse), Venice (lion of St. Mark), Augsburg (pine-cone); together in some cases with the individual mark of the maker. Occasionally not only is one piece of the armor thus marked but nearly every piece, including gauntlets and leg pieces. And in extremely rare cases (to show what store was set by tests of this kind) the same piece was hall-marked at many points. A Milanese armet in my collection bears the *poinçon* of proof on its back on the left side, on the right cheek and on the left, and the mark of "double proof" near the back on its right side. The double mark mentioned is believed to record a test of much greater strength. These tests were made with special crossbows and special bolts or quarrels; and tests of this

* Ch. Buttin, "*Les flèches d'épreuve*" . . . Annecy, 1917.

nature were still in force well into the sixteenth century.* Occasionally we read of armor which was tested in the presence of the purchaser, who brought with him special bolts and a "good windlass crossbow" to make sure that the proof was severe. This test, we may add, is not easily compared with a modern one, but it was fairly searching, for the projectile was heavy (four or five ounces), revolved in flight, and its point was well adapted to punching holes through metal plates (cf. page 297, that the effect upon armor plate is greater when a bullet is reversed). Such a bolt flew with an initial velocity of about 300 feet a second (writer's estimate) and it attained a distance of 400 to 500 yards; at 60 yards it would penetrate a deal plank three fourths of an inch thick.†

Early in the sixteenth century guns became used in large numbers and shattered much armor of "proof." Thus in 1517, Ariosto advised the soldier to send his armor and sword back to the forge and to adopt the musket or arquebus. ("*Orlando furioso*," Canto IX, stanza 29.) So, too, we find in 1523 a note in Montluc's "Commentaries" (*Ed.* 1821, Petitot, Vol. I, page 342) which deplores the death of "so many brave and valiant men, often at the hand of the most cowardly and timid, who did not dare to meet face to face the men whom they shot down with their miserable bullets!" Hence it came about that the conditions of proving armor were changed, and that by about the middle of the sixteenth century armor was made heavier, and the terms "proof" and "half proof" acquired a new significance, suits of the former type resisting the (war) musket, the latter the lighter firearms, including pistols. Sometimes a suit of armor was made up partly of "proof" (front of helmet, breastplate and upper thigh defenses and circular shield) and partly of "half proof" (backplate, arm defenses‡). To compensate for the increase of the weight of the breastplate it was even advocated that no armor for the back be worn, on the ground that it was unnecessary, and that its absence would discourage cavalry from turning its back to the enemy.‖

For the rest it becomes clear that testing by firearms was an important

* Crossbows were not discarded in the French army until 1566, when, indeed, many soldiers still preferred them to muskets; and in England the use of the musket did not become obligatory until 1596.

† *See* Payne-Galway, Sir Ralph, "The Crossbow, Medieval and Modern, Military and Sporting." 1903, London, XXII, p. 328.

‡ In instances all parts were designated as half proof, including even the groin-plate (brayette). v. Catalogue of the armory of the Dukes of Lorraine, 1629.

‖ A similar reason for abandoning the backplate was recommended by Alexander the Great. (Rollin, "*De la science militaire*," liv. XXV, § 3.)

factor in the decadence of armor, and that, little by little, each plate grew heavier, till at length the entire panoply became literally unbearable. During this time the competition became intense between the armorer and the gun-maker, whose clients added insult to injury by rejecting a musket if it did not shatter the armor, and rejecting the armor if it did not resist the musket. "Of course my fine armor failed," complained the armorer Colombo of Brescia (1574), "when my patron used an inch charge of powder!" And we can understand how the earlier armor, elegant in its lines, with its delicately adjusted curves, grooves and angles, designed especially to deflect the crossbow bolt, should in time give place to armor, solid and compact, rounded in contour. But even then the proof demanded by the wearer of the armor mounted always higher ("high-proof," "caliber proof," "musket proof") so the armorer was obliged constantly to resort to new devices. He knew little of the metallurgy of steel (see page 271), so he did not experiment with ballistic alloys; he did, however, like Vulcano of Brescia, strengthen the "fiber" of his heavy plates by the laborious process of hammering them out cold and by using various processes of tempering them; but in general he had either to make his armor of fewer and heavier pieces, or to use the earlier designed reinforcing plates by means of which a patron who had complete armor could strengthen his breastplate or headpiece and at the same time reduce the total weight of his equipment by discarding other pieces, according to his actual need. The result, however, tended ever in the same direction, the armor became far too heavy; and its wearer began to complain that he had become little more than a "living anvil,"* for he was so burdened with his harness that his value in active combat became small. Thus, even if dismounted, he could hardly get back into his saddle.† (ffoulkes, "The Armorer and his Craft," page 117.) In the end, throughout the seventeenth century, the best the

* La Noue in his *"Discours politiques et militaires,"* translated by "E. A.," 1587, writes on page 185, quoted by ffoulkes, "For where they had some reason in respect to the violence of harquebuzes and dagges (muskets and pistols) to make their armor thicker and of better proofe than before, they have now so farre exceeded, that most of them have laden themselves with stithies (anvils) in view of clothing their bodies with armour."

† Thus, Gaspard de Saulx-Tavannes, in his memoirs (*"Collection des Mém. relativ. à l'histoire de France,"* Paris, Didier et Cie., 1866), notes "that it is impossible for captains in their heavy casques and cuirasses to strike many times, as is their duty. If one who commands wishes the help of a casque and breastplate, proof to the musket ball, he must take them only at the moment he charges."

armorer could do was to keep his clients well mounted at the head of their troops where their presence and *beaux gestes* could inspire their men to further efforts. And they certainly found their way into the thick of the battle, for we recall that in those days princes and generals exposed themselves in a fashion which would seem to modern tactics little less than criminal. But while the opposing heroes rarely met in single combat in Homeric fashion, it is none the less true that they had often the opportunity of recognizing one another and at close range during the fortunes of battle.

Many suits of armor of the latest period (say from 1560 to 1750) bear dents of bullets;* certain of these are scars of warfare, but they are usually testing marks. Cf. Figs. 4-6. They were made prior to the finishing of the armor, for they are still apt to be below a russeted, blued or gilded surface, or even to form centers for etched or engraved ornaments. One, two or three of these marks may appear on the breastplate (sometimes at points concealed by large shoulder guards, as in the armor shown in Fig. 6), one on the backplate, one on each hip defense, one on each shoulder. The proof balls may have been shot in the presence of the person who had ordered the armor, at the time the plates were fitted to him but before they were filed and finished. In such a case the bullet was of lead weighing about one ounce, and the charge of black powder was sufficient to cover the bullet when held in the palm of the hand. (Cf. 1667 "Memorial of the Verney Family," IV, page 30, and the Gaya Reprint, by ffoulkes, Clarendon Press, 1911, page 30). There appears no record as to the distance at which the shot was fired nor the firearm employed, nor yet the mode of wadding,— although these are factors which influenced the test vastly. The ancient armorer, we fear, like makers of certain types of modern armor, was apt to gloss over details. Thus, he did not care to have the test made with cartridges specially prepared at the house of his client. "In general," wrote Pistofilo, "Heaven protect me from the musket which has been specially loaded at home!", and other writers comment upon the superior force of the first shot from a gun, a condition which, in days of poorly made powder, one may well understand, for a gun barrel would speedily have become clogged with carbon.

* As late as 1734 the bullet test was still in use for proving both back and front plates, as shown in the inventory of the Armory of the Château de la Rocca: breastplates bear the marks shown in testing bullets, in the second half of the eighteenth century, as in the armor museum in Turin, of Charles Emmanuel III (d. 1773) and Victor Amadeus IV (d. 1796).

In all tests a serious effort appears to have been made by early experimenters to find the best results which could be had in proportioning the weights of powder and ball. And they seem to have decided, as Cellini narrates in his autobiography, that the best penetration could be had when the powder weighed not more than one fifth of the bullet, a proportion, by the way, which has been confirmed repeatedly in later days—even for the last rifle of the French Government using black powder. Indeed, it may truly be said that the early authorities were dealing with problems of explosives in a very modern way. Experiments were in full swing with noiseless powder, and Cellini, for example, tells (*"Vita,"* Lib. I, Cap. VII) how by its means he was able in his hunting to keep from frightening away the most wary birds. Also shapes of bullets were being considered with up-to-date precision and there are records of models, including conical ones, which should have given excellent results. These followed the use of long projectiles shaped like crossbow bolts. Then, too, metals other than lead were employed experimentally. Iron, tin and copper were used, the last especially having a certain vogue (Admiral Coligny, by the way, was shot with copper bullets on the eve of his death). Clearly, too, the experts had ever before them the need of inventing armor-piercing bullets, and they came very close to solving their problem when they used steel bullets dipped in lead. But then, as in so many other instances, instead of following an excellent scent, they veered off in unscientific directions, as when they attempted to associate special metals with special grades of victims: thus, "only a bullet of gold could be used to cause the death of an emperor." And gun wads should contain cabalistic formulae.*

(E) *How heavy, irksome and even dangerous was armor to wear?*

If one examines Table I, shown on page 48, he may compare the weights of various kinds of body armor and helmets. Chain armor was almost as light again as plate armor.† Suits of plate, it will be seen, did not increase notably in weight during the century from 1450 to 1550; but during the century following they became heavier by perhaps 20 per cent. Tilting armor naturally attained extraordinary weight, since its wearer needed extreme protection and for only a short period,—thus a harness of

* The last superstition, with certain variants, was not extinct in 1901: while in the Philippine Islands the writer examined a collection of similar charms taken from insurrectos.

† This difference in weight is, however, deceptive; for with chain mail a much heavier supporting costume was worn.

a hundred and twenty-five pounds might be tolerated if it were to be taken off again within half an hour. Helmets, of which the various kinds are pictured in Fig. 8, may be divided conveniently into four groups, light, medium, heavy and very heavy. Light headpieces average three pounds in weight and include early bassinets, certain burganets, morions and cabassets, iron hats and hat-linings. Medium helmets weighing about six pounds occur in visored bassinets, salades, barbutes, armets and certain burganets. Heavy helmets weigh ten pounds, e.g., closed burganets and tilting armets. And very heavy helmets, say of twenty pounds, are represented by heaumes and siege burganets. The last-named headpieces would probably stand a good ballistic test with the most recent firearms. In their day they were proof to shot of large caliber, which were justly reckoned as most dangerous in crushing armor; they are said to have withstood a quarter pound ball, and even a one pounder when largely spent. In the matter of the discomfort of wearing armor, there can be no question that it was always irksome. But soldiers became used to it and the literature of the subject shows that they rarely complained of its burden until late in the sixteenth century. In earlier times the hardened wearer used it in active service all day long. If exceptionally active he could vault into his saddle (or over it) in full panoply, weighing, say fifty-five pounds, and while his horse was galloping he could jump to the ground without using stirrups;* he could throw himself on his back at full length and gain his feet in hardly more than double the time he could do it unarmed, the last a result which I have confirmed by actual experiment. But these things can be done only when armor fits the individual and is worn over the kind of costume adapted to it, with the necessary "points" for supporting the elements of the suit. See Figs. 9 and 9A. In fact, under these conditions armor is worn with surprisingly little discomfort. I can bear witness that a suit of half-armor weighing thirty-five pounds can be worn for a stretch of three hours, and by a novice, without extraordinary fatigue or subsequent lameness.

It was only from the latter part of the sixteenth century, when armor weighed over sixty pounds that we find the old-time soldier grumbling about his equipment. Pikemen would have none of it, "many throw it away," complained Saulx-Tavannes and Pistifilo. Horsemen would put it

---

* "The Bohemian Ulysses, v. Gentlemen Errant," by Mrs. Henry Cust, London, Murray, 1909, p. 23. Also, "this Spaniard, tho' clad in full armor, could run for six miles and beat all other men in ordinary clothes: placing his hand on Zehrowitz' shoulder he vaulted with feet together right over his head," etc. Ibid., p. 74.

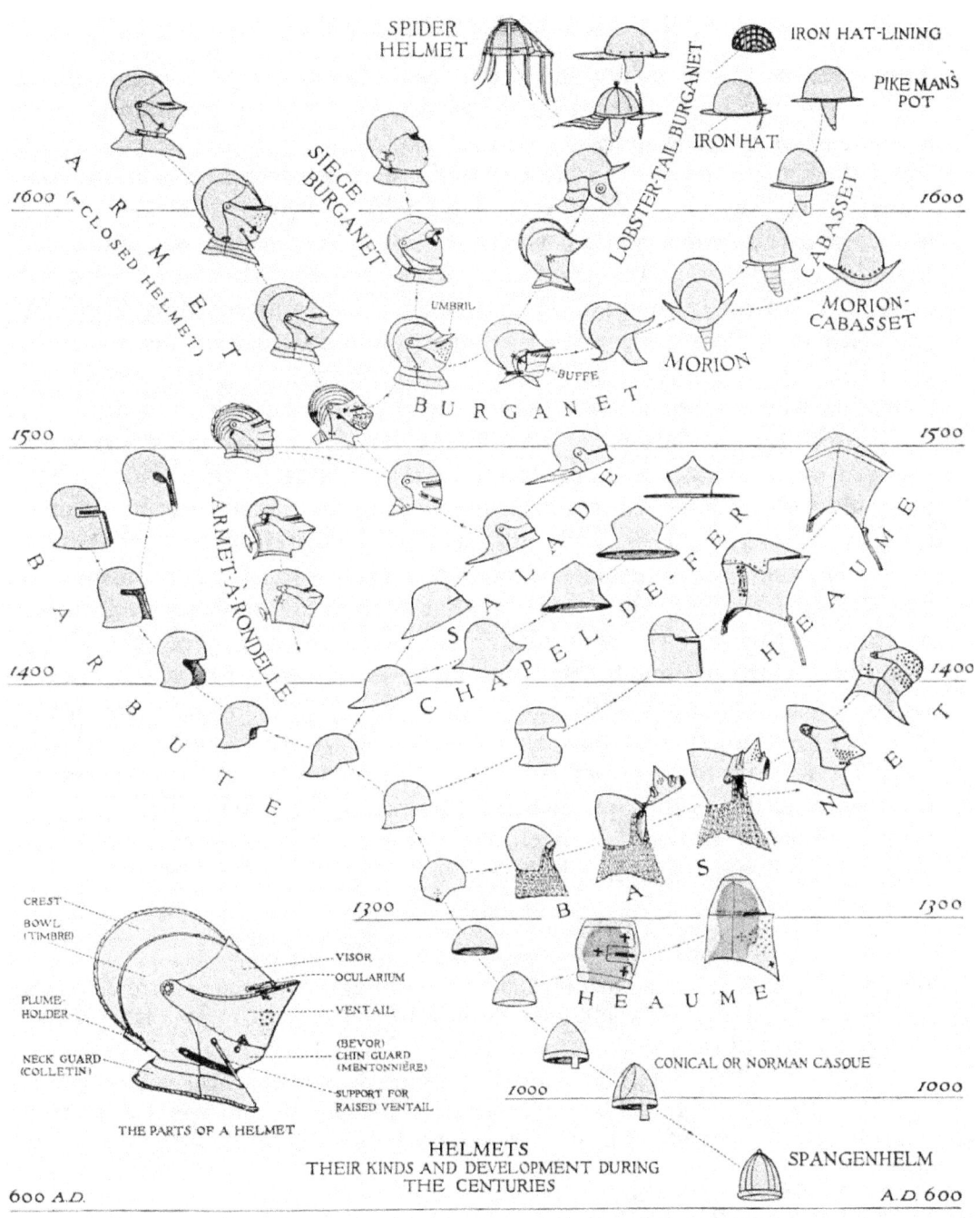

Fig. 8. Helmets and their developmental sequence

on only at the last moment; and Montaigne (1587, Essays) deplores "the vicious habits of his times and full of weakness to take up one's armor only at the call of extreme necessity, and to get rid of it at the very moment when the danger appears to have passed, for this gives rise to much disorder" . . . "the old fashion was better which insured that each soldier had on a part of his armor all the time." Still the fashion was spreading that the armor was to be carried as part of the equipment of the camp, rather than of the individual. Thus Saulx-Tavannes pleads that "captains and soldiers in close touch with the enemy should accustom themselves to carry their armor without confiding it to their servants in order to avoid the confusion which appears when there is need to look up their luggage."

But the fact of the matter was that so far as long marching service in war was concerned armor had become a physiological failure. Not merely was the wearer rendered inactive when wearing it, but in time he became actually crippled or "broken" by its use. A droll writer, whose stories were read everywhere, commented audibly upon the shortcomings of men who had worn armor. Brantôme declared that he himself had known them to be spent at thirty years. Montaigne says that "today (1587) the officer is so heavily armed that by the time he becomes thirty-five his shoulders are completely humpbacked." And La Noue (1587) repeats the same story.* The result of this was, according to Buttin, that "officers and soldiers not wishing to be crippled by thirty-five threw away their armor as often as possible, to the detriment of their discipline and to the advancement of much improvised quarrelling." This marked an important if not a final stage in the armorer's decline.

TABLE I
WEIGHT OF ARMOR AND HELMETS

WEIGHT in pounds: no allowance made for loss of weight after centuries of cleaning. Parade armor in each class would have weighed less by perhaps 50 per cent. Letters† refer to various collections.

* "*Discours politiques et militaires.*" "Neither was their armor heavie (those days) but that they might wel bear it 24 hours, while those that are now worne are so waightie that the peiz of them will benumme a Gentleman's shoulders of 35 years of age."

† Collections here referred to are:

B. Zeughaus, Berlin; D. Johanneum, Dresden; E. Rüstkammer, Wartburg, Eisenach; F. Bargello, Florence; G. Musée de Ville, Geneva; M. Real Armeria, Madrid; N. Y. Metropolitan Museum of Art, New York; P. Musée d'Artillerie, Paris; T. Tower of London; Tur. Armeria Reale, Turin; V. K. u. K. Sammlung, Vienna.

A. *Armor for man and horse*
    XVI century . . . . . E. 53 (man) + 101 (horse) = 154; 55 + 99 = 154; T. 65 + 69 = 134
    Tilting . . . . . . M. 106 + 101 = 207; 125 + 129 = 254; P. (Maximilian) 181

Fig. 9. Costume worn under armor. About 1510

Fig. 9A. Fluted armor of 1510. Weight 56 pounds

B. *Armor for man*
    Chain mail
        Suit . . . . . . N. Y. 31 (including coiffe)
        Shirt . . . . . . E. 14; N. Y. 32, 20, 19; Turkish 22
    Complete suit
        XV century—Gothic . . N. Y. 49; P. 53; V. 85
        Maximilian . . . . E. 71, 71, 56, 49, 56, 41, 52; N. Y. 48
        Complete suit for foot combat . . . . . . T. 94, 81

Middle XVI century . . .	E. 48, 59, 59; T. 67, 66
Tilting, XVI century . .	E. 70; T. 70, 79, 106, 80, 70; N. Y. 80
Half suits	E. (black and white) 54, 32, 35, 35, 35, 75; M. (bullet proof) (Philip III) 97; T. 35, (bullet proof) 93
XVII century	E. (bullet proof) 76; T. (3 pieces) 35, 43
Round shields	M. (Philip III) 35; N. Y. 36, 12, 10, 9 P. (diam. 61 cm.) 42

Helmets

Bassinet (early) . . .	T. 2.5
Bassinet (dog faced) . .	N. Y. 6.5, 7, 11; T. 5.5
Heaume	English, various, 13, 17, 18, 18, 22, 25; M. 42; N. Y. 19, 13, 17; T. 13, 10
Chapel-de-fer	N. Y. 10, 3, 4; T. 3, 6
Salade	N. Y. 6.5, 9.5, 7; T. 8, 3, 4, 3.5, 4.5, 5, 4.5
Barbute	N. Y. 6, 6.5, 6; T. 4, 5, 6.5, 4, 6
Armet-à-rondelle . . .	N. Y. 6.5, 6, 6
Armet Maximilian . . .	N. Y. 6, 4.5, 6; T. 7.5, 8
Armet late	T. 8, 9, 9, 7, 6, 8, 8, 5, 8, 5, 6, 6, 8, 9.5, 7, 7
Armet parade	T. 4
Burganet	N. Y. 9, 3.5, 4, 5, 9, 10, 11; T. 8, 12
Burganet siege	B. 25; D. 20; F. 25; G. 20, 18; M. 27; N. Y. 22; P. 22; Tur. 21
Burganet lobster-tail . .	N. Y. 4, 3
Morion-cabasset . . .	T. 2, 2.5, 3, 3, 3.5, 3.5, 2, 3
Iron hat	N. Y. 4
Pikeman's hat	N. Y. 3; T. 3, 4
Iron hat-linings . . .	N. Y. 1.5, 4, 5, 5, .7, 1.5

(F) *What in summary was the use of armor in later times, but prior to the Great War?*

In the preceding paragraphs we have seen that from the late sixteenth century the soldier complained bitterly of the weight of his armor: it crippled him, it prevented him from taking an active part in battle, and he threw it aside if he could. In spite of all this he admitted that armor was an extraordinary means of protection. It was for this reason that it did not disappear at the first flash of a gun, as is popularly believed, but remained in use for centuries while powder was being developed, and when it was in general use in warfare. In fact at the time of the highest development of armor at the end of the fifteenth century hand-guns had already been in use for a century; and there is no doubt that armor was used most frequently from the middle of the sixteenth to the middle of the seventeenth centuries when guns and pistols were in common use. At that time, indeed, powder had been notably improved in quality and already many "modern"

TABLE II
TABLE SHOWING THE USE OF VARIOUS TYPES OF FIREARMS IN EARLY TIMES. (GUNPOWDER AS A CHEMICAL INVENTION APPEARED IN EUROPE EARLIER THAN THE TENTH CENTURY)

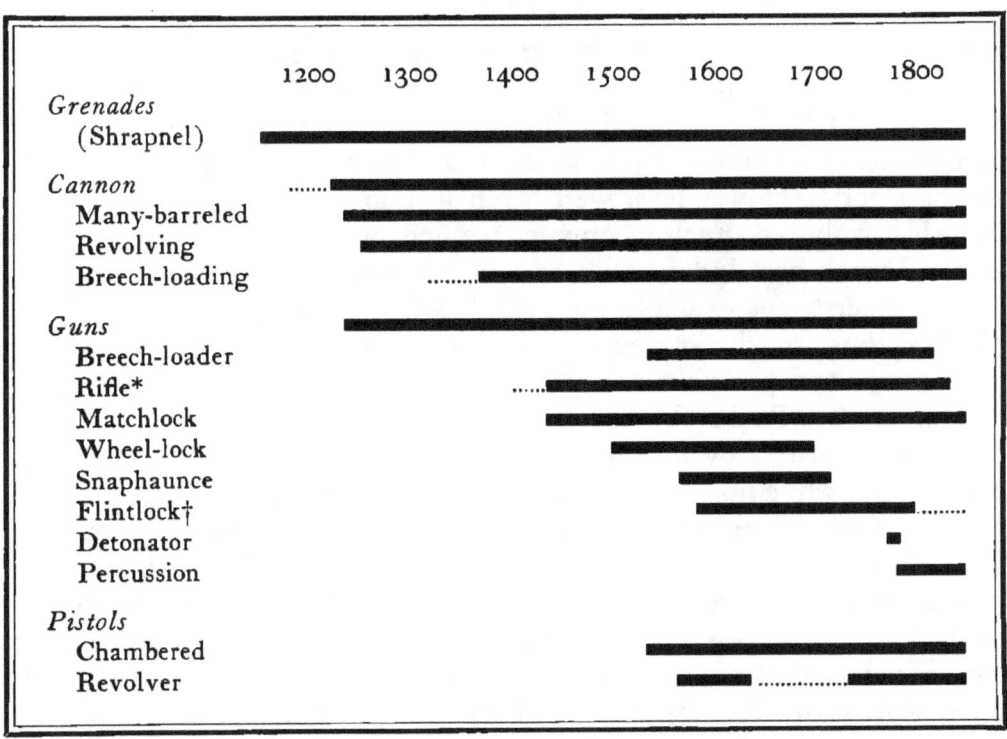

devices had been invented. (See Table II.) Hence we have reason to believe that the general disuse of armor was not due entirely to the failure of armor, in spite of its weight, to resist firearms, but to other causes as well. Here should be mentioned especially those changes in military tactics which were taking place at a time when armor was declining. Thus during the Thirty

* Survives in Orient.
† Survives in isolated localities, *e.g.*, Central Africa.

Years' War (which ended in 1648) the Swedes, especially, built up a military system wherein it became necessary for manoeuvring armies to cover long distances in short time,—a system which alone might have encouraged the infantry to throw away its armor, whether light or heavy. In fact I am inclined to believe that this factor is far more important in the disappearance of body defenses than is usually reckoned. For so soon as armor began to drop out of use it became unfashionable, then unpopular and in the end discredited. That it could still have been used to good purposes seems none the less clear if we examine attentively the comments of certain masters of war during the eighteenth century and there is no better case in point than that of Marshal Saxe († 1750)* who goes out of his way to recommend the use of armor, declaring that it is the more needed since in his experience casualties were caused in greater number by swords, lances and spent balls than by projectiles of high velocity. And we infer that such opinions were not exceptional since we find that suits of armor, lacking defenses for the lower legs, were worn in number up to the time of the French Revolution. Even in America we find such armor in use at the time of the French and Indian War and in rare cases during the Revolution. Lord Amherst, for example, in his Canadian campaign (1758-1760) is pictured thus armed, wearing even hip defenses, Fig. 10. Kosciuszko, also, wore armor and probably brought it to this country; and we have reason to believe that Rochambeau wore his siege armor at Yorktown (1781), for he is described by Joel Barlow as in "gleaming steel arrayed." And Paul Jones, while not in half-armor, wore a corselet under his coat during the fight with the Serapis, according to his fellow-Scotsman, Hyslop. (See Bull. Met. Mus. Art, 1912, Vol. VII, pages 26-28.) Possibly, the latest armor worn as a more or less complete suit appears in Reynolds' portrait of the Marquis of Townshend, and dates late in the eighteenth century; but we are not sure of the date of this harness, for it may have been merely a form of ceremonial costume which the painter adapted, or it may have been of considerably earlier date, *e.g.*, worn at Fontenoy, Dettingen or Culloden. During this late period part of the armor it appears was designed to resist bullets of fairly high velocity, shot often from rifled barrels and by good black powder. The bullets, however, had not a great range, rarely as much as seven hundred yards, and with great individual variation;

* Les Rêveries, Edit. 1756, p. 58. Among wearers of armor during a late period we may mention Luxembourg, Eugene, Louis XV (1750), George I (1718), George II (1758), Paoli (1780), Granby (1769). . . .

but they were usually of large caliber and proportionally more destructive than those in present use. Thus bullets of the Revolutionary musket

Fig. 10. Armor worn in Canada about 1760 by Lord Amherst

weighed about fourteen to the pound (= 500 grains), which is heavier by 50 to 100 per cent than the present rifle ball (Spitzer). (The latest Mauser weighs 227 grains.)

54 HELMETS AND BODY ARMOR

Armor of this kind showed, for one thing, that there was no evident ground for the common belief that the severe shock of a projectile against armor would in itself be fatal to the wearer—even when the armor remained unbroken. In fact, we shall see (page 242) that armor which resists a machine gun, say at fifty yards, did not cause its wearer grave discomfort from the impact even of a series of projectiles. In a word, from the study of the history of armor one can find no reason why it could not be used

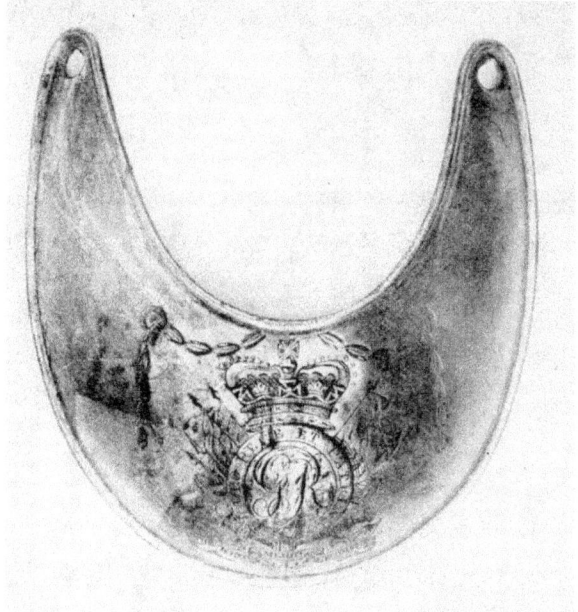

Fig. 11. Gorget worn during American Revolution

under certain modern conditions: hence it follows that if armor were required in actual warfare, there would be no need of developing a new system of wearing armor. We should advance merely a step further in its historical development.

There is no question, then, that armor passed out of general use not at once but gradually. Thus after the year 1620, leg armor rarely appeared and defenses of the hips and thighs are uncommon from about 1670. Defenses for the arms were abandoned piece by piece somewhat later, although complete arms continued to be used for about a century in ceremonial armor, *i.e.*, as worn by highest officers. For a long time the neckplate or gorget was retained as part of the regular equipment and it even became exaggerated in size; but it finally became so small that its function as a defense had practically disappeared. As shown in portraits of Colonial and Revolutionary times, it was little more than an ornament which was at-

Fig. 12. Gorget appearing in portrait of Washington, about 1772

tached to the officer's neck by a ribbon and usually bore his regimental number. See Figs. 11 and 12.* The corselet and helmet have remained ever in use in certain state guards or cavalry regiments. These plates were made of low carbon tool-steel and are fairly resistant even to modern explosives.

* It is even today in certain regiments; shown, *e.g.*, in portrait of Colonel Bates of the 71st New York Infantry, National Guard.

56 HELMETS AND BODY ARMOR

A heavy corselet (forty-one pounds), probably of the time of Napoleon, was recently tested by Captain Roy S. Tinney (National Service Magazine, January, 1918, pages 395-403) and gave good results; it resisted in turn Craig ammunition 30, 40 to 20 with muzzle velocity 1,970 foot seconds; at 100 yards—1,553 foot-pound blow; a Winchester 30, 30, 170, of 1,522 foot pounds; a Sharp's rifle of 45.90, 300, at 100 yards (muzzle velocity 2,644 foot seconds); and finally the 303 Savage firing a 195-grain bullet having muzzle velocity of 1,658 foot seconds. In a word, such a corselet

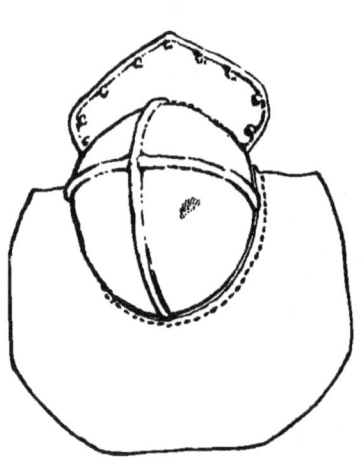

Fig. 13. Sapper's leathern helmet, 1750-1800

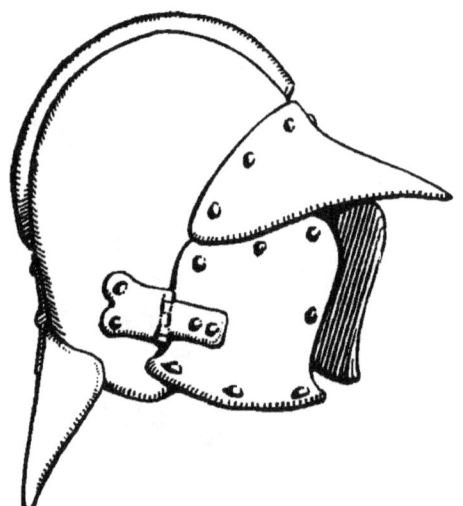

Fig. 14. Sapper's helmet, middle of nineteenth century

resisted projectiles which were scarcely inferior to those in use on present battle-fields. With this test in mind, we may well believe the early statements that the cuirass of the guardsman played an important part in bodily protection during the eighteenth and nineteenth centuries. During the eighteenth century, we recall that its use was fairly constant for cavalry (for the highest officers, especially, when parts of it, at least, degenerated into a ceremonial costume). And in the early nineteenth century, the corselet and headpiece appeared in great numbers in European armies. For one thing, Napoleon the Great favored their use. And there still exists his order to Requier, chief of the artillery museum of Paris, to send post-haste to Tilsit (1808) the corselets and casques which had been made for himself and the Prince of Wagram. There is no question, also, that armor was worn at a very late date in sieges and in naval warfare. Thus heavy helmets and shields of various forms were used during the eighteenth and nineteenth centuries, especially for the defense of sappers. In Fig. 13 is pictured one of the heavy leathern headpieces worn by sappers (and possibly by firemen), 1750-1800; specimen now in the Tower of London. In Fig. 14 ap-

Fig. 15. Body armor used in American Civil War, 1862-1864

pears a heavy helmet of this type drawn from a specimen in the Tower of London; its weight is over nineteen pounds and it dates from about 1848, judging at least from Raffet's picture of the siege of Rome in this year, when sappers are shown wearing helmets of this type. Perhaps, too, we should here mention the numerous types of metal "helmets" which have appeared as headgear for infantry and cavalry during the late eighteenth and throughout the nineteenth century which were of little value save ornamental, *e.g.*, the eagle headpiece of the fugitive German emperor.

In the Orient armor was used practically up to our own time and is probably still worn in out-of-the-way localities in Persia and India, more as a ceremonial costume, perhaps, than for use in warfare. Moreover, we know that the Japanese wore armor regularly until about 1870, and fairly good armor it was. Chain mail reappears in the East with curious persistency. As late as the Younghusband Expedition to Thibet (1903) cases occurred where natives were captured whose costume, reinforced with chain mail, had successfully resisted the bayonet thrusts of the English. Hardly earlier than this, chain mail appears to have been worn in the region of the Caucasus. Similarly, we note that coats of mail are still worn secretly wherever danger is dreaded from personal attacks, especially by sword or knife. The writer learns from good authority that a well-known armorer in Paris derived, until about 1908, a substantial part of his income from making shirts of chain mail which were shipped to South America and Africa for actual service.

To trace in further detail the use of armor in relatively recent times: It is known that breastplates were worn more or less frequently during the American Civil War. In the museum in Richmond, there is preserved such a "suit" of armor, Fig. 15, which at the time of the siege was taken from a dead soldier in one of the trenches. He was shot in the side or back, for the breastplate, it appears, was not penetrated. This armor was of northern origin. Further inquiry shows that a factory for the making of such defenses was established at New Haven about 1862. The metal employed was a mild steel, .057 inch thick, and the "suit" weighed about seven and one half pounds. While no tests of this armor are available,* we estimate from

---

* Since this was written Miss Helen Gibbs, curator of the Museum of the Virginia Military Institute, has very kindly forwarded to the writer a hip-guard belonging to this body shield. A test shows that it will resist a 45 Colt-revolver bullet of 200 grains at about 700 foot seconds velocity. A second test was made with standard ammunition (800 foot seconds), 230-grain jacketed bullet from the 45 automatic: one shot failed to penetrate at ten feet, two penetrated but without splintering the metal. The body shield was, accordingly, a surprisingly good one for its period—before the development of higher ballistic alloys. Again, thanks to General Nathaniel Wales of Jamaica Plain, Mass., I have just received very interesting data regarding this "steel vest" of 1862. He states that "it was worn more often than we had any idea of, but many officers felt they should not be protected better than their men, consequently those who wore the armor did not advertise it." . . . Thus "two of as brave officers as I ever knew wore it, my colonel . . . and my major who was killed, a bullet grazing the bottom edge of the vest and passing through his body." He states also that his life

the thickness of its metal, assuming that it is a "mild" steel, that it would have stopped a 230-grain pistol ball traveling at the rate of 500 foot seconds.

During the Franco-Prussian War several types of armor were used to a limited degree. The heavy corselet appeared, also the horseman's helmet.

Fig. 16. French body defense used in 1870

We have occasional reference to the use of a very heavy helmet in the trenches and also of varied types of armored waistcoats. One of these, manufactured in Paris, is shown in Fig. 16. This specimen is made up of small rectangular plates of low carbon steel and riveted to canvas. The was saved by it at Antietam (September 17, 1862). Quoting his letter: "I had been presented with a steel vest by my father when I left Massachusetts, but I left it in Washington. When I entered the fight a brother officer, who was wounded, insisted on my putting on his steel vest. . . . When I advanced [in the open to meet a rebel

entire defense weighs about five pounds and could be worn with a reasonable degree of comfort. It does not resist a 230-grain pistol ball at 650 foot seconds, and from its behavior in this test, one doubts whether it would have resisted a similar bullet at a velocity greater than 300 foot seconds. Its value, therefore, lay in protecting its wearer only from spent balls or splinters. Ballistically, it had much less strength than the light-weight shrapnel helmet in present use in the American Army.

In all later wars, armor appears to have been used sporadically, sometimes as body defenses, sometimes as helmets, sometimes again in the form of shields which were either carried by the soldier or pushed in front of him. It was due to small shields of the latter type (see also page 176) that the Japanese were able to take some of the most difficult outposts of Port Arthur. Also, in the Boer War armor appears to have been used. Thus in the siege of Ladysmith, helmets were used which are said to have been proof against machine guns. They were clumsy affairs and heavy, and were not firmly attached to the head. No details of these helmets have been recorded nor have we been able to secure photographs of them. From an officer (Lieutenant R. Miller of the Imperial Light Horse) who was present at the siege, the writer learned that the defenses in question were crudely made and were only moderately effective.

The most convincing historical instance of the use of helmets and body armor against modern ammunition dates from 1880. This was in the case of the Australian bandit, Ned Kelly, who long owed his freedom to the fact that he wore armor (Fig. 17). This, it appears, he had improvised; it was the "work of some skilled local artisan." It is said to have been made out of old plowshares, beaten into plates one quarter of an inch thick. It was

charge in the twenty-first Massachusetts regiment] a bullet [evidently at close range] struck me just below the heart . . . knocking me down. Getting on my feet I walked back to where General Ferrero was lying behind a ledge. As I passed him he said, 'Where are you going, adjutant?' I replied, 'I am hit, sir.' 'Where?' I pointed to the hole in my coat and he said, 'You had better go to the rear.' I sat down remarking, 'I'll see how badly I am hurt.' It was not until I grasped the cartridge-box belt to unclasp it that I realized I was wearing the steel vest. The convex side of the dent had cut through vest, shirt and undershirt making a small cut in the flesh. It was considerably swollen and for ten days or a fortnight I was unable to draw a long breath." The drawing of the armor which accompanies the notes of General Wales shows that his escape was the luckier since the bullet struck the breastplate very close to the point where four plates came together, a region of structural weakness in armor of this type, for the free corners of the plates are held together only by rivets.

badly fashioned and extremely heavy, weighing ninety-seven pounds, but it covered the body completely. On various occasions it was badly "shot up" but not penetrated. Its wearer was captured after a several months' chase and then only after he had been shot in the legs. To give one an idea

Fig. 17. Rifle-proof armor of Australian bandit, 1894

of the efficacy of this armor against Martini rifles at close range, we insert the following quotations from the official account of this case written by one of the attacking party.

"I have no hesitation in stating," writes Superintendent Hare, "that had the man been without armor when we first attacked . . . and could have taken proper aim, not one of us would have escaped being shot. He was obliged to hold the rifle at arm's length to get anything of a sight." "His armor included a great headpiece which was like an iron pot which rested on the wearer's shoulders and completely protected the throat. The outlaw as he advanced toward the policemen had taken the precaution to conceal his armor under a long gray overcoat." "The first policeman closed in upon him and a strange fight began. The soft Martini-Henry bullets dinted his armor but did not penetrate and he coolly returned the fire." "It appeared as if he were a fiend with a charmed life." "For one half-hour this strange combat lasted." "Then one of the party rushed in and shot the outlaw in the leg, then sprang upon him and disarmed him."

This instance of the use of armor against modern gunfire is of especial interest *since it shows that an armored man could stand in front of a squad of riflemen, even at close range, and be reasonably immune. He could even kill them all,* as Superintendent Hare admits, *if he were a skilful marksman.*

From the time of Kelly's practical "experiments" up to 1914 the matter of body armor had not been held altogether in abeyance. And he who follows the literature of the subject will be surprised to find how many types of "bullet-proof" devices have been invented. A breastplate known by the name of its promoter, Rowe, apparently patented, was experimented with extensively prior to the year 1901. It gave results so promising that it attracted the personal interest and support of the German emperor. Another body defense known as the corselet Loris was also "tried out" about this time; its inventor demonstrated its effectiveness, if I am correctly informed, in various theatres in France. So, too, a bullet-proof waistcoat (see page 290) was designed by Casimir Zeglin and worn about 1897 in spectacular tests in a New York theatre. And in London similar demonstrations, more or less serious, were made by inventors, whose results, by the way, Sir Hiram Maxim accurately followed up, he himself suggesting a certain type of high alloy plates (containing tungsten) for their armor.

Even chain mail was developed by these experimenters. Thus in the military retrospective exhibition of 1889 in Paris types of mail were shown which were "proof" to dagger thrust and to the lead ball (.433 inch) of a service revolver. The former mail was made up in alternate rows of links solid and open (*i.e.*, formed so that the tips of the wire merely butted together), made of tempered spring-steel; the better quality of mail had its links fused or riveted.

About the year 1900, in fact, a dozen or more types of armor were being exploited. A well-known establishment at St. Étienne was then advertising a light breastplate proof to service revolver. A cuirass made by Alphonse Payot of La Rochelle, Savoie, was in the market, and one devised by Ernest Benedetti was tried out in Rome (1901) before a military commission and was given a favorable report. And at that time military writers were impressed with the necessity of reconsidering the armor problem. "If out of a thousand soldiers not one can reach even an improvised trench when it is defended by machine guns we *must* arrive at the adoption of some kind of a portable defense," writes Captain Danritt (*"La Guerre de Demain,"* page 600). Ch. Buttin notes at that time (1901, *"Les Armures à l'épreuve,"* Annecy, pages 99-100) that the "question of proof, far from being a dead issue, is the order of the day," and that "nothing is more sure than that science has never said its last word. And perhaps there will be found,—even if it has not already been found,—a process of making again in a scientific way that which the earlier armorers were unable to produce in their day, in spite of the superiority of their workmanship,—a corselet, light and truly proof, this time to the test of an armor piercing bullet!"

I
THE EARLY USE OF ARMOR IN THE PRESENT WAR

WHEN war began, in August, 1914, a soldier, even under special conditions, was given no defenses for head or body, in the sense of personal armor. It is true that the Germans in certain formations wore their familiar "Pickelhaube," which was a stamped leathern helmet, sometimes reinforced by steel bands and weighing in general less than a pound and a half. In certain instances, also, the Germans were provided with shields which, during the rapid advance through Belgium and France, appear soon to have been cast aside. These shields, we learn, were a distinct protection against small projectiles of low and middle velocity (less than 1,500 feet a second) but they were difficult to transport, for they could not be carried by the individual soldier in addition to his regular equipment. They were said even to be dangerous to use since, when struck, the shock would be apt to injure the bearer seriously, *e.g.*, break his arm (although on what evidence the writer has been unable to learn). It is also true that in 1914 the cuirassiers of the present guards, German, French and English, wore their panoplies, as a reminiscence of the state guards of olden times, but as cavalry was speedily sent to the rear, no satisfactory data could be gathered concerning in what degree armor actually appeared. That the panoply of the cuirassier was of considerable protective value is learned from several sources (see page 56). If his headpiece or corselet were struck by a projectile, it deflected a bullet of high velocity if its angle of incidence were great (over sixty degrees to the normal), but in this case the bullet was apt to disintegrate completely, producing a "splash" which itself was capable of inflicting a dangerous wound. In one instance recorded, a cuirassier was nearly decapitated by a lead splash of this kind which passed upward over the border of his breastplate.

The French appear to have been the first to accept the helmet in actual service and thousands of soldiers today bear witness to the practical value of the casque which was provided for them, notably through the efforts of General Adrian.

A few words as to the work of General Adrian: During colonial service, in which soldiers were in danger less from the enemy than from diseases due to improper sanitation, this officer was known for his ingenuity in developing devices which aimed to protect his men. Their well-being became his hobby, and when the present war broke out, with its appalling

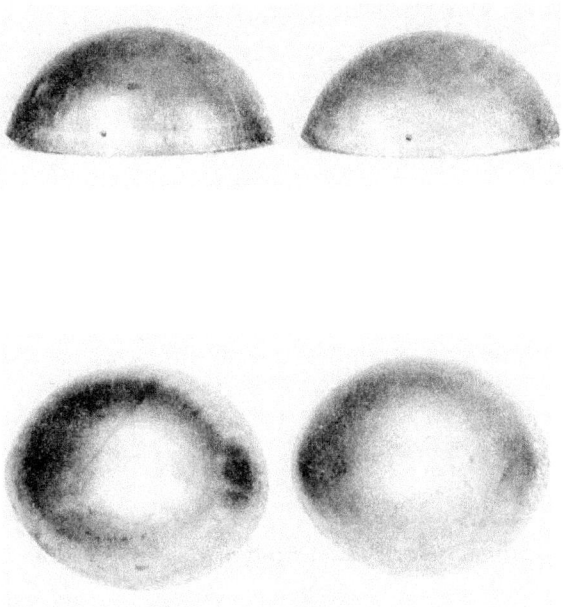

Fig. 18. Steel cap-lining, French model, 1915

casualties, General Adrian sought ways and means in all directions for reducing his losses. One day he stood before a stretcher and talked with a wounded man—"I had luck," said the sufferer, "I happened to have a metal mess-bowl in my hat and it saved my life." This incident impressed the General deeply. Here was the question of a device which might prove of universal value. So with his usual earnestness, he attacked the problem of a head defense. He promptly had a steel "calotte" made and fitted inside his cap; then he wore it constantly to find whether it would cause notable discomfort. Next he had many of them made and used experimentally.

See Figs. 18, 19. Good reports soon came in from the front. Thereupon, he developed the regular helmet which was manufactured in great numbers for the French Army. See Frontispiece. At first this defense was turned out hastily, stamped from dies which had already served in making the helmets of firemen.

Investigation showed that the new helmet was of actual value in the field; hence it became a part of the regular equipment and was used by every soldier on active duty. Its use naturally added to the burden of each wearer, causing at first considerable grumbling. During the period of pro-

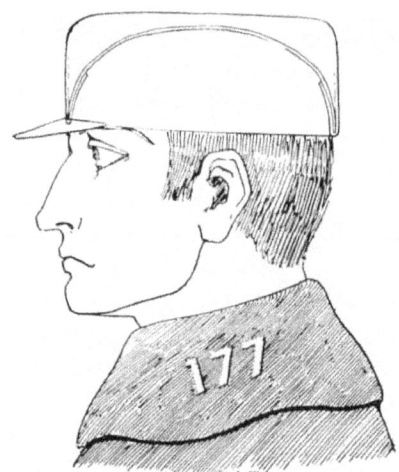

Fig. 19. French steel cap-lining, shown in position

bation of the helmet, some of the critics pointed out that the number of casualties with head wounds increased notably, but the advocates of the helmet, referring to statistics, replied that the vast percentage of those who were formerly wounded in the head found their way not to hospitals but to cemeteries!

It is interesting to note that almost from the beginning the "casque Adrian" was a successful experiment. It protected a measurable portion of its wearer; it was light and soldiers of all classes shortly "took to it." The casque was attractive in its lines and it added martial distinction to its wearer—which proved, in the opinion of many officers, a more important argument for its use than its ballistic value. Then, too, example was contagious and if one division wore it, the next was apt to follow suit. Presently it came about that the helmet was looked upon generally as indispensable. In 1915 the British Army adopted the type of helmet which it still wears. About the same time, so far as the writer can learn, the German helmet made its appearance. In 1916 the Belgians and Italians were wearing helmets and during this year they appeared in numbers on the Slavic line.

Body armor was used on all fronts from 1915 onward but its use was experimental rather than general. It was either so light in weight that it afforded too little protection, or was so heavy that its wearer, like his forebear in the Thirty Years' War, would throw it away in all cases where freedom of movement was needed. Only by sentinels or those engaged in short raids was body armor used successfully. Nevertheless, it is generally conceded by experts whom the writer consulted that this type of defense is of great potential value. But its future effectiveness will depend upon various conditions which further studies may be expected to solve. This matter is treated in a later section of this work and recommendations are made which are based upon the results of the experience which has been gained up to the end of 1918.

General Adrian

II

ARMOR AS PROTECTION AGAINST MISSILES OF LOW AND MIDDLE VELOCITY

THERE is no better evidence that armor is of practical importance in actual warfare than the testimony of physicians as to the value of the "shrapnel" helmet. In this case, at least, all criticism was overcome, although in the beginning there certainly were many objections to its use. Indeed, so severe was the criticism that had the French helmet not been introduced in very large numbers (the first lot included over a million copies), insuring it a thorough trial and under many conditions, the experiment might not have succeeded.

Various estimates have been made as to the number of casualties saved by the use of the shrapnel helmet. But these estimates are based on statistics obtained in different localities under different conditions, hence they are apt to be discordant. In a general way, however, hospital records (French, 1915) show that before the introduction of helmets about one head wound in four proved fatal. After the introduction of the helmet, however, statistics indicate that head wounds were fatal in, at the worst, one case in four and a half, and at the best one case in seven, a bettering of condition which is certainly appreciable. Add to this the saving of those men—and their number, although unreported, is great—whose helmets had resisted missiles which would otherwise have inflicted serious, if not fatal wounds.*

As a protection against missiles of low and middle velocity, there is no better evidence that armor has a definite usefulness in modern warfare than the fact that one type of armor (*i.e.*, the helmet) is accepted by many nations as a part of their military equipment; for if such a defense, even when made of light metal, is capable of resisting small missiles of middle and low velocity, it is clear that similar defenses must have a definite value when worn on chest, abdomen, or extremities. So far as the writer is aware,

---

* Major Samuel Getty, in charge of the American Base Hospital at Vittel, 1917-1918, was shown a helmet which had saved its wearer no less than seven times.

IN MODERN WARFARE

the only practical objections to the introduction of armor for these regions are its weight and the discomfort it causes its wearer—objections which, frankly, are grave, but they become the less serious if it can be shown that the advantages in wearing armor more than compensate for the disadvantages. Thus, important evidence as to the usefulness of armor is to be sought in the records of casualties.

(a) STATISTICS WHICH DEMONSTRATE THE USEFULNESS OF MODERN ARMOR, NOTABLY THE HELMET. THE MEDICAL VIEWPOINT

If it can be shown that a large percentage of the wounded soldiers in hospitals are suffering from wounds caused by missiles of low and medium velocity, it becomes clear that there is already a practical scope for the introduction of armor. The effort has therefore been made to collect data from various hospital sources, and it is now safe to say that the results of this inquiry have been conclusive. *The statistics which cover the casualties of the English through the year 1916 indicate that more than three fourths of the cases could have been saved if armor had been worn.** French statistics give similar results, the casualties caused by missiles of middle and low velocity averaging from 60 to 80 per cent in round numbers. The American statistics, so far as can be determined, vary from 65 to 80 per cent. In a letter to the writer, dated February 14, 1918, Major Charles H. Peck, Assistant Director General Surgeon, A. E. F., states that "wounds caused by missiles of middle and low velocity constitute about 80 per cent of all." In general, however, it should be admitted that complete statistics as to the percentage of the wounds caused by missiles of low and middle velocity are not always easy to obtain;† for the tabulation of wounds is not apt to be made from

---

* In a report from Colonel Walter D. McCaw, who has reviewed (June 30, 1918) the latest data at the Service de Santé, the following percentages are given:

Shrapnel or shell fragments	50.66%
Grenades	1.02%
Rifle or machine gun bullets	34.05%
Bombs from aeroplanes	.10%
Mine explosions	.15%
Accidental missiles, undetermined	14.00%

Certainly the majority of these wounds might have been avoided by the use of armor.

† According to the American surgeon, Dr. Walter Martin, whose experience was wide on the western front (1916-1917), "a large proportion" of wounds examined in

this point of view, although it is usually possible to determine from the nature of the lesion whether it was caused by a missile of high velocity. Summarizing the situation, we will come far within the mark if we state that the proportion of wounds due to middle and low velocity projectiles is not less than 60 per cent. In fact, this is the lowest estimate which we have been able to gather from medical experts who have sometimes declared that such a proportion would attain the surprising figure of 95 per cent! For, as Colonel Joseph A. Blake, director of one of the largest American military hospitals, notes in a letter to the writer, dated April 30, 1918, an accurate list of the "smaller wounds is not forthcoming because a large number of wounded whose injuries are not infected, are returned at the front and do not enter, therefore, in the statistics of the hospitals." If we accept accordingly that a large number of the wounded (estimates varying from 60 to 95 per cent) could have been saved by the use of armor it follows that the armor problem is a real and a very important one. One may note, also, that in cases not infrequent, armor might have saved victims of projectiles of high velocity. For it is well known that armor, if struck at an angle, will deflect projectiles of great velocity. In other words, from this source, too, the percentage of men whom armor would have saved becomes appreciably greater.

In this connection, we have at hand the medical report of a case which shows that a shrapnel helmet, which resists normally a projectile of 230 grains at 600 foot seconds, saved the life of its wearer when hit by a German machine gun bullet at a range of 100 yards—traveling, therefore, at the rate of not less than 1,800 foot seconds.

(b) FREQUENCY IN THE LOCATION OF WOUNDS AND ITS BEARING UPON THE ARMOR PROBLEM

There can be no question that the usefulness of armor is conditioned by a curve of frequency. In other words, if it is definitely established that a certain region of the body is particularly susceptible to injury, it is obviously that region which we should make an effort to protect. Hence the study of hospital statistics should furnish practical hints as to the sol-

the European war hospitals was due to missiles of low and middle velocity. Colonel McCaw states (June 30, 1918) "that in the hospital records, it is not the custom to note the probable velocity of the missile causing wounds in soldiers. As far as the writer knows, this is not done in any army."

diers' needs in the matter of protection. Unfortunately, however, from such a study we find that the statistics which are available are not usually classified on the lines we would have chosen, nor are they commonly accessible for large numbers of cases. Our deductions, therefore, must be made with a certain reserve. Moreover, it is clear that in various sectors at the front, the proportion of wounds may be different for various regions of the body. Nevertheless, the writer thinks that it is safe to state from the data collected that the proportional frequency of wounds in hospital cases may be arranged on somewhat the following lines:*

Lower extremities	35%
Upper extremities	25%
Head and neck	20%
Trunk	20%

In a word, certainly over 50 per cent of the hospital cases suffer from wounds in the extremities and rarely more than a fifth of the patients have been wounded in the head. The number of hospital patients wounded in the abdomen† is usually small—at first sight unexpectedly so. In fact,

* Colonel McCaw summarizes the latest data (June 30, 1918) of the Service de Santé as follows:

Classification of wounds according to anatomical situation:

Head	11.90%	Forearm	10.75%
Thorax	7.25%	Hand	8.95%
Spine	2.20%	Thigh	15.62%
Abdomen	3.97%	Leg	17.84%
Arm	14.07%	Foot	7.45%

In a word, the leg wounds would constitute 41 per cent of the total, arm wounds, 34 per cent, head, 12 per cent, trunk, about 13 per cent.

† Dr. Abadie (d'Oran) in his studies of wounds of the abdomen, published by Hongin, Masson et Cie., 1916, offers the following table:

			Due to projectiles	
Abdominal wounds	479 cases		low velocity	332
			high velocity	147
Thorax	15 lung cases		low velocity	13
			high velocity	2
	72 extracted			
	33 bullets			
	39 shrapnel fragments			

This authority notes that blood poisoning comes from low velocity projectiles, especially shrapnel. Bullets showed 4.5 per cent of the fatal cases, shrapnel, on the other hand, 40 per cent.

this proportion is the smallest of those injured, usually representing less than 3 per cent of the total. In such computations, however, it must be borne in mind that the frequency of wounds as shown in hospital records is by no means the frequency in which they occur in the field; for, as in the case of abdominal wounds, only a small proportion of these casualties survive long enough to be brought in. And this is true as well in the case of injuries of the head and of the thorax. We may note, however, that the consideration of these cases accentuates the importance of armor wearing, for it is evident that many a death occurs in the field from an injury to the thorax or abdomen where a missile of even low velocity readily enters the thin body wall.

The question of injury to the eyes has played also an important part in the discussion of armor. The peril of blindness affects the morale of troops and has led the general staff of almost every army to consider the problem of introducing visors for the helmet (see page 88). In fact, it may at once be stated that all experts agree as to the distinct usefulness of a visor of almost any type as a means of protection against eye wounds; for of such injuries over 50 per cent were caused by small fragments which could readily have been kept out by means of an eye-shield.*

We refer here especially to the extended studies of the French eye surgeons, MM. Morax and Moreau,† who show that over 43 per cent of

* Of those recorded in French hospitals about 93 per cent were due to missiles of low velocity.

† MM. V. Morax et T. Moreau in the *Annales d'Oculistique* of August, 1916, show that about 43.4 per cent of eye wounds are caused by very small fragments, 303 out of 698 cases. These experts also indicate that about 50 per cent (170 out of 341) of the cases of shell wounds are caused by small fragments and that a larger per cent of wounds are due to grenades and bombs. From the statistics in the hands of these writers, the following represents, in a general way, the frequency of wounds to the eye caused in various ways:

Shell fragments	341
Rifle or machine gun	191
Grenade	82
Fragments of bomb	63
Shrapnel ball	21
Bayonet	1

These authors declare that 50 per cent of these cases could readily be saved by the use of visors of various types. This result is corroborated by British specialists, one of whom, Captain Grove White, states that 50 per cent of eye wounds could be prevented by the use of the chain visor (see p. 133) designed by Dr. Cruise. LaPersonne

eye wounds in about 700 cases were caused by very small fragments and that 50 per cent of them were caused by small fragments, all of such a nature that they could readily have been prevented from entering the eye.

On the other hand, the question of armor for the eyes should evidently be given less attention if it can be shown that the cases of total blindness are extremely rare; for in this event the loss in efficiency would be costly if an army would be compelled to wear visors. In point of fact, eye wounds *are* proportionally rare, judged from statistics obtainable. The Canadian records are here extremely accurate and they show us that of 150,520 casualties there were only 20 cases of total blindness. That is to say, a case of blindness occurs among their casualties only once in seven thousand cases. In a word, following the statistics in question and taking into account the total number of troops involved, the chance of any particular soldier becoming totally blind is certainly very remote. Thus, in the English Army, in general, the percentage of cases of blindness is known to be low, and indeed not more than three thousand cases of blindness were recorded up to January, 1918, in an army of about three millions. In other words, the chance of any individual English soldier becoming blind is as one is to one thousand. And from the data concerning the armies of all nations, so far as the writer was able to determine, it seems clear that the number of cases of total blindness is not excessive, in no instance higher apparently than one in five hundred, or one fifth of one per cent. Hence in the work of war it would hardly be expedient to give to a thousand men an eye defense which would confuse them and which would possibly be a cause of slowness in action and consequent danger of casualties, to the end that only one person in this number should escape blindness.

and Terron note that 80 per cent of the eye lesions studied in French hospitals were due to missiles of low velocity; they also declare that in general the majority (75 per cent) of all wounds treated in military hospitals are caused by similar missiles.

III

FOREIGN TYPES OF HELMETS AND BODY ARMOR, THEIR ORIGIN AND FATE

(A) French
    (a) The French helmet
        1. Origin
        2. Description
        3. Manufacture
        4. Material
        5. Ballistic value
        6. Criticism
        7. Newer models
    (b) Face defenses, Polack and Dunand visors
    (c) Body shields
    (d) Defenses for arms and legs

(A) FRENCH

(a) THE FRENCH HELMET

1. *Its Origin*

FRANCE, as we noted in the introduction of this report, was the first nation in the present war to adopt steel helmets for its soldiers. The earlier form of this helmet appears in Figs. 18 and 19. This was a steel cap designed by General Adrian before December, 1914.

It was stamped out of soft steel .197 inch (5 mm.) thick and weighed but nine ounces. It had its initial inspiration in the metal hat-lining of the sixteenth century which was termed a "secrète." This metal lining was merely pressed into the cap and held in place by a sweat-band. It was a simple device but it was found to resist 60 per cent of the shrapnel hits. This was determined by experiments in the actual field in the "polygon of Bourges."

IN MODERN WARFARE

Early in February and March, 1915, 700,000 of these caps were made and issued. The success of this simpler type of head defense gave place within a month or two to the complete French helmet (Frontispiece). In its essential lines, this followed the design of the helmet of the cuirassier and of the "casque du pompier" as illustrated in the accompanying sketches

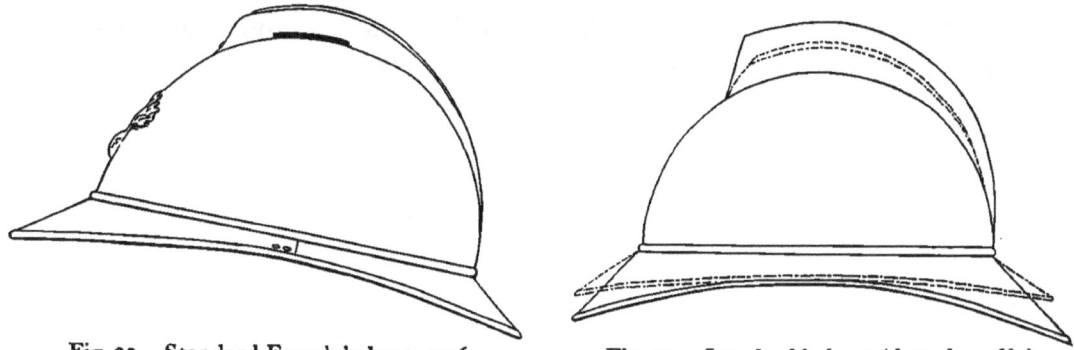

Fig. 20. Standard French helmet, 1916

Fig. 21. Standard helmet (dotted profile) compared with French fireman's helmet

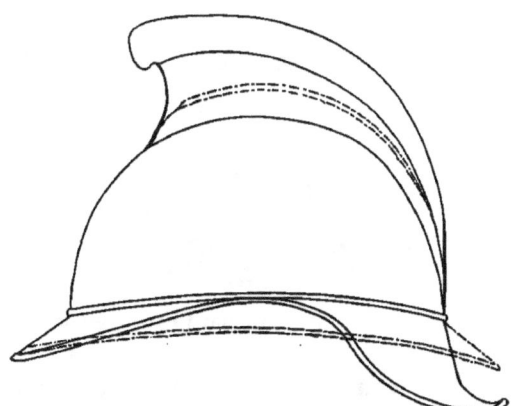

Fig. 22. Standard helmet (dotted profile) compared with French dragoon's helmet

(Figs. 20, 21 and 22), for by this procedure a model was at hand whose merit was fully established and whose speedy production was assured. In fact, certain of the dies which formed the earlier casques could be used at once. The thickness of metal recommended for the new helmet was 8 mm. (.315 inch). Its entire weight should not exceed 800 grams ($=$ 2 pounds) which was but two thirds the weight of the casque of the dragoon.

76 HELMETS AND BODY ARMOR

2. *Description*

The present hat-shaped helmet is worn by all French soldiers in actual service. Its light weight (which was reduced to one pound eleven ounces) enables it to be worn without fatigue, and its artistic merit, to which Edouard Detaille contributed, touches the pride of the soldier.

In general, it is hat-shaped, composed of a sub-hemispherical dome, a medium crest, and a down-bent brim which is narrow above the ears. On its forehead it bears the symbol, *e.g.*, grenade, crossed cannon, etc., of the

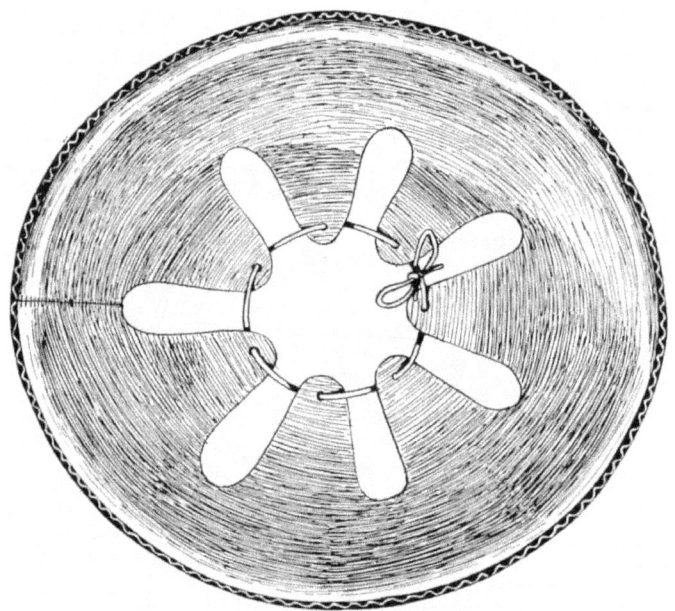

Fig. 23. Lining of standard French helmet

army group to which the wearer belongs. The casque is painted either the military blue of the French soldier or an olive drab. Its surface is not roughened.

It fits the head of the wearer nearly as comfortably as a "derby" hat and its size is, to this end, regulated with great precision. The steel shell is stamped out in three sizes, designated "A," "B" and "C": the first is adapted for heads of our hat-size $6\frac{7}{8}$, the second size corresponds to our $7\frac{1}{8}$, and the third to our $7\frac{3}{8}$. For each of these sizes, linings of four different measures are provided. The lining is separated from the shell of the helmet by a band of aluminum, which is crimped or corrugated—furnishing

IN MODERN WARFARE

a series of channels which run vertically when the helmet is in place, insuring a certain amount of ventilation. The lining consists of a sweat-band of "Cuban goatskin" from which arise tabs which line the dome of the helmet and converge to its apex (Fig. 23). Each tab is perforated near its free extremity by a metal eyelet through which a string passes. By the adjustment of this string, the head may be kept from contact with the top of

Fig. 24. Three stages in making French helmet, 1916

the helmet. The leather sweat-band of this helmet is kept from the steel shell by the intervention of a stout band of felt and by the corrugated band of aluminum mentioned above. A chin-strap, made of sheepskin, five eighths inch in width, is fastened to the helmet by means of two slender metal loops, each on its side attached by two small rivets. The latter serve, at the same time, to hold together the front and back halves of the brim of the helmet.

3. *Manufacture*

The French helmet, while apparently simple in structure, requires no less than seventy operations in manufacture. This number, moreover, does not include stages in the preparation of the metal for manufacture, cutting out the plates, etc. (Several stages are shown in Fig. 24.)

(a) *Dome:* The dome of the helmet is stamped out cold in two operations. "Blanking" (trimming) operations follow, then a hole is pierced at the apex for ventilation and other holes for attachment of the crest and the emblem. Last of all, a crimped border is formed around the dome, within which the brim of the helmet is attached.

(b) *Brim:* The brim of the helmet is stamped in two pieces, which, when fastened together, articulate with the dome of the helmet by means of marginal crimping. This upper or crimped border of the brim comes to lie in a horizontal plane and from it the brim slopes downward. The brow-peak bends downward at an angle of 22 degrees; the back of the brim, which forms a peak to protect the back of the neck, inclines at an angle of 45 degrees; while the sides of the brim are directed downward at an angle of 70 degrees. The peak at the brow is two inches wide, at the back of the head one and three fourths inches, at the side five eighths inch. The free edge of the brim is rolled over in the direction from bottom to top so as to make a neat finish.

(c) *Crest:* The median axis of the dome of the helmet is covered by an embossed convex plate of metal which extends from the region of the hind peak of the helmet over the dome forward to a distance of about three and one half inches from the base of the brow-peak. This forms a median ornament and is fastened to the roof of the helmet by four rivets. The crest is manufactured in two operations, in one of which the outer curved portion is formed. The emblem (bomb, crossed guns, initials of the republic, etc.) which represents the branch of the service of the wearer and which has already been embossed in steel, is now attached to the brow region of the helmet by means of cramping points.

(d) *Ventilation:* The French helmet is well ventilated. Air enters the dome of the helmet from the region of the brow-band through the channels provided by the encircling strip of crimped aluminum (cf. Fig. 23). The air then passes out of the dome through a median slot which is half an inch wide and an inch and three quarters long; thus it enters the hollow median crest of the helmet from under the margins of which it finally escapes; for here the crest has been so trimmed that its sides for a distance of about two inches do not come in contact with the adjacent dome of the helmet.

(e) *Lining:* The lining described above is fastened to the dome of the helmet by means of four wide staple-shaped fasteners. The backs of these staples are soldered to the dome; their points project straight inwards and perforate both the aluminum ventilating bands and the leather and felt sweat-band of the lining. They are then cramped together by bending and hold these elements in place.

(f) *Chin-straps:* These in the earlier helmets were attached to small loops which formed part of the back of the staple which fastened the lining mentioned above. In later models, these loops are fastened by small tabs of steel to the brim of the helmet by the same rivets which hold together the front and back halves of the brim. The chin-strap, with its loops, is considerably lighter than in the helmets of the English, Americans, or Germans. Its buckle is attached on the right side and is of the sliding type: it is simple in form, straight and light; it does not appear to give trouble by sliding over the strap even in well-worn specimens.

(g) *Painting:* The helmet is dipped in an oil varnish of a chosen color. It is then dried in an oven at a temperature between 257 and 284 degrees Fahrenheit for at least an hour and a half. At the end of this time, the paint will not scale off; nor does it soften in contact with water of 167 degrees Fahrenheit.

(h) *Size:* The greatest diameter of the dome of the helmet is 7.91 inches for size "A," 8.27 for "B," and 8.62 for "C." The width of the three sizes of helmets measures respectively 7.13, 7.48 and 7.83 inches. The height of the helmet measures similarly 4.13, 4.33 and 4.53 inches.

(i) *Production:* Two of the largest concerns manufacturing French helmets are Compteurs et Matériel d'Usines à Gaz (rue Claude Vellefaux, Paris) and the firm of August Dupeyron. The latter manufacturer is stated to have made prior to September, 1917, three million French helmets; the former turns out about 7,500 helmets per day and has the reputation of doing excellent work. The equipment of such a factory includes two hundred presses, among them four of one hundred tons and seventy of fifty tons, and has forty automatic and handscrew machines; its tool room employs eighty mechanics.

4. *Material*

The French helmet is made of mild steel, without scales or defects. It must be .0277 inch in thickness, with a tolerance of .002 inch. The steel should be clean and heat-treated. Its tensile strength is 62,000 pounds per square inch, its percentage of elongation 18 degrees. From this physical character, it may without special annealing be pressed into the needed form, and it is sufficiently tenacious not to be shattered when struck by a bullet—the last a feature of great importance, for if the helmet be penetrated, there must be no danger of the bullet carrying fragments of steel into the wound. Hence it is that "half hard" steel is safer to use than hard steel. The composition of the French steel, two types, A and B, considered, is as follows:

		Early	"A"	"B"
Composition:	Carbon	.225	.19½%	.10%
	Manganese	.490	.46%	.42%
	Phosphorus	.025	.025%	.03%
Thickness:			.026″	.026″

Treatment: "A" annealed once in course of pressing
"B" not annealed in course of pressing

According to information given the writer by General Adrian, the composition of the helmet steel is about to be changed; in the new steel the carbon content is to be .150, the manganese .450. It is noted that the French specialists lay less stress upon the composition of the metal demanded of contractors than upon the physical characters of the steel.

5. *Ballistic Value*

The French helmet, which is probably the most popular of headpieces in actual service, is functionally the least effective. So far as the writer can learn, it receives no ballistic test at the hands of the French Government; the contract merely prescribes that the metal sheet to be used in the manufacture shall have certain physical characters. It must show a tensile strength of about 60,000 pounds per square inch and an elongation of 18 per cent and it shall have a certain thickness. But nothing is stated as to the degree of the thinning out of the plate which may be tolerated in the crown of the helmet. In this and in some other details a sacrifice appears to have been made by the French Government in the interest of speedy production—which was of the utmost importance at the time the French helmet was introduced. In a general way, it may be stated that the ballistic value of the French helmet is about one half that of the British helmet. Thus, while the British helmet will resist perforation by an automatic revolver at ten feet, which has a bullet weighing 230 grains and a muzzle velocity of 700 foot seconds, the French helmet would be perforated by a similar missile having muzzle velocity of about 400 foot seconds. Sometimes a somewhat better result is shown, *e.g.*, 450 foot seconds, according to Mr. John MacIntosh of the British Ordnance Department. Similar results, we may mention, are recorded by French investigators. To cite one type of testing, we refer to the results obtained by Dr. E. Dupuy of the Chemical Laboratory of the Sorbonne, who found that the Browning revolver having a caliber of .25 penetrates the French helmets readily at two yards' distance. Even then, the ball is not spent, for it penetrates hard wood behind it to a depth of 3½ to 5½ inches. Dr. Dupuy, we note, devised a mechanism for determining the ballistic value of the metal without a firing test; his device is based upon the principle of a punch which descends upon the plate (or helmet) which, in this case, is cramped between rings 3½ inches in diameter. The punch is .28 inch in thickness, is round at its point, and is connected with a dynamometer to register the force of the blow. By the aid of this device, Dr. Dupuy examined the two types of steel used in the French helmets (indicated as "A" and "B" on page 80 of the present section) and found that "A" was perforated at a pressure of 756 pounds while "B" ruptured at 674. In one case, "A," the ball before rupturing the plate indented it to a distance of .25 inch, while in "B" it caused an indentation of .20 inch. In similar tests made by Dr. Dupuy on the English helmet, which was pressed from manganese alloy of 13 per cent and was .035 inch thick, the metal was ruptured only after a blow equivalent to 1,578 pounds had been given; it then showed an indentation measuring only .28 inch. His results, therefore, indicate that the French helmet has less than one half the ballistic strength of the English helmet, while it suffers an indentation almost twice as great. The latter condition we infer, since in the case noted above the French helmet indented .25 inch while the English helmet at more than double the shock indented only .28 inch.

6. *Criticism*

There can be no question, accordingly, that the French helmet does not take high rank ballistically. It is penetrated at about one half the blow which the English helmet is able to resist. On the other hand, it weighs nearly one fourth less and can, therefore, be carried with minor fatigue. Indeed, it can safely be said that in the matter of bearing a weight upon the head during protracted periods each extra ounce becomes an important matter; hence in any criticism of the French helmet, one should take into careful

consideration the type of missile which the defense is intended to resist; for it may be quite strong enough for its purpose. The French helmet is stated, as the basis of numerous and careful tests, to resist about three fourths of the shrapnel hits. The British helmet by similar tests would probably be effective against nearly all. Hence, it would seem that the superiority of the British headpiece was demonstrated beyond a doubt and that the French Government would speedily be led to improve the quality of its helmet. Not only is the French helmet less effective in its metal but in its construction as well; indeed, no one can question that it is greatly weakened by the numerous perforations in its bowl. We refer here especially to the long slot which pierces the crown of the helmet, which should have been avoided at almost any cost; also, every effort should have been made to gain strength in the helmet by fashioning the brim and the crown out of the same piece of steel, for one can only believe that many lives have been lost through the weakness of the brow line of the French helmet where the bowl and the brim are merely crimped together. In spite of this criticism, however, we note that its especial form of helmet was resolutely maintained by the French Government through four years of warfare. Hence, this headpiece must have been a satisfactory and a serviceable one. Perhaps it was not the very best for its purpose, for the French experts themselves are not blind to its shortcomings, but some of their most competent chiefs lay stress upon the fact that there is much to be gained in the management of the soldier's equipment by conserving standard patterns.*
It is by this means that speedy and economical production is maintained. Also it is fair to say that each helmet has a morale of its own. That of the French helmet is high: its wearer takes it seriously and it would do him no good to tell him that his is not the best model for his needs. He becomes fond of his helmet and his feeling toward it is a distinct asset in the problem. He is convinced that its shape is excellent, he is accustomed to its lighter weight, and he would gladly wear it under conditions in which he would probably cast aside a heavier and a better helmet. Hence, in the long run, the protective coefficient of the present casque is probably not far from that of a newer and improved design. Assuredly, there are many points to be

* This argument was recently emphasized by the Ordnance in Washington, and a circular was issued quoting the General Staff of Charles I, which deplored the many novelties in equipment which were then being demanded for the army! While the principle is a deserving one, the writer suggests that the illustration was chosen unfortunately, for one recalls the fate of the royal army at the hands of the innovators!

considered in this problem of changing a helmet; so it comes about that many things which seem to a foreigner to need speedy correction go on their way unaltered. As an example of this, one wonders vainly why the French helmet is allowed to remain narrow in brim over the ear and temple; for, obviously, the lack of protection in this vital region must have cost the lives of many wearers. A critic might also note that the casque Adrian might be lightened at least 3½ ounces (100 grams) by removing from it its various ornamental devices, a procedure which would also, by the way, considerably help to reduce the time and expense of its manufacture. But here, again, we touch the question of morale (in this case, aesthetical), which plays an important part even in the business of war.

Fig. 25. French helmet, experimental, having fluted crown

7. *Newer Models*

It is because of the obvious defects of the present helmet that armor critics in France have suggested a number of improved models, and some of these we may now briefly consider.

In point of fact, from the time the French helmet was adopted, modifications in its design were attempted and some of the newer models appeared in experimental lots in the field. In one of the earlier variants (Fig. 25), the crown of the helmet developed a series of horizontal ridges about ten in number, which were expected to increase the rigidity and hence the ballistic value of the helmet. It is even interesting to note that this device was also developed independently both in England and in the United States; indeed, it is fair to say that its origin is a very early one,

84   HELMETS AND BODY ARMOR

for those who know the history of armor will recall at once that cannellated surfaces in armor were used extensively by armorers in various parts of Europe during the late fifteenth and the first half of the sixteenth century. Indeed, they even gave rise to a style of armor known as "Maximilian" in honor of the Emperor Maximilian of Austria in whose court this armor was fashionable and by whom it is even supposed to have been invented. The physical principle which suggested that this fluted or corrugated type

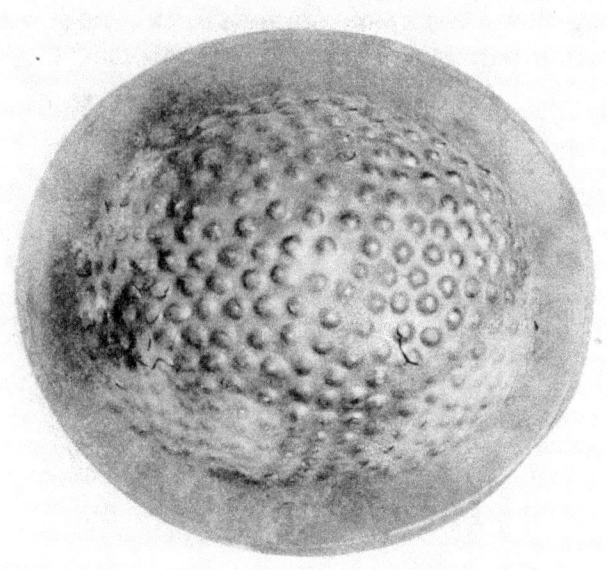

Fig. 26. British helmet, experimental, with bosses stamped on crown

of armor would be especially strong was evidently that of the arch which at a definite point was expected to sustain the metal against an impinging blow. The ridges, it is usually held, should be so close together that the impinging projectile would straddle, as it were, from one arch to another and thus meet greater resistance.* In a somewhat similar line a suggestion

* A somewhat similar principle was considered in the "honeycombing" of armor plate, or partly drilling it in lines, so as to reduce the weight yet with the possible effect of retaining the ballistic strength of the plate. Trials in this direction have not yielded positive results; it is certain only that the improvement in the strength of the plate under this condition is not substantial (W. A. Taylor).

was made both in England and in France that a type of helmet would be especially strong whose crown was covered with small bosses (Fig. 26), for these projections were supposed to serve the same function in supporting the shock of the impinging ball as the parallel ridges referred to above. In all these cases, however, actual tests of ballistic resistance have been disappointing. They have shown, notably, that the concave areas which separate the ridges are correspondingly weaker. In the final analysis, one may state that a surface which is smooth affords approximately as great

Fig. 27   Fig. 27A   Fig. 27B

Fig. 27. Experimental model (A) of French helmet, hand-made

a resistance to the projectile. In the matter of testing the strength of these small ridges, furthermore, the degree of movement of a projectile is probably a factor to be reckoned with; for when a missile travels as rapidly as a modern pistol ball, it may not have time to "feel" out accurately the delicate checks and balances of such a strengthening device.

Of the various substitutes for the Adrian helmet which have been recommended, no model has been definitely accepted up to the present time. We here show, in Figs. 27-30, several types or variants which have been suggested. These are hand-made specimens,* but they will later be reproduced in manganese steel by dies. All of the present models cover the sides

* Since this was written tests were made of die-stamped specimens (fall of 1918) but with what results we have not learned.

of the head far more completely than the French helmet in actual use; thus, it will be seen that the brim extends downward to the level of the ear-hole. Both the forehead and peak and the nape of this helmet are well developed and show but small variations. The models range from a straight-brimmed form (Fig. 27) through the types of Figs. 28 and 29, to a helmet (Fig. 30) which is indented at the side of the eye and better

Fig. 28   Fig. 28A   Fig. 28B

Fig. 28. Experimental model (B) of French helmet, hand-made

protects the temple. In the first of these forms, the brim is gradually rolled or tilted up, beginning from its line of union with the dome of the helmet; in the last type, the brim is developed downward at the sides and gives greater protection to the region of the temple. It is among these forms that the latest French helmet will possibly be chosen, although it is safe to say that the French soldier will not give up his attractive Adrian casque for a simpler and more efficient headpiece without a distinct struggle. Of the four forms here shown, the first (knowingly or unknowingly) is a copy of a fifteenth-century headpiece of the model known as a *chapel*.

Siege helmet. For sentinels and snipers, the French have used experimentally a type of headpiece shown in Fig. 31; it was found unsatisfactory in actual service (1916?) and discarded; few specimens were made and the writer has not been able to secure one for examination. It is said to have weighed twelve pounds.

Fig. 29　　　　　　　Fig. 29A　　　　　　　Fig. 29B

Fig. 29. Experimental model (C) of French helmet, hand-made

Fig. 30　　　　　　　Fig. 30A　　　　　　　Fig. 30B

Fig. 30. Experimental model (D) of French helmet, hand-made

A second type, also experimental, which we believe was never made in ballistic metal, is shown in Fig. 32; this was designed by M. Dunand in 1915; it was provided with a rotating and detachable face-guard.

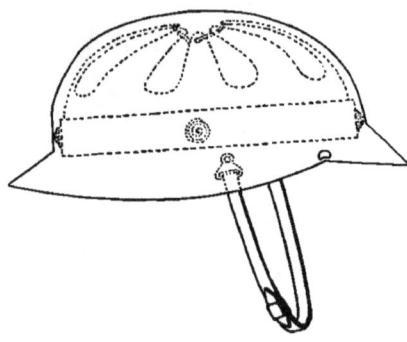

Fig. 31. Siege helmet, experimental. French, 1916-1917

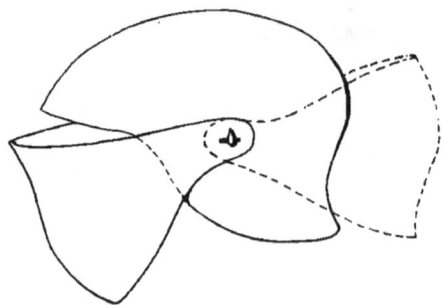

Fig. 32. Dunand experimental design for sentinel's heavy helmet

Fig. 33

Fig. 34

Figs. 33 and 34. French standard helmet with visor. Early Polack model

(b) FACE DEFENSES, POLACK AND DUNAND VISORS

The French Bureau of Inventions, organized as a Sub-Section of the Department of War (Paris, rue de l'Université, 26, bis), has had in its charge the development of helmets and body armor. In the matter of helmets, the experts of this Section, including General Adrian, Majors Le Maistre and Polack, have critically examined the various models presented to it and have themselves carried on a wide series of experiments in this field, especially in the matter of visors. While it is here inexpedient to review many types of defenses which these specialists have analyzed, the trend of their work should be followed.

After the helmet of the French Army had been definitely accepted, the efforts of various experimenters were directed toward developing a face-shield and eye-guard which could be adapted to the standard helmet. One of the first of these experimental defenses dated early in 1916: it was a reinforcing piece for the front of the French helmet; it corresponded to the upper portion of the face-guard in helmets of the sixteenth century, known

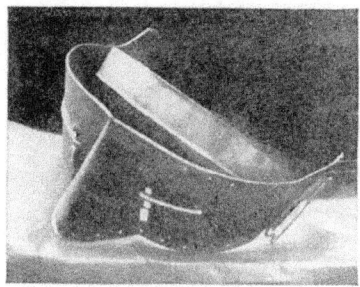

Fig. 35. French experimental visor. Early Polack model

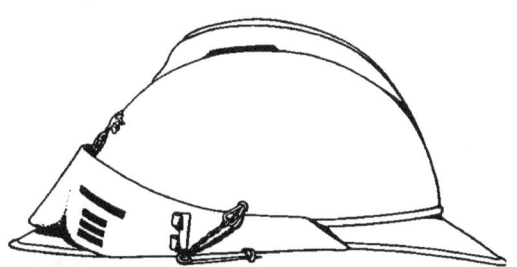

Fig. 36. Polack visor. Early form attached to French helmet

as the "visière," and like the latter rotated over the face by means of a rivet situated above the ears. This type, shown in Figs. 33 and 34, was designed by MM. Landret and Polack and stamped out of zinc. It was modeled close to the face in the nasal region and was provided with a narrow transverse slit for vision; this single slit, the inventors maintained, was quite sufficient to insure the wearer adequate vision and both experts advised against the use of a visor having many perforations, *i.e.*, like a pepperbox top.

Another type of Polack visor, however, dating from late 1916 or 1917, was based upon the principle of securing vision by means of separate slits developed in parallel series and strengthened structurally by vertical bands. An interesting visor shown in Fig. 35, which was arranged to be used with the standard French helmet and was detachable, shows a transitional type from a visor of a single slit to one having many. In the first specimen pictured, there are four slots; of these the second one is long, transverse, and is strengthened by a ridge made of metal which was bent out when the slot was formed. From this stage in development, we pass to that of Fig. 36;

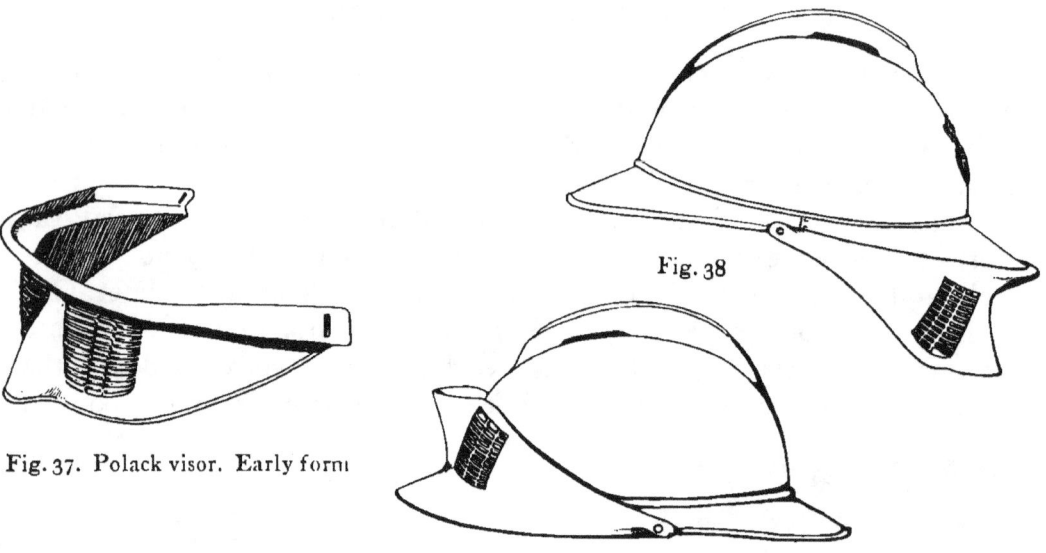

Fig. 37. Polack visor. Early form

Fig. 38

Fig. 38A

Fig. 38. Polack visor. Early form, attaches to brim of helmet

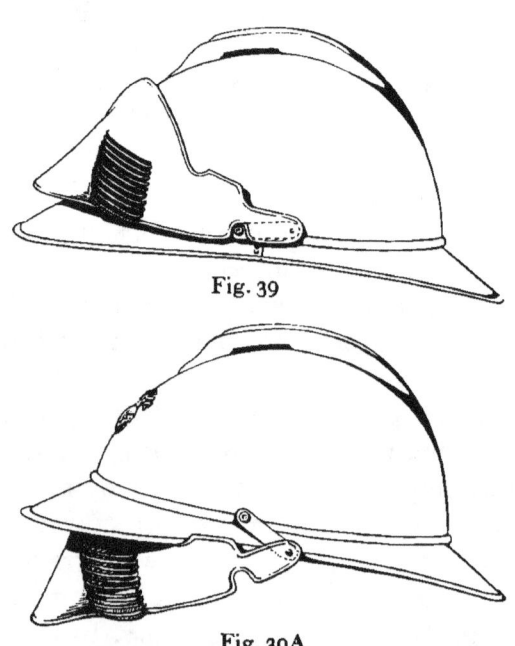

Fig. 39

Fig. 39A

Fig. 39. Polack visor, adapted to brim of standard helmet

IN MODERN WARFARE

then to a many-slotted visor capable of being attached to the French helmet. Here we note such types as shown in Figs. 37 to 41. Next there appear visors for which special helmets were designed (Figs. 42 and 43). Of these Polack visors, the earliest was attached to the standard helmet by

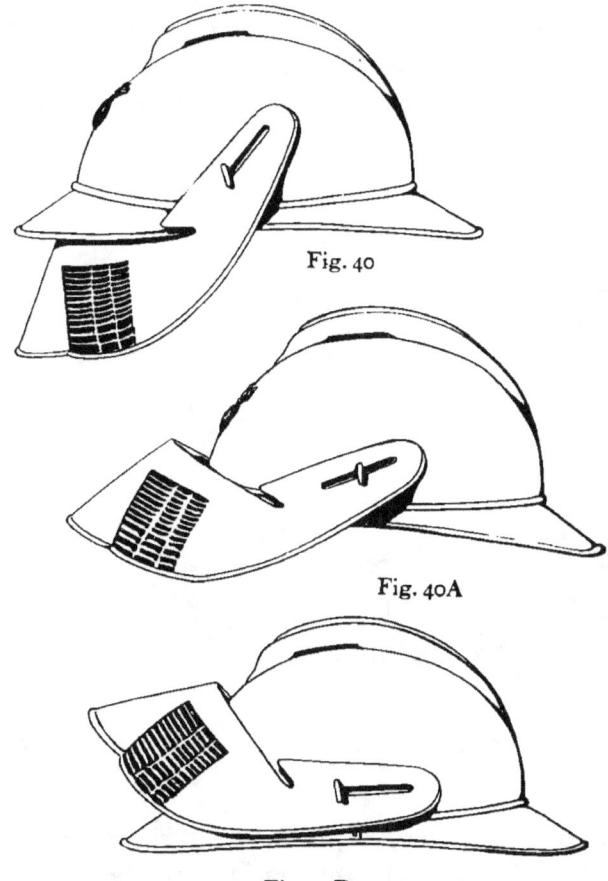

Fig. 40. Polack visor, fitting head below or above brim of helmet

means of rubber bands, and its slots for vision are still cut in the visor. In a later stage they appear in a definite cage built up of separate laminae and held together in a frame which is then inserted in the body of the visor. The laminae which are situated in front of the eye are set in a horizontal plane; those situated above the eye slant upward, and those below downward, all slants or planes having been designed to focus in a radial way on the pupil of the eye (Fig. 62). By this means, the wearer is given a remarkably clear range of vision in front, above, at the sides, and below, for the laminae are thin and are placed edgewise. Such a visor, it is evident, would be an exceedingly weak one were the laminae not strengthened by vertical bars. These are thin and are arranged vertically in such a way as to interfere very little with sight. The whole device is technically and optically excellent. The earliest type of the Polack visor could be demounted and carried upside down on the forehead of the helmet (Figs. 38 and 38A).

Fig. 41　　　　　　　Fig. 41A　　　　　　　Fig. 41B
Fig. 41. Polack visor with standard French helmet, 1918

Another model, when put in place, fitted neatly over the front brim of the helmet (Figs. 39 and 39A). A later variant of this visor, shown in Figs. 40, 40A and 40B, articulated ingeniously with the standard helmet by means of a peg and sliding groove and could be slid back on the brow region of the helmet when not in use. Still another variant, developed in 1917, is shown in Figs. 41, 41A and 41B; this takes the form of a mobile visor which when not in use is carried on the forehead. When dropped in place, its lower border extends as far as the tip of the nose. A final model, developed early in 1918, is shown in Figs. 42 and 43. Here the visor is adapted to a helmet entirely different in shape from the standard helmet. The models here shown are hand-made, but it is understood that this type of helmet will

Fig. 42   Fig. 42A

Fig. 42B   Fig. 42C

Fig. 42. Polack visor with new experimental French helmet (1918). Hand-made

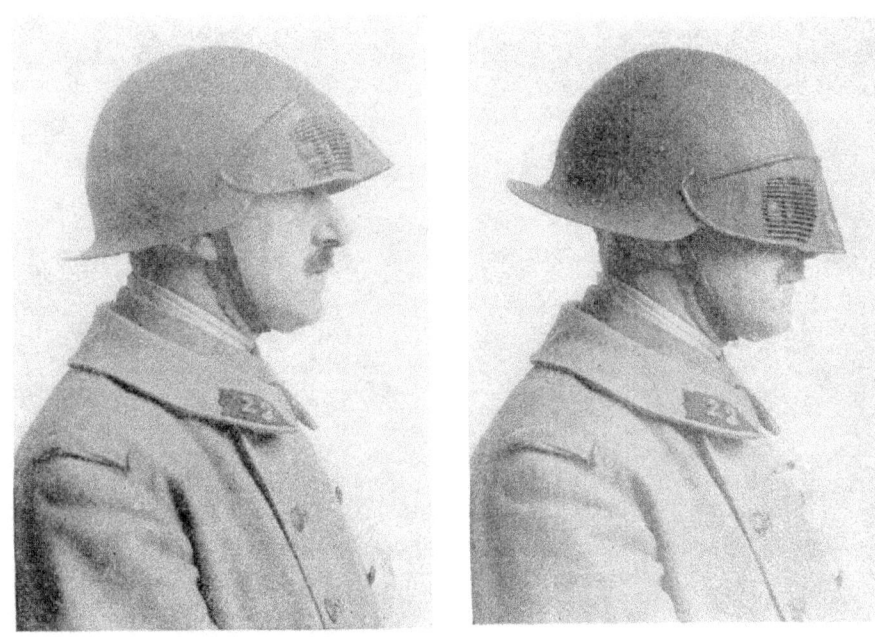

Fig. 43   Fig. 43A

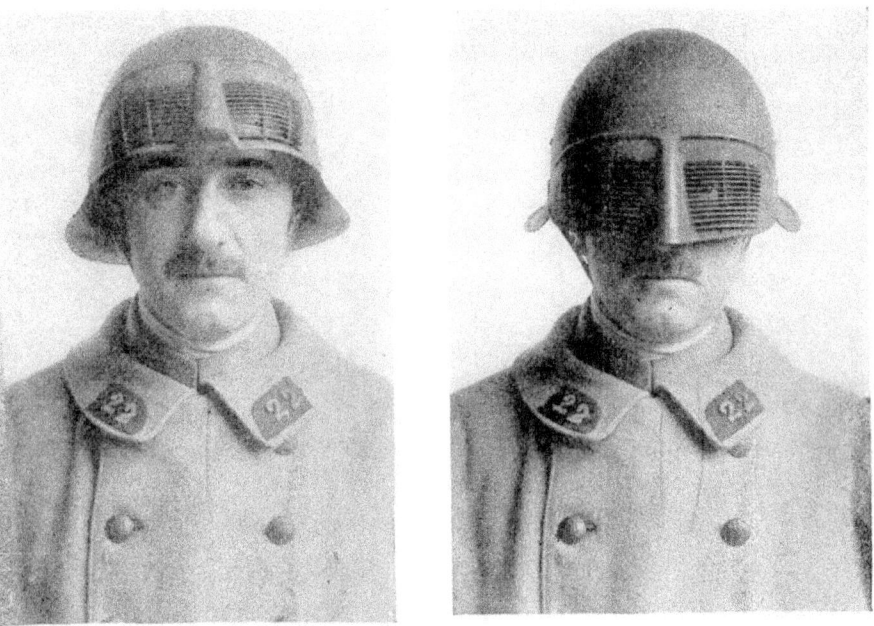

Fig. 43B   Fig. 43C

Fig. 43. Polack visor with new experimental French helmet (1918). Hand-made

be pressed in manganese steel* and that it will probably be chosen to succeed the Adrian helmet.

In the matter of the ballistic qualities of the Polack visor, tests made in France, England and the United States have not given altogether satisfactory results. It will certainly protect the eye region from metal splinters and shrapnel at low velocity. On the other hand, its great range of vision is its element of weakness, for, as was early pointed out, it is open widely

Fig. 43D. Polack visor with new experimental French helmet (1918). Die stamped. Specimen tested in H. A. E. F.

to small splinters and gives them ready access to the eye. In fact, the adjustment of the thin radiating slats or lamellae which compose this visor is precisely of such a nature as to draw into a direction of great danger to the wearer any fragments which are scattering in the neighborhood, very much in the same way that the mouth of a funnel would lead to its narrow end whatever falls within it. In general, however, this visor has found favor with the French Government and it is understood that many helmets have

* See also Fig. 43D, the first model stamped in ballistic metal received by the writer.

been provided with it and are being used in the field. The eye-shield was also given a favorable report from American Headquarters in France. It will be observed that the Polack visor covers only the upper part of the face and while therefore it is only a partial defense for this region, it retains the merit of lightness and balance, for in general a heavier visor tends to displace the center of gravity of the helmet and cause it gradually to tilt forward over the eyes. As a defense against such a missile as a pistol ball traveling at the rate of 600 foot seconds, the Polack visor is held to be worse than useless; it is penetrated, shattered, and an even more serious wound would be caused by the ragged ball and the inbent and broken ends of the visor's laminae.

In this connection reference should be made to the visors and helmets designed by the brothers Dunand.

During three years of the present war, M. Jean Dunand endeavored with great care and under discouraging conditions to produce a headpiece, and especially a visored headpiece, which would be the best of its kind. M. Dunand, it should be stated, has a European reputation as an artist in hammer work. His helmets are admirably embossed and he has produced a dozen or more variants of the type of helmet which he recommended. These, in most cases, he provided with a visor, or eye-shield, which he designed not less with sentiment than with art, for his brother, who has constantly aided him in his studies, lost an eye in French service early in the war. The MM. Dunand have carried on their work without subsidy from the French Government, which had already accepted its own standard helmet. They also early offered their services to the American authorities in France; in point of fact, many of their designs passed through the headquarters of the American Expeditionary Forces. An early type of Dunand helmet is shown in Figs. 44, 44A and 44B. It is a bowl-shaped helmet and its profile is not widely different from that of the British helmet; it is somewhat deeper, however (by three quarters of an inch), in the region of the ear and of the back of the head. The dome of the helmet is dilated in the brow region and is covered with a globose visor whose slots are pierced mechanically in transverse lines. The visor rotates on key-shaped pegs and retains its position when raised by means of a small peglike protuberance on the brow of the helmet which clings to the bent-in upper border of the visor, a "safety" device well known in automobile fittings. The early model of the Dunand helmet shown in this figure was exhibited at American headquarters and American authorities ordered that a number of these

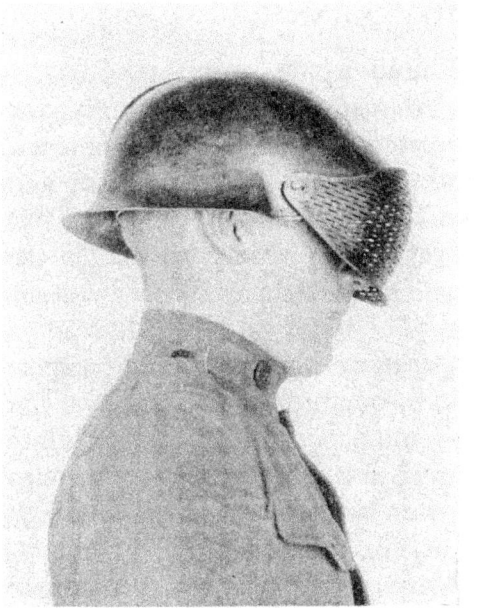

Fig. 44 Fig. 44A

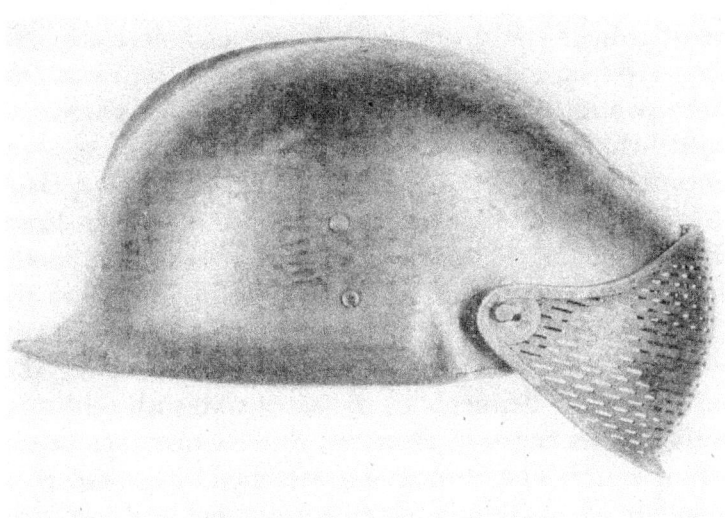

Fig. 44B

Fig. 44. Dunand helmet, hand-made model, 1916-1917

helmets (10,000) be prepared in the United States and forwarded to France for experimental use. This was in August, 1917. Accordingly, the Ordnance Department in Washington directed one of the most efficient pressing concerns in this country to undertake the work, Messrs. Crosby and Company of Buffalo. The dies for this work were promptly prepared, but great difficulty was experienced in the operation of pressing, so that in the end the Messrs. Crosby declared that the Dunand helmet could not be pressed in the manganese metal prescribed. They had called in vain upon their experienced die makers and press operators, and had sought expert advice upon their problem in other directions, but the verdict was ever the same. Their criticism of the helmet, as a pressing proposition, was that while the needed depth of the draw might be had in the desired metal, the sharp crest shown in the model could not thereafter be formed nor was it practicable to cause the metal at the side of the visor to be sharply inbent (it was already strained) without cracking. Now the difficulty with the crest could be avoided by simply omitting the median ridge, but unfortunately the indentation at the side of the visor could not be ignored since this in the model conditioned the attachment of the visor. Hence, it was found necessary to forward the word to American headquarters abroad that the present type of helmet could not be produced commercially. Shortly after this, early in 1918, the contract with the American firm was canceled.

In the meanwhile, however, Dunand continued his work energetically and developed his helmet on similar lines; and in January, 1918, a large pressing concern in Paris (the Compteurs et Matériel d'Usines à Gaz) undertook to produce one of his newly developed models in English manganese steel. In this model, the inventor, it will be seen, had modified certain technical details which had earlier been stumbling-blocks in manufacture. One of the later Dunand models is shown in Figs. 45 and 45A in which the side of the helmet is given a rounded lower border, causing it to resemble closely certain "hunting helmets" of the early sixteenth century. The model still retains the earlier comb or crest but this element has been rounded to facilitate manufacture. The visor is here attached by a rotating peg as in the earliest design but its position is somewhat higher; its form is the same but its sides are not perforated. Dunand developed finally the helmet which is shown in the Frontispiece and in Figs. 45 and 45A, which was ultimately pressed in manganese steel. It has approximately the same depth as the early model; its brim, however, is less abruptly out-turned and it is lower in front. The attachment of the visor was now ingeniously effected by means of pegs riveted strongly to the brim of the helmet in such a way that the tips of the pegs project at the side. The pegs, then, are no longer capable of turning and the visor is removable only when raised to a particular height. Specimens of this helmet were forwarded to the United States for the examination of the Ordnance Department and a statement was made by the committee on helmets in France to the effect that this type of helmet might be accepted as the standard helmet for the American forces in case a Polack visor could be used with it instead of the present one.

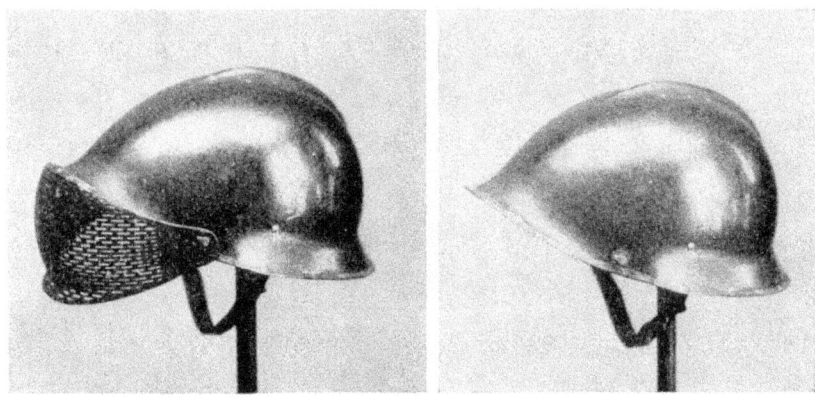

Fig. 45   Fig. 45A

Fig. 45. Dunand model, revised, 1917-1918. Hand-made

Critical Notes on the Dunand Helmet: There is no question that the Dunand helmet is designed attractively and that its models are made with great skill. It has, in fact, passed through a long series of progressive changes. Its visor, too, is the outgrowth of numerous (two score) experimental forms, some of which we represent in Figs. 49 to 60A. This series is an instructive one if only to show the complex nature of the problem which the designer of armor encounters. We note, for example, that in earlier experiments, an effort was made to provide the usual type of French helmet with a deep collar and face-guard of steel and that in this the eye region was perforated in bands of horizontal slits. In later trials, this collar was replaced by a narrow band containing transverse slits or by a shorter band bearing small transverse slots arranged either in a broad rectangular zone or in an elliptical area. In other cases folding visors were developed which were pierced for vision in various ways. All of these types, however, came to be rejected by M. Dunand in favor of the rotating visor now shown (Fig. 46).

The early model of this helmet (Fig. 44) was defective in several regards. The sharply outrolled corner of the brim beside the pivot of the visor was, as we noted, not capable of manufacture and the brim itself was slightly too wide at the nape to enable it to be worn with the pack of the

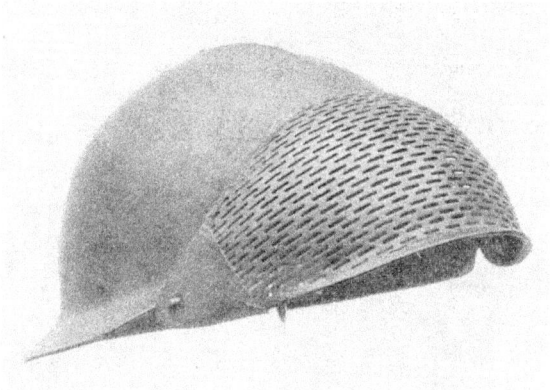

Fig. 46. Dunand helmet model, 1918, in ballistic metal

American soldier. Nor could the sharp crest of this helmet be reproduced in manganese steel without weakening the crown. Furthermore, the type of visor here used was criticized as producing a sensation of giddiness in the wearer; for the wearer when looking through the narrow slots which perforate his visor and through which he obtains an extended and fairly clear vision, soon becomes aware that the light areas in his range of view move up and down unpleasantly when the helmet wabbles—and wabble it will when the wearer moves about (cf. Major Polack's diagrams, Figs. 61 and 62). In a word, this type of visor is apt to produce more or less dizziness and cannot, therefore, be physiologically correct. In point of fact, the same type of visor was tried out at earlier times, notably in the first half of the sixteenth century (see Fig. 47) and was never widely accepted. In fact, it was used only when the helmet rested on or was attached to the shoulders of the armored soldier. Another and serious criticism of this type of visor is that it is relatively weak ballistically. It would unquestionably

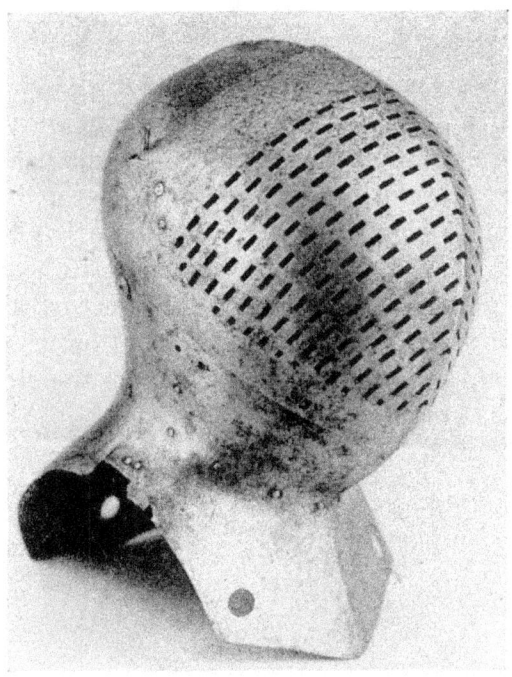

Fig. 47. Helm of 1514, whose visor suggests Dunand design

Fig. 48. Dunand helmet, showing result of tests

keep out many splinters and missiles of low velocity, but it would not protect the face against a pistol ball even at the range of 300 yards (Fig. 48). In a general way, the Dunand helmet possesses the demerits of all helmets of its class. The visor cannot be worn if the soldier is using his rifle and the entire helmet is apt to be ill balanced and heavy. (The Dunand helmet weighs about three and three fourths pounds while the English helmet rarely exceeds two pounds three ounces.) The fact of the matter is that the last model of the Dunand helmet (Frontispiece) has come back more nearly to the British model, and protects inadequately the sides and back of the head.

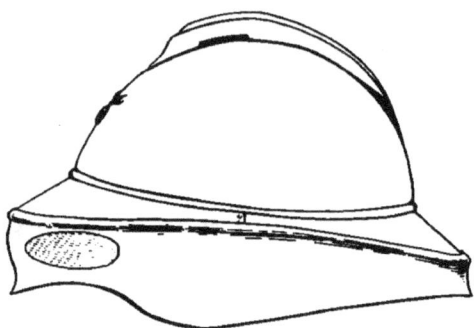

Fig. 49. Early Dunand visor, attachable to brim of standard helmet

Visors and Eye Wounds: (See also pages 72 and 133.) French armor experts early considered the need of protecting the eyes, and upon this theme the *Bulletin de la Société d'Ophtalmologie* and the *Annales d'Oculistique* have published a number of important papers. We note especially a memoir of MM. Morax and Moreau in the latter publication, August, 1918, pages 321-332, which considers this subject in detail. These authors gathered their data in the hospital of Laboisière, tabulating about seven hundred eye wounds, and have shown that of this number nearly half the cases were caused by splinters or small missiles of low velocity. Hence, it is clear that the use of a visor of almost any type would be an important means of protection. The authors also show very interestingly that the proportion of injuries to the eyes due to missiles of low velocity is approximately constant at various seasons and in various localities. Unhappily, however, they do

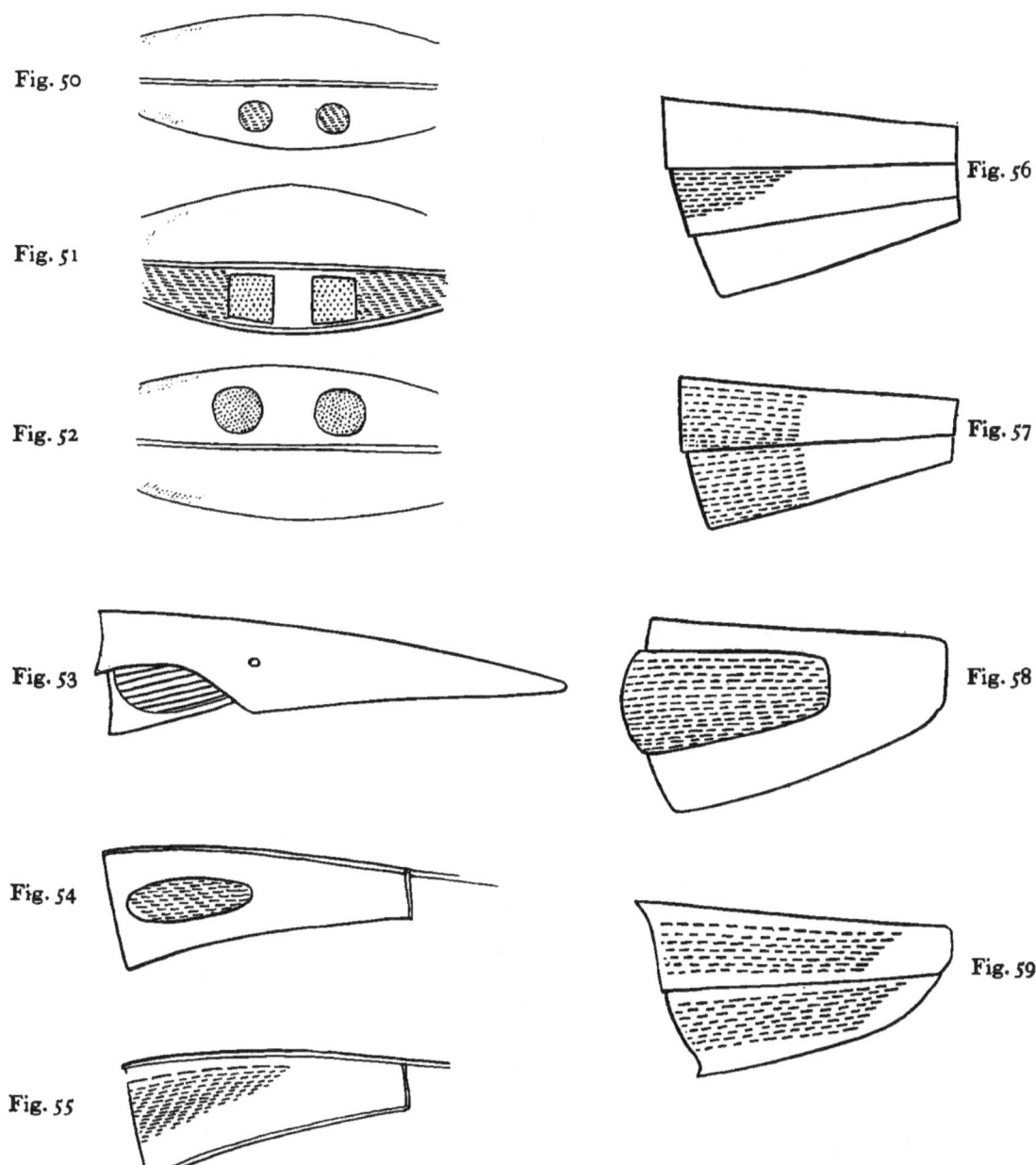

Figs. 50 to 59. Experimental visors designed by MM. Dunand, 1916-1917

HELMETS AND BODY ARMOR

not show us what the proportion of the eye wounds is to the total number of wounded. We have only a note (unverified) that in France, early in 1918, there were as many as 40,000 soldiers blind in either one or both eyes; nor do we know the French statistics which indicate what the probabilities are in the matter of total blindness. In the work of an active soldier it is

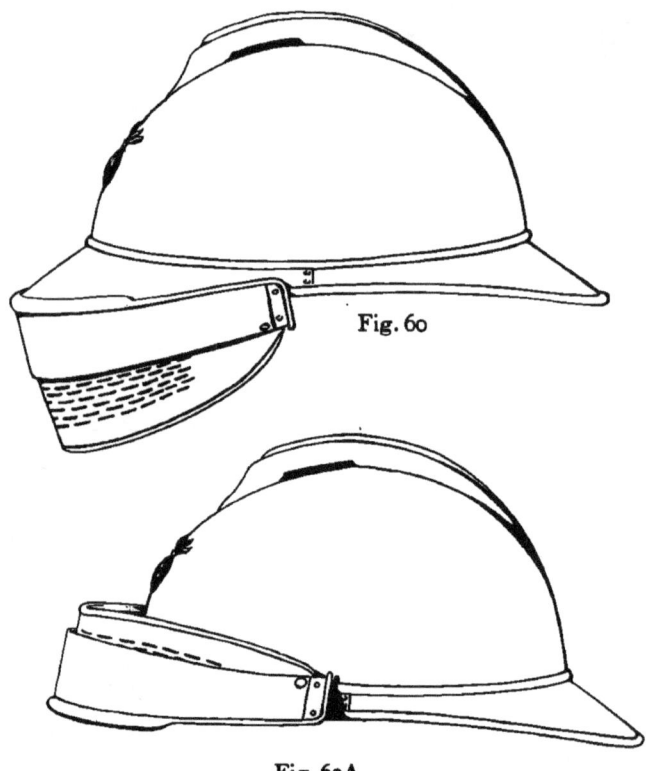

Fig. 60. Standard French helmet with early model of folding visor

clear that the use of a visor would be a decided handicap both in his actual fighting and in his morale—in the latter case leading him to think more of the danger to his eyes than of his immediate duty of destroying his enemy. Hence, viewed as a practical proposition, France might have been the greater loser if her soldiers had worn visors than if they had fought with their faces naked to the enemy. There is no question in the minds of all experts whom the present writer has consulted that under certain condi-

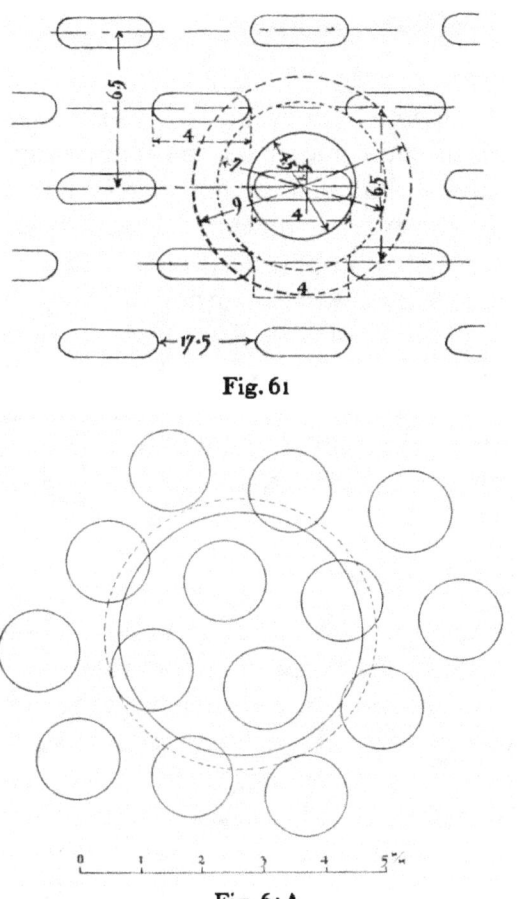
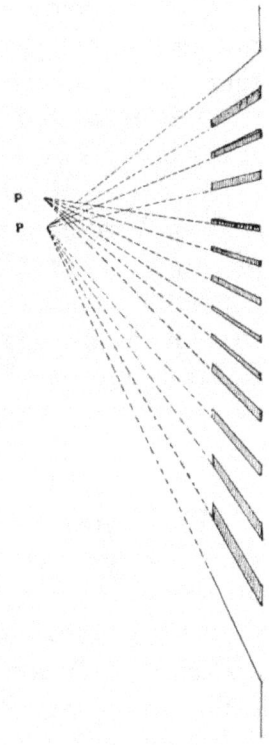

Fig. 62. Section of Polack visor

Fig. 61A

Fig. 61. Perforations of visor: dotted circle represents pupil of the eye

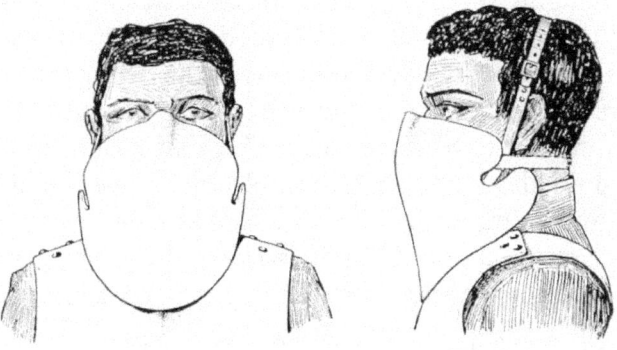

Fig. 63   Fig. 63A

Fig. 63. Sentinel's heavy face-guard

tions of bombardment a visor would be of very distinct value; unfortunately, however, one cannot pick and choose his equipment in actual warfare as occasion demands and the soldier soon finds that the requirements for a special attack or for a special defense may change not merely day by day but even hour by hour. Hence, in the present matter, he would have either to carry his visor with him constantly or, in practice, to go without it.

Face-shields for Sniper: The French used experimentally during the siege of Verdun, a type of heavy face-guard shown in Fig. 63, a specimen of which was seen by the writer in 1917. It was crudely fashioned to the face, modeled above more closely to the nose, and egg-shaped; it was said to be of chrome-nickel steel; was painted helmet-blue and was held in place by strap and buckle. It weighed about ten pounds. No information could be had as to its serviceability.

(c) BODY SHIELDS

The French have considered very carefully the possible value of body shields in the present war and they have issued them in considerable number at various times and places. In no instance, however, have they used them with conspicuous success. The corslet of the French cuirassier does not appear to have been worn, at all events in any number, even in the early period of the war. Nor do we note the appearance in actual service of such a jazeran as that shown in Fig. 16, which was used in the Franco-Prussian War.* Of the various types of body shields which were submitted to the Bureau of Inventions in Paris, none seems to have found special favor. Nevertheless, the French governmental experts recognized the need of an improved model of a body defense. In fact, General Adrian had himself given careful thought to the problem, for even at the beginning of the war he had noticed that soldiers when wounded in either of two regions had a scant chance of recovery; the one region was the head, for which he devised the present French casque, and the other was the abdomen, where even slight wounds were apt to be fatal. Accordingly, by the end of 1916 General Adrian had provided an abdominal shield (Fig. 64) which was light in weight (two pounds) and easy to wear. It was made of an oblong plate of metal bent in a curve and molded somewhat to the abdomen. This was held in place by a woven belt and was prevented from sagging by means of a

* Its weight was five pounds; test shows that it does not withstand a 230-grain automatic revolver at 600 foot seconds; its resistance will be scarcely more than half this figure.

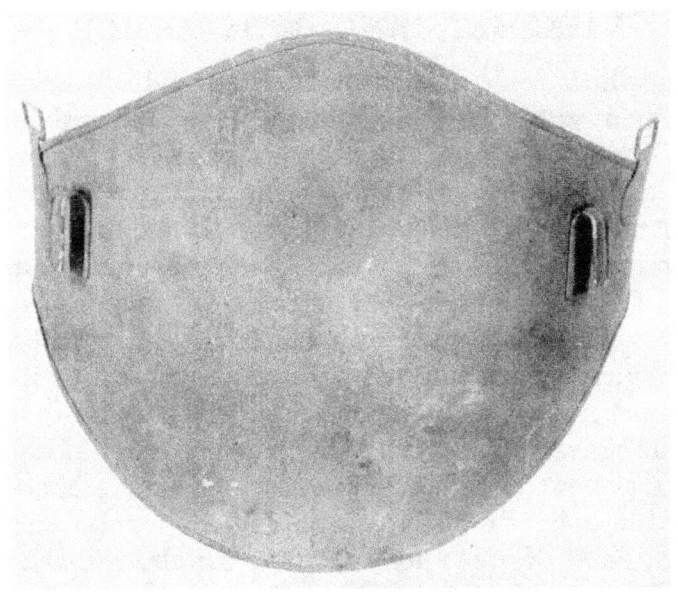

Fig. 64. Abdominal defense. French, Adrian model, 1916

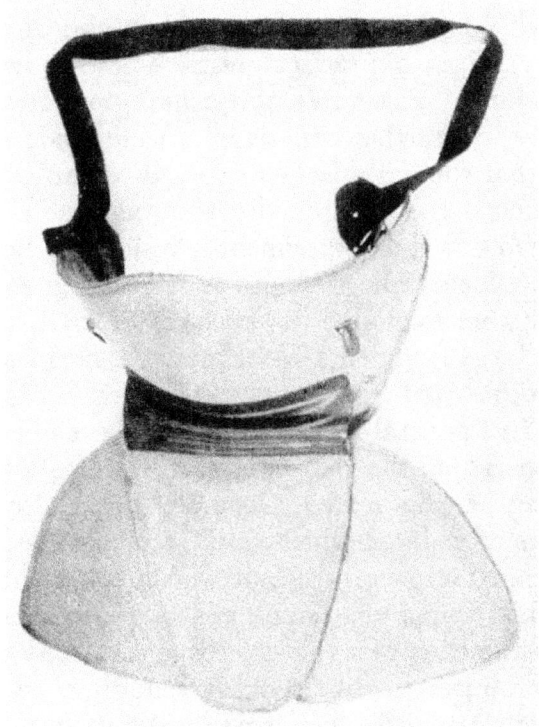

Fig. 65. Abdominal defense with tassets. French, 1916

pair of hooks which could be fastened to the soldier's belt. This defense was then covered with blue-gray cloth to harmonize with the uniform of the soldier. To an early type of the shield, hip and groin guards were added. These, three in number, approximately of the same size, were slung together and then fastened by a leather band to the abdominal armor. The groin guard, or sporran plate, hung in the middle; the thigh guards, or tassets, on either side (Fig. 65). The lower defenses proved cumbersome in active service and were soon discarded by the soldiers. Of the abdominal plate, 100,000 examples were manufactured and they were to have been used in the front line. A final report upon them, however, has not been seen by the writer, but he learned indirectly that the soldiers did not take to them as kindly as they took to the casque Adrian, and there is no evidence that they appeared in greater numbers, as part of the regular equipment. From the theoretical point of view, none the less, the abdominal shield deserved very careful consideration. Moreover, a carefully arranged series of tests (1917) showed clearly its ballistic value.

In addition to the body defense just described, General Adrian devised a breastplate which joined the abdominal defense below and which was provided above with a gorget. About three thousand of these defenses were made and they were given practical tests. These showed that the entire defense, which weighed about five and a half pounds, was too heavy for general use. Hence, no further experiments were made in such a direction. It may be noted that the armor when exposed to exploding grenades, even grenade "F," which is the most deadly form available (German grenades were not to be had for this experiment), resisted a large number of the missiles. In these experiments the shields were hung so as to form fences and the grenades were exploded at distances of from three to five yards. It was found that large fragments of the grenades perforated in the majority of cases, the middle-sized fragments perforated occasionally, the small fragments never. In a general way, two thirds of the missiles failed to penetrate. In many instances the percentage of failures showed a margin of safety greater than here indicated. General Adrian also attempted to produce lighter forms of defense which soldiers of all classes would not hesitate to wear. Here should be mentioned his steel epaulets which came to be used in very large numbers (hundreds of thousands) and which were unquestionably the means of avoiding casualties. They were small plates of steel which were inserted, like shoulder padding, between the layers of stuff in the soldier's tunic. Such defenses weighed but a few ounces; they gave the wearer no discomfort, yet served to ward off such missiles as a standard helmet would resist. They covered, moreover, a part of the body which was apt to be struck when shrapnel burst overhead. As a detail in the economy of manufacture, it was found that material for the epaulets could be obtained from the trimmings of steel cast aside during the manufacture of helmets.

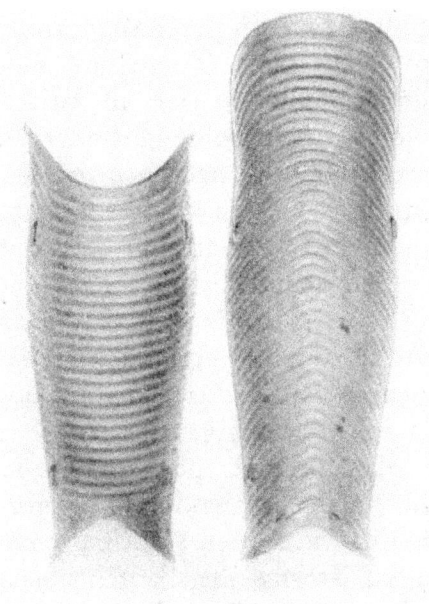

Fig. 66. Leg defenses. French, 1916-1917

(d) DEFENSES FOR ARMS AND LEGS

The French, so far as can be learned, never considered seriously the use of arm defenses. On the other hand, they manufactured leg defenses in some number and one of their models is shown in Fig. 66. This encloses the lower leg and consists of greave and calf-plate. It is made of helmet steel and is modeled competently. Its surface is pressed into ridges which are designed to offer greater ballistic rigidity after the fashion of armor in the time of Maximilian, as noted on page 84 of this work. It is not known whether this defense was used at the front; in any event, it was not adopted as part of the general equipment and no further effort seems to have been made to protect the soldiers' legs.

(B) ENGLISH

(a) Types of British body armor
(b) Helmets
(c) Face defenses

Of all the nations in the present war, the English have been the most persistent in their effort to solve the problem of light armor. Upward of eighteen designs of body shields have been produced commercially; and the Government has spent large sums in purchasing armor of various types and in itself producing revised models. There has, moreover, been no little expenditure in this direction on the part of British soldiers themselves. In shops in England, armor could be bought everywhere. Even the poorer types of it seem occasionally to have had good results, for all manufacturers received unsolicited letters from the front which tell of saving life and limb. It appears that defenses of the various models to be noted were worn only on special service and that he who wished the protection of armor must have been willing to carry it about with him, at the cost of no little discomfort, as part of his regular equipment. In view of this, several manufacturing companies endeavored to provide a body armor which would be light in weight and folded readily, so as to be carried in the soldier's pack. In the matter of general results, however, it should be stated that the British Government did not recommend body armor as a part of each soldier's equipment; it provided it only in sufficient quantity for arming about two men in each hundred. It was then kept at such points that it could conveniently be placed at the service of scouting parties, sentinels and bombers. Hence it was apt to be seen along the front as part of the regular *matériel*.

(a) TYPES OF BRITISH BODY ARMOR

Inventional work in Great Britain in regard to body defense has followed two lines of development which represent, for the rest, the types of armor known in early times, *i.e.*, "yielding" and "rigid." "Yielding" armor corresponds to the quilted or cushioned defenses and to the chain mail and banded armor of the Middle Ages; the latter corresponds to armor of plate.

"Yielding" Armor: The general subject of armor made of silk and other fibers, woven or padded, will be referred to in a later section of this report (page 282). A defense of this kind aims to prevent injury to the wearer by deadening the blow—that is, by yielding to the impinging missile yet at

the same time clinging to it, so that in the end it brings it to a state of rest. In the present section, we will refer only to the kinds of "soft" body armor which the British have actually used.

The first of these is a silken neck defense or necklet, prepared in London under the auspices of the Munitions Inventions Board. Its form, as shown in Fig. 67, suggests the high collar of an ulster, generous in its lines, thick (nearly two inches), and heavy (3¼ pounds). It is padded with about twenty-four layers of Japanese silk of six mommé (1.1 ounces) and wadded

Fig. 67. British silk-lined necklet, 1915-1916

with an additional amount of waste and floss silk. Its covering is canvas and khaki-colored muslin or drill, and its contour is stiffened with ⅛ inch iron wire. This defense is of about the same ballistic value as the English shrapnel helmet. Tests made by the Ordnance Department showed that it would stop a 230-grain pistol ball traveling at the rate of 600 foot seconds. The British authorities regarded the present necklet as a valuable defense and they issued it at the rate of 400 to a division. They later found it of less merit than had been supposed; it deteriorated rapidly as trench *matériel*, it was costly ($25), and the silk for its manufacture was difficult to procure.

A second type of soft body armor which has been used (but to a very limited degree) in the British Army is the Chemico Body Shield (Figs. 68

and 68A), manufactured by the County Chemical Company of Birmingham. This is a heavily padded waistcoat, weighing about six pounds, and, judging from a test made under the writer's direction in Washington, capable of stopping an automatic pistol ball, jacketed in alloy, at a velocity of about 300 foot seconds. The padding on this defense is about an inch

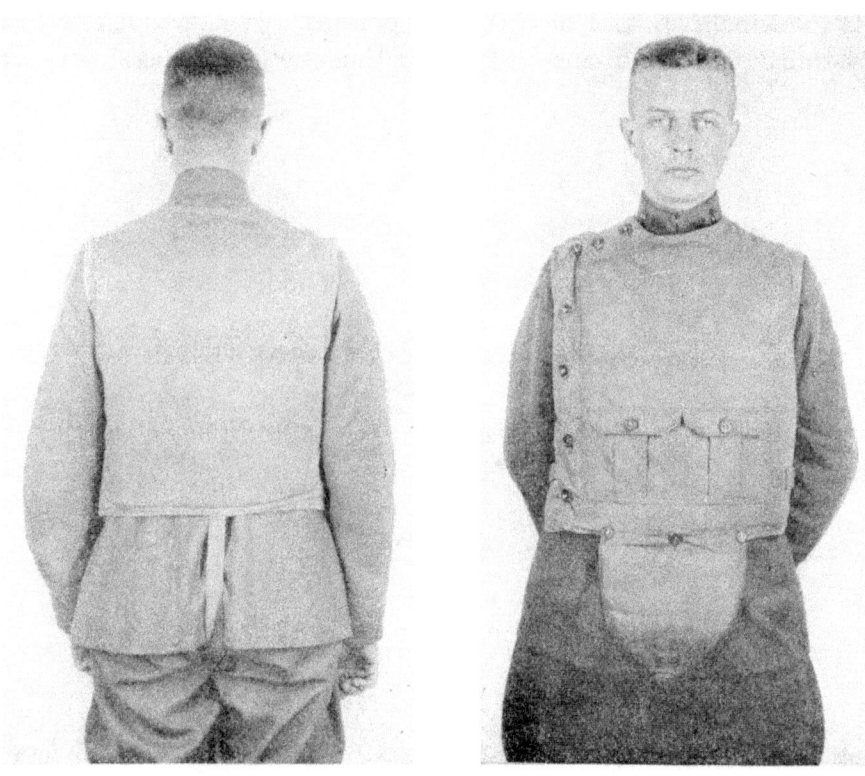

Fig. 68　　　　　　　　　　Fig. 68A

Fig. 68. "Chemico" body shield, 1916-1917

thick and is composed of many layers of tissue, scraps of linen, cotton and silk, said to be hardened by a resinous material; it is covered with brown muslin. It is not expensive ($15) and can be worn without serious discomfort. In one of its models the "Chemico" is provided with apron-shaped pieces which can be buttoned to the breast defense.

Plate Armor: Between the "soft" defenses noted above and the rigid armor of plate, there were early devised a number of intermediate types.

HELMETS OF VARIOUS MODELS:—
BY ALEXANDER McMILLAN WELCH, ARMOR

	Wt. Ounces Entire Helmet	Wt. Ounces Lining Only	Wt. Ounces Visor Only	Depth Over All	Width Over All	Length Over All	Width at Band	Length at Band
English	34-35	6		$4\frac{1}{2}''$	$11\frac{1}{4}''$	$12''$	$8\frac{1}{2}''$	$9\frac{1}{2}''$
French	26	3		$5\frac{1}{2}$	$8\frac{3}{8}$	$11\frac{1}{2}$	$7\frac{1}{2}$	$8\frac{1}{4}$
German	$39\frac{1}{2}$, 43, 48	4.5		$6\frac{3}{8}$	$9\frac{3}{8}$	$12\frac{5}{8}$	$7\frac{5}{8}$	$9\frac{1}{8}$
Dunand	$46\frac{1}{2}$	6	$10\frac{1}{2}$	$6\frac{7}{8}$	11	12	$8\frac{1}{2}$	$9\frac{1}{2}$
Belgian	$44\frac{1}{2}$	8	8	6	9	$12\frac{3}{4}$	$7\frac{3}{4}$	$10\frac{3}{8}$
American No. 2	$43\frac{1}{2}$	8 or $5\frac{1}{2}$		$8\frac{1}{4}$	10	$12\frac{3}{4}$	$7\frac{3}{4}$	$10\frac{1}{4}$
American No. 5	$39\frac{1}{2}$	8 or $5\frac{1}{2}$		$6\frac{5}{8}$	$10\frac{3}{4}$	$12\frac{3}{4}$	$8\frac{1}{4}$	$9\frac{7}{8}$
American No. 8	$51\frac{1}{2}$	8 or $5\frac{1}{2}$	10?	$7\frac{1}{8}$	$10\frac{1}{2}$	$13\frac{3}{4}$	$8\frac{3}{4}$	$9\frac{1}{2}$
American No. 10	$37\frac{1}{2}$	8 or $5\frac{1}{2}$		$7\frac{1}{4}$	$10\frac{1}{4}$	$12\frac{1}{2}$	9	$9\frac{5}{8}$

A COMPARISON OF MEASUREMENTS
EXPERT, ORDNANCE DEPARTMENT, U. S. A.

Space at Back	Space at Front	Rim from Center of Hole of Ear	Rim Above Center of Eye	Brim in Front of Nose	Rim Beyond Back of Head	Rim Beyond Ears at Side	Cubic Contents 4″ from Top in Cubic Centimeters
1″	$\frac{5}{8}$″	1$\frac{3}{4}$″ above	$\frac{7}{8}$″	1$\frac{3}{8}$″	2″	2″	2620 (2525 to edge of brim)
$\frac{3}{4}$	$\frac{5}{8}$	1$\frac{1}{4}$ above	$\frac{5}{8}$	1$\frac{3}{4}$	1$\frac{1}{2}$	$\frac{3}{8}$	2250
$\frac{3}{4}$	$\frac{1}{2}$	$\frac{5}{8}$ below	$\frac{3}{8}$	2$\frac{3}{8}$	1$\frac{7}{8}$	1$\frac{1}{2}$	2625
$\frac{7}{8}$	1	1$\frac{1}{8}$ above	1	2	2	1$\frac{5}{8}$	2560
$\frac{5}{8}$	1	$\frac{5}{8}$ above	$\frac{7}{8}$	1$\frac{7}{8}$	2$\frac{5}{8}$	1	2528
$\frac{7}{8}$	1$\frac{3}{16}$	1$\frac{1}{8}$ below	$\frac{3}{8}$	2$\frac{3}{8}$	1$\frac{1}{2}$	1$\frac{1}{2}$	2450 to base of ridge
1	$\frac{3}{4}$	$\frac{7}{8}$ below	$\frac{3}{8}$	2	2	1$\frac{7}{8}$	2650
$\frac{7}{8}$	$\frac{7}{8}$	1 below	1$\frac{7}{16}$	2$\frac{1}{2}$	2$\frac{3}{4}$	2	2750
$\frac{7}{8}$	1	1$\frac{3}{8}$ below	$\frac{5}{8}$	2$\frac{3}{8}$	2$\frac{3}{8}$	2	2750

ARMOR

Tabular Statement of Physical and Chemical Characters: Data furnished by various author

		Carbon	Manganese	Sulphur	Phosphorus	Nickel	Silicon	Molybdenum	Vanadium	Chromium	Zirconium	Elastic Limit per Sq. Inch	
1	Manganese Helmet Steel	1.20	12.	.....	.....	.....	.20	.....	.....	.....	.....	47,000	13
		1.50	15.	.04	.10	.....	.30	.....	.....	.....	.....	60,000	14
2	Lot 1 Sexonary	.32	.28	.....	.....	3.10	.....	.35	.20	1.05	.....	230,000	26
		.42	.42	.03	.03	3.50	.....	.....	.....	1.25	.....	250,000	27
3	Lot 3 Nickel-Chrome	.32	.20	.....	.....	3.50	.....	.....	.....	1.75	.....	230,000	23
		.42	.40	.04	.04	4.25	.18	.....	.....	2.25	.....	240,000	25
4	Nickel-Manganese (Baker)	.37	.90	.025	.015	1.75	.18	.17	.....	.....	.....	.....	..
		.50	1.35	.04	.04	2.35	.21	.28	.23	.06	.....	.....	..
5	German Silicon-Nickel "A"	.35	.05	.....	.....	1.75	1.50	.....	.....	.....	.....	180,000	20
		.45	.70	.03	.03	2.25	1.75	.....	.....	.....	.....	190,000	22
6	German Silicon-Nickel "B"	.20	.90	.....	.....	4.00	2.00	.....	.....	.....	.....	215,000	25
		.30	1.10	.03	.03	4.50	2.25	.....	.....	.....	.....	225,000	26
7	Chrome-Molybdenum (Sargent)	.30	.60	.....	.....	.....	.....	.50	.15	1.00	.....	210,000	25
		.40	.90	.....	.01	.45	.25	1.00	.25	1.25	.....	225,000	27
8	Nickel-Molybdenum (Sargent)	.30	.45	.....	.....	5.00	.....	.75	.....	.....	.....	215,000	25
		.40	.64	.....	.....	6.00	.14	1.00	.....	.92	.....	225,000	26
9	Manganese-Chromium (Howe)	.....	.....	.....	.....	.....	.....	.....	.....	.71	.....	.....	..
		1.64	.15	.03	.12	.....	1.04	.....	.....	.73	.....	.....	..
10	Zirconium Alloy (Ford)	.34	.75	.216	.62	2.62	1.25	.....	.....	.....	.25	236,000	28
		.44	1.00	.....	.....	3.25	1.32	.....	.....	.....	.50	240,000	28

Mr. Aigeltinger maintains that the elastic limit is not proportional to the ballistic strength. This is apt to be greater when ultimate strength and elastic limit are widely different. Respecting this note, Dr. George W. Sargent queries whether Mr. Aigeltinger had not in mind results from tests with "pistol ball, which has a very decidedly different action upon the impact than either the soft rifle projectile or the armor-piercing ball."

Mr. William Smith, Captain John T. Unton o observations obtained with possessing the highest elonga

ALLOYS

ities, notably Dr. H. M. Howe, Dr. G. W. Sargent, A. Aigeltinger and W. T. Wrighton

Ultimate Strength	Elongation	Reduction of Area	Quenched at Fahrenheit	Drawn at Fahrenheit	Brinnell Test	Results on Helmets .036" Thick: 230 gr. Jacketed Bullet	Source
0,000 7,000	35-40% 25	35-45%	1800°-2000° Water	....	217-302	800 f.s.	American Sheet & Tin Plate Co.
0,000 5,000	9-10	30-35	1400°-1600° Water	300°-475° Oil of 70°	495-512	1000	American Sheet & Tin Plate Co.
0,000 0,000	8-9 9-10	30-35	1400° Oil of 100°	257°-120°	495-512	1000	American Sheet & Tin Plate Co.
....	....	....	1250°-1800° 30 min. Oil of 100°	450°-530°	578	1000	Universal Rolling Mills
0,000 0,000	 3-5	 10-12	O. T. 850°	450°	444-500	....	Cyclops Steel Co.
0,000 3,000	7-9	25-30	850°	450°	460	....	Cyclops Steel Co.
0,000 5,000	10-12	30-40	O. T. 1600°	900°	495-555	....	Carbon Steel Co.
0,000 0,000	10-13	30-40	....	495°-555°	495-555	....	Carbon Steel Co.
....	....	....	1500° Oil	....	....	....	Taylor Wharton
0,000 5,000	10 13.5	30-37	....	400° Oil	512-557 578	....	Ford Motor Co., Detroit

expert of the Ford Motor Co., holds that "a low elongation, together with great ultimate strength and elastic limit, should produce good armor plate" (helmets?). f the same Company features elongation as the desired physical property, at the expense of elastic limit. Mr. Smith's note, Dr. Sargent believes, was based upon armor-piercing ball at high velocity, and "rather thinks that Mr. Smith holds to the view that steel with the greatest ultimate strength and elastic limit and tion, even though that elongation be relatively low, produces the best light armor."

One of these was the scaled waistcoat, or jazeran, known as the Flexible Armor Guard of John Berkeley (Newcastle). This consists of a breast and back (see Figs. 69 and 69A) formed of square plates of metal riveted from the center of each piece to a canvas support. It is easy to wear but its ballistic value is slight; its metal plates (in the specimen seen by the writer) are not of high alloy; and as they do not overlap, they give little protec-

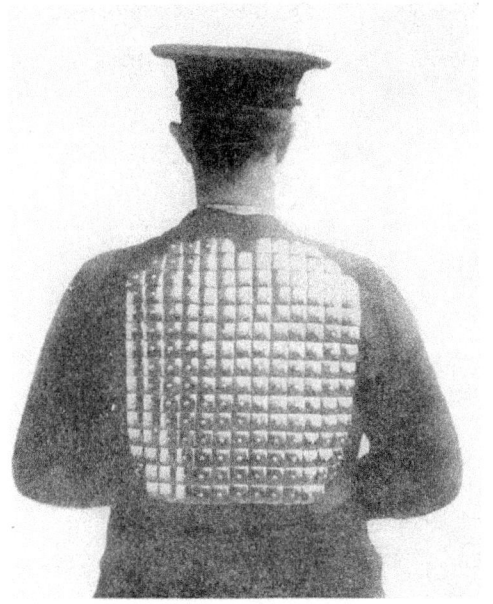 

Fig. 69   Fig. 69A

Fig. 69. Berkeley's "Flexible Armor Guard," 1916

tion save to projectiles of very low velocity. Struck by a bullet, one of the small squares, instead of indenting, is apt to be pushed into the wearer's body. Experiments made by the writer on a three-pound breast defense of this model show that it has but about one quarter of the protective value of such a body shield as the "B. E. F." hereafter described. The Berkeley body shield is said, however, to be furnished in thicker types of metal, extending its range in weight to four pounds.

One of the earliest types of body shields appearing in the British market was also a flexible one; this was known as the Franco-British, since it was first manufactured in France and sold to British soldiers (Fig. 70). It was made up of eight vertical rows of rectangular plates which were linked together by steel rings, every plate on each of its four sides. Like the Berkeley jazeran, such a plastron could readily be worn under the tunic. Its weight was not great and it afforded protection from splinters and from low velocity shrapnel. As a defense against other missiles, it was well-nigh

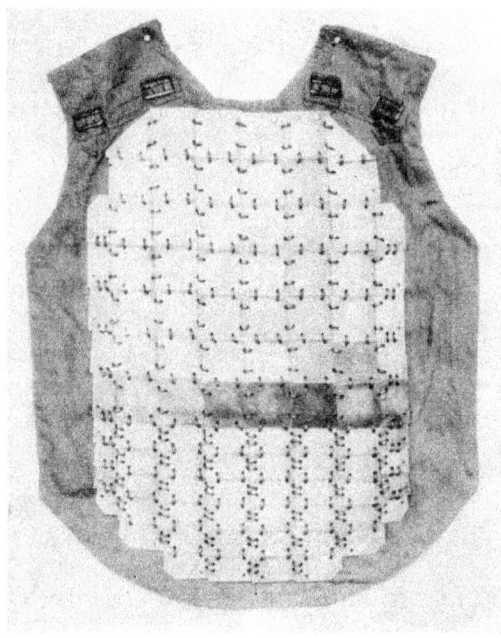

Fig. 70. "Franco-British cuirass," 1916-1917

valueless; its plates were unsupported, their marginal areas readily penetrated, and their material by no means of the best. Even under favorable circumstances, as when a bullet struck the center of one of these plates, it could resist scarcely more than a pistol bullet at the rate of 200 foot seconds, which is but about one third the strength of the British helmet. This breast defense, sometimes known as a "cuirass" or the "life-saving waistcoat," had, it appears, considerable sale among soldiers. It appeared at military shops and retailed for about $25. A variant known as Wilkinson's Safety Service Jacket is shown in Figure 71. It weighs about three pounds (front defense only) and costs forty-odd dollars.

Fig. 71   Fig. 71A

Fig. 71. "Wilkinson Jacket." Detail indicates test

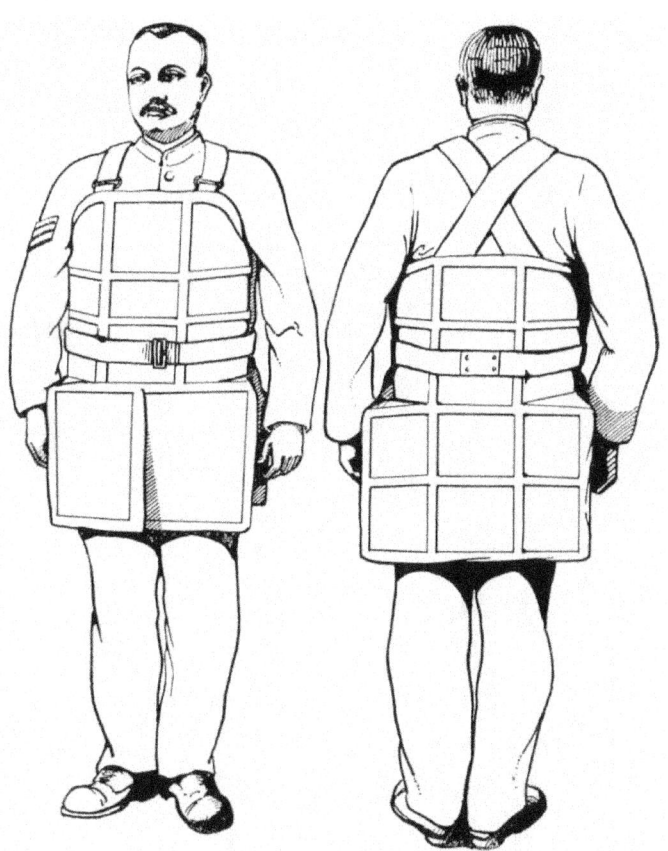

Fig. 72   Fig. 72A

Fig. 72. "Dayfield body shield," heavy model, 1916

Fig. 73   Fig. 73A

Fig. 73. Dayfield body shield, 1917, also silk neck defense

Fig. 74   Fig. 74A   Fig. 74B

Fig. 74. Dayfield body shield, simple model

IN MODERN WARFARE

The Dayfield Body Shield should next be mentioned. This was one of the earliest and most widely known of British body defenses. It is shown in Figs. 72-75 both in front and rear views. It consists of a plastron formed of a number of separate plates, a pair of tassets which hang from the waist-

Fig. 75   Fig. 75A

Fig. 75. Manganese-alloy basis of Dayfield body shield, 1917

line, a backplate made up of a number of pieces, and guard-reins of two or three plates. This defense is held in place by means of shoulder straps and belt. It is covered with brown canvas, the separate plates slightly overlapping one another and having their borders covered with separate bands of stuff. The heaviest type of the Dayfield Body Shield weighs from fourteen to eighteen pounds (Fig. 72). At one time it was found useful for scouting or wire-cutting parties, bombers, sentinels, and advanced guards or garrisons of crater holes, but its clumsiness and weight caused it in the end to be discarded. We note that in October, 1917, about 20,000 sets of armor of this type, including a shield of lighter weight, were in use in France (Fig. 73). The lighter form of this shield was also tried out but found unsatisfactory. In the latter model the plates meet one another end to end instead of overlapping.

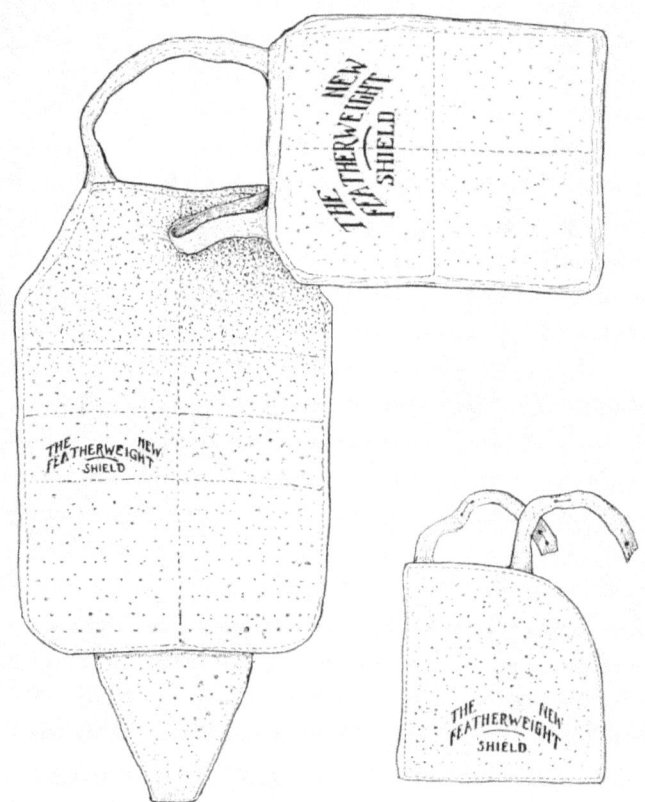

Fig. 76. "Featherweight" shield. Also shoulder defense

A still simpler form of the Dayfield shield appears in Fig. 74; its metal plates are pictured in Fig. 75. The plastron bears testing marks; its weight is about four pounds.

In general, it is evident that English inventors made strenuous efforts to solve the armor problem by devising a defense which should be light in weight and easy to wear. Their best experts declared that no armor could be used successfully which was heavier than six pounds. Unfortunately, however, no body shield of this weight, even made of the best ballistic metal, could do more than protect its wearer from shrapnel at low velocity, an occasional hand grenade, or a spent ball. So, clearly, the lightest type of body shield could not find general favor. Thus the Canadians, who had abandoned their armor of the heavy type (sixteen pounds) in favor of a light Dayfield model which weighed but five and a half pounds, soon de-

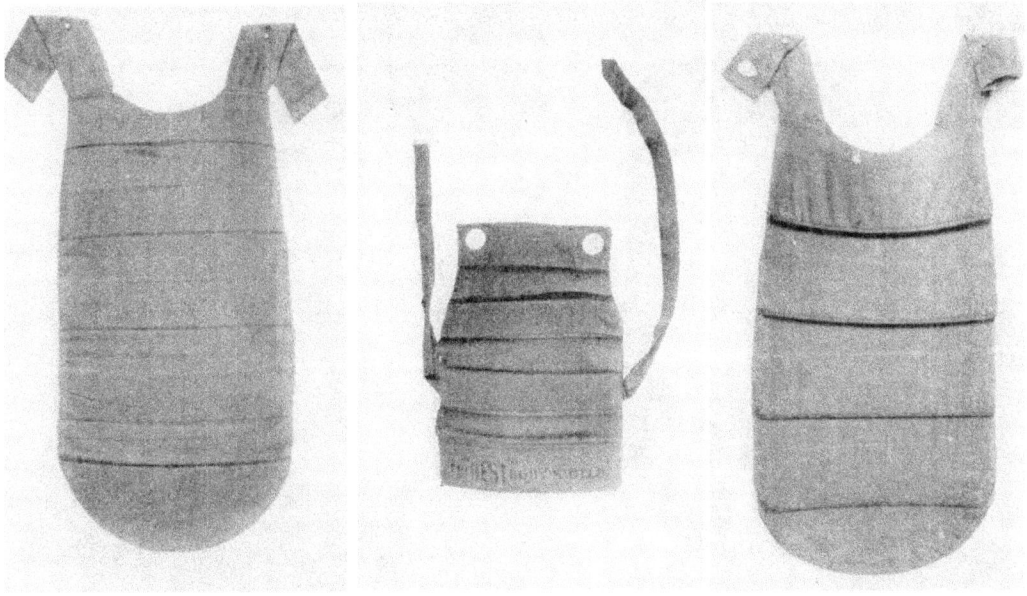

Fig. 77   Fig. 77A   Fig. 77B

Fig. 77. "Best" body shield, showing front, lining of front and backplate

cided that the newer model was equally unsatisfactory. It was too light to be of service; it needed to be strengthened by a few more pounds of metal. The light type of shield which aimed to fill the need is illustrated in the New Featherweight Shield (Fig. 76). This is made up of a similar number of plates and covered with khaki drill; it may have with it a "sporran plate" to protect the groin, making the entire weight about seven pounds. If one considers that such a defense as the "Featherweight" can be perforated in nearly every case by an automatic pistol bullet at eighty feet, one concludes that it would hardly prove of the greatest service.

The type of defense represented by the Dayfield and Featherweight shields seems, nevertheless, to have become generally standardized for the use of the British Army. A variant of it is "the Best Body Shield" (Figs. 77, 77A and 77B), in which the plates are arranged in a vertical row; five

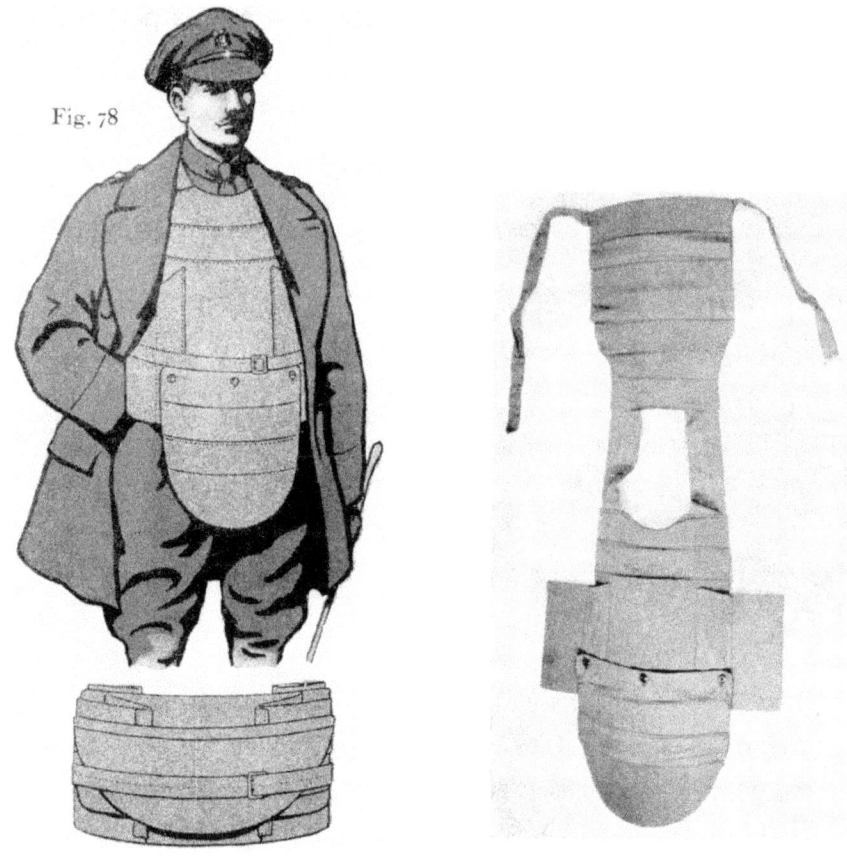

Fig. 78A   Fig. 78B

Fig. 78. British body armor. "B. E. F." model, 1917-1918

behind and four in front. This model is a dangerously narrow one, for it protects only the middle line of the body; it has the advantage, on the other hand, of folding up in a fairly small package for convenience in transport. It is well made, its plates are of 12 per cent manganese steel, and it resists the tests prescribed for the British helmet. Its weight is six pounds. A similar but better shield is the B. E. F. (British Expeditionary Forces), which is manufactured at Willenhall, Staffordshire. This, shown in Figs. 78, 78A and 78B, has corrected the narrowness of the Best shield. Its large plate is placed over the chest and it is flanked by two small ones. An abdominal defense, which consists of two plates, is attached by buttons to the breast-

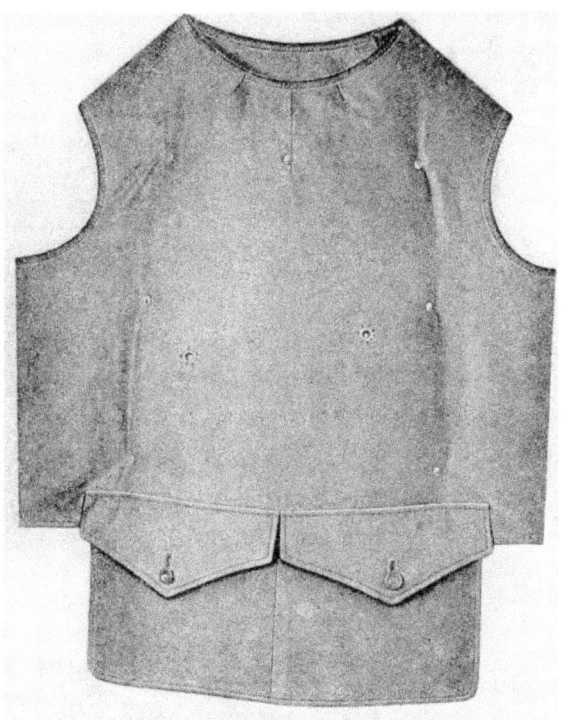

Fig. 79. British "Portobank" armored waistcoat

plate. Its backplate is similar to the one in the Best shield but is somewhat smaller. This defense is not expensive ($20), and like the former one can be folded up for easy carrying. In a general way, it is one of the most efficient body defenses which has been devised up to the present time; it is made of 13 per cent manganese steel, covers a considerable part of the body, and prevents penetration of a pistol bullet at about 700 foot seconds. Its weight is seven and one half pounds.

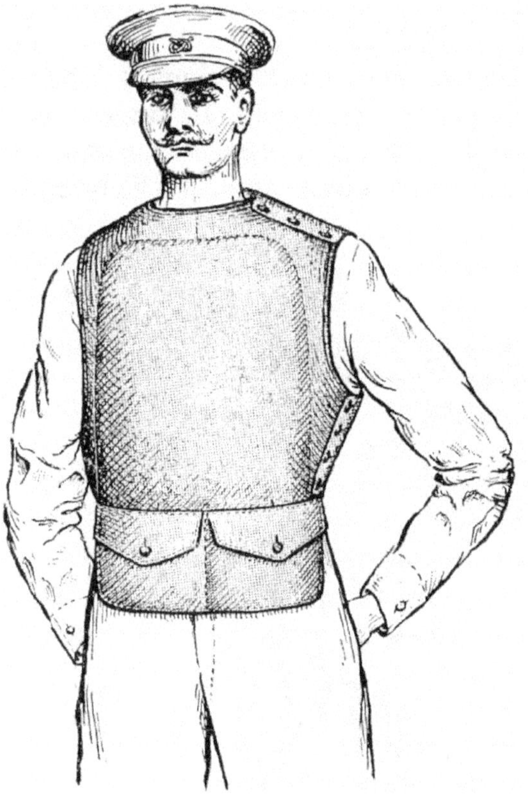

Fig. 80 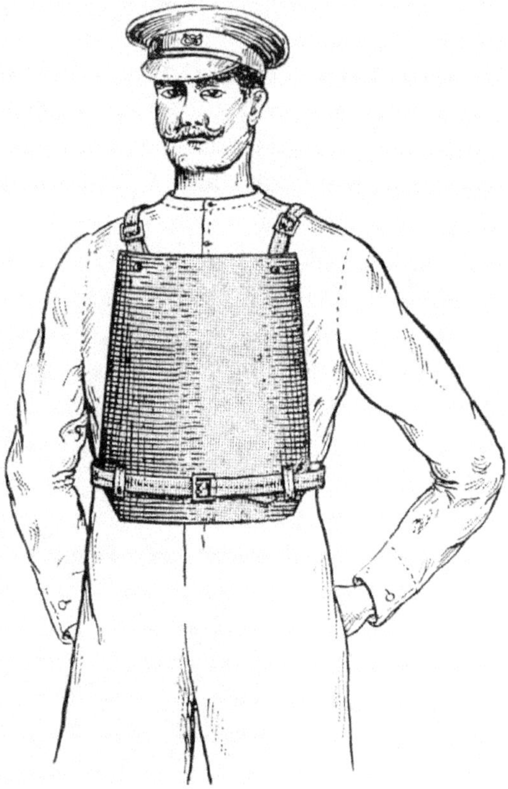   Fig. 80A

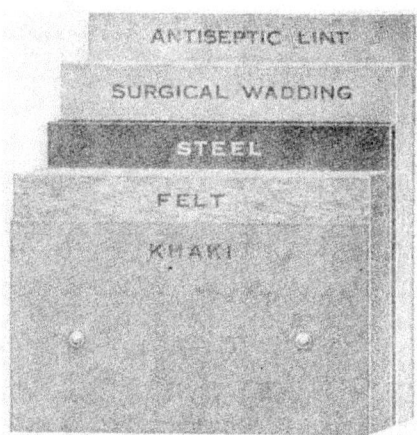

Fig. 80B

Fig. 80. British Portobank body shield. 80B gives detail of construction

IN MODERN WARFARE

Among other types of khaki-covered body defenses we may mention the Military shield (see page 156), the Portobank, and the Army and Navy (Figs. 79 and 80), which are produced by the same firm which provides the Best Body Shield. These defenses are made of manganese steel, but are more simply finished than the "Best." The Portobank in its simplest form

Fig. 81   Fig. 81A

Fig. 81. "Star" body shield

is for the breast only and weighs $2\frac{1}{4}$ pounds; with a backplate it weighs $4\frac{1}{4}$ pounds; in its khaki-covered form it weighs three pounds, with breastplate only, and five pounds with breast and back; its cost is from four to seven dollars. The "Army and Navy" body shield affords greater protection in its attachable skirt. Also to be mentioned among simpler models is the Star body defense (Figs. 81 and 81A); this is made of Whitworth's "rustless" steel (chrome-nickel) cut in strips and riveted together; its single shield is said to weigh less than three pounds; the breastplate costs $8 and the breast and back $17.

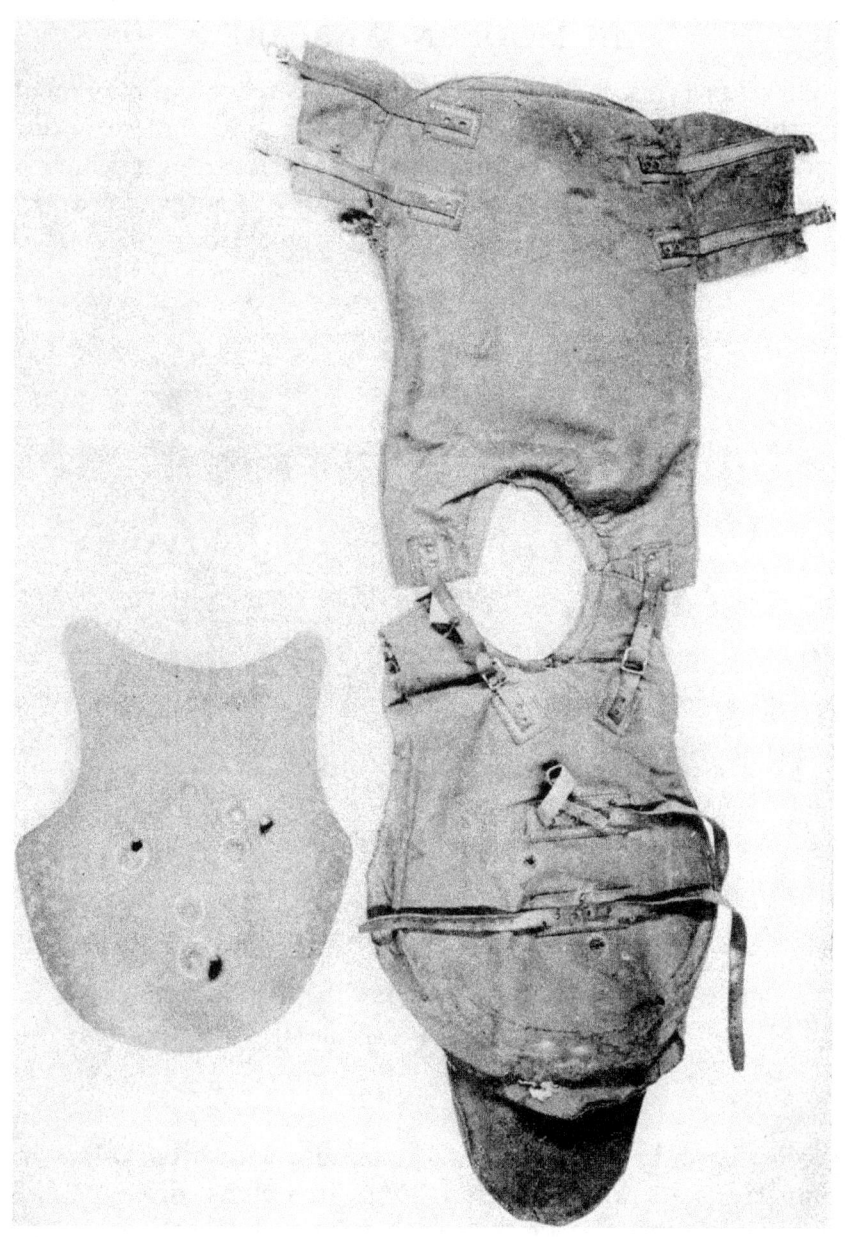

Fig. 82. British standard model body armor, 1917-1918. Also metal foundation of breastplate

In its effort to furnish an improved type of body defense the British Government through its Munitions Inventions Board finally manufactured the corselet ("E. O. B.") shown in Figs. 82, 83. Its weight is 9½

Fig. 83. British breastplate, standard model, 1918.
Also silk necklet

pounds and it is formed of three elements, a breastplate, a backplate and a sporran piece. These are covered with khaki drill and are somewhat padded. The figure pictures the breastplate removed from its cover and shows the marks of the tests which have been made upon it. It will resist the ball of the automatic pistol, also shrapnel and grenade. It is not penetrated by a rifle ball traveling at the rate of 1,000 foot seconds. Its plates are made of 12 per cent Hadfield's manganese steel of 18 gauge. The 1917 model was issued in "pretty large quantities."

Smaller body shields of greater weight have been employed but not in great number. The Corelli British bullet-proof body shield, shown in Fig. 84, measures 11 x 16 inches. It is said to resist German standard ammuni-

Fig. 84. "Corelli" body shield

tion at ten yards and is guaranteed to stand six shots spread within a six-inch circle. Its material is "special alloy steel manufactured by the Siemens-Martin open hearth process." Its weight is seventeen pounds—a weight regarded by English critics as too heavy to warrant a defense which covers so small a part of the soldier's body.

A shield similar to this is the "Roneo," shown in Fig. 85, which is made of .3 inch chrome-nickel steel, encased in brown canvas and hung by straps over the shoulders. In specimens used in the experiments of the British

IN MODERN WARFARE

Munitions Board in March, 1916, shoulder plates were added and were so bent as to support the weight of the shield and at the same time protect more effectively the wearer's shoulders; also an air cushion was provided in its lining to resist concussion. This shield weighed twenty-two pounds; its resistance was great but it was heavy considering the area it protected;

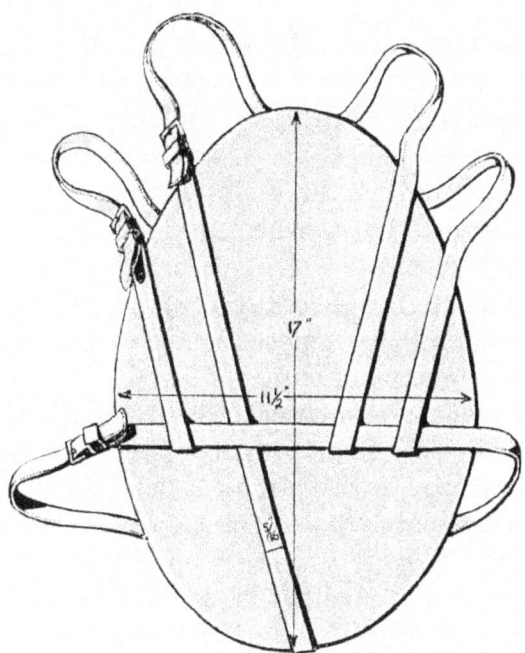

Fig. 85. "Roneo-Miris" body shield

hence, the report upon it was not favorable. Also the heavy body shield is to be referred to which was designed by Colonel C. F. Close. This is of the same type of steel as the "Roneo" and is of similar weight (eighteen pounds), but its steel is enclosed with a layer of woodite one eighth inch thick which is stated to reduce the danger to the wearer from lead splash. The shield was tested by the British Munitions Inventions Board and was found to be proof to British service bullets at a fifty-yard range. The report of the Armor Committee, which then dealt with this matter, considered, however, that the Close shield was unduly cumbersome and that it covered too small an area of the body to be of practical value.

(b) BRITISH HELMETS

The use of a helmet for the modern British soldier is by no means recent. The headpiece of certain mounted regiments has been a "casque" sometimes in steel, sometimes in brass or other alloy. These casques, although of value to a certain degree, cannot, of course, be compared with the present helmet as a means of defense. On the other hand, heavy helmets were in recent use, *e.g.*, at the siege of Ladysmith. And the various specimens of "Giants' helmets" (twenty-five to thirty pounds) which one sees in various arsenals, *e.g.*, at the Gun Wharf in Portsmouth, in the Tower, or at Malta, show that during the early nineteenth century sappers were provided with these head defenses when they exposed themselves above the top of the sap-roller* when pushing it before them in the trenches.

The present British helmet (Frontispiece), shaped like an inverted bowl with narrow shelving rim, was devised in 1915 by an English inventor, Mr. Brodie, who after many experiments came to the conclusion that this simple type of head defense would probably be found the most serviceable; he emphasized especially the fact that it could be cheaply and rapidly produced, for its simple shape enabled it to be pressed in metal of high ballistic quality. His representations to the Government in the matter were accepted and the British Army was soon provided in great numbers with its "tin hat." In point of fact, the British helmet was an eminently successful device. We query whether its designer was at first aware that he had selected a model which had already been tried out by infantrymen in earlier times, but such was certainly the case; its form was that of a simple "chapel," well known in the wars of the fourteenth and fifteenth centuries. For ease of manufacture it left little to be desired; its shallow dome could be stamped out in a single operation without unduly thinning the metal in the crown; its brim was made wide enough to protect the wearer's face

---

* The sap-roller, it may be recalled, is in itself an armored defense—a large cylinder made of wattle and filled with earth, affording protection to soldiers who are digging trenches; it is pushed forward by two or more men according to the width of the sap or communication trench desired. For this purpose, hand-pikes or crowbars are used and as the workers "prise" the roller along, their heads with the upward lift of the crowbar rise above the surface, hence the necessity for protection. (Cf. note by General Desmond O'Callaghan, *London Times*, 1916, July 22.)

and shoulders from splinters and shrapnel; and its shell was far more resistant than that of the French helmet. In the matter of its steel the recommendation of Sir Robert Hadfield was followed, who pointed out the many virtues of a high percentage (roundly 12 per cent) manganese steel. This alloy, rolled in sheets of twenty gauge or .036 inch, would resist with remarkable uniformity pistol bullets of 230 grains jacketed with cupro-nickel, traveling at the rate of 600 foot seconds. Such a bullet, it is true, produced a deep indentation in the metal, but it did not break through (Fig. 86). Moreover, if at higher velocity the projectile passed through the plate, no shattering or splintering occurred to aggravate a wound. The

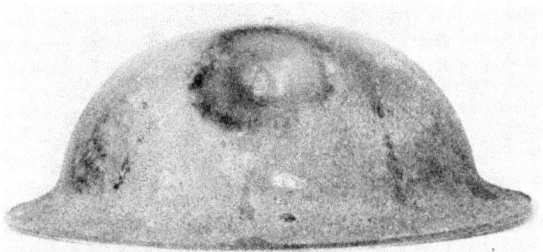

Fig. 86. British helmet showing indentation caused by glancing machine gun bullet

demerit of this metal was its liability to indent deeply, for this would be apt to cause fatal injury to the wearer. On the other hand, the value of manganese steel in producing helmets in large numbers and quickly was of counterbalancing importance; the metal was found to be pressed readily without splitting or fracturing; it required no annealing at the time of the pressing operation and no heat treatment afterward—features of great practical moment. They insured the production of helmets at a rate far more (possibly twice as) rapid than if subsequent heat treatment were given. They meant, also, that cheapness in production was assured as well as the uniformity of the product—for in heat treating a helmet alloy if pyrometers are not operating accurately, or if the work of the attendants is at fault, helmets are apt to be produced which from their brittleness are unduly dangerous to the wearer. In the matter of price it was found that a

British helmet could be turned out with lining complete (Fig. 87) at the rate of less than $2 apiece.

We may note, however, that the specifications for the manufacture of the British helmet in 1917 do not stipulate that manganese steel shall alone be used. They prescribe merely that the steel shall not be thicker than twenty gauge (.036 inch) nor shall it be heavier in the stamped-out shell

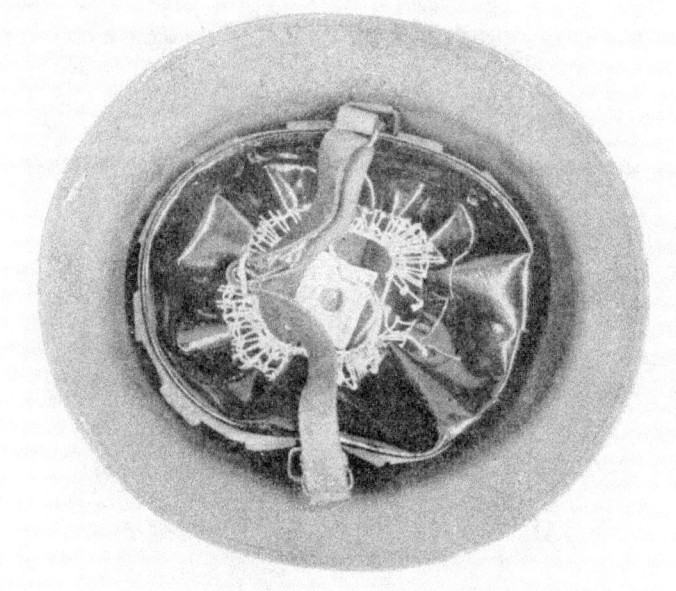

Fig. 87. British helmet viewed from below

than one pound eleven ounces. In point of fact, a ballistic test was made the criterion of the quality of the steel, rather than a physical or chemical analysis (contrast the specifications for the French helmet, page 80). The manufacturer was required to demonstrate that his product was proof to shrapnel ball, forty-one to a pound with a striking velocity of 700 foot seconds. This test was given to ten helmets in the first thousand, three helmets in the second and third thousand, and two helmets in each succeeding thousand. No requirement was given as to the depth of indentation or the deformation allowed, the decision in this regard having apparently been left to the discretion of the inspecting officer. All helmets, however, were to bear the initial of the manufacturer and the heat number of the steel. The foregoing test, it may be remarked, is far less searching and apparently less uniform than that required from American manufacturers; for to resist a bullet of 170 grains (which is the same as forty-one to a pound) traveling at the rate of 700 foot seconds is, ballistically speaking, by no means as severe as the test of a cupro-nickel encased pistol ball of 230 grains traveling at the rate of 650 foot seconds.

Fig. 88. Face defense, early device. British, 1915-1916

The details in the manufacture of the helmet in England probably differ little from those developed in the United States, hence for convenience they may better be considered, together with further details regarding the British helmet, on page 196.

(c) FACE DEFENSES

Numerous experiments were made by the British in the direction of producing a shield for the face. One of the earliest forms, so far as the writer has learned, was devised by John Berkeley of Newcastle and is shown in Fig. 88. It was merely a steel plate which fitted under the peak of the soldier's cap and was pierced with vertical and transverse slits

132 HELMETS AND BODY ARMOR

in front of each eye. This design is only one of many which never passed beyond an experimental stage. We should, however, mention a fairly good

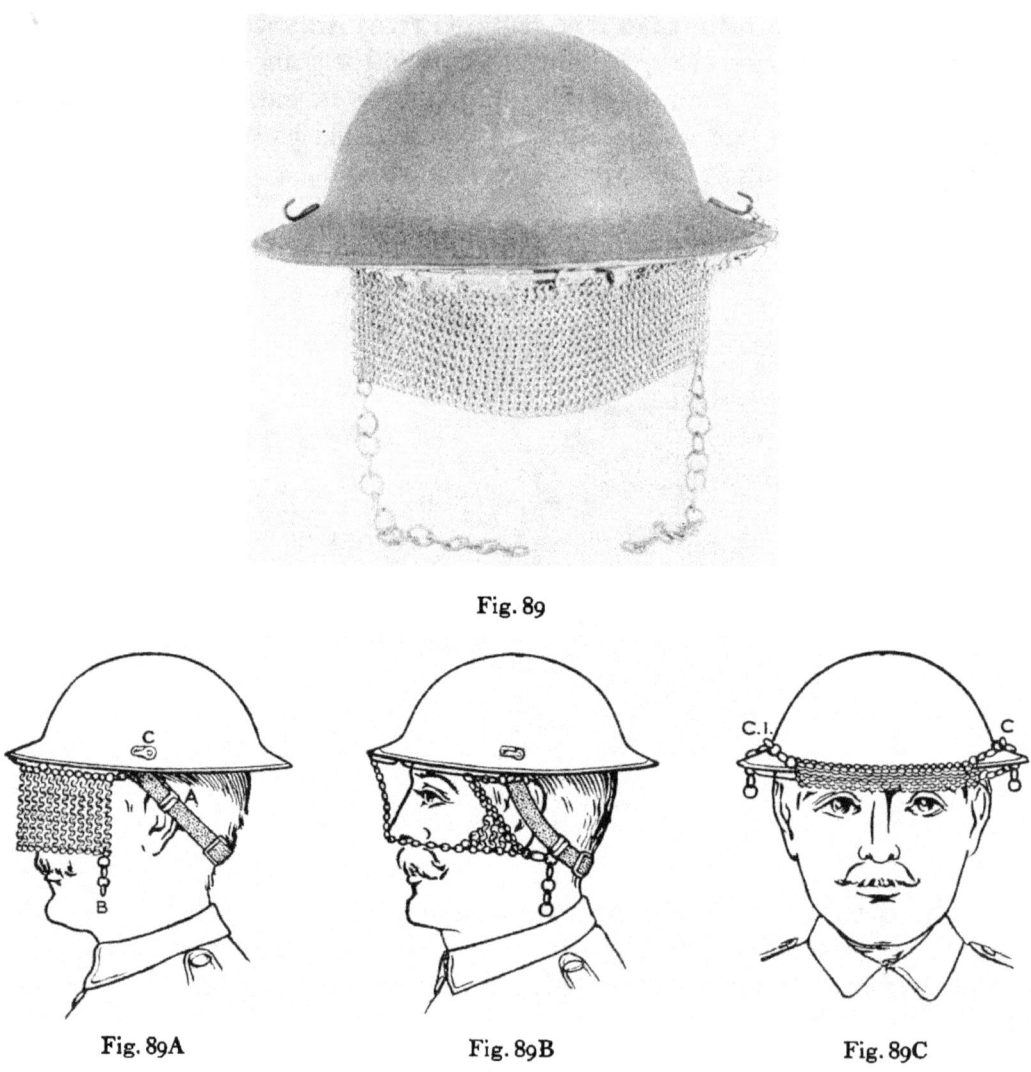

Fig. 89

Fig. 89A Fig. 89B Fig. 89C

Fig. 89. British helmet provided with chain mail visor, 1917

eye defense produced in steel in 1916, which had a considerable sale among English soldiers (see page 233). This, as shown in Fig. 182, is in the form of metal goggles, weighing five and one half ounces, which could be tied to the head by tapes. It was slotted for vision and, although the slits were narrow, they were situated close enough to the pupil of the eye to give a remarkably clear and wide vision. No regular issue of these goggles to soldiers in the field was made. The only eye defense which the British produced in large number was the chain-mail veil, as shown in Figs. 89 and 89A to C, which was devised by Captain Cruise, R. A. M. C., oculist to the King. This visor was made of closely woven links and was attached to a metal rod which passed immediately under the brim of the helmet. In Fig. 89A, the visor is shown hanging in front of the soldier's face. One notes a hook at the point "A" on the helmet strap, also a hanging chain at "B" and a hook on the brim of the helmet at "C." In Fig. 89B, the visor is shown in correct position; it is drawn taut, touching the nose and cheek region, and is fastened firmly in position by looping the chain "B" on the hook "A." When not in use, the visor may be detached from the point "A," then turned up over the brim of the helmet and fastened again by the side chains to the hook "C," as shown in Fig. 89C. In 1916-1917, this type of visor found favor with English authorities and was manufactured in large numbers. Some of the lots found their way to the front but we do not know to what degree they were actually worn. Certain it is that they were not given a kindly reception by the soldiers, who are said to have found them annoying and soon cast them off. A report states that in actual use they produce dizziness, for the links of the visor change position in front of the wearer's eyes, following every movement of the helmet. In designing this visor, it should be explained, the British authorities took into careful account the statistics as to the nature of the eye wounds, and it was demonstrated that about 50 per cent of the eye cases were of such a character that they might have been prevented by the use of the chain veil. On the other hand, it should have been pointed out that as there were only from two to three thousand cases of blindness reported in the entire British Army, which included about three million soldiers, the use of such a visor would probably be inexpedient—on the ground that it might hamper the efficiency of the men. (Cf. pages 72-73.)

(C) GERMAN

No information, unfortunately, is at hand dealing with the experimental results of the Germans in this field. There is no doubt, however, that they have considered this subject in an extended way, for a careful study of their present helmet and body armor shows clearly that they have consulted not only able metallurgists but technical experts in the field of armor.

HELMETS AND BODY ARMOR

They have probably secured the best results for the protection of the soldier during the present war.

(C) German
  (a) The German helmet
    1. Description
    2. Lining
    3. Chin-band
    4. Thickness
    5. Weight
    6. Composition
    7. Manufacture
    8. Ballistic tests
  (b) Siege helmets
  (c) Breastplate and tassets
    1. Chemical composition
    2. Physical characters
    3. Ballistic tests
    4. Use
    5. Criticism
  (d) Austrian helmets and armor

(a) THE GERMAN HELMET

The leathern helmet sometimes reinforced with steel in the familiar form of "Pickelhaube" need not be considered in the present discussion. The actual "trench helmet" (see Frontispiece and Figs. 90 to 93) while the heaviest of those in actual use—weighing two pounds ten and one half ounces, against the two pounds two and one half ounces of the British helmet—protects a lower zone of the head; it covers, in fact, the neck region, temples, and ears to a depth over two inches greater than the British helmet. We may, therefore, fairly assume that from this reason alone it has saved a greater proportional number of its wearers. Its metal, we may note, is hardly inferior to the British manganese alloy.

1. *Description*

The German helmet consists of dome, peak and neck-guard. The dome is cylindrical, somewhat flat at the top. Its measurements are $9 \times 7\frac{5}{8} \times 4\frac{1}{2}$ inches. Its peak is $6\frac{1}{2}$ inches broad and $1\frac{3}{8}$ inches long. Its neck-guard, which is $2\frac{1}{4}$ inches high, flares below at the brim, where its greatest diameter is 9.28 inches. These measurements concern the usual specimens of German helmet. A smaller model is, however, recorded. This arrangement,

IN MODERN WARFARE

it will be seen, differs from the British one in which helmets of different sizes do not occur, the fitting being regulated by the size of the helmet lining.

2. *Lining*

The helmet lining (Fig. 92) is borne on a sweat-band of cowhide, which is fastened to the helmet at three points. To this band are attached

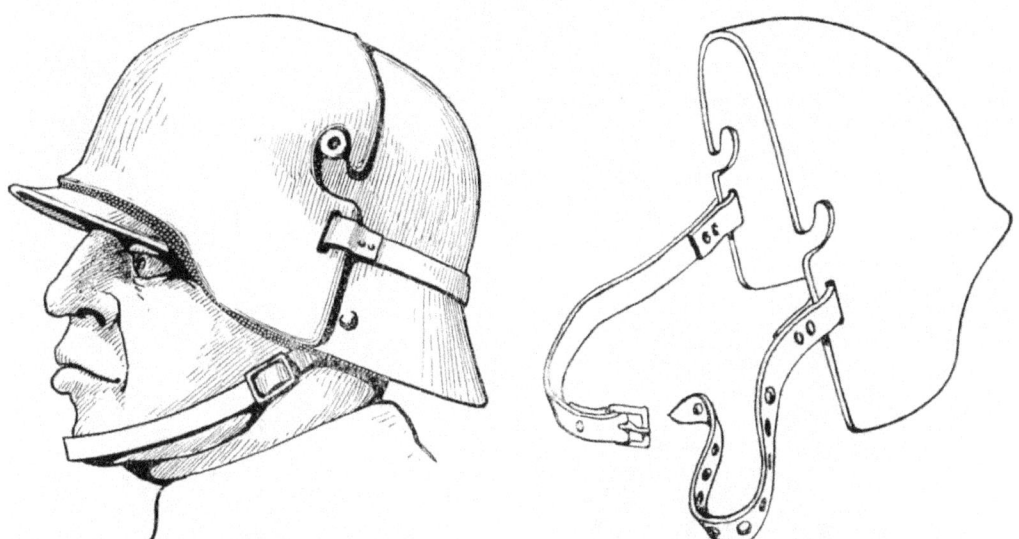

Fig. 90. German helmet with frontal plate for sniper

Fig. 91. Frontal plate detached

three pads which fold upward within the dome of the helmet and are backed (*i.e.*, next to the helmet shell) each by a cushion. The pads are then so arranged that one comes to lie against the forehead and one against each side of the head. In the specimens examined, the pad has been formed of calfskin so cut that the end which is attached to the sweat-band is the wider part; the opposite end divides into two lobes, each of which is pierced and threaded by a string which is so arranged that it draws together the free ends of all the tabs and forms an elastic carrier for the weight of the helmet. It should be noted that each tab bears an inner pocket which contains a small mattress filled with curled hair. This mattress is kept in position in the pocket by means of tapes which can be tied. The entire lining weighs 4½ ounces. It is so designed that it fits the head easily and allows free

136 HELMETS AND BODY ARMOR

spaces (one on either side of the forehead and one at the back of the head) through which ventilation is secured and by means of which the weight of the helmet upon the head is carried on the three cushions above described.

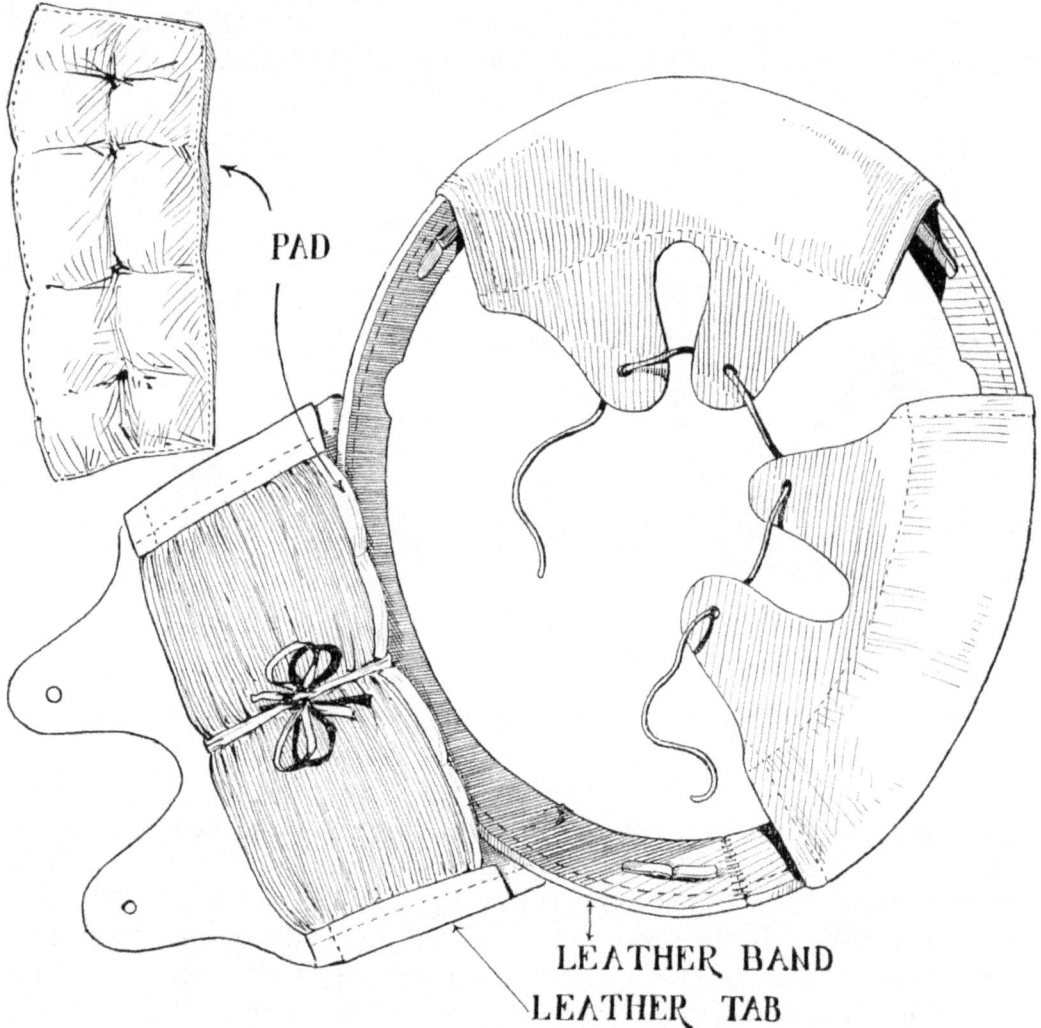

Fig. 92. Lining of German helmet

The scalp or the top of the head may thus still receive its supply of blood freely; for the vessels (and for that matter the nerves) which transmit the blood along the sides of the head upward or downward are not compressed by the constricting rim of the usual "hat-lining" of a helmet but have open passageway, thanks to the three spaces between the cushions. Another advantage of this type of lining is the way in which a wearer can adapt it comfortably to his head. Thus, if he feels that the supporting cushions are too hard or too thick, he is quite at liberty to remove some of their stuffing to the desired degree; if, on the other hand, he finds that the helmet sits upon his head too loosely, he has merely to open the drawing strings of the enclosed pads and thrust behind each mattress the needed amount of stuffing, in the shape of a bit of burlap, a folded strip of a handkerchief, a layer of cotton wool, etc.

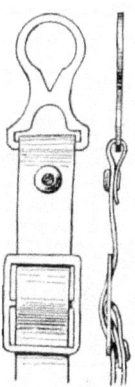

Fig. 93. Buckle and chin-strap fastener of helmet

3. *Chin-band*

The chin-band of the German helmet is adjusted by means of a simple buckle; it is attached on either side to brass loops which can at need be removed from the helmet shell. They have merely to be separated from their turning peg (Fig. 93).

4. *Thickness*

Several specimens measured showed a thickness of .040 inch at the top and .045 inch above the brim.

5. *Weight*

The shell of the German helmet weighs two pounds six ounces.

6. *Composition*

A sample analysis of a helmet shell showed:

Carbon	.37
Silicon	1.54
Manganese	.90
Nickel	1.94

7. *Manufacture*

No definite information could be obtained in this matter. The helmet is said to be pressed hot, probably on electrically heated dies. In confirmation of this statement, it is known that the Budd Manufacturing Company (Philadelphia) tried in vain to press steel of this formula cold; they failed to give it even the simpler shape of the British helmet. The surface finish of the helmet, according to studies made for us by the Schenectady Laboratory of the General Electric Company, is a coating of japan in which the helmet was dipped. It was air dried without artificial heat.

8. *Ballistic Tests*

A German helmet tested at British General Headquarters was not penetrated by:

Special rifle cartridge	Cal. .45	G. B. 117	vel. f. s. 670
Colt revolver	Cal. .38	G. B. 148	vel. f. s. 750
Automatic pistol	Cal. .45	G. B. 230	vel. f. s. 800

Test made in the Ordnance Department at Washington (several specimens) (Captain Simonds, 1917) showed that the helmets resisted the Government automatic revolver, 1917 model, and automatic pistol, model of 1911, bullet weighing 230 grains and velocity up to 900 foot seconds. The present writer confirms this result and notes that a helmet tested at Ford's plant in Detroit gave even better results—or about 1,000 foot seconds; he learns, however, that considerable variation exists in the ballistic strength of German helmets. Thus, Mr. William A. Taylor of the British Inventions Board states that he has seen instances in which the German helmet failed at 650 foot seconds.

(b) SIEGE HELMETS

Each standard German helmet can be used at need as a defense against rifle fire at close range. On its forehead appears, above and on each side, a deep peg formed of cylindrical tubing, which serves to attach a brow-plate (Figs. 90, 91) as a reinforcing piece, *e.g.*, for snipers. This plate is .23 to .25 inch thick and fits closely to the forehead as far down at least as the level of the frontal peak of the helmet. It weighs from five to seven pounds and naturally overbalances the headpiece considerably. From information collected in the field, this heavy brow-plate is not often used; its weight evidently makes it an unsatisfactory defense.

A siege or sniper's helmet (Figs. 94, 94A) said to have been taken from the Germans at Verdun in 1917, was seen by the writer at an exhibition of war objects sent by the British Military Mission to New York; it resembles very closely and is probably copied from a Saxon siege helmet of

Fig. 94   Fig. 94A
Fig. 94. Siege or sentinel's helmet. German, 1917

the sixteenth century. It has a sub-spherical dome, a somewhat straight peak, and a short straight neck defense which together at the sides merge into broad ear lappets which extend down from the dome of the helmet to below the level of the ear. This headpiece weighs fourteen pounds. It is held in place by a chin-strap adjusted by a simple tongue-bar buckle and is provided with a quilted lining about half an inch thick (see Fig. 94A). It will resist service ammunition at 200 yards when a normal hit is scored; it fails at 200 yards when hit similarly by an armor-piercing bullet, but will deflect a bullet of this type when struck at a slight angle.

Another type of sniper's defense which has lately been reported from the front is a mask rather than a helmet. This is a plate of steel which covers the entire face and is crudely fitted to it, buckled in place by means of a leather strap. It is thick (.227 inch) and heavy (13¼ pounds), deeply padded in the forehead region, and painted gray-green outside and in. It is provided with a pair of eye-slits, each .7 inch long and .3 inch wide. The lower right-hand corner of this defense is proof to service ammunition

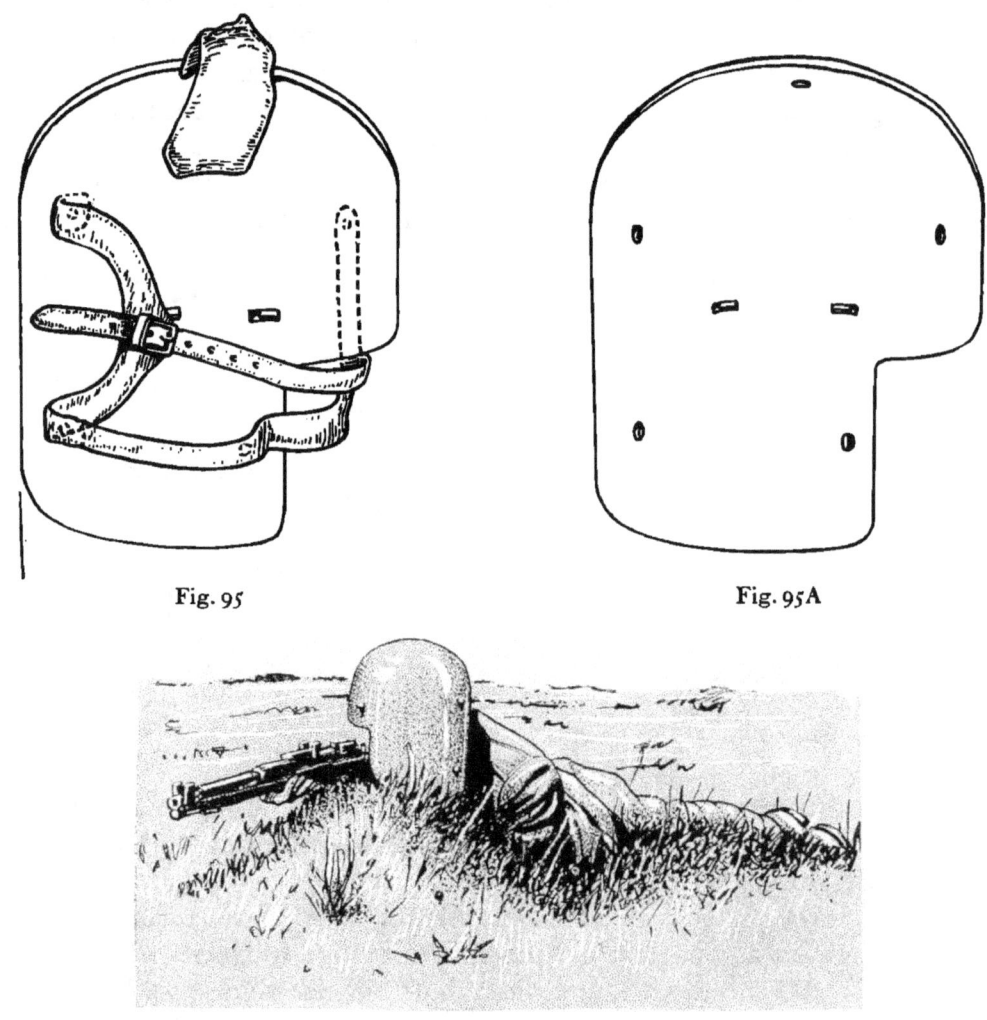

Fig. 95　　　　　　　　　　　　　　　Fig. 95A

Fig. 95B

Fig. 95. German sniper's head shield, 1916-1917. Fig. 95B. Variant?

even at close range; it fails with armor-piercing bullets at normal impact at 200 yards. In composition, it is not unlike the standard helmet described above (C.33, Si. .37, Mn. .49, S. .04, Ph. .060, N. 3.65, Chr. .24, Va. .20,

Tungsten and Molybdenum .0); it is well heat-treated; its Brinell hardness is 430.

The writer has not seen a specimen of this defense, nor yet a similar (or the same) sniper's head-shield which is pictured in Figs. 95, 95A, 95B, but upon which no special report has as yet been received; it is said to weigh seventeen pounds and to be proof to standard rifle ammunition at close range; it is stated to be provided with a handle by which it can readily be carried and with a "foot" by which it is anchored firmly to the ground.

Fig. 96. German helmet, 1918 model (variant ?)

New Model German Helmet: Photographs have recently (1918) been received in this country of a German helmet* which is probably a new

* Through the courtesy of his friend, Lieutenant Charles K. Bassett, the writer has had the opportunity of examining a German helmet of late model, captured among the equipment stores at St. Mihiel (November, 1918). This helmet has not the changes in curvature noted above; it weighs three pounds complete; its total depth is 6¾ inches, its total length 12, its width 9¾. It is therefore heavier by five ounces than the earlier model, deeper by nearly half an inch, and somewhat shorter. Its lining shows several changes: a steel sweat-band replaces the leathern one; the chin-band is of a woolen woven braid, and the cushions are made more tightly and cheaply; they lack the drawing strings and are held in place by a wide braid sewed in place. The

142 HELMETS AND BODY ARMOR

model: it has a sloping brim and a neck-shield which merges gradually into the cranial dome (Fig. 96). A German helmet camouflaged in green, buff and white, may here also be figured (Fig. 97): it was taken from the head of a sniper in August, 1918.

(c) BREASTPLATE AND TASSETS

We have no evidence that the Germans made use of a light type of corselet. On the other hand, they issued "in large numbers" a heavy body defense which can be worn on front or back indifferently (Figs. 98, 98A, 99 and 100). This defense is made up of four plates of which the three

Fig. 97. German helmet, 1918. Camouflaged green, buff and white

lower dangle freely, and the largest or uppermost is attached to the wearer's shoulders. The uppermost plate follows broadly the shape of the chest; its front is 18½ inches high and its upper border is rolled outward so as

chin-strap is of a heavy braid made of coarse cloth folded and sewed; its mountings are of leather and its eyelets of iron; a common tongue-roller buckle finishes this trapping.

Colonel Hans Zinsser, also recently returned from the front, has kindly furnished the writer with additional notes concerning the latest issues of German helmets. The lining-pads of the standard model now contain "first aid" dressings: when these are used, the helmet becomes too large for the soldier, who then, however, has probably little need for wearing it. The Colonel also reports the use of an extremely heavy type of helmet for machine gunners, which is said to be proof to American service ammunition at very close range. It follows closely the lines of the standard German helmet. Possibly this is the model shown in Fig. 95.

IN MODERN WARFARE

to protect the region of the throat. Riveted to each upper corner of this front plate is a shoulder plate, 9 inches long and 4½ inches wide, which bends backward and serves as a hook to support the armor on the shoulder. The abdominal plates, which together form an apron, are three in number; the uppermost measures 17¼ inches long and 6 inches wide; the second is of the same height but is less than 14 inches in length; the lowest ("sporran

Fig. 98. German heavy breastplate

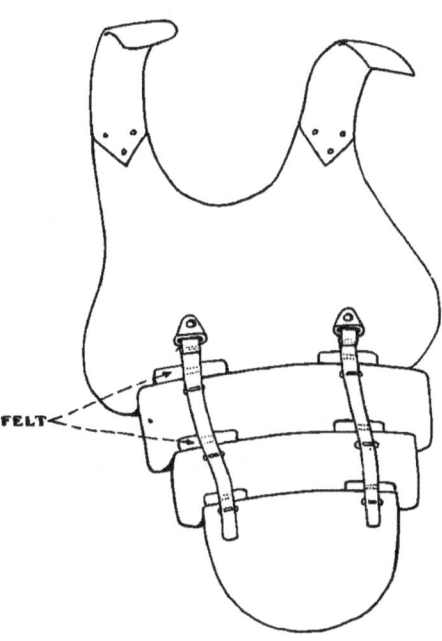

Fig. 98A. German heavy breastplate. Inner view

plate," as the Scots would call it) is almost flat, 10 inches long and 7½ inches high. These three plates are hung on each side to a band of webbing which is made fast above to a loop riveted to the breastplate. To keep the abdominal plates from jangling, pads of felt (cow's hair) are inserted between them and sewed to the webbing supports. There are two sizes of this armor used. The first weighs from 19 to 22 pounds, the second is larger (31½ inches high) and weighs about 24 pounds. The plates in the smaller size are somewhat the thicker, averaging .140 inch as against .131 inch.

HELMETS AND BODY ARMOR

1. *Chemical Composition*

This body armor is made of a silicon-nickel steel, of which the formula is as follows:

	I*	II†	III‡
Carbon	.38	.20	.39
Chromium	.22		.21
Copper	.17		
Manganese	.60	.98	.58
Nickel	1.55	4.12	1.55
Phosphorus	.022	.013	.20
Silicon	1.75	2.135	1.95
Sulphur	.006	.073	.01

2. *Physical Characters*

Unaltered by annealing and capable of being drilled. Tensile strength (square inch) 65.69; elongation 1 per cent; hardness, Brinell test, 360-520.

3. *Ballistic Tests*

American rifle ammunition at 2,140 foot seconds pierces at 30 yards but is resisted at 60 yards.

Service ammunition of full velocity (2,780 foot seconds) shatters at 60 yards, is resisted at 300 yards.

In cases of failure lamination of metal was noticed.

4. *Use of the Present Sentinel's Armor*

At the various points on the western line armor of the present type has been observed in considerable quantity during the "pushes" of 1916-1917. It is referred to in an order taken from a captive German officer which may be translated as follows:

"CGS of the Field Army,
"11 Nr. 56938 op.   5.6.17

"Infantry armour has been issued on a large scale to the Sixth Army; a report of that army on the experience gained with this armour is attached.

* Analysis of an abdominal plate (model 1917) made by Universal Rolling Mills.
† Analysis made by order of British General Headquarters in France. Model 1916.
‡ Analysis received (February 1, 1918) from H. A. E. F.; the composition of the main plate is here given.

With regard to this report, an endeavor will be made to carry out the proposed improvements but in order not to delay the issue, this can only be done in the case of later deliveries.

"The armour is not generally intended for operations, but it will prove valuable for sentries, listening posts, garrisons of shell holes, gun teams of machine guns scattered over the ground, etc., especially as a protection for the back.

"I request that the armour be issued to units destined for threatened sectors of the line, so that they can become familiar with its use before they go into line.

"(signed) LUDENDORFF.

"Sixth Army H. Q.
11 B Nr. 19718"

5. *Criticism of German Sentinel's Armor*

Another captured document is translated as follows:

"To the C.G.S. of the Field Army:

"Infantry armour has, on the whole, proved serviceable for sentries in position warfare. Universal complaints have been received that the armour makes it difficult to handle the rifle and is a considerable handicap to bombers.

"On the other hand, it is admitted that the armour is very useful, especially as a protection to the back, for individuals (listening posts, advanced posts during a heavy bombardment) and has prevented casualties.

"It should not be used for operations which entail crossing obstacles by climbing, jumping, or crawling, especially as it makes it difficult to carry ammunition. When the enemy attacks, the armour has to be taken off, as it decreases the mobility of the soldier on account of its weight and stiffness.

"As regards the resistance of the armour to penetration by various projectiles, sufficient experience has not yet been gained.

"The following improvements are suggested:—[compare Fig. 99]

"1. The edge of the armour below the shoulder should be hollowed out at (b) and (a).

"2. In order to provide a support for the butt of the rifle and so facilitate aiming, a plate should be attached to (c).

"3. The iron shoulder plates (g) do not fit close to the shoulders and back. In order that they may so fit, it is recommended that these plates be attached to the breastplate by means of bolts and nuts, round which they will be free to revolve.

"4. The armour should be provided with two straps (d) and two eyes (e) so that it can be secured by means of hooks or spring hooks, as otherwise the armour is liable to slip from the shoulders when jumping and especially when lying down, crawling through obstacles, etc.

"5. When lying down or crawling, the edge of the armour presses against the body unless the edge is hollowed out at (b).

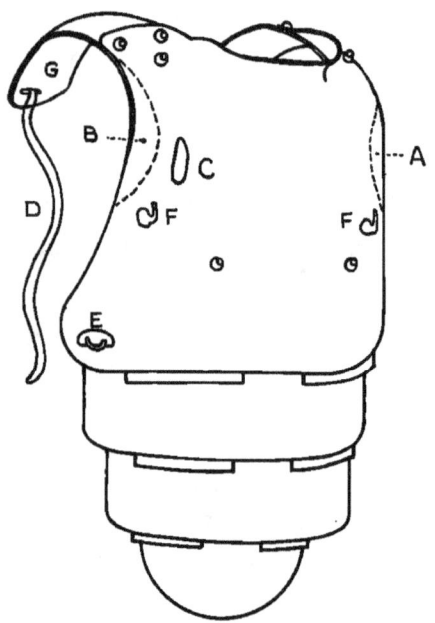

Fig. 99. German breastplate.
Improvements suggested, 1917

"6. In front of the armour two hooks should be provided at (f) from which bags for tools or for carrying bombs, etc., can be slung.

"7. If worn for any length of time, the weight of the armour becomes very oppressive. As a remedy for this, it is recommended that the shoulders should be padded, which would relieve the pressure considerably. An issue of this armour, even in small quantities, is requested.

"Note: The scale of issue to the 2nd Battn. 95th Inf. Regt. on the 19th June 1917, was 2 per company, including the machine gun company."

IN MODERN WARFARE

From the foregoing evidence, it is clear that this type of armor was found serviceable for sentinels in position warfare; and from the testimony of officers returning from the front, the writer learned during the summer of 1918 that this defense was appearing in greater proportional numbers among the Germans. In Fig. 100, an entire machine gun unit, its officers excepted, is shown wearing this armor. In a general way, it offered protec-

Fig. 100. German machine gun squad armed with new model helmet and heavy body armor, 1918

tion against bombs exploding within a few yards; it did not interfere seriously with the wearer's movements, nor was it excessively heavy.

(d) AUSTRIAN HELMETS AND ARMOR

The Austrians appear to have introduced a helmet at a later period than the French, English, Germans and Italians. Falling under the orders of the German General Staff, they adopted their ally's model, and during the last campaigns in Russia and in Italy, they were provided with German helmets in large numbers. No data is at hand concerning their use of body armor.

148 HELMETS AND BODY ARMOR

(D) ITALIAN

The Italians are reported to have used experimentally many types of headpieces and body shields during the present warfare, but exact data

Fig. 101. Italian helmet, also Ansaldo body shield, 1918

on this Italian work proved difficult to obtain; the present résumé must therefore be regarded as provisional.

From the beginning of the war, the Italian General Staff is stated to have taken great interest in the development of armor for assault. In 1915, before any special defenses could be provided, the Italian infantry under certain conditions carried with them or rolled in front of them bags of sand to serve as shields, or "sap-rollers" (see page 128)—a primitive defense which is said to have saved numerous casualties.

(D) Italian
    (a) The Italian helmet
        Service helmet, helmet for shock troops
    (b) Body defenses
        Body shields, Ansaldo, Fariselli, Frati, Gorgeno-Collaye
    (c) Armor defenses for other parts of the body

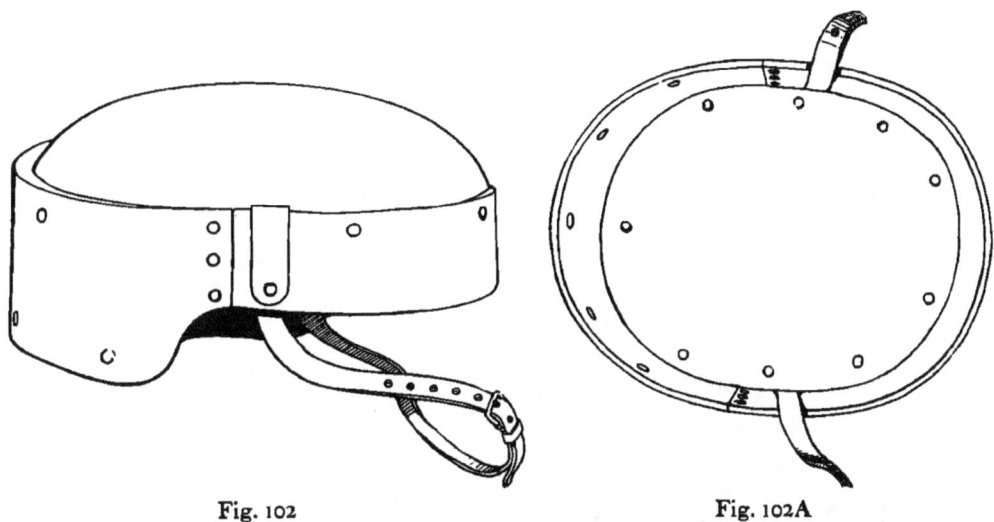

Fig. 102   Fig. 102A

Fig. 102. Italian helmet, heavy model, 1917

(a) THE ITALIAN HELMET

Following the traditions of a kindred stock, the Italians were led to adapt their helmet from the French (Figs. 101, 102, 104 and 105). This is evident from photographs taken in the war area, for no actual Italian helmet has come into the writer's hands which would enable him to compare definitely its weight, manufacture, lining, etc. He examined, however, a heavier type of Italian helmet, shown in Fig. 102, while visiting the Munitions Inventions Board in London. This helmet, it was stated, was used for shock troops and was issued "in fairly large number." It weighs four pounds and is made of chrome-nickel steel. Its heavy vertical rim is made up of three separate strips of alloy held together by riveting; to this

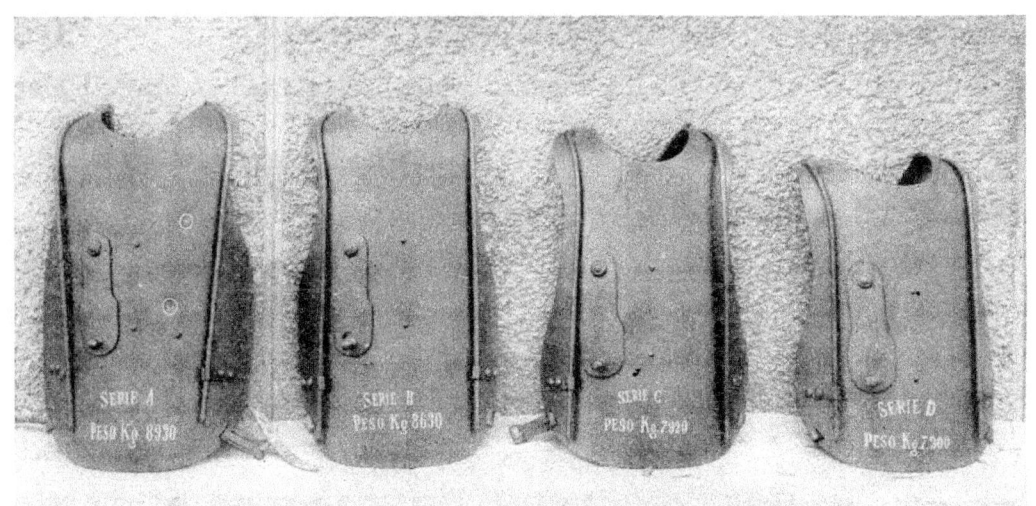

Fig. 103. Italian body armor, 1918. Weights represented

Fig. 104. Italian helmet and body armor, Ansaldo model

rim the convex top of the helmet is riveted. Unfortunately, no specimens of this headpiece are at hand for actual tests. It is learned, however, from Mr. William A. Taylor, the armor specialist of the Munitions Inventions Board, that this helmet is ballistically disappointing. The third type of Italian helmet is a small skullcap, evidently lighter in weight; it appears in photographs which have come to the writer's attention, but no details concerning it are to be had.

(b) BODY DEFENSES

The body shield "Ansaldo" manufactured by the Società Anonima Italiana (Gio. Ansaldo et Cie. of Genoa) ranks among heavy defenses

Fig. 105. Italian body armor used as rifle shield

(Figs. 101, 103 to 109). It is made of chrome-nickel-vanadium steel and will resist a service rifle ball of 2,500 foot seconds at 100 yards; its official test requires that it shall be neither pierced nor cracked when struck by five shots of the Italian service rifle at the distance of 110 yards. Its thickness is about .25 inch and its weight about 21 pounds. It is, however, made in lighter weights, respectively 19, 17 and 16 pounds, as indicated in Fig. 103. As shown in Figs. 104, 107, this body defense may be worn either in front or back or when demounted it may be used as a rifle shield, Fig. 105. When employing it in the latter way, the soldier sights his rifle through a slot in the shield which is otherwise closed by a sliding door (Fig. 106 [1916-1917]) or by a rotating device (Fig. 109). The present defense is formed plainly in a single piece which extends between the regions of collar bone and groin; it probably, therefore, impedes the active movements of the body. For supporting the present breastplate, shoulder straps are used (Fig. 108) which cross the back diagonally; the right strap buckling near the left hip and vice versa. A novel feature of this breastplate is its pair of "legs" which, where the breastplate is used as a rifle shield, may be rotated downward and become the support by which the defense may be held upright on the ground in front of the soldier (Fig. 105). When not in use,

Fig. 106. Italian body armor, 1917 model

these "legs" are merely rotated forward and are held in place under the soldier's cartridge belt (Fig. 101). It is not known in what number the present shield has been issued.

A second type of body defense is the armored waistcoat of Fariselli, the property of the Astori Company in Milan. A specimen of this, examined by the writer in the Munitions Inventions Board in London, appeared simple in principle but quite effective (Fig. 110). It takes the form of a waistcoat of heavy stuff, provided with three pockets, two covering the breast and one the abdomen. Each pocket contains a plate of chrome-nickel steel; here it lies unattached and for this reason the defense is said to be easier to wear. Certainly such a device, one notes at once, lends itself readily to the use of plates of different thicknesses. The waistcoat examined by the

Fig. 107. Italian body armor, 1918

writer weighed altogether 17 pounds; its plates were .30 inch thick and their weights were as follows: abdominal about $7\frac{1}{2}$ pounds, right and left breastplates about 5 and 4 pounds respectively. The ballistic test of this

Fig. 108. Italian body armor. Inner view

Fig. 109. Italian body armor used as rifle shield

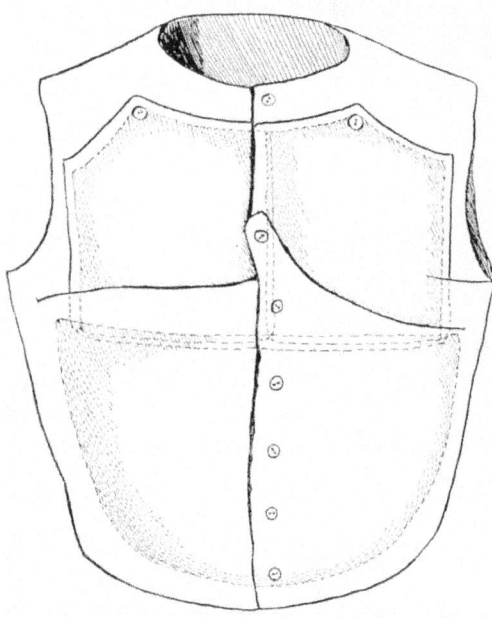

Fig. 110. "Fariselli armored waistcoat," 1917

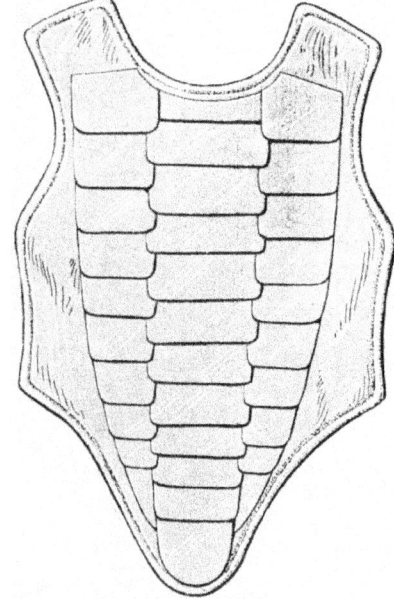

Fig. 111. Italian body armor, "Gorgeno-Collaye," 1916-1917

defense resisted the bullet of the Austrian Männlicher rifle at distances greater than 20 yards; it was pierced, however, by the service ammunition of the German Mauser at less than 200 yards; it was proof to the bullet of the Italian rifle of 1891 at muzzle velocity. About 200 specimens of this defense were ordered by the English for service in France. No report is at hand concerning its use in the field.

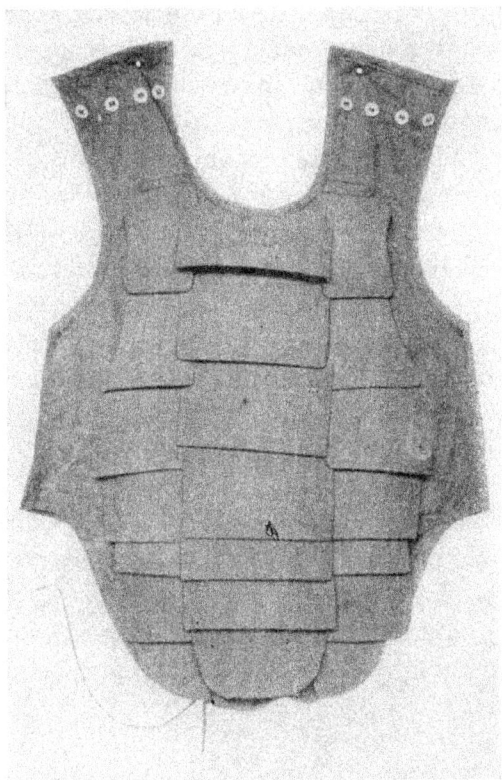

Fig. 112. Italo-British "Military" body armor

Still another Italian body defense is the cuirass of the Frati Company of Milan. The plates of this defense are .20 to .22 inch in thickness. We have seen no specimen of this defense or photograph of it. We assume from a French report that its plates are worn very much as in the Fariselli breastplates. Its material, however, is of greater resistance, for when tested at distances from 20 to 200 yards, its plates withstood successfully Italian, German and Austrian service ammunition without showing even a pronounced indentation on its under surface. The test was a good one even when shots were concentrated on a surface one inch square. This type of breastplate weighs 15½ pounds.

A light breastplate of an Italian model, which the writer examined while in London, is shown in Fig. 111 and is known as the Gorgeno-Collaye model. It is said to date from 1916. This defense is known technically to armor experts as a jazeran but differs from this defense in having its plates covered separately in cloth; the plates themselves, it will be seen, overlap one another freely, as in ancient jazerans, on the outer side of the defense. No data is at hand regarding the inventor of this defense or its place of manufacture. We know, however, that this defense appears both in France and England. The "Military" waistcoat shown in Fig. 112 is merely a variant of this plastron. The last-named defense weighs eight pounds and it is easy to wear; it resists the automatic 45, 230-grain bullet at a foot-second velocity of over 800. We should here mention that the Italians appear to have used trench shields (see page 180) as a type of heavy body defense (Fig. 113), judging from photographs taken in the Italian war area. Such shields are proof to machine guns but they are obviously difficult to carry—even for a short distance. They overbalance the soldier on account of their great weight, averaging from thirty to sixty pounds.

(c) **ARMOR DEFENSES FOR OTHER PARTS OF THE BODY**

The only evidence at hand that such defenses were employed is shown in photographs of Italian troops at the front. In some cases shock groups are pictured wearing épaulières (Fig. 114) formed of single pieces of steel held together on the back by means of a strap and attached in front to the plastron.

(E) BELGIAN

After their country was invaded, the Belgians became dependent upon the British and French for equipment of all kinds. In 1916 they were receiving through the French Quartermaster Corps a large number of trench helmets of the Adrian model. These appear to have been made by the firm of Aug. du Puyron, one of the best of the French manufacturers, in whose establishment as many as 12,000 helmets were turned out per day. It was, nevertheless, the constant wish of the Belgian Staff to provide their soldiers with a helmet which should be distinctly different from either the French or the British. They desired especially a model which should protect not merely the cranium but the face of the wearer. This need for the national army, it appeared, soon attracted the attention of the Queen of the Belgians, who spoke with enthusiasm of her wish "to provide her soldiers with a helmet which should protect their faces and especially their eyes," and in behalf of her project, she offered all necessary financial aid. Experiments in the direction of producing a visored helmet were accordingly undertaken by both French and English inventors. It is understood, for example, that

Fig. 113. Italian trench shield used as body armor

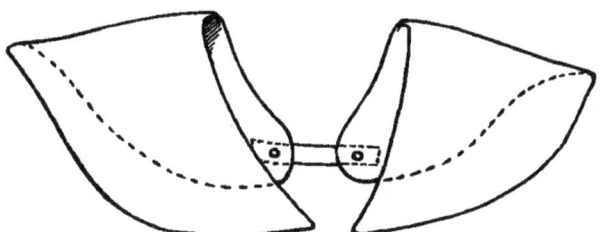

Fig. 114. Italian shoulder defense

M. Dunand produced a design which was considered critically in this matter. But up to the end of 1917, none of the models furnished was accepted. A report in this matter which came to the attention of the writer, showed that the Dunand helmet was considered too heavy and too high in the neck, and that its visor was too fragile. In 1917, the question of making a visored helmet* was placed by the Queen in the hands of Mr. John MacIntosh,

* According to information received recently from M. Ernest Henrion, of the Belgian General Staff, Professor Weckers, ophthalmologist of the University of Liège, furnished the model recommended. About 40,000 helmets were made and were used for special service.

158 HELMETS AND BODY ARMOR

director general of British trench warfare, supply department, and through his efforts the firm of Messrs. Sankey of Wolverhampton produced the helmet which is shown in Figs. 115 and 115A.

(E) Belgian
    (a) The Belgian helmet
        1. Description
        2. Manufacture
            Ballistic results, weight, thickness, critical notes
    (b) Belgian body armor

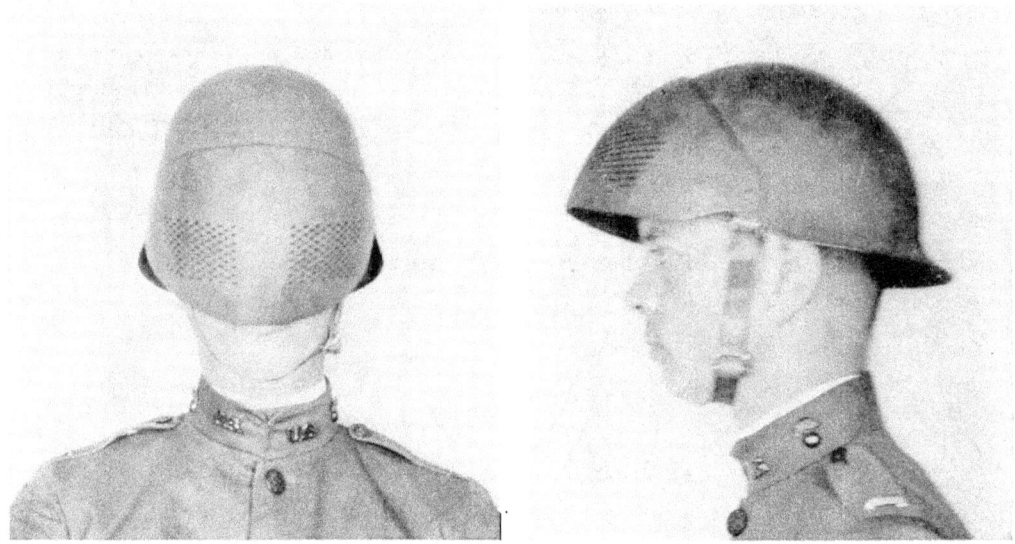

Fig. 115   Fig. 115A

Fig. 115. Belgian helmet. Experimental model, 1917

(a) THE BELGIAN HELMET

1. *Description*

This model was, apparently, inspired by the Dunand helmet, although in certain directions it is an improvement upon it. The visor fitted the helmet more closely and was considerably stronger than the French inventor's although similar in principle; it was, however, provided with small elliptical perforations for vision instead of long slit-like ones. Then, too, the perforations in the Belgian model were brought together into a rectangular area in front of each eye, leaving a strip of metal nearly two

IN MODERN WARFARE

inches wide between the two visual areas. In the Dunand helmet, it may be recalled, the visor extended its perforations over its entire surface, even at its sides, where perforations could not actually be needed and where in fact they would materially reduce the strength of the defense.

The bowl of this Belgian helmet is somewhat narrow and high, broadly rounded above, without crest or ornament. The neck region flares somewhat further outward than in the Dunand model.

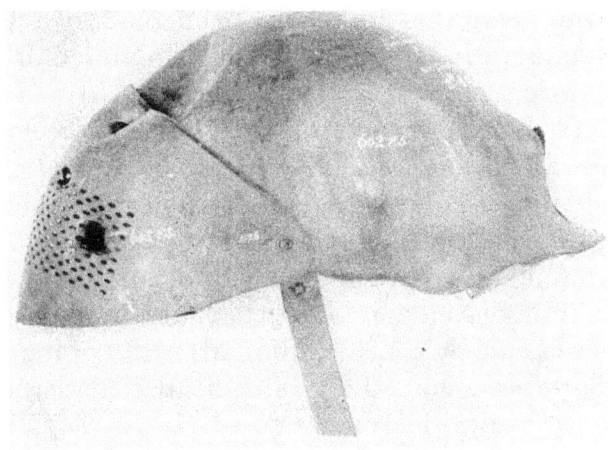

Fig. 116. Belgian helmet. Result of tests

2. *Manufacture*

It was evidently found difficult to reproduce so deep a model in the manganese alloy which had been used for the regular British helmet, still the present model is probably pressed in this steel. It could not, however, have been made of it, if we accept the report from Major Dunning that this helmet has been "retempered," for this would imply that it had been given a heat treatment during its manufacture, a process which would have injured a helmet if made of manganese alloy.

Ballistic Results: Actual tests of the helmet have yielded good results, according to Mr. MacIntosh's data. In a report from the Woolwich Arsenal, it was shown to be proof at 730 foot seconds (bullet weighing 230 grains, automatic revolver) and sometimes to resist at 820 foot seconds. The visible result of a test of this helmet in Washington appears in Fig. 116; an impact of 602 foot second automatic revolver bullet failed to penetrate but produced an area of indentation which indicates strongly that the helmet is made of manganese steel. A shot in the forehead was resisted but showed again a very great indentation. The visor perforated readily at 602 foot seconds and the perforated visual areas were found to have relatively little resistance, probably not as high as 200 foot seconds.

Weight: The weight of this helmet is twenty-eight ounces without lining, thirty-six with lining, and forty-four with visor complete.

Thickness: The helmet is well pressed although thinned out considerably at the crown. Near the rim of the helmet, its metal measured .044 inch in thickness and at the top .035 inch. The minimum indentation noted in the above ballistic test is one half inch measured from a line connecting the sides of the crater. The thickness of the visor is .026 inch.

Critical Notes: This Anglo-Belgian helmet is comfortable to wear and in general, considering that it is a visored helmet, its balance is good. Its lining is in the French style, that is, having a continuous leather head-covering which terminates above in a number of small lappets held together by a string. The lining is supported by a separate carrier which is attached to the shell of the casque by coiled springs, after the fashion of the Dunand model. In the matter of shape, the present helmet is criticized as being too narrow and flat to insure the maximum safety in use. Even a relatively slight shock in the temple region would be apt to produce grave injury to the wearer. In another direction, the form of the bowl of the helmet is faulty, for it is highly arched at the back where the head almost touches the helmet shell. No statistics are at hand to show in what number this helmet was introduced in the Belgian Army. (Later specimens examined are provided with lining after the English model.)

(b) BELGIAN BODY ARMOR

The writer was told that during the campaign of 1916 the Belgians received a supply of English body shields (Dayfield model) but they found them difficult to wear and soon cast them aside. Thereafter they appear to have taken no further steps in the way of developing body armor.

(F) PORTUGUESE

A helmet designed for the Portuguese General Staff was submitted in 1917 to the British Director of Munitions Supply, Mr. John MacIntosh, who caused it to be supplied in some number to the Portuguese troops. It is a hat-shaped casque ("chapel" or wide-brimmed "cabasset") weighing about two pounds (Fig. 117). It is corrugated on its sides and its general appearance suggests somewhat the Portuguese headpieces of the late sixteenth and early seventeenth centuries. It is made of a mild steel and has about the ballistic resistance of the French headpiece, or 300 to 400 foot seconds for shrapnel ball, forty-one to the pound. Its appearance is distinctive, rather good-looking, its fluted surface offering a range of shadows—but not materially strengthening the casque. The fluting may even have rendered the helmet more apt to be injured, for its ridges tend to hold

Fig. 117. Portuguese helmet

the fragments of shell, etc. (of low velocity), which might have otherwise glanced aside. The measurements of this helmet are as follows: height, 5½ inches; length, 11¾; width, 9⅞; width of brim, 1⅝.

Body armor does not appear to have been provided for Portuguese troops; in case of need they had at hand the light breastplates furnished to the British forces.

(G) SLAVIC

Details concerning helmets and body armor in Slavic countries are not accessible. We know, however, that the Russian and Polish regiments were provided with helmets somewhat after the French model, as shown in Fig. 118. The visor, however, appears to have been less produced above the eyes and the bowl of the helmet is apparently wider. No data are at hand concerning its ballistic resistance, lining, attachment to the head, or manufacture.

162　　HELMETS AND BODY ARMOR

From photographs of Russian troops at the front, there appears no evidence that body defenses of any kind were employed. A trench shield was used to a certain degree (see page 185) and one form of shield was developed in the United States at the instance of the Russian Commission which visited the United States in 1916. The firm of W. H. Mullins and Company of Salem, Ohio, prepared this, which, however, was not carried to production on account of the collapse of the Russian front. The shield in question,

Fig. 118. Slavic helmet (Polish), 1917

when made of alloy, proof to machine gun at fifty yards, would have weighed about thirty pounds. It could be carried on the soldier's breast or back or could be stood in front of him when he assumed a prone position.

An early effort of the Russians should be recorded in the matter of armor. During the Russo-Japanese War, bullet-proof waistcoats were issued in considerable number to Russian officers. These were manufactured by Captain Aveniro Czemcrzin in Petrograd. This defense covered only the front of the body and weighed about nine pounds (Figs. 119, 119A, 119B); it was made up of a chrome-nickel plate, one eighth inch thick, which was covered and lined with a silken fabric, or mat, measuring respectively one eighth and one half inch in thickness. This was of Zeglin fabric (see page 290). The corselet, we understand, gave fairly good results; it resisted the Russian service rifle ball of about 2,300 foot seconds at a distance of 200 yards. A lot of 50,000 breastplates of this type was ordered for the army of General Leniewitch at a cost of about $75 each. The writer may here express his conviction that a breastplate agreeing with the defense here noted in size, shape, weight and ballistic resistance could have been furnished even at that time but without the silk, at not more than one quarter the cost.

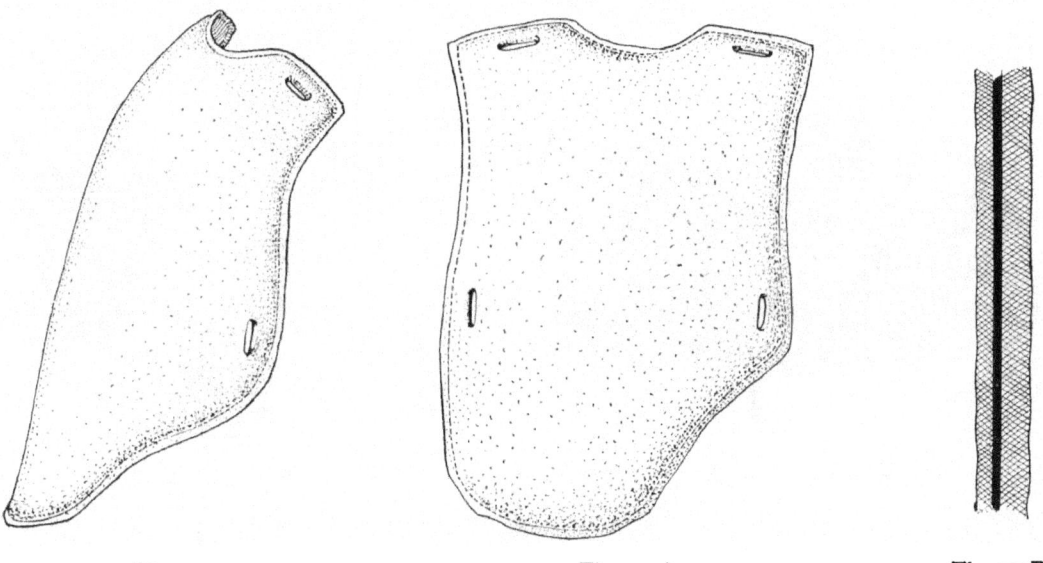

Fig. 119   Fig. 119A   Fig. 119B

Fig. 119. Russian breastplate. Section shows a core of ballistic steel: the covering and lining are of heavy silk matting

(H) SWISS

The Swiss Government has as yet considered the use of armor only in an experimental way. In the matter of body armor, it has done little, so far as can be learned.

In an effort to produce a distinctive helmet for the Swiss Army, the work of several inventors should, however, be mentioned, though as yet (spring, 1918) no model has been officially chosen, according to Colonel

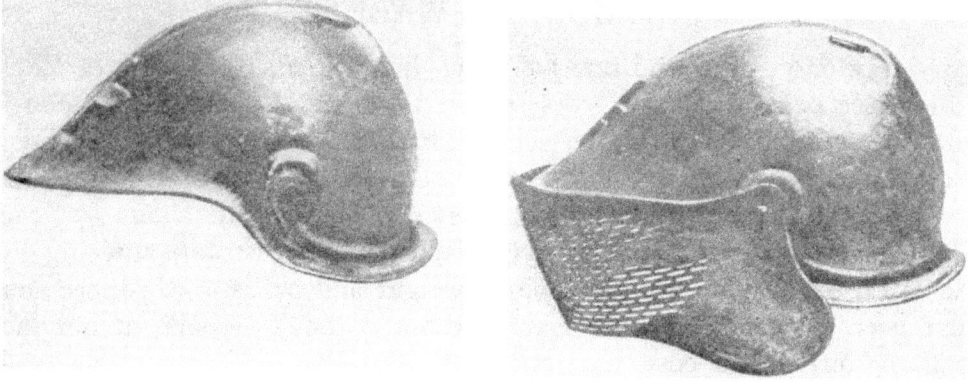

Fig. 120 Fig. 120A

Fig. 120B Fig. 120C
Fig. 120. Experimental Swiss helmet. Le Platenier model, 1917

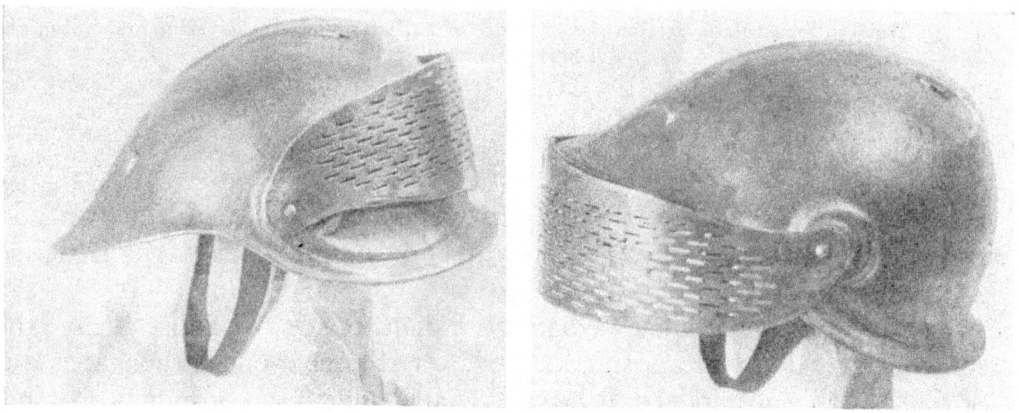

Fig. 121. Similar model with shallower visor, 1918

Sprecher of the Swiss General Staff. The helmet shown in Figs. 120, 120A-C, 121, 122 and 123 has been referred to in various publications as the national helmet. But apparently it has never been produced in ballistic

Fig. 122. Le Platenier helmet, 1917-1918

steel. This helmet suggests in broad lines the Dunand helmet. It differs from it, however, in being somewhat deeper at the sides and longer in the brow, having a peak which extends to the front of the nose as in the burganets of the sixteenth century. The form is well modeled, and is provided with a small median crest. It bears a demountable visor which is appar-

166 HELMETS AND BODY ARMOR

ently inspired by the Dunand design. Like the latter, it has a series of small transverse slots in front of the eyes and face. Nevertheless, it differs from the Dunand visor in having a wide marginal flange which holds it in place against the sides and back of the helmet, and when not in use it can be rotated backward to a position of rest over the top of the helmet. The lateral flanges then, at least in one model, project upward and form ornamental processes suggesting the wings of the hat of Hermes! Two

Fig. 123. Swiss experimental visor in place

ornaments appear on this helmet; the first is a repoussé scroll centering on the point which pivots the visor, the second is a Swiss cross embossed on the forehead. The lining is detachable by means of a clasp; it is held on a carrier made of rattan which has a circular brow-band and above it two intersecting arches; at their point of intersection a small cushion is placed which supports the main weight of the helmet. The brow-band of this carrier is provided with pads or cushions which alternate with spaces in order to insure comfort in wearing. The cushions are arranged in separate pockets and can be stuffed to fit the size of the individual head—a type of cushioning well known in the German lining. The chin-strap is also similar to the German. It is said that the cushioning of this helmet is elastic and that it resists adequately the shock of a blow.

The present helmet is criticized as being badly balanced and this may well be the case; for the visor extends far in front of the helmet and would naturally cause it to tilt forward when in use. Also, it is noted that the perforations of the visor are so numerous that while tending to restore the balance of the helmet, they notably diminish its value as a defense. The ornaments on this helmet are also regarded as undesirable.

A model embodying suggestions for a Swiss helmet is said to have been made by M. Dunand in December, 1916. It was sent to Switzerland and on February 17 it was returned to the French inventor. Shortly thereafter, the helmet described above appeared as the design of Charles le Platenier of La Chaux de Fonds. Be this as it may, the Swiss inventor may claim with considerable justice that nothing appeared in his casque that was not known to armor makers of the sixteenth century. Even the type of visor he employed was of an early type.*

Since the foregoing notes were written, a letter has been received (December 30, 1918) from the writer's friend, Dr. Edward A. Gessler, Directorial Assistant of the Swiss National Museum in Zurich, Switzerland, from which the following extract may be translated:

"The Swiss Army during the World War has not changed its type of equipment in essential directions, since it adopted its new rifle model in 1912. We should mention, however, the steel helmet which was introduced into the army in 1918. To your questions I answer as follows:—

"(1) Aside from the steel helmet, no form of armor has been used in the Swiss Army.

* Compare the helm of Sir Giles Capel which dates from 1514 and is now in the Metropolitan Museum of Art. A photograph of the visor of this helm is reproduced in the present report and one may compare with it instructively the Dunand visor (Figs. 47 and 48). The ancient visor loses nothing by comparison; its lower rim fits snugly into a depressed band in the chin region of the helmet and is therefore stronger; also the visor's pivot is concealed below the surface. Its slots, as the pictures show, correspond with singular completeness to those in Dunand's visor. The present writer could therefore hardly be blamed for believing on this evidence alone that M. Dunand had copied the visor of this early helmet or of a similar one—were it not that he is convinced on excellent testimony that the French artist had never even heard of this helmet and had developed his visor (see p. 99) through a series of experimental stages in an independent and altogether praiseworthy way.

"(2) In the following documents sent you, you will have at hand the desired details in the matter of helmets:—

    Züricher Post No. 250—1918
    Züricher Wochen Chronik 20B No. 24—1918
    Schweizer Illustrierte Zeitung Nos. 24, 28, 32—1918
    LaRevue Nos. 200, 298—1918.

"The first experiment in the way of a steel helmet to be seriously considered by the Bundesrath was the model designed by the painter Le Platenier. This is the helmet which was pictured in numerous journals. It was, however, in no way chosen and was known only in experimental models. It copied inadequately a model of the sixteenth century. The mobile visor which was pictured in various positions was never introduced. After this time, the Technical Warfare Section of the Military Department of the Swiss Government caused a review of the whole helmet matter to be made in the National Museum, and, in broad lines, the new helmet was thereupon chosen (Figs. 124, 124A, 124B, 124C). This is now being introduced for the entire army and it is pleasant to note that it finds great favor with the soldiers. The helmet was designed by myself and First-Lieutenant Paul Boesch of the General Staff, who at the same time is a sculptor and who executed the model. The Swiss War Technical Division added a few improvements during the manufacture of the first model.

"From the illustrations which accompany this letter, you will see exactly the form of this headpiece. It is not provided with a visor, for this we found could not be used in actual warfare; also, the Swiss cross in the forehead region was not introduced, since the entire helmet was pressed from a single plate of nickel steel and its mode of construction did not lend itself to this embossing. Besides the articles sent you, nothing has been published in the matter of armor. The new steel helmet, model 1918, at first found a lukewarm reception in non-German-speaking cantons. Now, however, they have taken to it as kindly as have the rest of our soldiers."

In the present report, we show in Figs. 124, 124A, 124B, 124C pictures of the new Swiss helmet taken in various positions. Also compare Figs. 125, 125A, which show its outline in terms of American helmet model No. 5. It resembles our helmet so closely that it could readily be mistaken for it—yet there is no doubt whatever that the two models were designed independently on either side of the ocean. American model No. 5, it will be observed, has its side produced farther forward as a protection to the orbit.

Fig. 124.

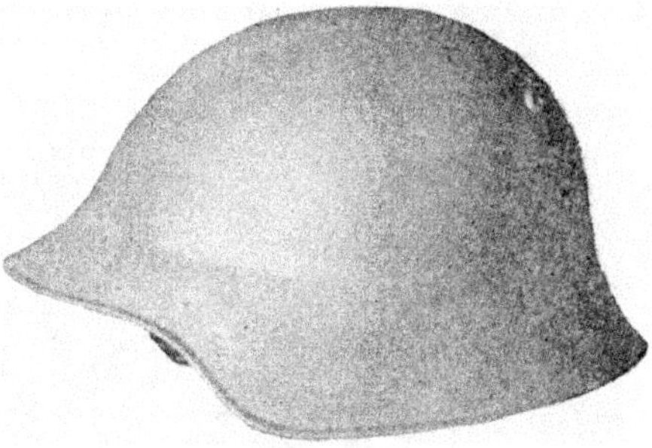

Fig. 124A

Fig. 124B

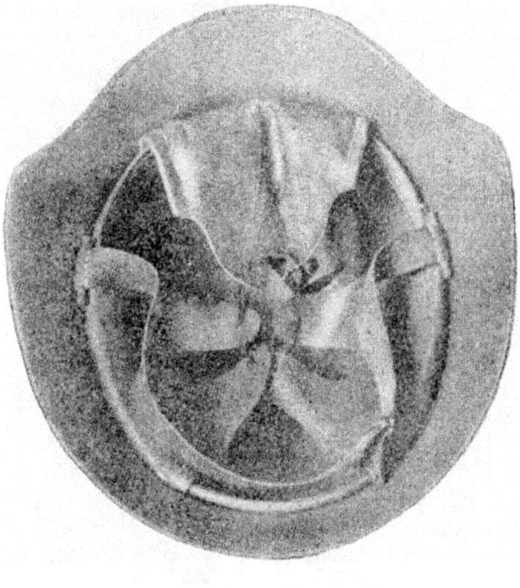

Fig. 124C

Fig. 124. Swiss helmet. Standard model, 1918

Fig. 125

Fig. 125A

Fig. 125. Swiss helmet, compared with American helmet model No. 5—the latter represented in dotted lines

Fig. 126. Swiss standard helmet in process of manufacture

IN MODERN WARFARE

In the accompanying illustration (Fig. 126) we show a photograph of the interior of a Swiss factory, in which the helmets are being prepared; also a cut (Fig. 127) copied by consent of the Schweizer Illustrierte Zeitung, in which Swiss soldiers are shown using a machine gun and wearing both helmets and gas masks.

Fig. 127. Standard Swiss helmet worn with gas mask

(I) SPANISH

As yet Spain has not selected a ballistic helmet for her army. The matter of its choice, however, was taken up by a military commission in 1916, which, after examining types of headpieces in the Royal Armory of Madrid, came to the conclusion that the "chapelle" worn by the Spanish Army in the fifteenth century could be so modified as to produce an effective model for present use. Alas, however, they did not know how difficult such a form would be to press in ballistic metal! The Director of the Royal Armory, it may be mentioned, Don José Florit, had earlier taken up the problem of the modern helmet and had produced in non-ballistic metal the burganet shown in outline in Fig. 128. This reproduces essentially the late model of the lobster-tailed burganet of an earlier century. It is, however, provided with a detachable visor which, after the fashion of the seventeenth-century headpieces, was held in place by a channel-groove and thumbscrew. Señor Florit, it will be seen, fluted the surface of the dome of the helmet, aiming thereby to increase its ballistic strength. (Cf. page 84.) It will be noted that in the Spanish expert's design the chin-strap was arranged with a double attachment on either side. This would certainly prevent the casque from rotating uncomfortably on the head. On the other hand, it would be apt to hold the helmet so firmly that it would endanger its wearer in case the headpiece received a severe jolt, for thus the jolt would be communicated directly to the bones of the neck.

(J) JAPANESE

Bullet-proof armor in old Japan
Chain mail as a defense against musket ball
Trench shields for the Russo-Japanese and for the present war

The Japanese, in a sense, never abandoned the practice of wearing armor. Until about 1870, it was still in use in various parts of Japan; since then, it has hardly been out of sight, in some form or another. In many households the young Japanese learned to dress themselves in it cap-à-pie; parts of it were sometimes used as defenses in sword-play, although of course it was no longer worn for service. During the Tokugawa Shogunate (a period of over two centuries) the empire was not at war; yet, paradoxical as it may appear, military affairs continued to flourish and many experiments were made as to the value of various defenses. The ruling caste wore armor on ceremonial occasions and the testing of armor was a part of the regular training of the soldier. The practical exclusion of Europeans, however, kept from Japan noteworthy improvements in matters of armor and firearms. A number of western helmets and suits of complete armor, nevertheless, found their way to Tokyo and they there enjoyed high reputation. A number of helmets for daimyos were adaptations of European headpieces (cabassets), and a particular form of bullet-proof breastplate (hatomu-nédo) had unquestionably its origin in Europe. But the Japanese appear not to have taken kindly to improvements in firearms. So far as we know, they introduced no wheel-locks, snaphaunces or flintlocks. Their matchlock, however, which came to them through the Portuguese in the late sixteenth century, underwent a series of improvements which resulted in guns and pistols of diversified designs, sizes, calibers and ranges in shooting. Un-

IN MODERN WARFARE

fortunately, we have no record of the actual tests of these arms to enable us to compare their results in different directions with European firearms. We know, however, that similar testing methods were in vogue in Europe and Japan and many of the armored defenses of the Japanese show the marks of testing bullets very much in the way they appeared on French or German armor. A Japanese bullet-proof plastron* dating not later than the eighteenth century is shown in Fig. 129; it is fourteen inches high, made of bands of steel riveted together; its form is well designed, slightly arched

Fig. 128. Helmet suggested for the Spanish army

in the median line, and modeled somewhat to the body; it weighs 5½ pounds. It bears the marks of seven testing bullets, and while we have no analysis of its metal, it will probably resist our standard automatic ball traveling at the rate of 900 foot seconds. This conclusion assumes that the metal in question is a good low carbon steel, having a thickness of .093 inch. In certain regards, the design of the present shield is noteworthy; thus its edges are carefully upturned so as to deflect splinters or lead splash, also the perforations of the plates occur very close to the borders with the holes so small that they do not weaken the plates notably, yet numerous enough to insure that the plates be firmly riveted together. In a word, the present breastplate was made by a well-trained armorer.

* Both this and the plastron below are in the Metropolitan Museum.

174 HELMETS AND BODY ARMOR

A second type of Japanese body defense which may now be mentioned (Fig. 130), is a plastron of chain mail closely woven of triple links and so heavy that it was evidently designed to resist the impact of a musket ball. This breastplate is sixteen inches high and weighs 5⅜ pounds. It shows no evidence of having been tested. We doubt, however, in spite of its costly manufacture whether it possessed more than one half the strength of such

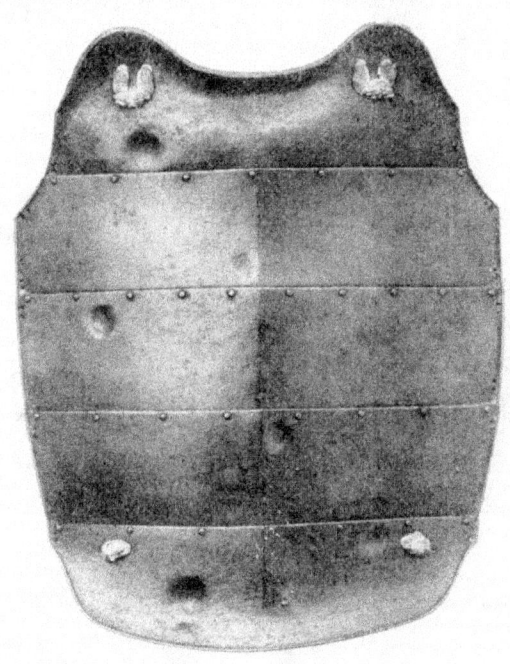

Fig. 129. Japanese breastplate with marks of bullets, 1750 ?

a defense as the British B. E. F. body shield, which is about one half its weight.

In their war with Russia, the Japanese developed trench shields and used them in considerable numbers. Indeed, in their attacks upon the defenses of Port Arthur, they appear to have been greatly aided by these devices. We mention here the work of Mr. Chiba Chosaki, president of the Nihon Budo Kai (Japanese Samurai Society), who played a prominent part in developing the Japanese shield (bodan-jun). This is a small defense, measuring 19 x 12 inches, made (in the earlier specimens at least) of a British armor plate .22 inch thick, and weighing 17¾ pounds (*fide* Mr. William A. Taylor). It has a backing of hair and is covered with leather. The hair, known as uralite, acts with the leather to prevent the scattering of splinters when the shield is struck.

Since the Russo-Japanese War, Mr. Chiba has experimented actively on his shield and early in January, 1917, he is said to have perfected his model and made use of the latest metallurgical improvements in its manufacture. We have at hand no data as to its resistance; but the earlier

Fig. 130. Japanese breast defense of triple-linked mail

Japanese shields were decidedly inferior to the European. They were tested in England in 1916 and were penetrated at 35 yards with British rifle ammunition; they were safe at 50 yards when the surface of the shield was inclined 55 degrees; they resisted German and English armor-piercing ammunition at 100 yards only when backed one against another and separated by an interval of an inch; at longer range a shield was badly broken when a number of shots (seven to ten) were concentrated upon it, this in spite of the fact that it weighed 30 per cent more than the corresponding shields of the English. To explain this, it is not unreasonable to assume for one thing that the Japanese had not the same skill in heat-treating their steel. It is very probable that the Chiba shields have improved in quality; this is noted in a Japanese paper (Jiji-Shimbun) and of similar testimony is the information lately received that a large number of these shields (one half million?) were to be manufactured in Tokyo by the French Government and that the Chinese had also placed an order (10,000).* Jiji states that these shields had lately passed the official test made at Omori near Tokyo.

For a general review of armor matters in Japan, the reader should consult the monograph of Professor Shozo Arisaka of the Department of Engineering, published by the University of Tokyo in July, 1916, vol. 7, no. 1, entitled "Illustrated History of Improvements in Arms and Armor."

* Note from the Japan Society, New York:

Further information regarding the work of Mr. Chiba, in Tokyo, shows that he is the holder of three patents which concern armor. The first covers his body armor, patented June 17, 1905, the second his portable shield, the third his "defense cart," patented October 26, 1915, defenses all of which are said to have passed successful tests.

The first of Mr. Chiba's defenses was given a practical trial by the Japanese Government during the Russo-Japanese War, when three hundred specimens were placed in actual use. In 1908 four hundred were purchased by the Government of Formosa. This armor weighed thirteen pounds, and was formed of $3/8$ inch (chrome-nickel) steel. They cost 25 yen ($12.50) each. It is this armor in which Mr. Chiba is pictured in Fig. 130A.

The second defense illustrates the type of shield which has been referred to in this report on p. 179. (See also Fig. 130C.)

The armored cart appears to have been purely experimental. No details are at hand concerning its usefulness (Fig. 130D).

In addition to the defenses described above, Mr. Chiba has designed a pistol-proof jacket, which can be worn under the ordinary Japanese costume, and it is now being developed by the inventor. It weighs seven pounds, and is $1/8$ inch thick.

It may be mentioned that Mr. Chiba's interest in bullet-proof defenses arose from his study of old Japanese armor. His bullet-proof cart is said to be a device developed from an early Chinese model, *fide* Dr. Naohidé Yatsu, of the Imperial University of Tokyo, who was so kind as to visit Mr. Chiba in Tokyo, at the instance of the present writer, and to send him a report on the work of the Japanese inventor.

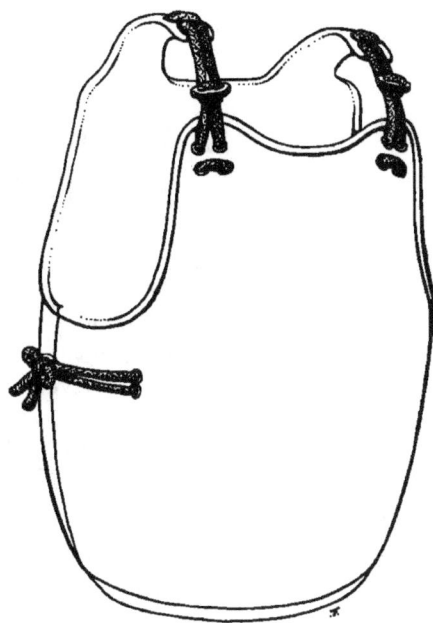

Fig. 130A　　　　　　　　　　　　　　Fig. 130B

Figs. 130A and 130B. Body defense. Chiba model, 1905

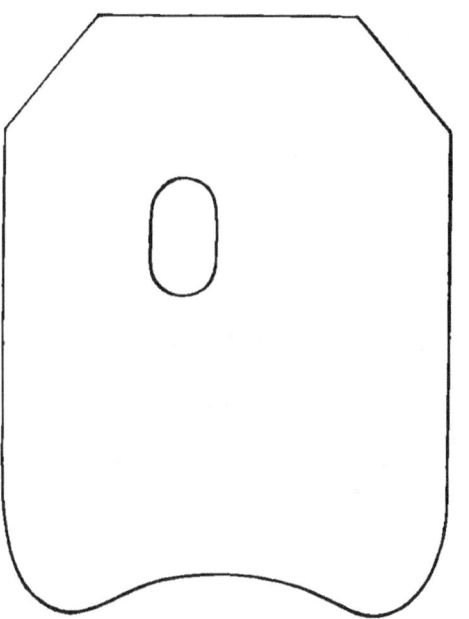
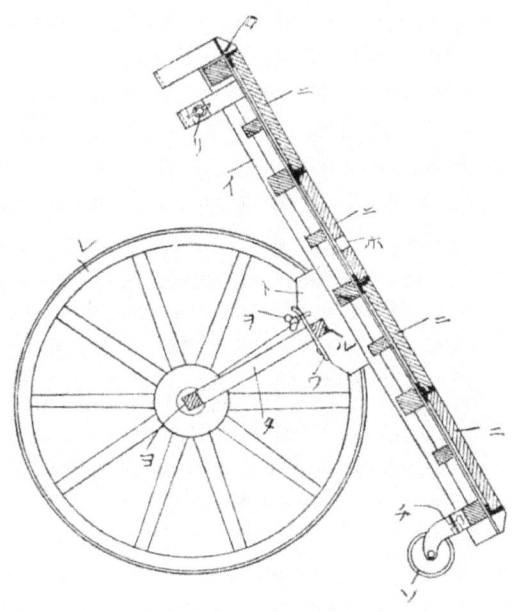

Fig. 130C. Portable shield. Chiba model, 1908

Fig. 130D. Mantlet mounted on wheels. Chiba model, 1915

IV

SHIELDS AND THEIR USE DURING THE PRESENT WAR

(a) Portable shields
(b) Set-shields
(c) Push-shields
(d) Shields propelled by horse power or by mechanical devices (gasoline-driven tractors or tanks)

IN the foregoing classification one may trace the development of the forms of shields used in the present war, or, in many cases for that matter, in earlier wars; for the first two types of shields were used in many phases of ancient warfare and the third appeared in considerable numbers in early sieges.

In a general way, it may be stated that the principle of the shield is the one which underlies every development in the armor problem, for upon it, as the simplest form of defense, arose modeled body armor. The weakness of the shield in old-time wars lay in three directions: (1) if carried by the soldier, it prevented him from using his left arm in combat, (2) it was apt to interfere with his balance in actual fighting, and (3) it defended him from an enemy attacking in only one direction. Now it is clear that these disadvantages in the use of shields are intensified under conditions of modern warfare; for any defense which can resist a ball even of medium velocity must in the nature of things be so heavy* that it can be carried

* Regarding the weight of steel for "trench shields," it is found that any good alloy steel to resist at 50 yards service ammunition, German, English or American, should be at least .25 inch thick; this entails the weight of a pound for each 14 square inches of surface. To stop a German bullet reversed, the plate should be .30 inch thick, giving a weight of 12 square inches to the pound. To stop an armor-piercing bullet, a plate of the best alloy should be at least .4 inch thick or a pound for each 9 square inches of surface. (Since the foregoing was written, the results of governmental tests on new molybdenum-nickel plates have been received from Dr. G. W. Sargent of the Ordnance-Engineering. These show that a thickness of but .30 inch is necessary to stop service A. P. ammunition at 50 yards; or .26 at 100 yards; or .24 at 150 yards.)

IN MODERN WARFARE

by the soldier only with great difficulty; it would overbalance him seriously, and it would afford him little protection against an enemy who shot from any direction save from directly in front. In spite of these disadvantages, which are obvious, it appeared that shields of various types might still be useful under certain circumstances, *e.g.*, during quick approaches or in passing points of danger or in giving protection for a brief time, in order that a soldier might dig himself in.

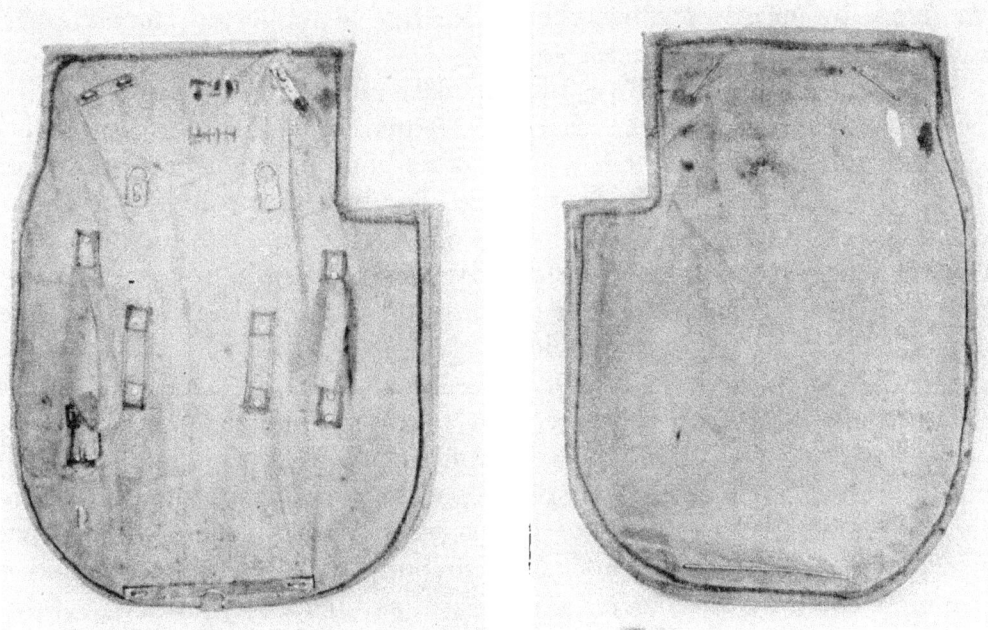

Fig. 131   Fig. 131A

Fig. 131. French (Daigre) shield and body armor, 1917

(a) PORTABLE SHIELDS

At the outbreak of the war, the Germans were provided with small portable shields which are said to have been cast aside during the rapid march through Belgium.

One of the early forms of shields of this type is known in France under the name of its inventor, M. Daigre. This is shown in Fig. 131 and may be described as follows:

It is roughly rectangular with corners rounded save at the right-hand upper corner where the border is squarely indented to form a rest for the rifle. Its height is 23 inches, its width 14 inches, and it furnishes a protected area of about 190 square inches. It weighs about 21 pounds and encloses a nineteen-pound plate of chrome steel; this is .275 inch thick and is covered on either side with a thick layer (half an inch) of gelatinous material (woodite) which is continued over the edge of the shield so as to furnish a marginal cushion which helps to stop lead splash or flying splinters. Over all is a sheath of blue tent-cloth which firmly adheres to the surface of the shield. For ease in handling, arm straps are provided and also loops by means of which the shields can be supported from the neck and belt and carried as a breastplate.

That the Daigre shield was of practical value there can be no question. Tests at close range showed that the German service bullet, even when reversed, failed to penetrate it. On the other hand, it is not proof to armor-piercing bullets even at moderate range. The present model of the Daigre shield is said to have been early produced in some numbers for the French Government, 65,000 having apparently been ordered. The firm manufacturing it is said to have been in the position to furnish lots of 2,000 per day at a cost of about $22 per shield.

In the Daigre defense, it will be seen that the effort was made to provide a shield which could be used not as a portable shield only but as a breastplate and a set-shield as well. And this idea of combining different purposes in a single shield was developed by other manufacturers. Thus, the Italian breastplate Ansaldo (see page 151) was a shield of this character. And certain French and English body defenses were modeled so that they could also be carried on the arm as shields.

(b) SET-SHIELDS

Set-shields, or *mantlets*, were used in great numbers in earlier times, especially during the fifteenth century. In later wars (nineteenth century), they appear occasionally as shelters for sappers, as in Fig. 132, a model (V. 76) now in the Tower of London. Such a mantlet was made of a dozen or more hides riveted and framed together and provided with sling and struts. In the present war small shields which could be set in place were employed so soon as the type of warfare became stabilized. In approaching the enemy's trenches, in wire-cutting service, etc., it was necessary to protect attacking soldiers from rifle fire until a new trench could be established or other protection given. In some cases, therefore, shields were intended to be used for short intervals only. Apparently they were provided by the

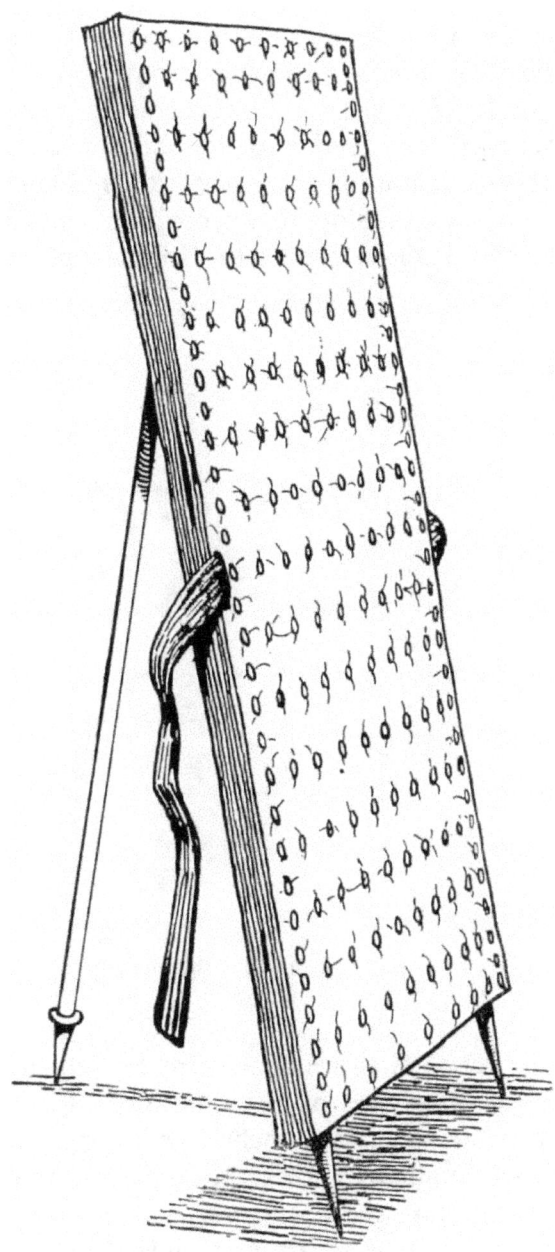

Fig. 132. Sapper's mantlet, nineteenth century

Allies in great numbers; a note given the writer by Captain Simonds stated that in 1917, 200,000 were in use on the western front. The British, it appears, were among the foremost to develop shields of this type. As early as 1915, they provided for their infantry shields which weighed about twenty pounds and were provided with loophole and shutter. They were proof to German service ammunition at fifty yards. There was no question, therefore, that they offered considerable protection, but they were found so difficult to handle and transport that the soldiers generally would have none of them.

Fig. 133. German trench shield, 1916

Several types of set-shields are shown in the adjacent figures, 133 to 136. The first of these was used by the Germans (Fig. 133); it weighed about 30 pounds, measuring 24 x 18 inches, and was arranged with a firing slot 2 x 6 inches. It was made of a silicon-nickel steel .23 inch thick and was proof to machine gun fire at about 100 yards, even when the bullets were reversed. It failed, however, with armor-piercing shells. A variant of this type of shield, shown in Figs. 134 and 135, is also a German defense (1916 and 1917 models). This shield weighed about 50 pounds and measured 26 x 12 inches, presenting a firing slot about 2 x 5 inches. It differs from

IN MODERN WARFARE

the former shield in covering a wider space and in being provided with hinged cheek-plates which keep it upright and help to stop lead splash and the ricochet of bullets. It was nearly double the thickness of the preceding

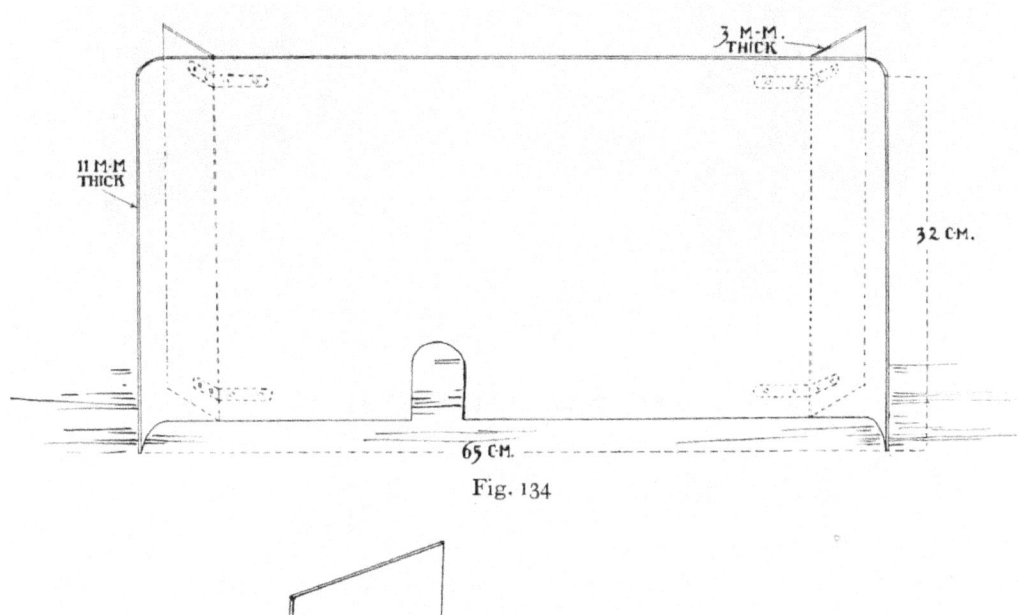

Fig. 134

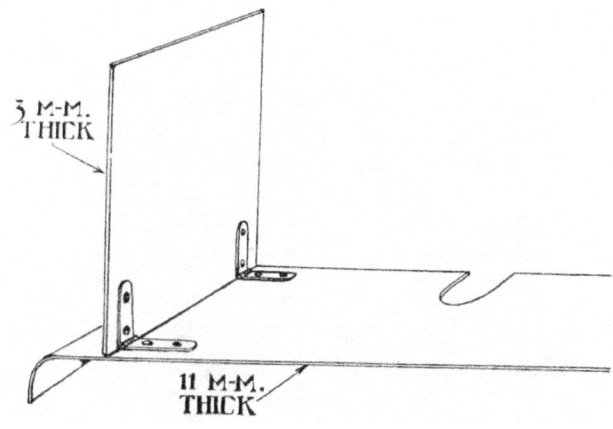

Fig. 134A

Fig. 134. German trench shield, 1916-1917 model

shield (.42 inch). It was designed to stop an armor-piercing bullet at close range.*

Both of the foregoing models of shield appear to have been used in large numbers.

* The resistance of German armor plate may be summarized as follows:

Fig. 135. German trench shield, 1917-1918 model

Fig. 136. Belgian trench shield. American manufacture

The trench shield shown in Fig. 136 was manufactured for the Belgians by or through the firm of Rosenwasser Brothers of Brooklyn. This is of the same width but higher (24 x 31 inches) than the German shields mentioned. It is proof to service ammunition at six yards and to a reversed bullet at 50 yards. It is made of a chrome-nickel plate .29 inch in thickness, and is enclosed in a canvas jacket. It weighs about 60 pounds; it can be

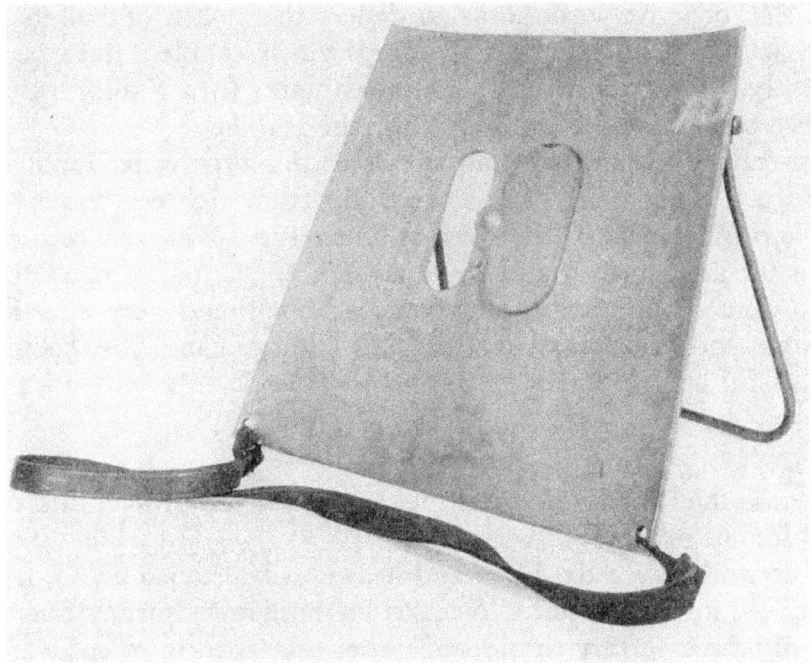

Fig. 137. Russian trench shield. American manufacture

supported in an upright position by means of a pair of legs articulating from the back.

Still another type of shield (Fig. 137) was ordered for the Russian

.40 shield penetrated up to and including 150 yards of British and German armor-piercing bullets.
.25 occasionally safe at 100 yards.
.28 penetrated at 100 yards by German A. P. bullet.
.20 shield safe at 100 yards from British service ammunition. Penetrated at 100 yards by German service ammunition. Safe at 100 yards against Lewis machine gun with British armor-piercing bullet.

Tests made by the English Munitions Inventions Board.

Army from an American manufacturer, Mr. W. H. Mullins of Salem, Ohio. This is a small shield (16½ x 15 inches) with a thickness of .232 inch. It was provided with a firing slot similar to the one shown in the German shield. It was to have been formed of chrome-nickel steel but it failed to reach the stage of production, since the Russian Government fell out of the war about the time the contract for this shield was being issued. The present figure shows that the upper part of the shield was slightly concave, *i.e.*, bent forward, so as to deflect the splash of bullets. It was provided with a shoulder- or neck-strap which enabled it to be carried conveniently, or even be worn as a breastplate. In a similar way trench shields appear to have been employed by the Italians.

In general, it is admitted that shields of this type were troublesome to carry and use. They were heavy, weighing from eighteen to seventy-five pounds, and overbalanced the wearer. Their type, however, recurred as a shield for the artillerymen and we find them appearing in many forms attached to cannon. For this use they have been found very effective. For trench work, and for mobile warfare, on the other hand, the set-shield has been successful only in a modest degree.

(c) PUSH-SHIELDS

These are shields provided with rollers or wheels, pushed into position, and used for one or more soldiers.

Shields which were too large and heavy to be carried could, nevertheless, be moved into the required position by mechanical means. Such shields in fact had been carefully considered rather than used in recent wars; thus, during the Spanish-American War, as the writer has learned from Colonel Fiebeger of West Point, shields* mounted on wheels were used experi-

---

* Cuban War Portable Shields, 1898, under General Nelson Miles.
See *Washington Star*, June 14, 1898; *Washington Post*, June 15, 1898.
Made by Belt and Dyer of Washington, who did woodwork for these shields. Cost of shields, $60,200.
These "portable breastworks" consist of two large wooden wheels, about six inches thick, at either end of a wooden axle about six feet long. To this axle is attached a twenty-foot ladder, the ladder being fastened about eighteen inches from one of its ends. The ladder is used as a lever for the shield, which is fastened to the short protruding end, while the longer portion can be used for pushing the affair along, the soldiers being protected by the shield, which swings in an upright position, or for climbing breastworks, while raiding rifle pits.
This shield is designed to protect the charging soldiers from the raking fire of the

mentally under the direction of General Nelson Miles. During the second year of the present war, however, determined efforts were made to develop heavy shields of mobile types; and in this field the French appear to have been foremost. Various types were designed, made in proof alloy and used experimentally,* notably in training camps, but none were found effective on account of their great weight; for it was learned that these shields could not be pushed forward rapidly unless the terrain was exceptionally favorable. In nine cases out of ten, roughness of ground caused these shields soon to be brought to a standstill, for their weight was great and their wheels would be driven into the sod or gravel. Moreover, in the case of heavy mobile shields, where progress was apt to be slow, danger was ever present from accurate artillery fire. Among the devices which aimed to overcome the difficulty of moving such a defense quickly over rough ground was a small mobile shield mounted on wide wheels (Fig. 138). This was a model used in considerable numbers by wire cutters during the year 1917-1918; it was merely a gun shield of St. Chaumont alloy, mounted

sharpshooters, and it is believed that, with this apparatus, a small detachment of men can take a rifle pit filled with soldiers. When up against the breastworks, the ladder is let go, the shield swings down in a horizontal position between the wheels, while the ladder is brought to a perpendicular position. One of the machines has been put together, and stands in front of Belt and Dyer's shop on Thirteenth Street. This one machine will be shipped as it is so as to show the army how to put the rest together.

All the woodwork for the protector was made by this firm of woodworkers, and the steel plates by a New Jersey foundry. The whole affair is constructed in a strong but rather rough manner, so that the plan can be followed and new protectors built by soldiers in the field. The wooden wheels, made of seven layers of plank, are four feet six inches in diameter, the rims being six inches wide and eight inches deep. Four boards at right angles take the place of spokes. The wheels are made wide and light, in order that they may be easily pushed through the soft earth and sand. The axle is about six inches in diameter and is turned of hard wood.

The shield is constructed of two plates of Harveyized steel, one eighth of an inch thick, bolted on either side of hardwood seven eighths of an inch in thickness. This shield has been tested and found to be absolutely bullet-proof, although a small machine gun would doubtless play havoc with it. The ladder levers are well-made affairs of oiled wood, with round rungs. Pushing from between these rungs the soldiers will be safely protected from any infantry fire from the front, the shield at the other end of the ladder being 5 x 6 feet in size.

(Mem. furnished by Nathaniel Hazen, Chief Clerk of Office, Chief of Ordnance, April 8, 1919.)

* The Japanese inventor, Mr. Chiba, holds a patent (1915) for a wheeled shield shown in Fig. 130D.

between two wooden wheels made like boxes and filled with sand to give them weight. A similar but more elaborate device was a "man-power tank"

Fig. 138. Mobile shields. French. One-man type, 1917

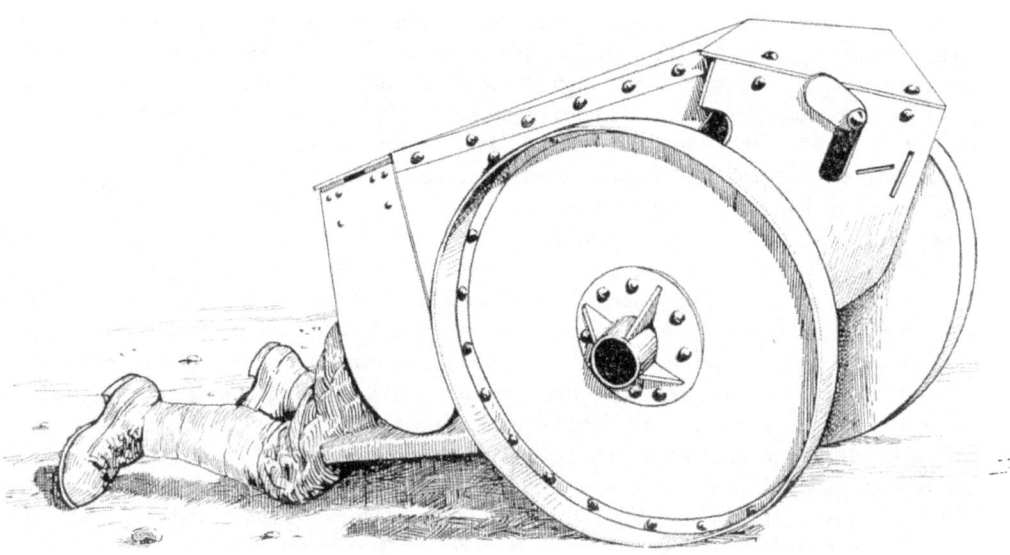

Fig. 139. Mobile shield, or one-man tank. English model, 1917

used by the French and British in 1918. This was made entirely of metal, even to its wheels, its armor consisting of chrome-nickel steel, and its front region so modeled as to present angles well arranged for deflecting bullets (Fig. 139). Aided by this device, the operator, who was protected as far back as his thighs, could creep about quite actively and do serviceable work destroying wire entanglements. No notes are at hand as to the number in which these "tanks" were employed.

A somewhat similar device but intended for the use of a party of riflemen is shown in Fig. 140. It is a movable rifle shield, a kind of glorified sap-roller (see page 128), pierced for the use of five soldiers; a heavy machine at the best—and while it might be used effectively on a good road,

Fig. 140. Mobile shield for five riflemen. British model, 1917

e.g., where a village had to be entered against a machine gun defense, it would soon be apt to become a target for artillery. This device, so far as can be learned, was used only experimentally by the English.

Numerous mobile shields in the model of the preceding ones have been suggested in different countries. One of them, curiously like a chariot, was recently patented in Washington (patent number 1,261,518). Another, also American, a four-wheeled affair, was designed for the Singer Motor Company of New York City by Mr. Dimond (Fig. 141). Still another was devised by Mr. Bockman of Carlonville, Illinois, especially for trench warfare. The shield was so made that it could be slid from side to side wherever needed. Such a device, however, could be used only under conditions too rare and too special to warrant that it be given serious consideration.

The most ambitious invention in the field of push-shields was a man-power "mobile-fort," called a "pedrail" (Fig. 142), of which experimental specimens were made under the auspices of the Munitions Inventions Board at London. This was a small platform, wheeled, mounted with machine gun and armored in front and on the side. The front or gun shield was six feet wide and five feet high; sides or wings which could be pushed out or drawn close to the sides of the gun platform were ten feet long and four feet high, increasing to five feet high at the junction of the wing and the shield. Such a machine gun fort was a heavy affair, weighing about 3,000 pounds, and it required at least three men to start it and keep it moving. At the best, it could be used only under very favorable conditions, as when the road was hard and when rapidity in the attack was not of the greatest importance.

(d) SHIELDS PROPELLED BY HORSE POWER OR MECHANICAL DEVICES INCLUDING GASOLINE-DRIVEN TRACTORS OR TANKS

Of the former type is the Lèbe light-armored car for infantry, which appeared in France in 1917 and was used experimentally under the direction of Major LeBlanc. It is mobile, has low elevation, and its small size renders it a difficult mark for artillery. The function of this car was to enable machine gunners to find a position outside the lines quickly and to occupy it without the need of extensive emplacement work, for the armor plate afforded considerable protection and the car could be camouflaged to such a degree that its position could not be located by photography. For offensive measures, the Lèbe car, for obvious reasons, was not employed; in fact, only with difficulty could it find its way over ground which was broken by shells. On the other hand, it was actually used in bringing ammunition to the front, thus aiding to safeguard the position of lines which had recently been taken. In mobile warfare, as when the enemy was in retreat, the car could be used in supporting the advance of the infantry. (From a report, dated September 5, 1917.)

In all the foregoing devices, it will be seen that the object in view was to protect the soldier while in combat, yet not to weigh him down with personal armor. It was, in a word, to give him a small mobile fortress in which he could attack the enemy. Such a device was of course an eminently desirable one, but it could not, alas, be consummated until a better mechanical means was devised for pushing the shield more rapidly, even over the roughest ground.

Fig. 141. Mobile shield for nine riflemen. American, 1917

Fig. 142. Mobile shield or "pedrail" for machine gunner and riflemen. British model, 1917

The solution, however, was at hand when a certain Canadian, viewing a shell-shattered field in Flanders, suggested the use of shields mounted on a particular type of American farm tractor with which he was familiar—

a machine which would find its way with some degree of speed even over the roughest ground. It was this hint which furnished the military engineer the needed stage for the development of the "tank."* The tractor, in point of fact, even in its first trials demonstrated that it could do the work—which, needless to note, was of the utmost practical importance in penetrating the enemy's lines and in saving the attacking forces. Indeed, it is hardly too much to say that had movable shields of this type not been brought into use, the armies on the western front might still be locked together in battle. It was the "tank" which demonstrated that even the strongest works could be taken.

To consider the tank in further detail and to discuss its variants would require a special work. We need merely to recall that within a few months we have seen the development of tanks of various degrees of movement, some of the small models ("whippets") operating at a fair rate of speed, and all of the types making it practicable for their operators to carry with them a large stock of ammunition and to travel over almost impossible ground. We have here only called attention to the successive steps which resulted in the evolution of this new engine of war. Thus, we have seen the various types of bullet-proof shields advance structurally and functionally in the direction of small mobile forts. And in the pedrail we have clearly reached a stage in the development of such a defense which foreshadowed tanks. It had developed armored and loopholed walls built upon a mobile platform which mounted a machine gun. It required, in fact, only a gasoline-driven motor and endless "caterpillar" bands for progression to insure its transformation into the completed tank.

* From the historical development of the land-forts, land-ships, mobile shields and armored vehicles, we are not surprised to learn that the question as to who was directly responsible for the origin of tanks is closely contested. The British Commission on Awards to Inventors is now dealing with the claims of eleven inventors who are seeking honor and bounties. Secretary of War Churchill testified (October 7, 1919) before the Commission that eighteen working models of these mobile defenses were constructed during the war and tried out, and that the original tank, first used in the Somme offensive in 1916, was the result of collective experience.

V
AMERICAN HELMETS AND BODY ARMOR

    (a) Introduction
    (b) Description
    (c) Material
    (d) Manufacture
    (e) Assembling
    (f) Experimental types of helmets
    (g) Face defenses
    (h) Shoulder defenses
    (i) Body armor, heavy and light
    (j) Leg armor
    (k) Arm defenses
    (l) Aviator's armored chair

(a) INTRODUCTION

IN June, 1917, the American General Staff considered the selection of a type of helmet for general use in the American Army. A helmet committee was appointed and its report aimed to consider the virtues and failings of various designs, including French, British and more recently devised types. In view of the need of production, the decision was shortly made to adopt the British helmet. The committee agreed, nevertheless, that their choice was only a provisional one; they noted that the model selected was by no means ideal. They deplored the fact that it protected so small an area of the head and that it was heavier than the French helmet. On the other hand, the ballistic value of the British helmet, as we have noted on page 80, was great. It had also the especial merit that it was simple to manufacture in hard metal, hence a considerable number of these helmets were ordered through the Ordnance Department, Equipment Section, at Washington, with the view of meeting the immediate needs of the American Army. It was learned also that a considerable number of these helmets could be purchased "ready made" through the British Quartermaster's Department, and in this way, the first 400,000 of our helmets were secured in England and shipped to France, the first lots in July, the last in November, 1917. This arrangement, it will be seen, gave the Ordnance Department in Washington the necessary time to develop the manufacture of these helmets in the United States. Accordingly, from the fall of 1917 it became possible to ship abroad American-made helmets. Of these, the first hundred thousand were forwarded packed in special cases; the rest, from the early summer of 1918, were carried on the heads of the soldiers.

When the first examples of the British trench helmet were received in this country, the authorities in the War Department showed them to a number of manufacturers of objects in alloy steel in order to secure bids for their production. Among the experts consulted in this matter was Mr. A. T. Simonds, president of the Simonds Saw Company of Fitchburg, Massachusetts, who showed the greatest interest in the necessary technical details which governed their manufacture. It appeared that the Simonds Saw Company had already entered largely into armor work for the Government, especially in the manufacture of rifle shields in chrome-nickel-vanadium steel, and through its efforts it seemed possible to procure the needed helmets without loss of time and to insure for them even better ballistic results than the British headpiece offered. Accordingly the Simonds Saw Company set to work at once on its own account to secure the pressing of sample helmets, and in order to effect the needed production through associated manufacturers, Mr. Simonds was attached to the Ordnance Department with grade of Captain. It was under his supervision that our first helmets were manufactured. It should be stated at once that the task which was undertaken by the Ordnance Department was by no means an easy one; for the art of pressing harder alloys into the deep shape of a helmet was altogether undeveloped in this country and to get results required many fruitless experiments and the closest cooperation with expert manufacturers. Among the firms to be mentioned for their pioneer work in this field is the Crosby Company of Buffalo, which succeeded at last in pressing a helmet in chrome-nickel steel in five operations. Here, even, wrinkling could not in all cases be avoided in the region either of the sides of the helmet or of its brim. In fact, from the difficulty in handling the tougher alloys, which entailed delicate processes of annealing and heat treatment, it presently became evident that an effort should be made to secure steel of the 12 per cent manganese type for experimental use in manufacture. But here again difficulties were encountered, since the manufacture of manganese steel in thin sheets had first to be developed. Hence for the earlier experiments 4,000 sheets of it were imported from England. We should mention that the American Car and Foundry Company and the Taylor-Wharton Company in Pittsburgh were among the first of those called upon to make experiments in pressing this material for the Government. In the end it was found, as the English declared, that the manganese steel lent itself readily to pressing and that a result which in tougher alloys was to be accomplished only in several operations could in manganese be secured by a single "draw." Hence the idea was abandoned of using vanadium steel (C. .35, Mn. .097, Van. .15) for the first lot of helmets, and every effort was made to produce an adequate supply of manganese plates according to the British formula. This supply was presently assured from the mills at Gary, Indiana, through the efforts of the American Sheet and Tin Plate Company, and the work of pressing the helmets was thereupon distributed in lots of 200,000 each among a number of American firms, including the Crosby Company of Buffalo, the Budd Manufacturing Company, Philadelphia, the Taylor-Wharton Company, Pittsburgh, the Worcester Pressed Steel Company, the American Can Company and the Sparks-Withington Company. Through their efforts good helmet shells were soon being stamped out in large numbers—due allowance of time being made, of course, for the production of dies and for the manufacture and delivery of the manganese steel. The first lots were being produced in October, 1917, *i.e.*, six months after the entrance of the United States into the war. From that time onward helmets could be obtained, not always as promptly and in as huge lots as were called for, yet always in the quantity needed for active service. Thus, such a firm as Messr. Budd and Company of Philadelphia would readily turn out as large a number of helmet shells as 12,000 in a day and was presently able to maintain this number in average production.

The manufacture of helmet linings had also to be carefully organized before production was assured. Among the firms contributing to this work may be mentioned the Leatherwear Company of America, the Progressive Knitting Works, both of New York, the Taylor Company of Buffalo and the Curtain Supply Company of Chicago. The work of these firms soon assured the appearance of the finished helmets in the desired numbers.

To give an idea of the production required, it may be mentioned that 6,500,000 helmets were to have been made by January 1, 1919. Thereafter contracts were to be issued for the immediate production of 2,000,000 more.

(b) DESCRIPTION

The American helmet is a faithful copy of the British one (Frontispiece); it has the same inverted bowl, a similar border of metal, the same type of chin-strap and lining; it has even the same general type of roughened surface to prevent reflection of light. As a means of causing this roughening of the surface, the American helmet was coated with sawdust during the process of painting, while the British helmet in earlier lots at least was sprinkled with such materials as sand and chopped fiber. In thickness the helmet shell is precisely that of the British and its ballistic resistance is approximately the same, although tests indicate that the American are stronger by about 10 per cent than the British helmets which were received in Washington.

(c) MATERIAL

With the exception of a single lot, all American helmets were made of Sir Robert Hadfield's manganese steel, as noted on page 277. In the exception noted, 200,000 helmets were produced by the Columbian Enameling Company of Terre Haute, Indiana, in an alloy whose formula was recommended by Mr. W. H. Baker, the metallurgical expert and head of the Universal Rolling Mills Co. (Analyzed in table opposite page 274.) This lot of helmets, it may be remarked, passed an extremely good ballistic test, the indentation in the majority of cases showing scarcely one half the depth recorded in manganese helmets. In some cases the indentation was scarcely noticeable. In a test of several hundred specimens made in the writer's presence, scores of helmets were so little injured by this test that they were authorized to be placed among the perfect helmets for finishing and shipment. The slight mark in these cases was regarded not as injuring the helmet but as adding to its value—just as were the testing marks on well-made armor of the seventeenth century.

(d) MANUFACTURE

The American helmet shell (Figs. 143 and 143A) may be pressed in either one or two operations. If pressed in a single operation, the shell is apt to be thinned unduly at the crown. In a majority of cases, this thinning leaves the helmet shell about .030 inch in thickness at some points of the crown. In certain instances helmets as thin as .027 inch have been noted which, nevertheless, passed the required test. On the other hand, the Columbian Enameling and Stamping Company of Terre Haute, Indiana, produced a helmet which retained the maximum thickness of metal in the

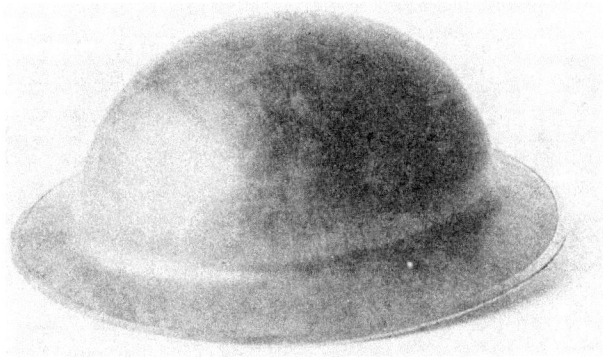

Fig. 143

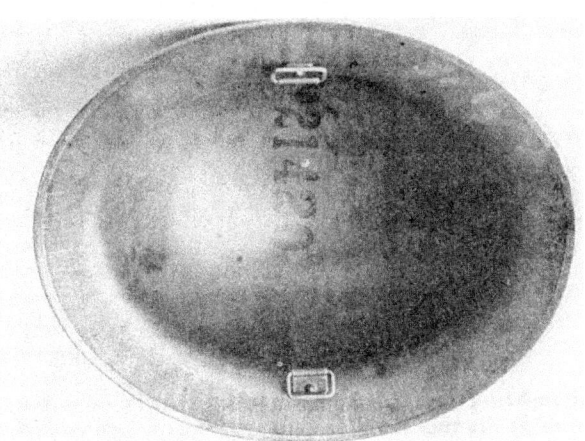

Fig. 143A

Fig. 143. British-American helmet. Completed shell
with attached rim and chin-strap loops

crown, a technical feat which deserves honorable mention. The reader may here be instructively referred to two photographs of the interior of a large pressing shop, in the present case that of the Budd Manufacturing Company of Philadelphia. One here sees, in Fig. 144, behind the operators a huge press of the "double-action" type where two plungers pass down from the position indicated close to the head of the man standing at the right in the picture. The first of these plungers holds the plate securely against the brim of the heavy die, the second thereupon passes down through the first

Fig. 144. British-American helmet in process of manufacture. The double-action press, shown in background at the right, stamps out the helmet in a single "draw."
Budd Manufacturing Co., Philadelphia

plunger and stamps the helmet into its form in a single operation. In this figure, one sees a great pile of helmet shells ready to be transferred to a press where a blanking or trimming operation takes place. Such a press is seen in Fig. 145, and a pile of the trimmed helmets appears near the center of the picture. Near by a helmet rim is being put on and spot-welded to the helmet shell. Such a rim appears beside the helmet shell shown in Fig.

IN MODERN WARFARE

146, and beside it are the loops and rivets which are attached one to each side of the helmet in the region of the sweat-band.

It will be noted that the metal plate in which the form of a helmet has just been stamped (Fig. 145) shows at the corners curious little knobs. These had earlier been given in order to test the quality of the individual

Fig. 145. Manufacture of British-American helmet. The plate is being "blanked out" so as to form the helmet rim; in another part of the picture the thin separate metal rims are being spot-welded in place

sheet, *i.e.*, to learn whether or not it would stand the operation of pressing the helmet. To this end, a punch was driven into each corner of the plate to a certain depth. If this ruptured the plate (Figs. 147, 148) the manufacturer was given a practical hint that he could not press a helmet from it. If, however, it is perfect, as shown in Figs. 147A and 148A, the plate of steel may be drawn into a helmet with an excellent result assured. In Figs. 143 and 143A appears a helmet shell as it passes from the hands of the manufacturer; its rim is in position, the loops for the chin-strap are riveted in place and the helmet shows by its number to what heat of steel it belongs.

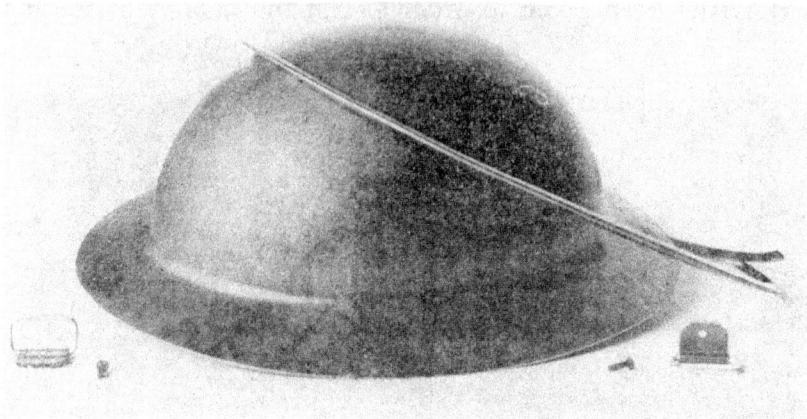

Fig. 146. Manufacture of British-American helmet. Helmet shell, metal rim, chin-strap loops and rivets ready to be put together

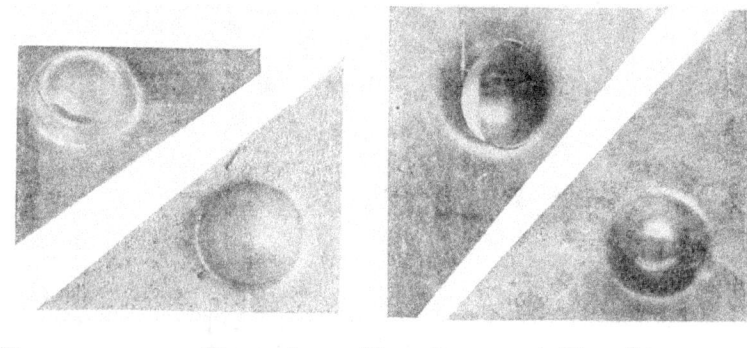

Fig. 147   Fig. 147A   Fig. 148   Fig. 148A

Figs. 147 and 148. Test of a plate of helmet steel. The corner of the plate is given a punch-mark; if the metal cracks, the plate is rejected

Breakage: In stamping helmets the American manufacturer is allowed a wastage of not more than 3 per cent. In point of fact, the loss in nearly all cases is much less than this, rarely exceeding 2.5 per cent.

Test: As with British helmets, an actual ballistic test is required. Helmet shells are selected from different heats of metal and "shot up."

From the first 50 helmets a single shell is taken for this purpose; from helmets 51 to 250, two shells are tested; from this number up to 500, three shells; from this in turn to 2,000, four shells; from this to 3,000, six shells; and from 3,000 onward, one shell for each 500. A shell so selected is placed in a testing machine, which consists merely of an iron pipe ten feet long,

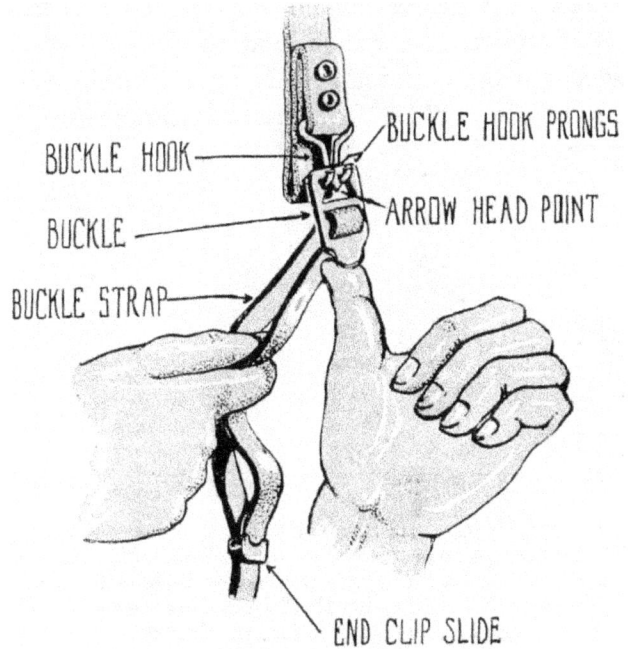

Fig. 149. Diagram showing the mode of tightening the new chin-strap; also the new buckle-hook is pictured, by means of which the chin-strap can be "broken" when passed under the tube of the gas mask

having at one end a firmly supported automatic pistol and at the other end a box to contain the helmet. By this apparatus the testing bullet can be made to strike each helmet at a definite point. It may be mentioned that this test is carried on without risk to the operator; for each bullet, when deflected, is stopped by the lid of the box in which the helmet is placed. After the test shot is fired, the helmet is inspected and if it has resisted penetration, the degree of indentation is measured. This is usually less than one inch, when measured from the original contour of the helmet by means of a standard gauge which the Government furnished to inspectors. The testing pistol is the American automatic caliber .45, model 1911 or 1917, carrying a 230-grain cupro-nickel jacketed ball, with a striking velocity of 600 foot seconds (special cartridge). The shot is direct or "normal" to the surface. To pass the government test a helmet shell when struck shall "show no cracks on the surface or on the reverse side" and must yield an indentation no deeper than $1\frac{3}{16}$ inches. In order to insure uniformity both in the manufacture of the helmet and in its test, each helmet shell is numbered as a means of showing to which heat of steel it belonged. Figs. 150 and 151A show a testing cartridge with its cupro-nickel jacket; in the neighboring picture (Fig. 151B), one sees a bullet restored to its position

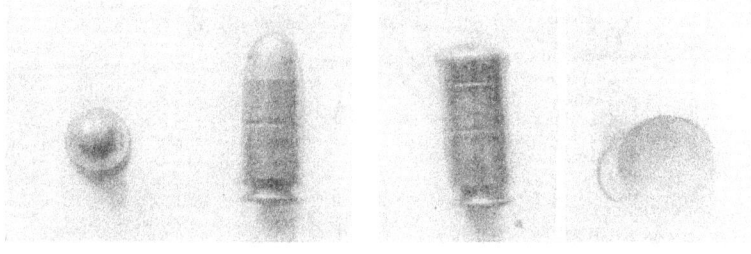

Fig. 150   Fig. 151A   Fig. 151B   Fig. 151C

Figs. 150 and 151A. Special cartridge for testing helmets—600 foot seconds. In B. Test cartridge in which the alloy-jacketed bullet has been flattened against the helmet, then replaced (to be photographed) in the empty shell. In C. End view of testing bullet after it has been flattened against a helmet shell

in the shell after having been blunted upon impact with the helmet. Sometimes, as in Fig. 151C, a bullet will be quite flattened upon such contact.

In the latest model of the American helmet, certain details in manufacture are modified. Especially noteworthy is a change which has been made in the chin-strap. This is no longer of cowhide; but is replaced by a carefully woven braid or webbing, olive-drab,* provided with a special buckle which enables the wearer to tighten the helmet cord readily (Fig. 149). This device also permits him quickly to detach and to readjust it when it has to be passed under the tube of the gas mask.

* Tensile strength 375 pounds, as against 300 in the case of the earlier strap; when wet, over 400 as against 275; it is a more durable chin-band, more comfortable in use, and cheaper (only one third the price of the leather).

Fig. 152. British-American helmet. Assembling. The helmets are shown arranged in rows on metal racks, front and back, ready to be immersed in the paint trough shown in right of picture. (Ford Mfg. Co., Philadelphia)

Fig. 153. British-American helmet. Assembling. Freshly painted helmets being passed along over drip-boards

(e) ASSEMBLING HELMETS OF BRITISH TYPE

Abundant production was the keynote of the instructions given to the Ordnance Department for providing an American helmet. Hence every effort was made to link up the work of the manufacturers of helmet shells with that of the makers of linings and then to see that the assembling processes were promptly organized and that the helmets were efficiently packed for transit—not a small undertaking when we consider the large supply of helmets which were to be furnished in a brief time. We should here record the excellent results which were secured by the officers of the Ford Manufacturing Company, which offered to the United States Government the facilities of their Philadelphia plant and organized on large lines the painting, assembling and boxing of helmets for shipment. This firm, it may be mentioned, was soon able to pass through its factory 10,000 helmets a day.

The helmet shells were received on the top floor of the Ford plant practically in bulk; thence as they were assembled they passed, literally gravitated, downstairs till they found their way out of the building. When they came in they had their metal rims already in place and the loops to which the chin-strap was to be attached. Such "shells" as these may be seen under the table in Fig. 152. The first operation in assembling consisted of placing the shells on rectangular iron frames or carriers, each of which held ten helmets, that is, five in a row affixed to each side. In the picture noted, a number of empty racks stand near the window and one of them lies on the table with five helmets attached to it; on the right side of the table the second row of helmets has been put in position, the first five helmets, now turned upside down, lying against the top of the table. The next process, illustrated in Fig. 153, is painting; a paint tank is shown in which each group of helmets is immersed and a draining board which lies just beyond it. An ingenious arrangement overhead enables the helmets after they are dipped to travel along continuously. In the following process the top of each helmet shell is given a thin layer of sawdust while the paint is still wet. Thus an entire rack of newly painted helmets, as shown in Fig. 154, is placed on a special board or table (appearing in the foreground of the same picture) in such a way that the helmets on this rack fit separately into the holes in the table (Fig. 155); thereupon sawdust is scattered over them by means of a current of compressed air turned on by a foot lever which blows the sawdust about within the box. The upper row of helmets

Fig. 154. British-American helmet. Assembling. Freshly painted helmets about to be given a coating of sawdust in the sprinkling box shown in the foreground

Fig. 155. British-American helmet. Assembling. Freshly painted helmets being given a coating of sawdust. (Front, right)

Fig. 156. British-American helmet. Assembling. Shells arranged on racks about to be passed into the heated drying chamber

Fig. 157. British-American helmet. Assembling. Helmet shells being passed down an inclined plane to tables where linings and chin-straps are put in place

IN MODERN WARFARE

having thus been dusted, the entire rack is turned over and the second tier of helmets is given its coating of sawdust. In the next stage of assembling, the paint is dried by heat. For this purpose a large cage is employed (Fig. 156) which is capable of containing about 600 helmets on their racks; and this cage, when filled with freshly painted helmets, is pushed bodily into a

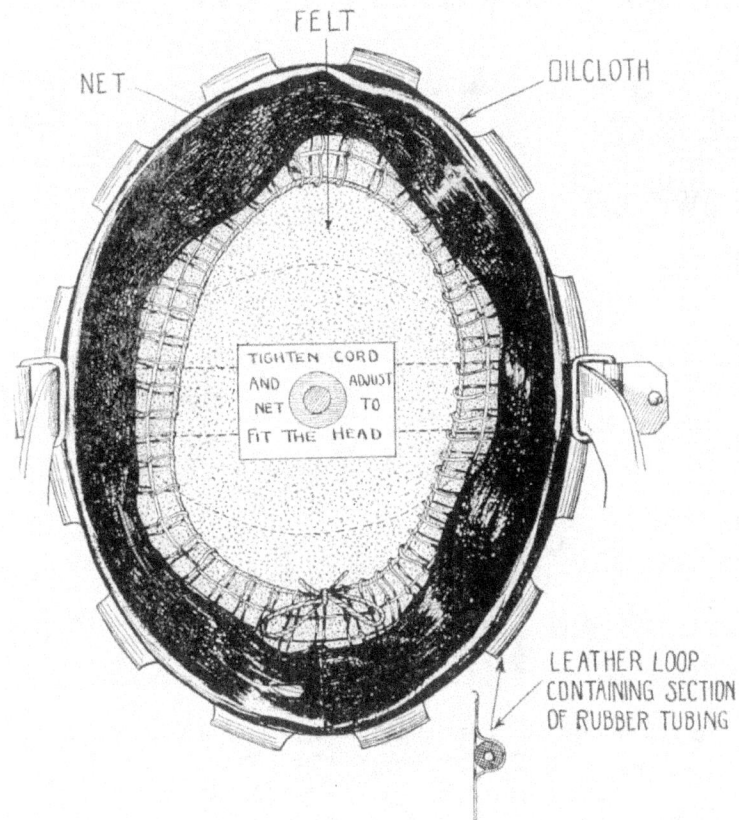

Fig. 158. Lining of British-American helmet. From below

heat-drying pantry. Here a temperature of 200 degrees Fahrenheit is maintained for one hour. After this process the helmets are again dipped and dried. They are then detached from their racks, passed down an inclined plane to the room where the linings are assembled, and here (Fig. 157) they are speedily distributed to the tables of operatives. One may distinguish in the picture piles of helmet shells on the right-hand side of a worktable

208 HELMETS AND BODY ARMOR

and helmet linings on the left. The workman must now fit each lining with its chin-strap and attach it to its shell with a rivet (shown in middle of lining, Fig. 158), which he stamps in place by means of a riveting machine. This completes the processes of assembling. The helmets are thereupon packed (Fig. 159). An ingenious device now comes into play: this is a hydraulic compressor (shown in the picture) which pushes and holds together a group of helmets with their linings while a packing case is auto-

Fig. 159. British-American helmets being packed for shipment. Note hydraulic compressor (center)

matically lifted and receives them. The case is then passed along on a track (Fig. 160) and finally comes to rest on the ground floor of the building (Fig. 160A) in storage piles, awaiting shipment oversea.

(f) EXPERIMENTAL TYPES OF HELMETS

The American General Staff, as we have seen, adopted the British helmet as a measure of expediency; it had, none the less, borne in mind a plan to secure for the troops a distinctly American helmet. Its desire to bring this about was strengthened not only by patriotic motives, but by

Fig. 160. Cases of British-American helmets passed along a track for storage and shipment

Fig. 160A. Cases of British-American helmets ready for shipment

reasons diplomatic, for the acceptance of the British model might be interpreted by their allies as expressing the American opinion that the French helmet was an inferior one. One of the first models considered by the American Staff in this connection was the Dunand helmet (Figs. 44, 45 and 46) already described on page 96 to 102. This was presented to the Helmet Board, A. E. F., in Paris in August, 1917, and in the report of this board it was stated that the Dunand helmet "gives much better protection to the temples, ears, back of the head, from fragments traveling in a horizontal direction than do the English and French helmets, but with less protection to the back of the head than does the German." An especial feature of the Dunand helmet which appealed to the American Board was the visor, for it noted that "the number of men who have become partially or completely blind as the result of wounds has been especially large and anything which will aid in reducing these unfortunate cases has a special importance." It adds, moreover, that "experiments with the visor have been made in both the English and French Army but so far nothing which proved satisfactory has been found." This board considered the merits of the Dunand visor and found it more advantageous than the style of visor submitted by Dr. Polack of the French Mission d'Essais. On the basis of this report an order was sent (August, 1917) to the Ordnance Department in Washington to produce 10,000 Dunand helmets in the United States, and another was sent to England, asking that a number of Dunand helmets be there manufactured in manganese steel and tested. Results subsequently showed that the Dunand helmet as at first designed was not suited to pressing on account of its peculiar shape in the brow region, for here the metal invariably cracked in the operation of forming. Hence this order was ultimately canceled (see page 98). Moreover, it was subsequently found that the Dunand visor (page 100) did not yield satisfactory tests. It was too fragile. Hence the Helmet Board in France recommended (August, 1917) that a combination arrangement should be made so that the Dunand helmet should be provided with a Polack visor (cf. Fig. 41), and in this direction various experiments were carried out. Meanwhile M. Dunand caused specimens of his helmet to be manufactured in Paris in ballistic metal; and in the new model he succeeded in overcoming the structural defects which were earlier noted. In this model, the helmet became reduced more nearly to the shape of the English helmet in use. In a word, as time went on, the sentiment of the Helmet Committee became less favorable to the adoption of the Dunand helmet as the American standard type.

In the meanwhile, the Ordnance Department in Washington endeavored to produce helmet models which should be better suited to the American needs. Of these helmets several forms may now be referred to. All of these, it may be said, were developed under the auspices of the Armor Committee of the American Council of National Research—the chairman of the committee becoming a member of the Ordnance Department (Engineering Division, Equipment Section). This committee consisted of many prominent American students of armor and metallurgists, including Dr. G. O. Brewster, George K. Burgess, William F. Durand, Henry

Fig. 161   Fig. 161A   Fig. 161B

Fig. 161. Helmet model No. 2, "deep salade." This protects the head more completely than any other modern helmet

M. Howe, Edward H. Litchfield, Clarence Mackay, Thomas Robins, David B. Rushmore, A. T. Simonds, and its chairman, Bashford Dean. In this connection it may be mentioned that the Metropolitan Museum of Art, New York City, placed its armor workshop and its important collection of helmets at the disposal of the Government. Thereafter throughout the war, numerous models of armor were here designed and made. In connection with the work on experimental helmets, compare the accompanying table, opposite page 212.

American Helmet Model No. 2
(Figs. 161, A and B, and Frontispiece)

This form, designed in June, 1917, aimed to protect more completely the sides and back of the head and to present the best arrangement of "glancing angles" or surfaces adapted to turning aside an impinging missile. To this end, the designer followed the lines of helmets which had been approved by centuries of actual use, especially the "Standard" helmets of classical Greece and of Italy in the fifteenth century. Non-ballistic specimens of this model were prepared by the armorer, Daniel Tachaux of the Metropolitan Museum of Art, and its lining was carried on a thin steel band (Fig. 164) having three supporting pads arranged after the German model, which, for the rest, in theory and practice was the best of those submitted to the American Armor Committee. Such a helmet was found comfortable to wear; for one reason, its center of gravity was low; hence, although it weighed 10 per cent more than the British model, the weight was better distributed and it had less tendency to change position when on the head. The objection to this type of helmet was that it was difficult to produce. For its deep dome, which at the beginning was hardly to be drawn in mild steel, could be formed in hard alloys only after much experimental work by the die makers. Thus, in the summer of 1917, this helmet, after having been shown to the experts of several manufacturing concerns, who feared that it could not be made, was turned over to the Worcester Pressed Steel Company with directions to produce it in an experimental lot in 12 per cent manganese steel. Dies accordingly were prepared and every effort was made to deliver the helmets needed. Unfortunately, however, the dies which this firm employed were inadequately designed and in the end the only helmets produced were defective, having their sides wrinkled and their tops thinned out. Later, however, this helmet was shown to Messrs. Ford and Company of Detroit who declared that it could be pressed and pressed well without an important breakage of metal. Accordingly, this firm, receiving an order from the Ordnance Department, produced a set of experimental dies. On these, during the fall of 1918, a couple of thousand helmets were turned out. It may be mentioned that the principle upon which Messrs. Ford and Company proceeded was quite similar to that which an armorer would have used in olden times, for the top of the helmet was pressed not as a final but as an earlier operation. The brim and brow of the helmet were thereafter formed by the Detroit experts by the aid of "stoving" dies. The material used was the standard manganese steel .038 inch to .040 inch in thickness, which becomes thinned out in the crown to about .030 inch, the average thickness at this point of the British helmet. The helmets finally produced were found to stand a satisfactory ballistic test; they were, moreover, as had been expected, excellent in their deflecting angles. They were hard to hit "straight on"; but in the testing machine, when struck normally, they resisted the impact of the regulation automatic bullet with standard ammunition—that is, of 800 foot seconds. It may be mentioned that a model of this helmet was shown to the Commander-in-Chief of the American Forces, who commented upon it favorably.

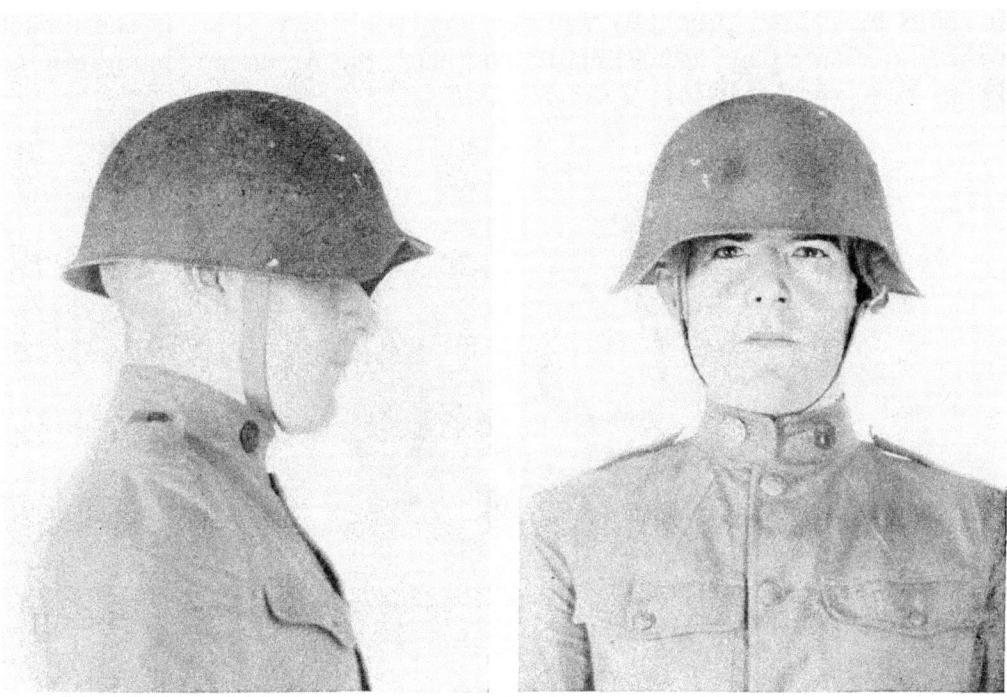

Fig. 162   Fig. 162A

Fig. 162. American experimental helmet No. 5

(The figure of this helmet shown in the Frontispiece as model No. 2A is slightly narrower in the brim.)

American Helmet Model No. 4
(Frontispiece)

This helmet was made in non-ballistic metal by the armorer, D. Tachaux, during the summer of 1917. It aimed to furnish a somewhat deeper model than the British helmet and to be roomier around the cranium.

214 HELMETS AND BODY ARMOR

This helmet was furnished with a lining similar to the French model (Fig. 23). It was criticized as being too nearly like the British helmet and not covering enough of the head. No ballistic specimens of this helmet were, therefore, prepared. As first designed, it would undoubtedly have proved a difficult model to draw even in manganese alloy; simplified, however, by rounding out the apex and enlarging somewhat the region of the hat-band, it could have been produced without great difficulty. This is the model which later (see page 232) found favor with the American Committee at H. A. E. F.

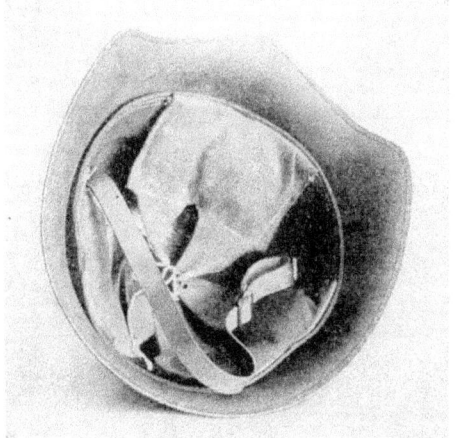

Fig. 163. Lining of preceding helmet

American Helmet Model No. 5
(Frontispiece and Figs. 162-165)

This model aimed to provide a helmet which combined the virtues of helmet No. 2 and the ease in production of the British helmet. Its dome surrounded the cranium generously and its sides descended to the lower lobe of the ear. It protected the temple and brow region, and in spite of the impression which the accompanying figure gives, it insured the wearer a fairly extended vision, enabling him without changing the position of his head to see in a horizontal plane from one side to the other through an angle of about 140 degrees, while the normal angle of vision in this plane is about 200 degrees. This helmet, it will be seen, protected the vital region of the back of the head better than the British helmet. The type of lining now provided was again a variant of the German model but with a choice of two types of sweat-band: one of these was a wide band of leather to which the supporting pads were riveted (Fig. 163); the other, a thin circlet of steel which was riveted close within the shell of the helmet

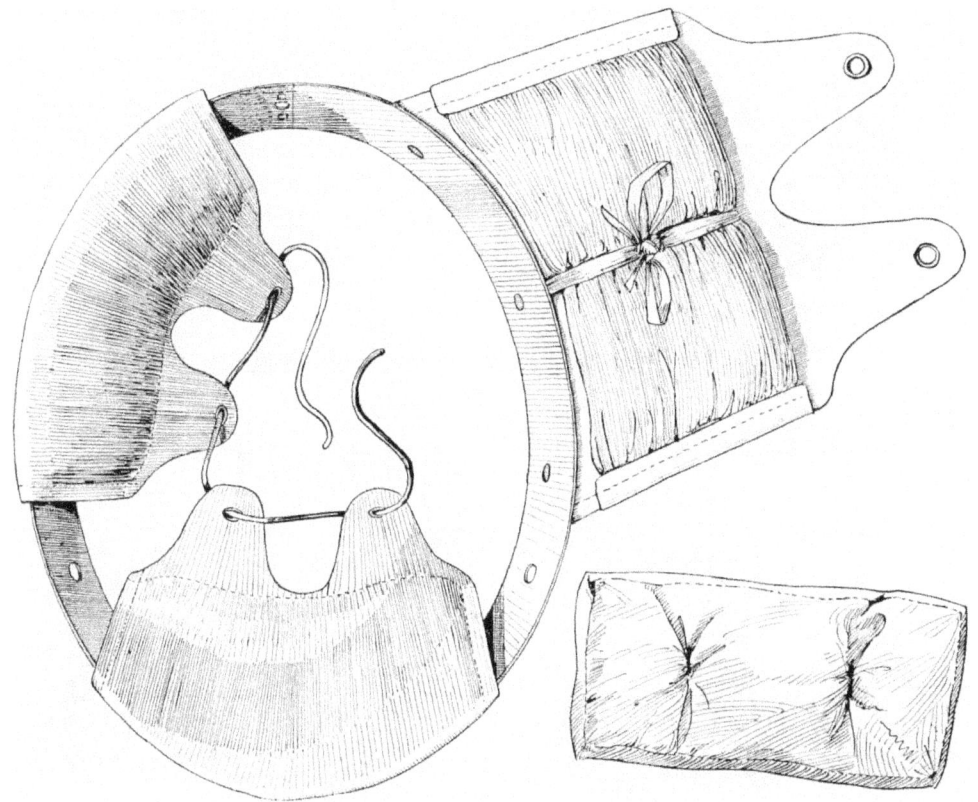

Fig. 164. Improved lining of experimental helmet model No. 5. A sweat-band of light steel replaces one of cowhide

(Fig. 164). The latter type proved the better and altogether this style of lining was found quite satisfactory. A woven chin-strap was used having the type of buckle shown in Fig. 149,* by which the strap could be quickly "broken" so that it could be passed under the tube of the gas mask and readily rehooked in position. This style of chin-strap found general favor. Dies for this helmet were prepared by the firm of Hale and Kilburn Com-

* Developed by Captain H. D. Mainzinger of the Ordnance, Engineering, in Washington, with cooperation of Mr. Tabler.

pany of Philadelphia, and several thousand specimens were manufactured. The first lot of them was favorably commented upon at American Headquarters; it was later rejected as being, on the one hand, not sufficiently different from the British helmet and, on the other hand, too similar to the German model. It was found also by no means as easy to produce as

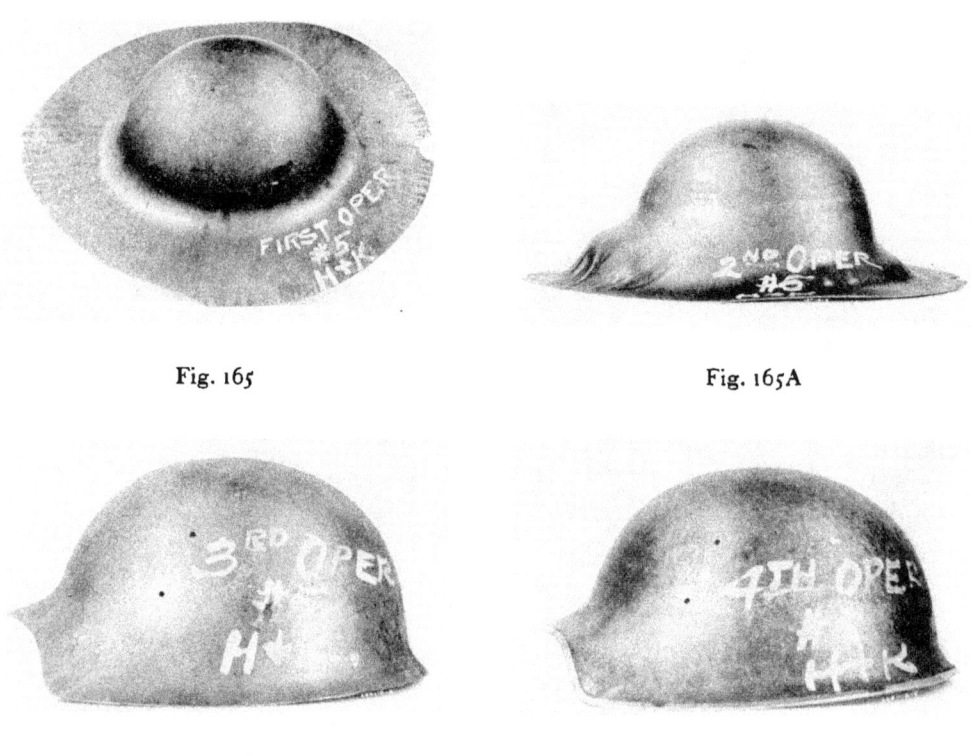

Fig. 165   Fig. 165A

Fig. 165B   Fig. 165C

Fig. 165. Helmet No. 5. Stages in manufacture by Messrs. Hale and Kilburn, Philadelphia

the British helmet, although the experts of Messrs. Ford and Company declared that if this type of helmet were wanted in large number they would willingly guarantee its production. They were sure that a breakage hardly greater than 5 per cent would ultimately be had as against the breakage of about 3 per cent in the British helmet. The various stages in the making of this helmet are shown in Figs. 165 A to C. The first operation in pressing was a simple one: it was the second which gave the greatest number of failures, for considerable wrinkling was apt to occur in the region of the brow.

In a general way, helmet model No. 5 has much to recommend it. Covering considerably more of the head, it would unquestionably have saved the lives of many of our soldiers. Its sloping peak and well-developed sides distinguished it clearly from the German model—seemingly for all practical purposes—and the precaution had even been taken of placing in the forehead region a slight median ridge (it could have been

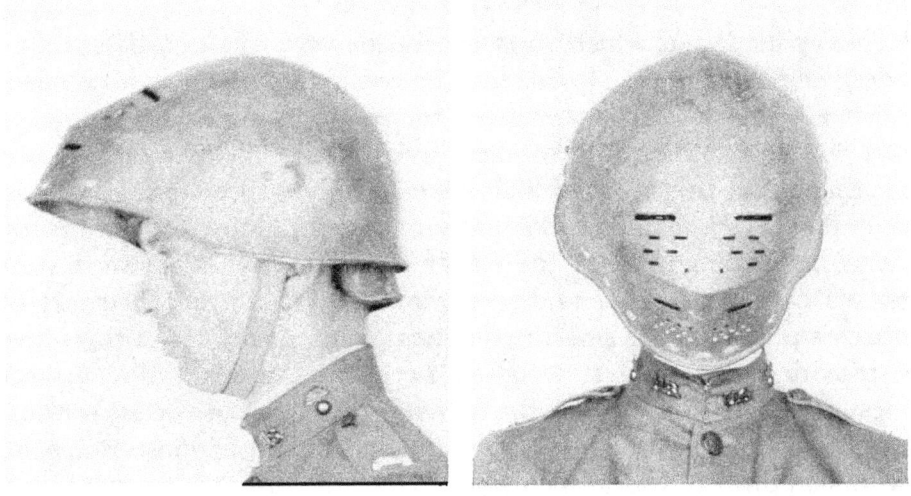

Fig. 166   Fig. 166A

Fig. 166. Experimental helmet (No. 6) with tilting dome

made greater), which cast a shadow and served as a recognition mark even at a considerable distance.

(The figure of this helmet shown in the Frontispiece as model No. 5A is slightly narrower in the brim.)

American Helmet Model No. 6
(Figs. 166 and 166A)

This form, purely experimental, was devised by the armorer, D. Tachaux; it is referred to here as bringing out an idea which, so far as the writer knows, is novel in the history of helmets. In order to protect the face, the entire helmet may be tilted forward so that the frontal border comes to lie below the chin. This helmet is provided with a calotte which bears the lining and becomes also the defense for the back of the head when the helmet is rotated forward above the ear. In practice such a helmet is uncomfortably balanced and from the need of having a double protection at the back when the face region is not protected, it is needlessly heavy. No ballistic specimens of this helmet were prepared.

American Helmet Model No. 7—Sentinel's Helmet
(Figs. 173 and 173A)

A heavy model, of which forty specimens were made in ballistic metal, was designed for the use of observers or machine gunners, whose need was vital for a helmet of great strength—for assuredly under no ordinary conditions would a soldier care to experiment with a helmet of this weight. The specimens of this model which were sent to France were pressed in the shop of the W. H. Mullins Company of Salem, Ohio; they were formed of nickel-manganese steel of the Baker formula, page 277; were stamped by means of a lead drop, and were heat-treated at the Pittsburgh Saw Company's plant. In this small experimental lot, examples in three weights were provided; the lightest weighed 11 pounds, the middle 15, and the heaviest 18. Tests showed that the heaviest helmet would resist service rifle ammunition at 200 yards with normal impact, and at close range, if the hit were less direct; thus at 15 degrees from the normal the wearer would be safe at 150 yards. In helmets of all weights furnished, the forehead plate was .185 inch in thickness. The other plates ranged from .065 inch to .185 in thickness, the lightest of these resisting rifle ammunition at about 1,200 foot seconds. The present helmet retains in general the lines of the siege helmets which in spite of their great weight (up to 25 pounds) were used everywhere in Europe during the seventeenth and eighteenth centuries. In certain regards, especially in the development of cheek-plates, it suggests an Italian armet of the fifteenth century. In spite of its apparent cumbersomeness, it could be worn without grave discomfort for a considerable length of time. Its weight is supported on the head by a padded lining which includes three cushions. These cushions are attached to a light metal frame which in turn is riveted to the helmet by means of certain of the rivets which hold its plates together. In designing this helmet it was thought possible, judging from data furnished by line officers, that under certain conditions, *e.g.*, when a machine gunner was to hold a position at all costs, this helmet would prove useful. Its weight seemed not an insuperable objection, for a considerable burden can be borne upon the head without grave discomfort; witness in this regard the weights, three or more times as great as our heaviest helmet, which are thus carried, sometimes for hours, by European peasants. Tested at American Headquarters in France, the present helmet was reported upon adversely.

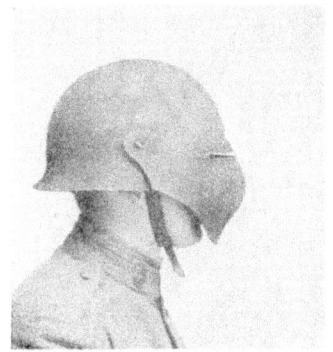  

Fig. 167   Fig. 167A   Fig. 167B

Fig. 167. American experimental helmet No. 8. Die stamped. Ballistic

American Helmet Model No. 8

(Frontispiece and Figs. 167, 167A, 167B, 168, 168A, 168B, 169, 170, 171, 172)

This model aimed to produce a helmet on the lines of helmet No. 5, but with a stout visor. Like the former helmet, it is roomier and protects a greater area of the head than the British helmet. Its visor protects the face almost entirely, and through its ocular slit the wearer obtains an extended vision—for the slit, although narrow, lies close to the pupil of the eye. The visor is not provided with openings lower at the sides, which would enable the wearer to see the ground immediately in front of him; for a soldier, it was reasoned, when moving forward would not consent to be hampered with a visor lowered. On the other hand, he would be willing to wear it down while in a position where casualties were great and where there were long periods of waiting. It is fair to say that the present visor is the only model among the many which is of considerable ballistic strength (Fig. 169). Specimens are at hand which have resisted the penetration of service ammunition of the automatic revolver (at 800 foot seconds), yet are not so deeply indented as to have caused a fatal wound to the wearer. In contrast with the Polack model, this visor protects the eye from splinters which scatter over a large area; it is certainly several times stronger ballistically than the Dunand visor, and it is weak not at all

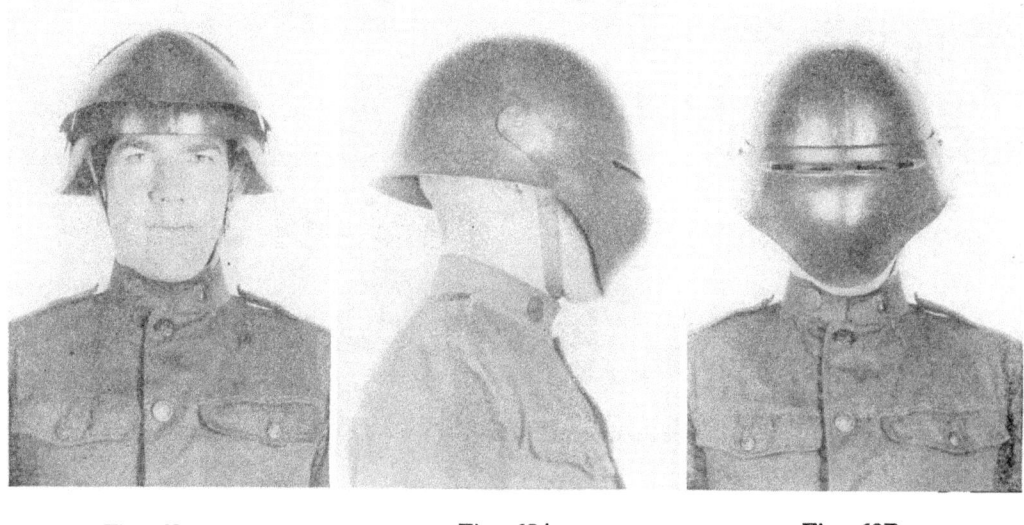

Fig. 168   Fig. 168A   Fig. 168B

Fig. 168. Experimental model of helmet No. 8. Hand-made

points but only in the immediate line of the ocular slit. Thanks to the accurate manufacture of this visor, it can readily be raised or lowered and be kept in position.

The manufacture of this helmet was undertaken by the Ford Motor Company, which furnished us in November, 1918, about 1,300 specimens. As a productional proposition this helmet was found to suffer about the same degree of breakage as helmet No. 5. The type of lining adopted for this helmet is pictured in Fig. 171. A narrow metal carrier or sweat-band was stamped out, which bore three tabs as in helmet No. 5 or as in the German helmet. With these tabs, however, no cushions were provided. In their place slabs of felt were used which could be folded by the wearer to the needed thickness and held in position by tapes. They were so arranged that they could be mounted in either of two ways—outside the metal carrier or inside (cf. the sections of these tabs in Figs. 172 and 172A).

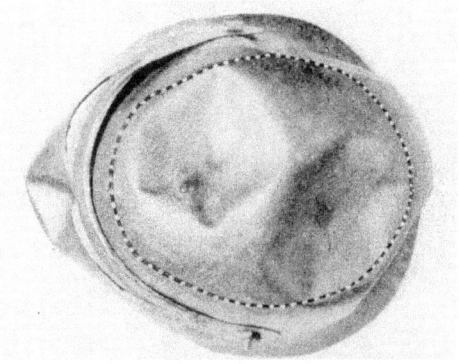

Fig. 169. Experimental helmet model No. 8. Result of test by pistol bullet at 800 f. s. Outline of head within helmet is shown by dotted line. This helmet bears marks of six testing bullets

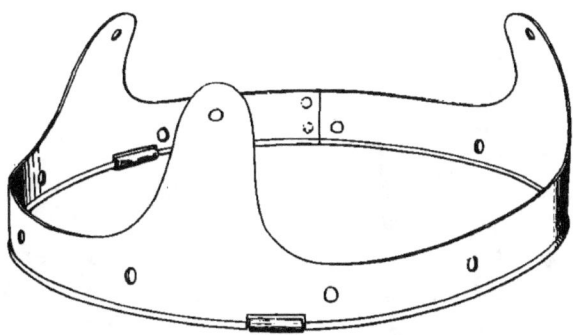

Fig. 170. Light steel frame for carrying lining of helmet No. 8

In the former case, the helmet was adapted for heads of size No. 7⅛ or larger, and in the latter for the size of No. 7 or smaller. So it will be seen that by increasing or decreasing the number of folds of the piece of felt, the size of the helmet could readily be altered to fit its wearer. The helmet of this model was made of manganese steel of .038 inch. Its ballistic value

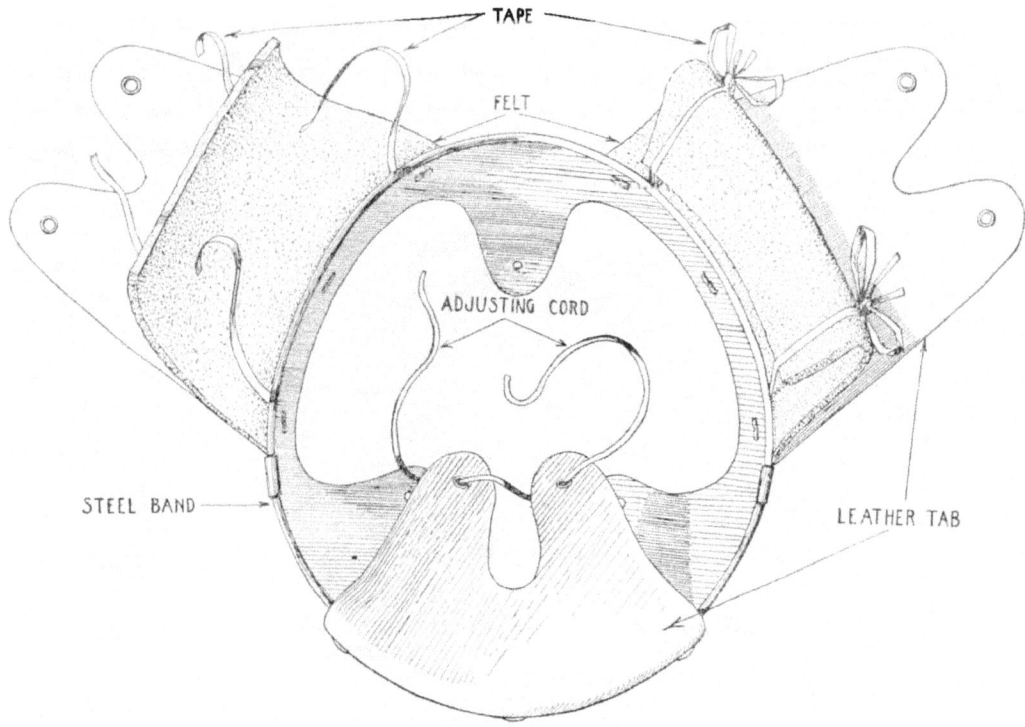

Fig. 171. Carrier of helmet model No. 8, showing lining pads or tabs

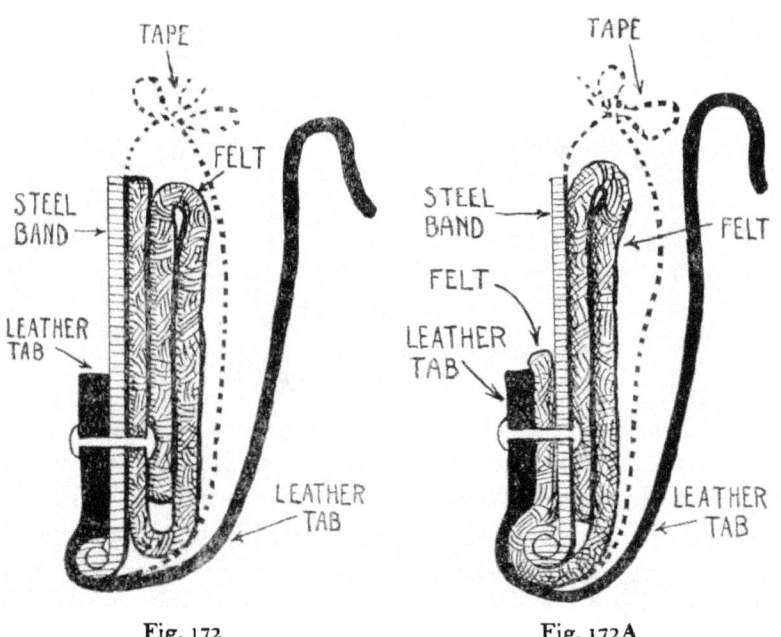

Fig. 172.   Fig. 172A

Fig. 172. Section of lining carrier showing arrangement of tabs for head sizes 7 and under, for 7⅛ and over

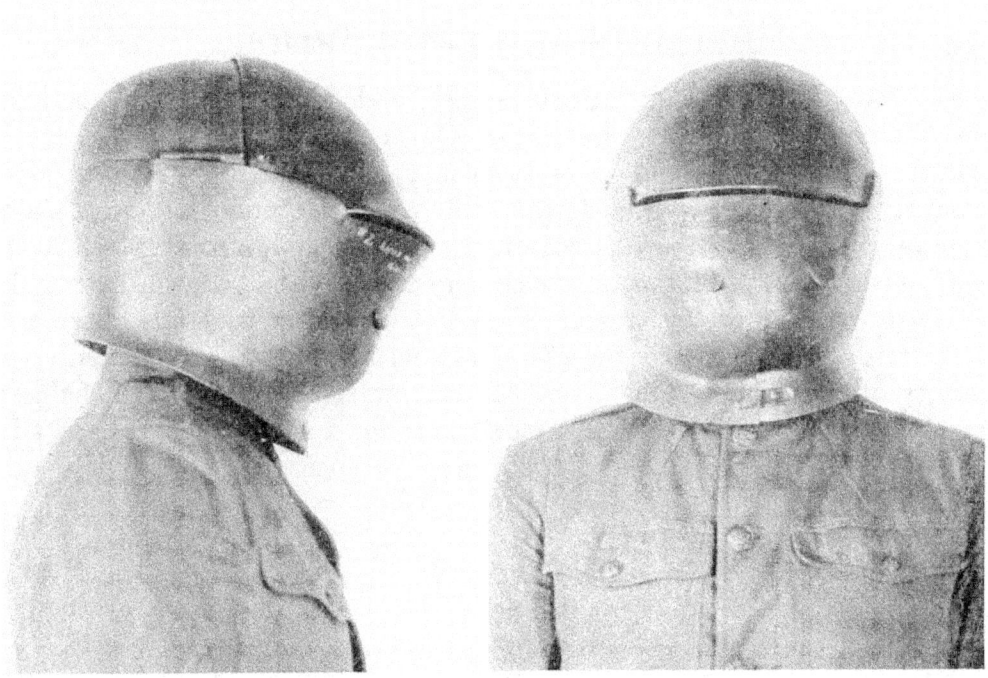

Fig. 173   Fig. 173A

Fig. 173. American sentinel's or machine gunner's helmet. Experimental model No. 7, 1918

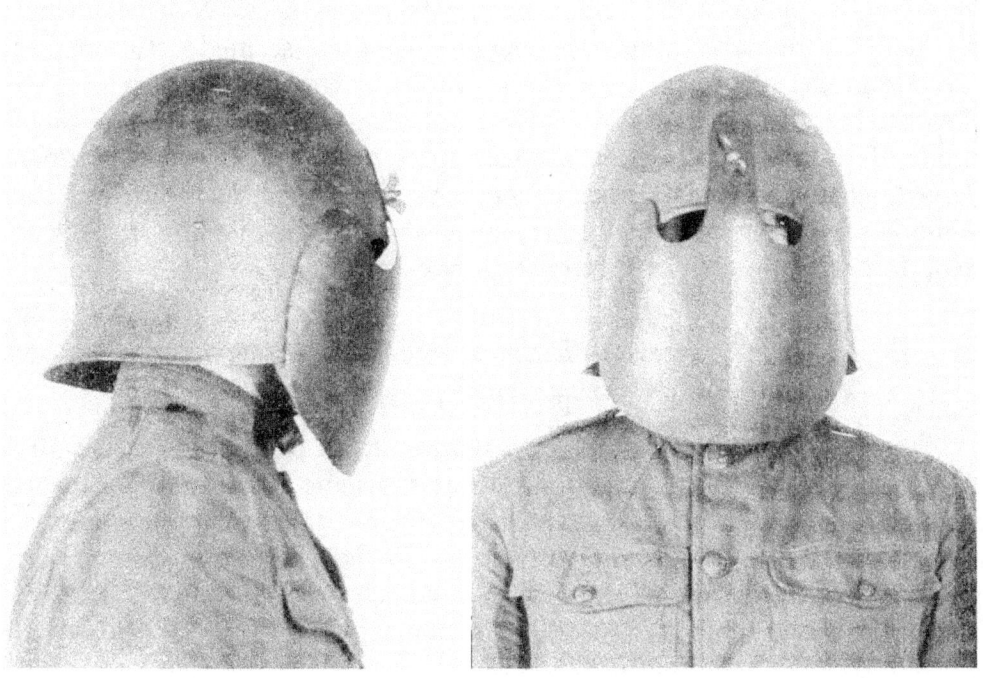

Fig. 174   Fig. 174A

Fig. 174. American sentinel's or machine gunner's helmet. Experimental model No. 9, 1918

was as high as that of the British helmet, and it had the added merit of covering considerably more of the head. On the other hand, it was a heavier helmet, weighing 51½ ounces as against 35 ounces. Its visor alone, however, accounts for 10 ounces of this difference. We note that great pains were taken to perfect the balance of this helmet; in spite of its relatively heavy visor, it keeps its position with very little difficulty, even during the active movements of the wearer, a result which is in part attributable to the careful adjustment of the chin-strap with reference to the center of gravity of the helmet. The same type of chin-strap is used as in helmets No. 2 and No. 5. This helmet model does not appear to have been adequately tested at American Headquarters in France.

American Helmet Model No. 9—Machine Gunner's

(Fig. 174)

The present model copies in essential lines a siege helmet of the seventeenth century preserved in the Riggs Collection in the Metropolitan Museum of Art. The bowl of this helmet is formed in two pieces riveted together strongly in the median line. Its face-guard, which can be raised, lowered, or removed by means of a thumbscrew, is a shovel-shaped affair protecting adequately the region of the face and neck. No specimens of this model were made in ballistic metal, since there seemed little hope that a second model of so heavy a defense would be considered, even if it were shown to be proof to rifle or machine gun fire at close range, *e.g.*, if pressed in one of the newer alloys developed under the auspices of the Ordnance Department—in point of fact, it is estimated that such a headpiece could be made proof to machine gun fire, even when armor-piercing bullets were used, at a total weight no greater than twenty pounds.

American Helmet Model No. 10

(Figs. 175, 175A)

This model provides a greater space around the head than helmet model No. 2; it is easier to manufacture and at the same time would be proportionally lighter than the second model mentioned. In a word, it aimed to smooth out the incurved or indented zone in the "hat band" region of the earlier helmet and thus to gain space with economy of weight. The cubic volume of this helmet is extraordinary, containing at four inches from the apex 2,750 cu. cm. as compared to 2,450 in helmet No. 2, 2,628 in the German helmet, 2,250 in the French helmet, and 2,525 in the British-American helmet. This headpiece was developed in June, 1918, but no ballistic specimens were ordered. Hand-made specimens were sent to H. A. E. F. abroad during the summer of 1918.

Fig. 175   Fig. 175A

Fig. 175. American experimental helmet model No. 10

American Helmet Model No. 13—Tank Operator's Helmet

(Figs. 176 A to C)

An effort was made (1918, summer) to protect the tank operator from injuries in the head caused either by heavy bumps or by lead splash which finds its way into the tank from disintegrating rifle balls. To this end, a helmet, in an experimental lot of thirty, was produced by the Equipment Section of the Ordnance Department under the advice of the officers of the Tank Unit, Engineering Division. This helmet was made from the "first operation" stage of helmet No. 5, described above (Fig. 165); it was cut and trimmed around the brim and provided with a crown-like ring of sponge rubber, which was found to furnish an admirable buffer in case the wearer of this helmet was struck on his head during the excessive jolting of his car. In this helmet, again, a lining of the three-pad system was employed, and a woven chin-strap with detachable clasp (Fig. 149) to enable the helmet to be promptly fastened, or detached and reattached under the tube of the gas mask. This type of helmet, it was suggested, could be used by tank operators while behind the lines and during the period when the tanks were being brought together a few miles from the

Fig. 176

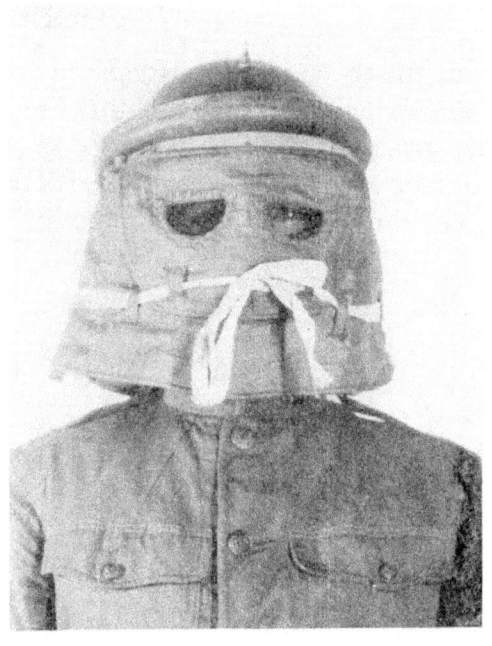

Fig. 176A

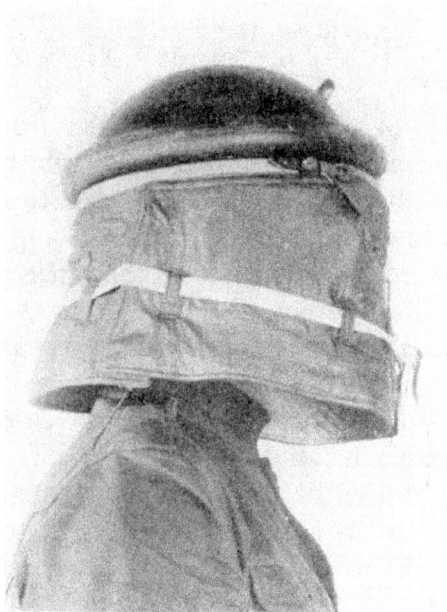

Fig. 176B

Fig. 176C

Fig. 176. Experimental helmet model No. 13 for American tank operator, shown with and without detachable padded-silk curtain and visor, guarding against lead splash

front. When the tanks came to closer quarters, the operator could buckle in place a special face- and neck-guard which is shown in Figs. 176A-176C. At this time, the visor would be raised and locked in position by means of a turning clamp. Where considerable risk was incurred from the penetration of lead splash in the turret, the operator would drop the mask and

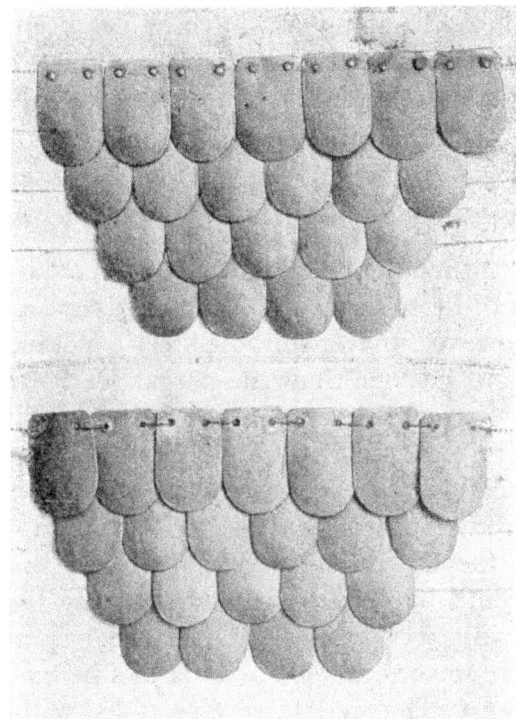

Fig. 177. Thin steel scales arranged as substitute for the silk curtain of tank operator's experimental helmet

fasten it in place either within the neck-guard or outside of it; in the latter event it could be tied securely in place. The bowl of the present helmet was formed in manganese steel and furnished for the region covered the same protection as the service helmet. The neck-guard was shown by tests to keep out a considerable amount of lead splash; it is formed of about twenty layers of Japanese silk* and is covered with a closely woven American silk

* Efforts were made to produce a neck screen which would be a safer defense against lead splash than the silk curtain described above. In Fig. 177, a device is

prepared especially for this purpose by Mr. Paul Gerli, a New York inventor. The visor in use is formed of layers of raw silk precisely as the neck-guard; its eye region is protected with triplex glass held in a narrow metal frame, and the latter is at the top ingeniously arranged so that the glass can be conveniently replaced. The entire helmet, as above described, weighs two pounds fourteen ounces; without its splash guard, it weighs less than two pounds. No official reports have as yet been received as to the practical value of this model; the writer learns, however, that it was used in the tanks during the last push and that it was well spoken of.

American Helmet Models No. 14, No. 14A and No. 15—Aviator's Helmets
(Figs. 178, 178A, 179, 179A and 179B)

Up to the present time the head defense of the aviator has been a leathern casque. He has hitherto been unwilling to accept a helmet of steel. In view of the fact, however, that a suitable steel headpiece would weigh but about one half pound heavier than the actual leathern model and would have many times its strength, it was suggested that his type of headgear might be revised. For one thing, actual tests showed that a helmet shell of .036 inch in thickness of manganese steel would resist as much as twenty-one layers of chrome-tanned leather $\frac{3}{32}$ inch in thickness. It also became clear from the use of the standard helmet that many balls even of high velocity would be deflected by a relatively light helmet of alloy steel. The Engineering Section of the Ordnance Department was, accordingly, led to prepare several models of aviator's helmets and submit them to the Aircraft Defense. The models were provided with linings of different types; some were cushioned on the three-pad system (Fig. 178A) and some with a soft lining as in the leathern casque (Fig. 179A). All proved comfortable and well balanced. The total weight of these helmets made of steel .036 inch in thickness, was from one pound ten ounces to two pounds. In each case the ear region of the helmet was so hinged that it could be equipped with the telephone receiver. The chin-strap was then attached to the lower edge of each ear-plate and the hinge of the latter was fastened above by a single rivet. By this means, the inclination of each ear-piece

figured, consisting of thin scales of manganese steel, broadly overlapping. While this device furnishes an excellent screen against lead splash, its weight would be an insuperable objection to its successful use; for, made even of thin metal scales, it would weigh nearly as much as the helmet itself.

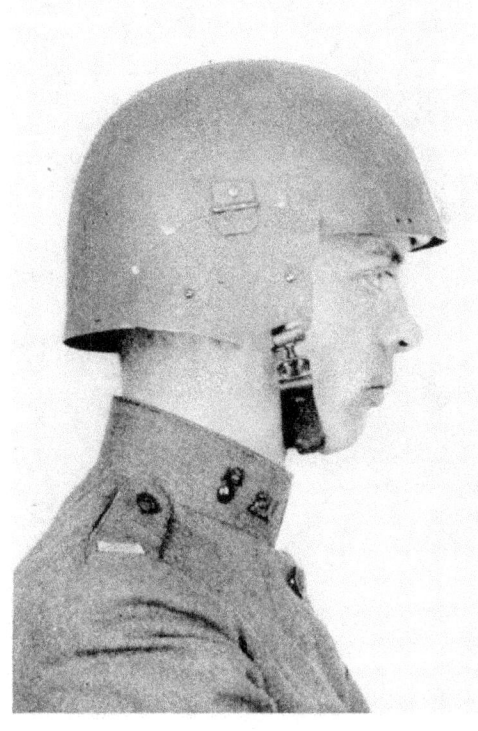

Fig. 178

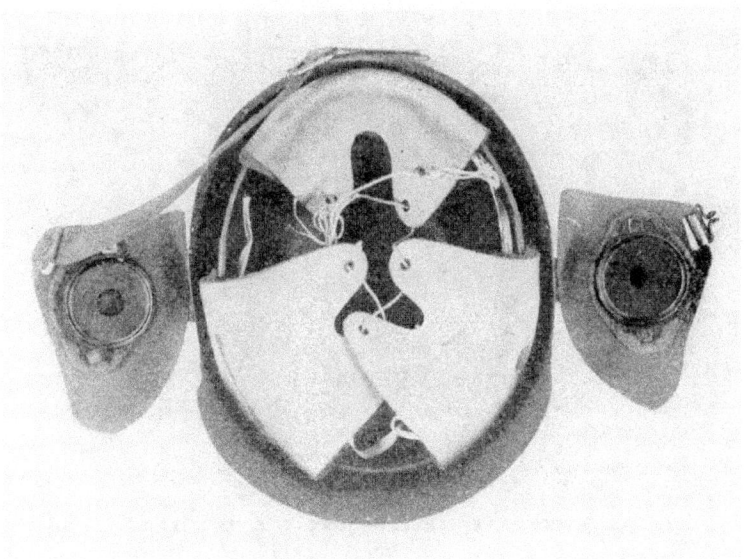

Fig. 178A

Fig. 178. American experimental helmet. Aviator's model, 1918

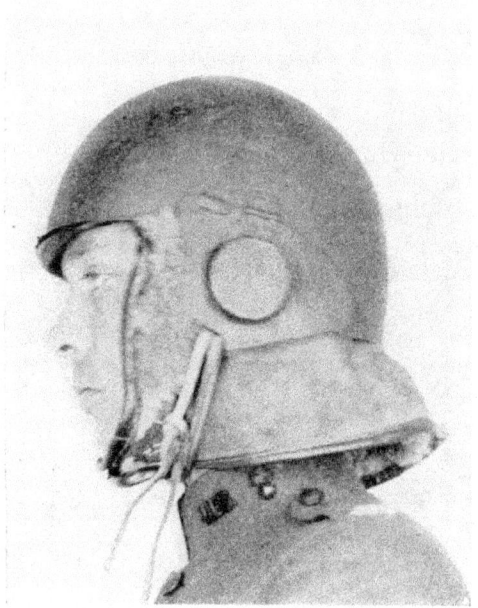 

Fig. 179   Fig. 179A

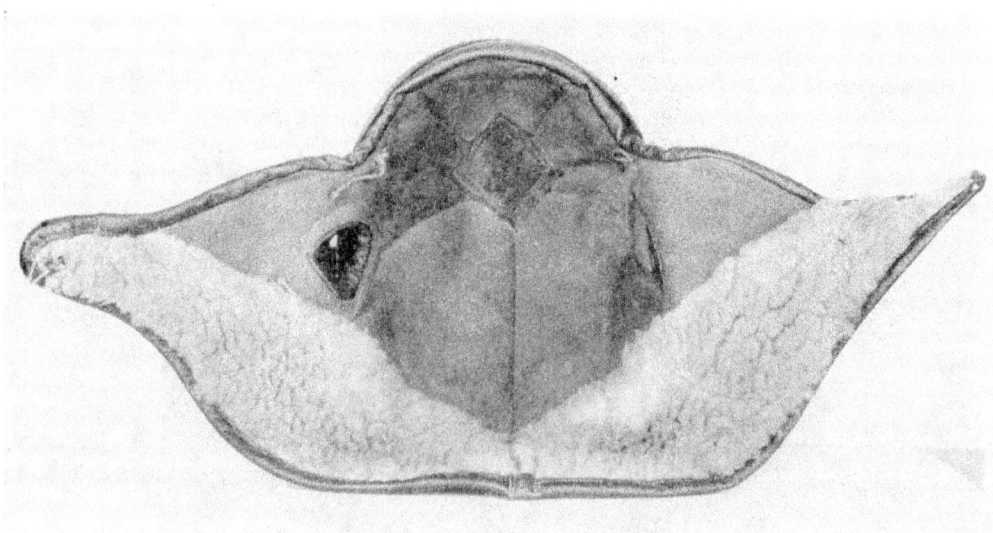

Fig. 179B

Fig. 179. American experimental helmet. Aviator's model, 1918

would naturally be maintained in accordance with the shape of the face of the wearer—for the tightened chin-strap would cause these ear-plates to be drawn into their serviceable position. The model of aviator's helmet shown in Fig. 178 was made of ballistic metal from the first operation die of helmet No. 5. It allows a space for indentation of about one inch around the cranium. It is possibly too large to be worn with maximum comfort,

Fig. 180. American experimental helmet. Aviator's model No. 15, 1918

even when provided with the thick fleecy lining of the usual aviator's helmet (Fig. 179B).

Still another aviator's headpiece is shown in Fig. 180, and it has probably the best lines of all the helmets designed in the armor workshop. It is more closely modeled to the head, having intervening space of only from one half to three quarters of an inch. Such a helmet, if made of Baker's nickel-manganese steel, insures great rigidity and minimum indentation and should furnish a light and serviceable defense. This model is well balanced and is provided with the new-type tissue chin-strap. Its lining is of the continuously cushioned type to prevent troublesome ingress of air. If, however, a lining based on the three-pad system were recommended, the pads could readily be mounted on a thin circlet of steel and be riveted to the bowl of the helmet at three points; but, in this event, an additional outer rim of leather or fur should be provided which would serve to keep out a current of air. These aviator's helmets were prepared at too late a date to insure their being used at the front. Official tests, however, were given them at Bolling Field in Washington and the first model (14A) received an especially favorable report.

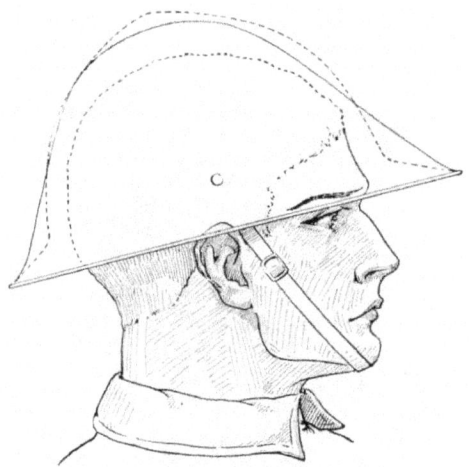

Fig. 181. Liberty Bell helmet. Fall, 1918.
Shown over profile (in dotted line)
of American experimental
helmet model No. 4

Liberty Bell Helmet

Finally to be mentioned is the "Liberty Bell" helmet which just before the close of the war was accepted "provisionally" as the standard helmet for the American Army, and of which a few thousand specimens were made by order of the General Staff, through the Equipment Section of the Ordnance-Engineering at Tours. This helmet (Frontispiece and Fig. 181) is essentially a variant of model No. 4 (compare the lines of these two helmets shown in Fig. 181), which was prepared under the direction of the Washington Armor Unit in June and exhibited at H. A. E. F. in December, 1917. The present helmet is soon to be given an extensive test in connection with other models. Already, however, it has been found unsatisfactory in the following regards: (1) it rests too high on the head to be well balanced; (2) it does not protect adequately the sides and back of the cranium; (3) from its sub-conical shape it gives greater space than is needed at the top, which entails unnecessary weight; (4) its shape, also, makes it a difficult model to manufacture, for its broadly conical dome is formed only after a severe stoving operation, which tends to thin out the sides of the crown dangerously: in point of fact, the latest model of this helmet presents a thickness of .029 inch to .030 inch at the sides of the crown, as against .046 inch to .047 inch near the brim; (5) as at present manufactured, it is probably too heavy (39½ ounces, against 34 or 35 ounces in the British helmet); (6) its present lining is unsatisfactory, for it follows a model which exerts continuous pressure on the scalp instead of a three-pad system. Its latest variant is without the reinforcing plate which is seen in the figure (Frontispiece). The merits of the Liberty Bell helmet are easy recognition and reversibility, for it can be shifted fore and aft at the will of the wearer. It must be noted, finally, that the aesthetic value or "morale" of this helmet is low; it suggests less a helmet for serious service than the dome-like hat of a Chinese fisherman.

(g) FACE DEFENSES

Defenses for the Eyes

The peril of blindness has stimulated inventors of all countries to produce protective shields for the eyes. One of the earliest devices was a pair of goggles which were made of metal and slotted for vision. A horizontal slit was intersected by a vertical one which was designed to be opposite the pupil of the eye; and to insure still better vision, one or more oblique slots were added. Such slots, although extremely narrow, .02 to .06 inch, gave a surprisingly extended and clear vision. The first example of this armored goggle (Fig. 182) is English (see page 132). It is made of ballistic steel and weighs about 5½ ounces. It can be adapted to foreheads of various shapes by means of a median hinge. Such a device would obviously be a useful defense against splinters—under certain conditions it would even deflect a bullet; and there is no doubt that its general use would have prevented casualties. Its use, however, as in the case of most armor defenses, was never general; it appeared as a privately manufactured article and is known to have had a certain sale among the soldiers of the Allies.

The second type of armored goggles, shown in Figs. 183 and 184, was manufactured by several inventors and had a limited sale. This device gave an extended range of vision; it was easily folded and carried; but ballistically it was weak. It could be of service only as a defense against splinters.

The third type of eye-shield is designed by one of the officials, Mr. Thomas C. Harris, in the Engineering Division in Washington. It is similar to the foregoing but simpler (Fig. 185); it is merely a spectacle-shaped plate of metal, embossed over each eye and there provided with a horizontal slot. Through this single aperture a very fair degree of vision can be obtained. This design was never manufactured in ballistic steel.

Other eye defenses have been suggested, some of them furnished with "resista," "triplex," or similar patented glasses, which afford considerable protection. (Cf. Fig. 176C.) The principle of this glass is that by separating its layers of glass by celluloid a complex may be built up which will sustain a considerable shock without shattering dangerously the fragments of glass. Of this material goggles were produced in large numbers which were worn by aviators and others. This type of eye defense, it should be stated, was introduced into the service from technical workshops where measures had long been developed in the direction of protecting the eyes.

One might mention additional eye defenses but they would be found to be merely variants of the types mentioned above; that is, they are either metal goggles with slots for vision or spectacles provided with some form of transparent eye pieces.

Visors: The British helmet was early criticized by the helmet board at H. A. E. F. as not providing a face defense or visor. Accordingly, as noted before, on page 210, efforts were made to introduce into the American Army the Dunand visor, the Polack visor, or a visor having a single slot, *e.g.*, in helmet No. 8. Of these three types the preference should, in the writer's opinion, be given to one having a single slot; for in this model the wearer not only enjoys a wide range of vision but is insured a considerable degree of protection for his face. Indeed, in the nature of things, no perforated face-guard can be strong, and when a visor is needed at all it is fair to assume that it should be so strong as to resist the greatest range of impacts. Of course, the wearer of the single-slitted visor has not the height of vision which a "pepperbox" visor would yield, but he has vision enough for practical purposes, and, from what has been learned at the front, it is quite safe to conclude that the American soldier would never consent to "go over

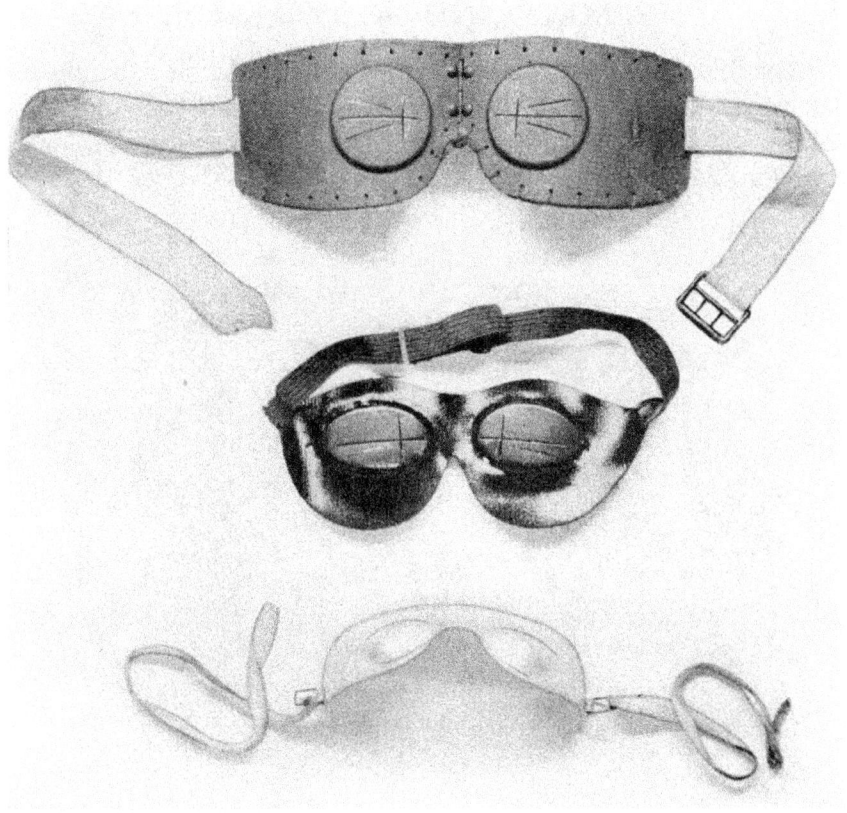

Fig. 182. Splinter goggles and face defense. British, 1917

Fig. 183. Splinter goggles, American : reproduction of French design, 1918

Fig. 185. Splinter goggles having single visual slit. Model by Thomas C. Harris, Washington, D. C.

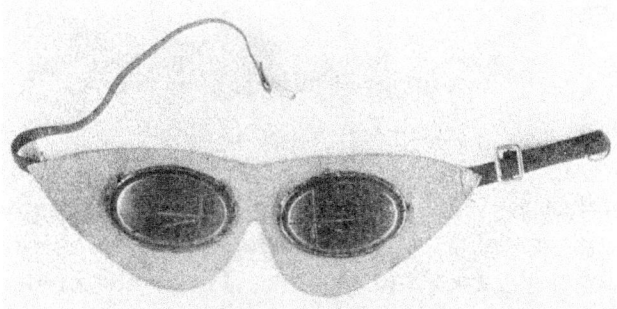

Fig. 184. Splinter goggles. Variation of preceding model. Manufactured through Mr. Arthur Dunn of Quincy, Ill.

236 HELMETS AND BODY ARMOR

the top" with his visor down. His face defense would most be needed when he was waiting, hour long in many cases, in exposed positions, in danger from splinters and shrapnel. In such a case the solid type of visor would surely be best of all.

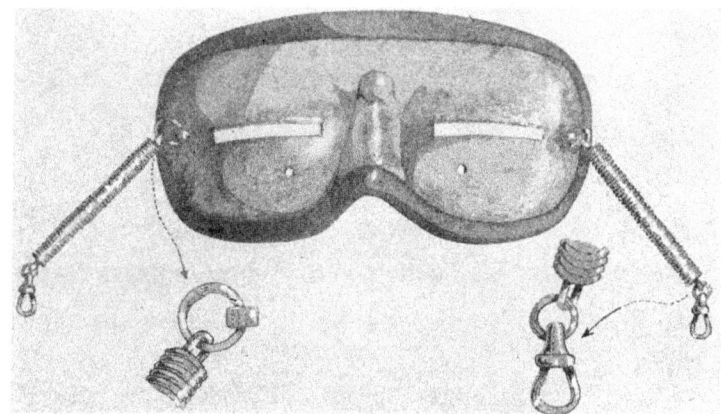

Fig. 186. Eye-shield. Wilmer model, adaptable to British-American helmet

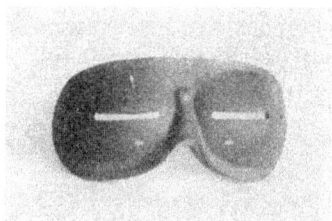 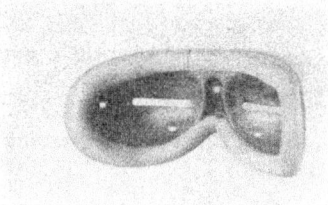

Fig. 187A.   Fig. 187B

Fig. 187. Wilmer model eye defense. The last figure showing a marginal supporting cushion of sponge rubber

We should here refer to a face-guard or visor (it could also be classed among eye defenses) which was designed to accompany the standard British helmet; it was suggested and endorsed by the distinguished American oculist, Colonel W. Holland Wilmer. The model of this was borrowed from the single-slotted eye-shield which is used against snow-blindness by the Indians of our Northwest. The present model, shown in Figs. 186, 187A and 187B, is pressed in soft steel of the same character as in the

IN MODERN WARFARE

French helmet; it fits against the brow and cheeks snugly by means of a marginal band of sponge rubber; and it is held in place by means of springs which are attached above to the sides of the helmet. When not needed, this visor is lifted from the face and snapped in position on the forehead region of the helmet. The defense, by the way, is a light one (seven ounces) yet will safeguard the wearer against the type of missiles to which a French helmet is proof. The present visor has the additional merit of furnishing its wearer a wide range of vision, for its ocular slit is close to the pupil of

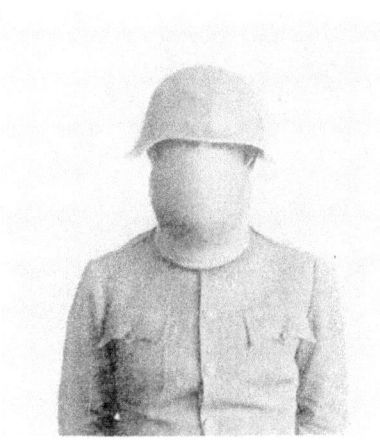

Fig. 188. Face defense or bavière. American experimental model, 1918

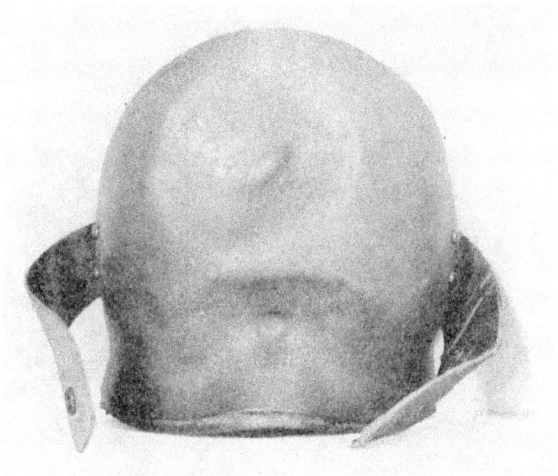

Fig. 188A. Result of test on foregoing face-guard, with pistol bullet at 850 f. s.

the eye; it has also a small aperture on either side and below, through which the wearer may see the ground immediately in front of him—and he sees it through apparently a single hole, since the opening under each eye is placed at the correct distance from its fellow to insure stereoscopic vision. The present visor was manufactured in an experimental number of thirty thousand by the order of H. A. E. F.; when the lot was made, however, it was rejected by a special committee at H. A. E. F. The report stated that these visors were not readily kept in position.

We should refer also to a second type of face-guard (Figs. 188, 188A and 188B) devised to accompany a helmet of the British type. This is merely adapted from the usual type of face-guard (bavière) of the fifteenth century. It encloses the face, rests on the chest, and is held in position not too tightly by leather bands provided with snap fasteners. These catches can be instantly pulled open and the face-guard thrown off in the event of the gas mask being needed. A point of special interest of this face-guard is its lining, which was formed of sponge rubber vulcanized at low temperature or by what is technically known as a "cold cure" to the ballistic metal. The arrangement of this cushioning is such that the shock is borne by the strong "landmarks" of the face, the sponge-rubber cushion extending

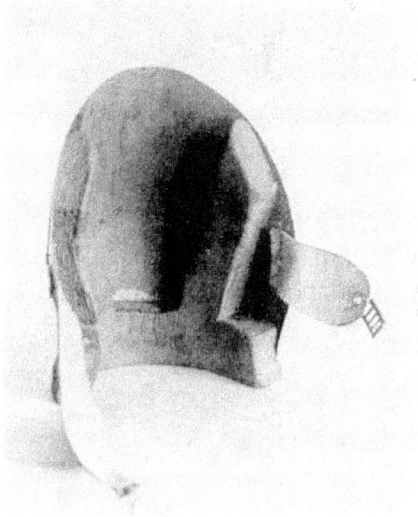

Fig. 188B. Inner view of face-guard

between the cheek-bone and the angle of the jaw. Such a face-guard made of helmet steel (12 per cent manganese, .038 inch thick) was found in actual tests to give good results; it stopped the automatic revolver bullet at ten feet (Fig. 188A) yielding a degree of indentation which would not have resulted in a dangerous wound to the wearer, for the rubber cushion kept the metal guard about one inch away from the face. No experiments were made with this face-guard in the field. A number were sent to training camps where the soldiers, declaring that they were stuffy, did not take kindly to them. None the less, there can be no question that in active service, where gas was not experienced, such a defense would prove of value; for as a type of face-guard, there can be little doubt that the present model is

IN MODERN WARFARE

the easiest to wear and the strongest which has been devised up to the present time. That it is practical, indeed, seems clear, since the same form was in general use in Europe for about a century (roundly 1450-1550).

(h) SHOULDER DEFENSES

The necklet or gorget, shown in Figs. 189, 189A and 190, was designed to afford considerable protection to the region of the upper chest. It is a defense which in practical armor-wearing was found of minimum discom-

Fig. 189. Defense for neck and shoulders.
Experimental, 1918

fort; in fact, it was the common type in use during the seventeenth century. The present model differs, however, from the old defense in having no backplate to accompany it; its back consisting merely of two flanges which arise from the front of the plate and are bent down to such a degree as to hold it comfortably against the body. Pressed in manganese steel .038 inch to .040 inch in thickness, it resists an impact of an automatic bullet of 230 grains traveling at the rate of over 900 foot seconds. Its weight is but 1½ pounds. In order to guard the wearer against the shock of a missile it bears near its lower border a cushion of sponge rubber about three quarters of an inch thick. This is vulcanized to a thin plate of steel which in turn is spot-welded to the necklet. It is due to the shape and position of this plate of sponge rubber that an impact will be distributed over the lower chest of the wearer. It will be seen that the shoulder region of this defense is provided with eyelets through which a thong may be passed which attaches the necklet to the wearer's shoulder strap—to prevent it from "riding," though this may in great part be guarded against by bending the shoulder plates so that they will fit the wearer snugly. Another point to be noted is

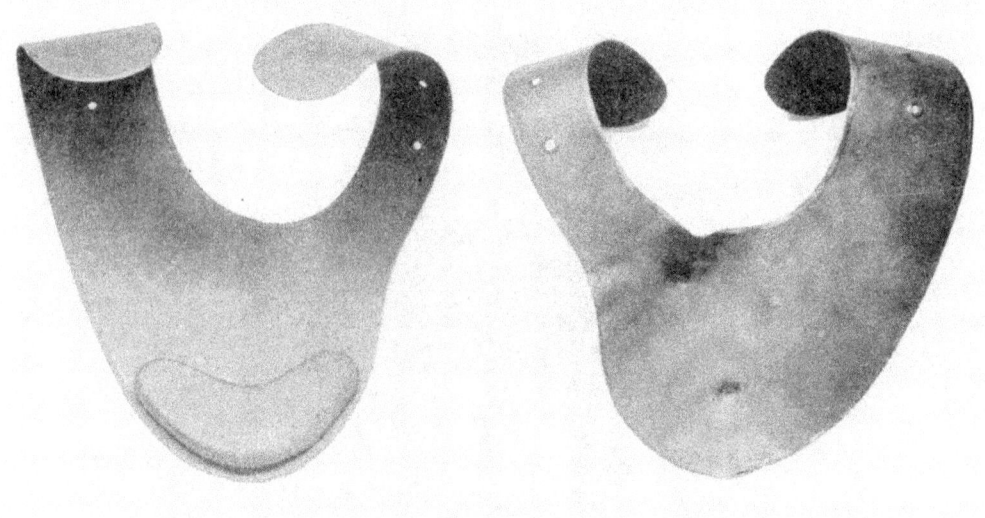

Fig. 189A. Inner view of same defense showing cushion of sponge rubber

Fig. 190. Similar necklet, showing result of pistol bullet at 850 f. s.

that the necklet is given a narrower border on its right side in order to allow the soldier free shoulder space for the use of his rifle. A lot of these necklets were prepared in ballistic steel by the New England Enameling Company and sent to France; an excellent report of them was given by the examining committee at American Headquarters, which declared them to be "the most practical of all body armor examined." A larger experimental lot was immediately ordered and we are led to believe that this type of body defense would have had a fairly general use had the war lasted.

Another type of shoulder defense is shown in Fig. 191. This épaulière consists of two plates held together by a transverse strap on the back and by inclined straps in front through which these plates could be buttoned to the tunic. Since these plates are developed largely over the shoulder blades, the present defense would possibly prove useful when the wearer advances under barrage, in which case its area of protection would become

Fig. 191. Shoulder defense. American experimental model, 1918

far more important than at first apparent. A small lot of ballistic specimens of this defense was manufactured and tried out in an infantry training school in France. The report upon it declared that the region which it protected was not sufficiently large to warrant its use. Since it is known, however, that a large number (said to be 10 per cent) of fatal and dangerous injuries are suffered in the region protected by this defense, one regrets that more extended tests of this defense were not made.

(i) BODY ARMOR, HEAVY AND LIGHT

A communication received from General Pershing in the summer of 1917, referred to the importance of developing an effective body armor and directed that experiments to this end should be continued. The Ordnance Department accordingly made an extensive review of the work in this field, examining upward of thirty types of body shields which were submitted to be manufactured, and sent abroad several models in greater or smaller lots. None of these types of body armor, however, so far as can be learned, was given a favorable report from American Headquarters.

Heavy and Light Armor

Two general types of body defenses were considered; the first aimed to be a reasonably adequate protection against service rifle and machine gun. The second was to be worn with minimum discomfort and was to protect the body from missiles of low and medium velocity—in other words, to be proof to shrapnel and the automatic revolver. The former type of armor could evidently be worn only for a short period and would render the wearer practically immobile; it would be an armor of defense, suited for sentinels, machine gunners and defenders of shell craters. The latter armor would serve for shock troops and in general for advancing infantry. In explaining the experimental work on body armor carried on in the United States, we may consider these two types in order.

Heavy Body Armor

The first armor of this type to be developed practically in the United States was the Brewster Body Shield, shown in Fig. 192; this consists of a shield-shaped plate of chrome-nickel steel (Bethlehem Steel Company) supported by a complex frame or cradle of wire which in the shoulder region develops bands which pass one over each shoulder and spring in position close to a shoulder blade. By means of these shoulder clasps the heavy shield is borne with a minimal degree of discomfort, for the weight is thereby widely distributed—in fact, most of it is borne apparently on the wearer's back. The inventor of this armor, Dr. Guy Otis Brewster of Dover, New Jersey, lays great stress upon the spring frame which supports the breastplate. This he devised to distribute the shock of the impinging bullet and in point of fact the wearer of such a defense can support readily the shock of a heavy blow, *e.g.*, given by a sledge-hammer. Experiments were made with this body defense at Picatinny Arsenal in April, 1917, when Dr. Brewster stood in front of a Lewis machine gun and received an impact of a number of bullets at full-service velocity (about 2,700 foot seconds). His armor weighed about forty pounds. It is interesting to record that the wearer gave no sign of the great impact to which he was subjected.

Fig. 192. Brewster body armor, 1917-1918

He declared that it was "only about one tenth the shock which he experienced when struck by a sledge-hammer." An interesting feature of this test was that the breastplate which resisted the impact became hot through the conversion of the energy of the impinging bullets. It must be admitted, however, that in this test the breastplate was not struck normally but at an angle of 35 to 45 degrees. To this body armor, Dr. Brewster had affixed a heavy helmet which also was cushioned (*e.g.*, to the forehead of the wearer). This was provided with adjustable eye-shields.

In demonstrations given by Dr. Brewster, this armor was shown to be capable of being worn under varying conditions. The wearer could advance rapidly, change position, and use a rifle, although evidently his aiming would not have been of the best. The thickness of his armor, .21 inch, made it a fairly safe defense from rifle fire, and the spring frame which formed the lining was held to reduce notably the shock of the impinging bullet. The Brewster armor could have been improved in the following details: it might have been worn more comfortably if it had been modeled to the body of the wearer; its headpiece should have been designed after a better model; as it stood it was clumsy and needlessly large. The main objection to the armor was that it was too heavy to be profitably used. The American soldier, critics maintained, could not be induced to carry its weight. Nor in wearing it would he be adequately protected, for even if he were immune from a bullet from in front, he could still readily be shot from the side and back; then, too, at close range, his unarmored legs would make him an easy mark for a machine gunner. To arm a soldier so that he would be proof to machine gun at thirty yards, his breastplate alone would weigh forty pounds and his complete suit of armor would represent a total burden of at least 110 pounds. Dr. Brewster, it should be mentioned, is an armorer expert of wide experience; he has devoted himself for over a decade to the development of body defenses and, so far as the writer is aware, he is the only inventor who, firm in his faith, has stood in his own armor in front of service ammunition fired from a machine gun.

Heavy Breastplate—Ordnance Model
(Figs. 193, 194, 195, also 231)

A heavy breastplate designed to include the virtues of the German model (page 142), and to be worn more easily than the type of armor designed by Dr. Brewster, was prepared in the armor workshop of the Metropolitan Museum of Art in February, 1918. Its lines followed those of the breastplates of the fifteenth century, which for the rest are known to have been excellent expressions of the ancient armorer's art. The model was sent to Messrs. Mullins and Company of Salem, Ohio, who produced dies for its manufacture and "turned out" the first lot of fifty ballistic specimens in a remarkably short time. In point of fact, within twenty-six days from the time they began work upon this defense, the specimens were on shipboard leaving for France. The steel for this work was produced promptly through the personal cooperation of Mr. W. H. Baker of the Universal Rolling Mills of Bridgeville, Pennsylvania, and by the similar help of Mr. Grayson of the Jessop Steel Company. These defenses weighed in all twenty-seven pounds. The breastplate alone weighed about sixteen pounds and was .185 inch in thickness. The two waist-plates, or taces, weighed together six pounds and were .625 inch in thickness. The steels furnished by Messrs. Baker and Grayson were similar in formula (see table

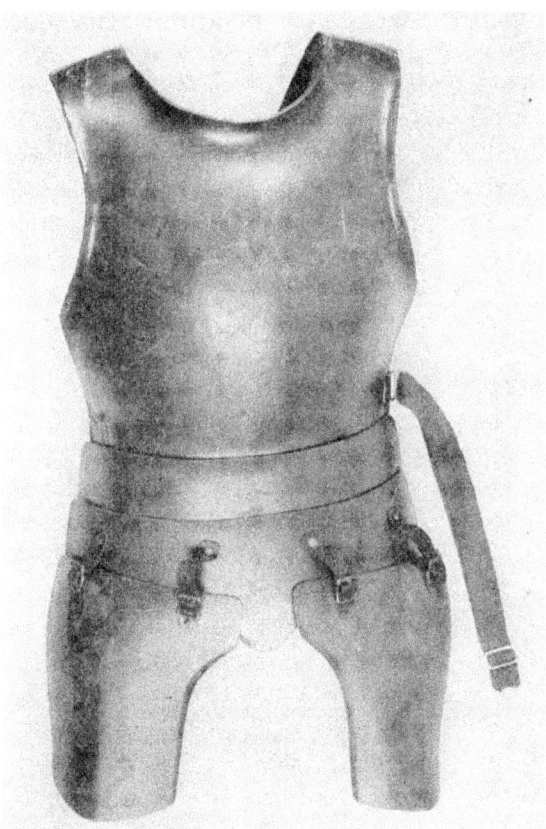

Fig. 193. American experimental model of sentinel's heavy armor

opposite page 274), that of Mr. Baker giving slightly better ballistic results. These breastplates were held in position by means of plates or bands which rounded backward over the shoulders of the wearer and terminated over the middle of his shoulder blades, giving a firm support and distributing the weight over a considerable region. To the end that the breastplate should seem as light as possible, a padding was vulcanized within the region of the upper chest, shoulders and hips (Fig. 194). This was of sponge rubber manufactured by the Miller Rubber Company of Akron, Ohio, whose aid and interest contributed notably to the prompt completion of this experimental lot.

Tests upon this type of breastplate were made at the armor school at Langres and an unfavorable report upon it was given. The various soldiers who wore it stated that the weight of the armor caused considerable fatigue

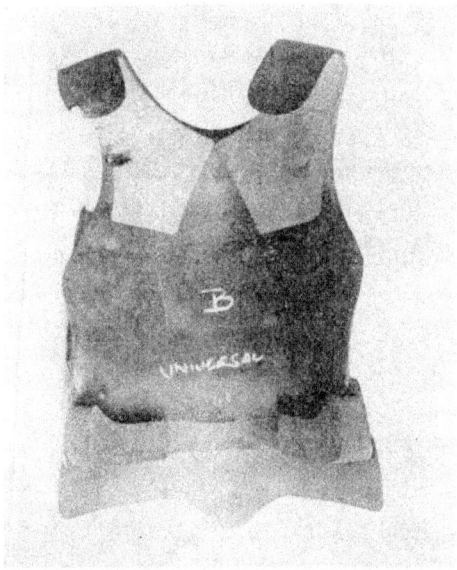

Fig. 194. American sentinel's armor showing cushions of sponge rubber

in shoulders and back, that it was not noiseless, and that it bothered them in the manipulation of their machine guns. In a word, they declared that its disadvantages overweighed its advantages. Ballistic test showed that it would resist a machine gun bullet, German, at about 300 yards and American service ammunition at about 200 yards. The critics admitted that it might prove of value to machine gunners if a backplate was added and the thigh pieces omitted. While their official report was adverse, they nevertheless recommended that tests should be made on the battle-field and that armor of this type should be issued to machine gun troops of a selected

IN MODERN WARFARE

division, apparently to the brigade battalions and to the machine gun companies of the regiments, but in any event a backplate should be provided.

In addition to the foregoing types of heavy body armor, the Committee of the General Staff of H. A. E. F. considered a model which had been prepared for their committee in France. Of this no specimen or photographs have come to the United States. It is built up of five separate plates, one

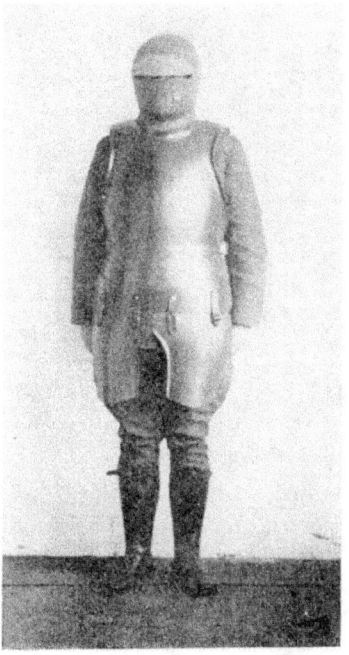

Fig. 195. American sentinel's armor shown in connection with sentinel's heavy helmet, 1917-1918

covering the chest, two the shoulders, and two the waist region. The shoulder plates are riveted firmly to the breastplate; the waist-plates are attached very much, it appears, as in the body armor of the Germans. It is not known of what ballistic alloy the samples were made which were tested in France, nor is the weight of the armor given. The test showed, however, that the breastplate was proof to .30 service ammunition, including the German, at a range of over 100 meters, but that it could not be relied upon to be a complete defense at a distance less than 200 meters, a result which

248   HELMETS AND BODY ARMOR

apparently does not differ widely from that given by the heavy breastplate described above.

In a general way, there appears to have been no insistent call for a heavy armor of this type.

Fig. 196   Fig. 196A

Figs. 196 and 196A. American light body armor, 1917-1918. Experimental model. Also arm defenses and British-American helmet

Light Body Armor
(Figs. 196 A-D, 197, 198, 198A, 199, 200)

Reports from American Headquarters in France indicated the need of producing a body armor which would protect the front and back alike and which was of such a weight that it could be carried by an infantryman with minimum discomfort. Trials had earlier been made with several types of British body shields but they had proved unsatisfactory. For the new defense a maximum weight of seven or eight pounds was recommended. A body armor which was aimed to meet this requirement was produced by

Fig. 196B   Fig. 196C   Fig. 196D

Figs. 196B, 196C, 196D. American experimental light armor, with arm defenses and helmet model No. 5

the Engineering Division of the Ordnance Department. This defense consisted of a plastron which was attached to the backplate by means of shoulder straps; these terminated in metal plates having openings like keyholes which fitted to pegs on the breastplate. The breastplate was formed of three plates held together by leather strips, to the lowest of which was laced a "sporran plate" protecting the groin. Between each pair of plates

250 HELMETS AND BODY ARMOR

a small piece of leather was inserted attached by the same rivets which held the plates together on the back of the breastplates. These aimed to prevent rattling when the breastplate was worn. The present defense covered the front of the body of the wearer quite completely and its size was so arranged that it could be worn by men of various heights and weights. In

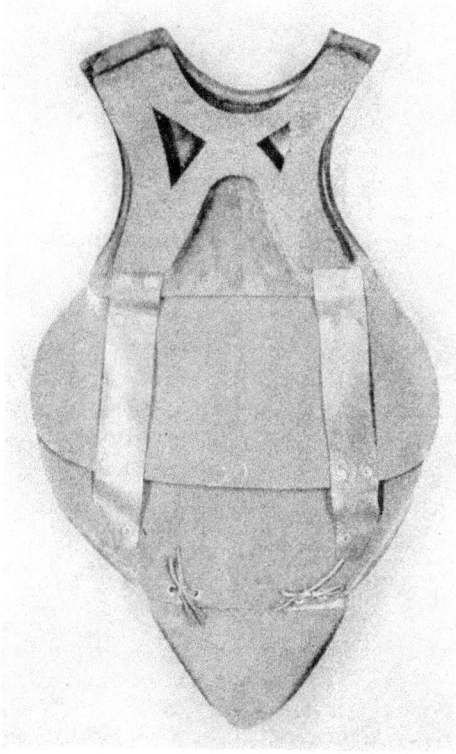

Fig. 197. Light body armor. Inner view of laminated breastplate. A heavy cushion of sponge rubber lines the uppermost plate

the case of a man of short stature, it might be worn without the sporran plate. In modeling the uppermost element of this breastplate care was taken to allow considerable latitude for the movements of the shoulders and arms of the wearer: thus, space was given, especially on the right side, to enable the infantryman to use his rifle. A cushioning was arranged within this breastplate in the form of a sponge-rubber pad nearly one inch in thickness (Fig. 197). This kept the uppermost part of the defense at a sufficient distance from the body of the wearer to render him safe from an injury which might be caused by the indentation of the plate. This cushion was vulcanized to the metal by means of a new process, the so-called "acid cure," wherein it is not necessary to heat the metal and run

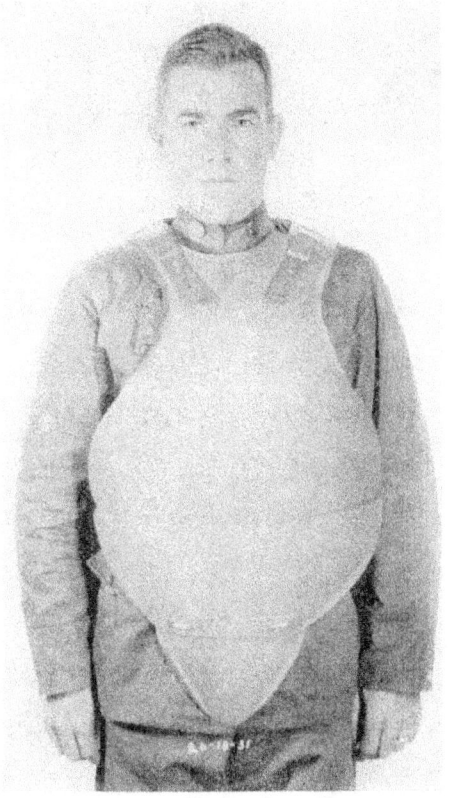 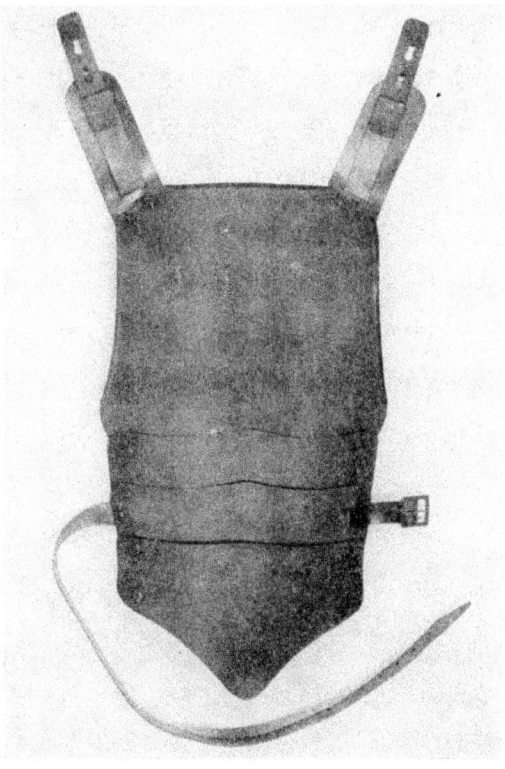

Fig. 198. Light body armor   Fig. 198A. Laminated backplate of experimental model, 1918

the risk of drawing its temper. The metal used for this defense was manganese steel .036 inch to .040 inch in thickness. Its ballistic test showed that it would uniformly resist penetration of revolver ammunition at 850 foot seconds. Such a defense would render the wearer reasonably immune to shrapnel, splinters, spent balls, and even to rifle fire, in case the bullet impinged at a considerable angle.

252 HELMETS AND BODY ARMOR

The backplate accompanying the foregoing defense (Figs. 198 and 198A) is also laminated; it is made up of a large upper plate, two intermediate pieces, and a lowermost plate or garde reins. These elements are riveted together and made interflexible by the use of slotted grooves in which the rivets can travel as in the old-fashioned "alemayne rivets." The

Fig. 199. Light body armor. Experimental backplate. American model, pressed in single piece

backplate like the breastplate is designed to suit wearers of many sizes and to be worn with a considerable degree of comfort. It is cushioned with sponge rubber (Figs. 197, 200), which protects the wearer against injuries caused by the indentation of the metal. The backplate is provided with belt straps which pass between the breastplate and the main leather straps, holding together the wide plates of this defense. A second type of backplate is shown in Figs. 199 and 200. This is modeled in a single piece and so designed that it will fit backs of various sizes. It can be worn comfortably under the pack, if need be, and furnishes a considerable degree of protection. Like the former backplate it is made of manganese steel .036 inch to .040 inch in thickness and is not penetrated by service ammunition of the automatic revolver at 850 foot seconds.

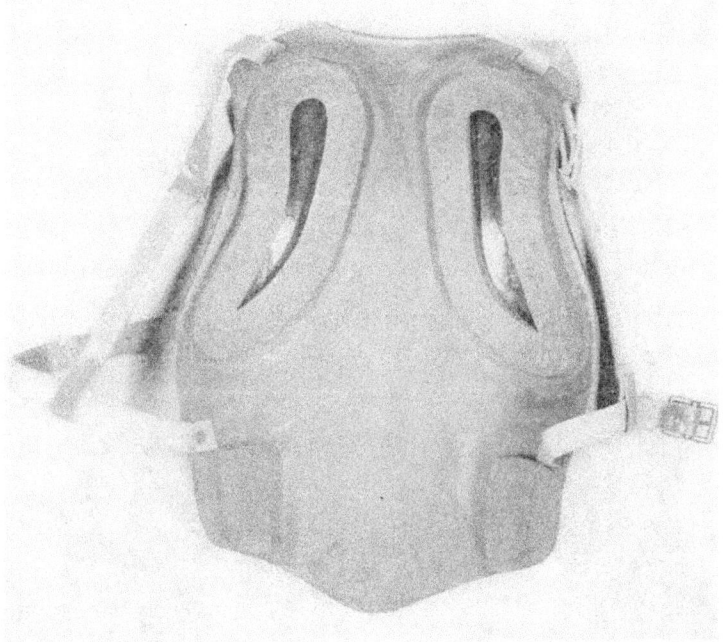

Fig. 200. Inner view of light body armor, 1918, showing cushions of sponge rubber

We note that with the experimental lot here described some of the breastplates were furnished with shoulder plates similar to those seen in Figs. 189 or 192 but of greater length. These could be so molded by the wearer that they would lie close to his shoulder blade and help to keep the defense in position without further attachment. There can be no question, however, that the corselets provided with the type of shoulder plates shown in Fig. 196 are the better from the armorer's point of view, since the other type of attachment did not prevent the breastplate from "hiking up" or from becoming detached in case the wearer threw himself on the ground or even when he made certain movements in bending. The present defense weighed, front and back together, eight and one half pounds.

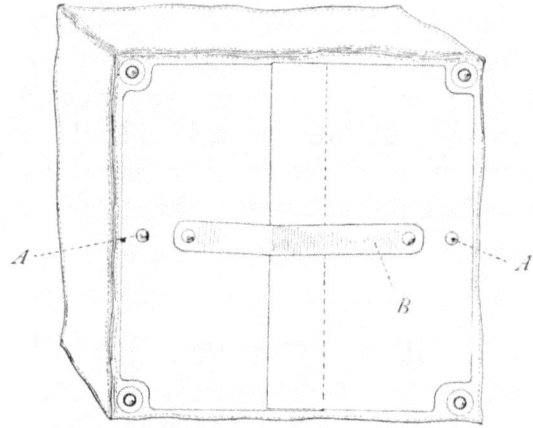

Fig. 201. Haversack or box respirator of gas mask, the back of which is reinforced by plates of steel. American model. Fall, 1918

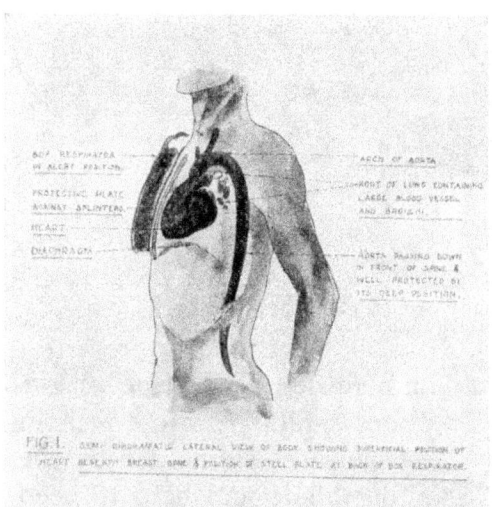

Fig. 202. Drawing provided by British Trench Warfare Division (Captain Rose), showing area protected by armored respirator of gas mask. Fall, 1918

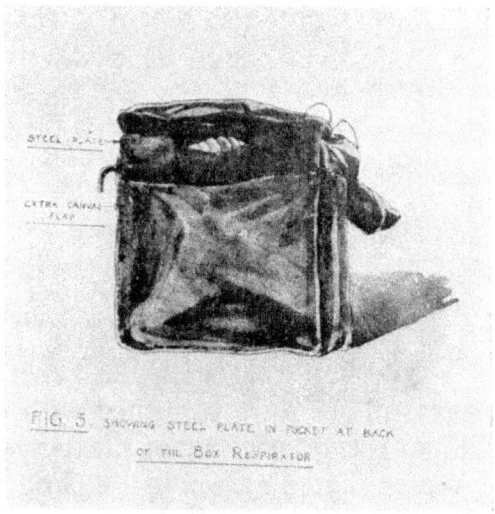

Fig. 203. Drawing provided by British Trench Warfare Division (Captain Rose), showing armored back of box respirator of gas mask. Fall, 1918

IN MODERN WARFARE

Armored Case for Gas Mask
(Fig. 201)

As a simplified form of body defense, we may here mention an armored haversack which was prepared by the Ordnance Department in Washington at the instance of the Gas Defense Service. It provided merely a false back to the existing standard gas-mask haversack and placed within it two plates of helmet steel. These were riveted to the haversack at the points "A" and held together by a leather band ("B"). The use of two plates for the pres-

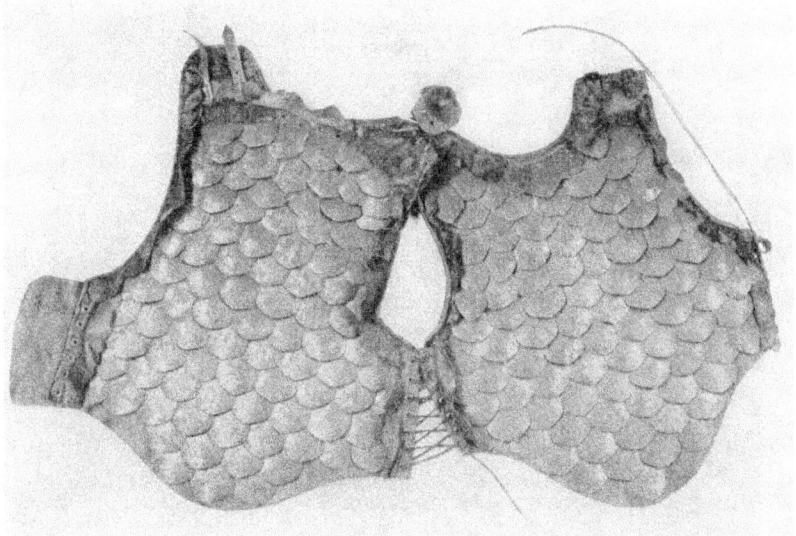

Fig. 204. Body defense or jazeran made up of overlapping scales of manganese steel

ent purpose instead of one insured a degree of flexibility to the back of the haversack, which was found to be of practical importance. Haversacks of this type were produced in number just before the close of the war. The writer subsequently learned that the British experts had considered a similar device, but had provided it with a single plate of metal instead of a pair of plates (cf. Figs. 202, 203).

Jazerans

A small experimental lot of scaled waistcoats or jazerans was also produced by the Engineering Division of the Ordnance, designated as Jazerans A and B. The former (Figs. 204, 205, 205A, 205B) was formed of overlapping scales riveted to a leather lining. The latter was made of a combination of plates and scales (Figs. 206, 206A and 206B). In the breast region these plates were so articulated that the wearer was given considerable freedom of movement in the shoulder and upper arm. This particular form was designed by the armorer Daniel Tachaux, under the supervision of the Ordnance Department.

The jazerans illustrated herewith furnished a remarkably comfortable body defense; they were worn hours at a time and under difficult conditions

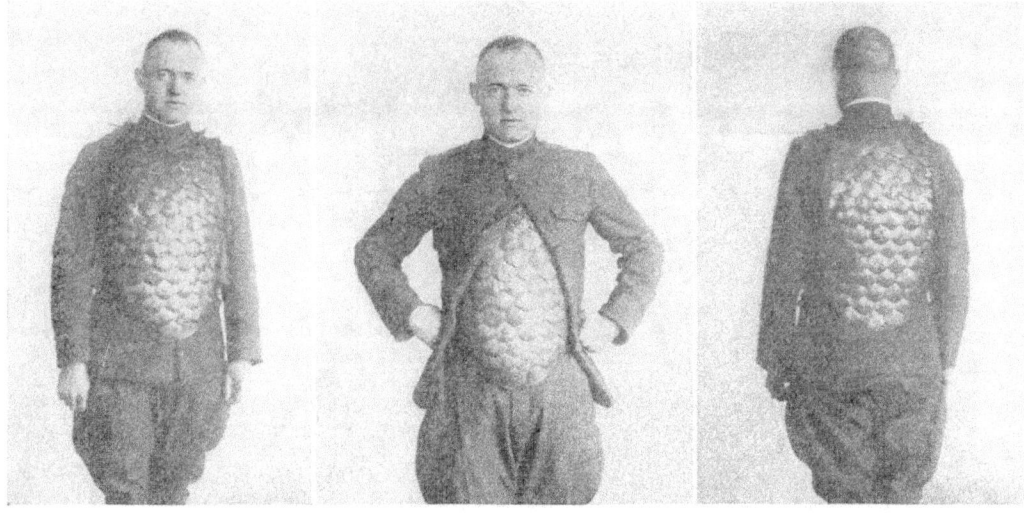

Fig. 205   Fig. 205A   Fig. 205B

Fig. 205. Scaled body defense, as actually worn

by various experimenters. The reports declare that they did not cause great discomfort, even though their weight was considerable (eleven pounds). The scales or plates of which they are made up were pressed in manganese steel of helmet thickness and were then riveted to a leather lining; they withstood the test of service ammunition with revolver. These defenses of both types were sent abroad and tested at American Headquarters. The report upon them stated that they have "excellent qualities" and were "recommended as a body armor, thoroughly practicable, no inconvenience to wearer, comfortable, silent." They were later criticized, however, as being ineffective against a bayonet thrust when the point entered

Fig. 206   Fig. 206A   Fig. 206B

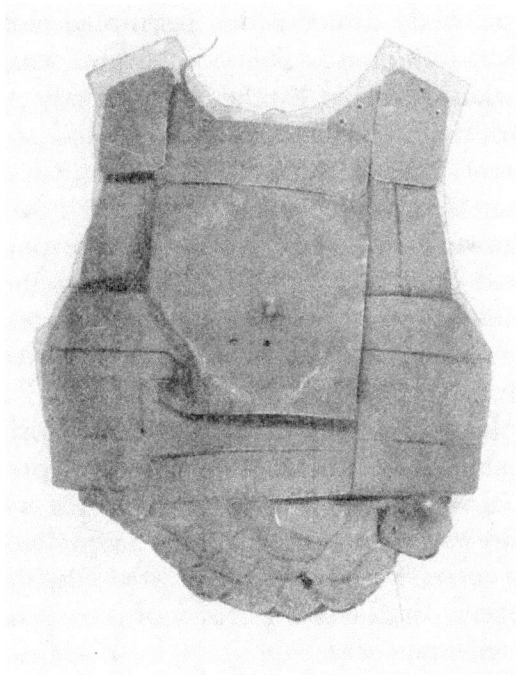

Fig. 206C

Fig. 206. Body defense formed of overlapping plates of manganese steel combined with scales as in Fig. 205. The plates of the breast defense slide together making possible free movements of shoulders. A jazeran of this type is pictured in 206C, which has been tested by automatic bullet at 850 f. s. While in this test scales became detached, no bullet succeeded in penetrating

at a great angle below. Under usual conditions, however, it is still believed, from careful tests which were made under the Ordnance's supervision, that this defense is proof to the bayonet, especially when worn under an officer's tunic, which would naturally tend to hold the scales tightly together. We can only regret that these defenses were not given a test under conditions of actual combat. Indeed, in the fighting that took place during the last weeks of the war, it is by no means improbable that jazerans of the present type could have saved many wounds and lives.

Other Body Defenses

In addition to the foregoing body shields which were made in ballistic metal and subjected to trial abroad, there should now be mentioned a number of defenses which were submitted to the experts of the Ordnance Department at various times during the war. Some of these were merely variations of types manufactured abroad, others were distinctly novel in principle, and others still were revolutionary. In the first category, we may mention the "Selecta" body armor which resembled closely the "Featherweight Body Shield" of England. This body armor was produced, though we do not know in what quantity, by the Selecta Body Armor Company of Long Island City. Another type (Figs. 207, 207A and 207B) is the jazeran of the Columbia Steel Tank Company of Kansas City, Missouri, which resembles closely the "Anglo-French" body armor shown in Fig. 70. It is somewhat longer, however, in the hip region. We understand that this defense was produced only in a small experimental lot. We should also mention the "Whyler" jazeran of steel bands or plates, these encased in fabric with the intervening joints covered again with steel strips somewhat after the plan of the Dayfield Body Shield.

In the second category, *i.e.*, of defenses novel in principle, we include a number of body shields in which springs play a prominent part—not springs in the sense in which they appear in the frame which supported the body armor of Dr. Brewster, but coiled springs having a considerable degree of elasticity. Among these, we refer to the plastron designed by Mr. Horter of the American Museum of Natural History of New York: this was scaled defense in which each scale was supported by a series of coiled springs. We refer, too, to the ingenious shield-like devices of Mr. Van Allen, which include intercoiled springs whose combined elasticity aimed to soften the impact of the projectile; to the armor of Mr. Montez, in which springs were interwoven with fabric and furnished a mattress-like defense; and to Mr. Telley's body defense, which was not unlike that of Mr. Horter. Of types of jazerans many were suggested. The Duncan model was a composite affair made up of horizontal splints of wood, steel and felt, which

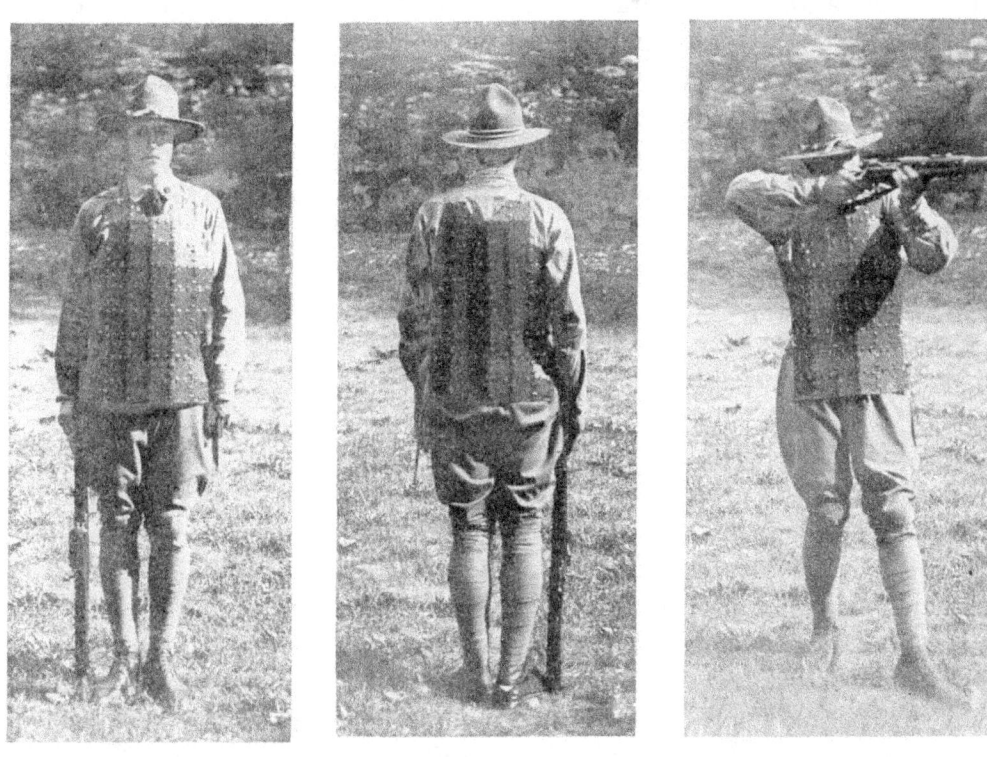

Fig. 207   Fig. 207A   Fig. 207B

Fig. 207. Body defense of small plates and links. Model of Columbia Steel Tank Co., Kansas City

formed together a long apron extending from the neck to the groin. The Horwitz "bullet-proof shield" was made of a series of spring plates ingeniously hinged together. And the Senyard body defense was a laminated jazeran made up of three sets of horizontal splints encased in fabric. Then there was the Worisbeverfeld defense, which employed elastic strips of alloy steel elaborately meshed together so as to distribute the force of the blow. We should mention here, also, the Carlson jazeran made of rectangular bits of steel; and finally the Fraser Collapsible Breast Shield, shown in Figs. 208, 208A, which is formed of vertical bands of steel ingeniously articulated and folding into compact space. This form of defense is one of the most finished of the designs submitted to the Ordnance Department. It weighs four and one half pounds, is easily worn, and when made of helmet steel affords considerable protection. Its demerit is that it does not protect a large area of the body and that, when placed in position, it separates its plates somewhat widely along their outer edges, so that if struck at an angle, it would not be difficult to penetrate.

Of defenses of a still lighter type, Prince's "Armored Belt" should be mentioned, which proves, however, to be but a variant of the abdominal armor recommended by General Adrian (see page 106). Also, Duryea's bayonet shield, which covers the body from chin to groin and is made of a woven belting, deserves notice. For bayonet practice it should prove fairly satisfactory. The smallest defense of all was the "Ryto heart protector," manufactured by a Boston company and sold in some number. It hardly was larger than the wearer's fist—entirely too small to be of practical value.

Belonging to the third type of body defenses, *i.e.*, those of revolutionary design, which were submitted to the Ordnance Department in models or drawings, we should mention the glass armor of Szmyt, which endeavors to utilize the great hardness of glass as a means of protection. In this curious device a "non-fragile" glass is placed over a cushion-like layer of cotton material and with it is encased in a fibrous material heavily paraffined. So, too, we should refer to the pneumatic armor of various inventors, Keegan and others, or the body defense suggested by the Lee Tire Company, which is really the model known in ancient times as "penny plate armor." In the recent model the metal disks were banked between layers of a fabric saturated with rubber—after the manner of certain puncture-proof automobile tires. We may finally notice a type of armor in which the device of ball-bearings plays a part and is believed to cause the plate when struck to rotate in such a way as either to deflect the projectile or else to reduce greatly its impact.

In the various forms of armor mentioned above, certain ballistic principles are found to be involved which the inventors had evidently not considered in a practical way. Thus in those defenses whose value depended upon springs, tests would have shown that the more rapid the course of a bullet the less it would be apt to be stopped by a yielding spring. For, clearly, while the spring would deaden the force of a blow given, for example, by hand thrust, it would not have time to act if the velocity of the impinging object were as great as 1,000 foot seconds; in other words,

Fig. 208　　　　　　　　　　　　　　　　Fig. 208A

Fig. 208. Experimental defense—Fraser collapsible breast shield, 1918

the degree of yielding of the spring would be so slight in this small space of time that it could have no practical effect in spending the blow. Thus, experiments made under the direction of the Munitions Inventions Board in London, referred to on pages 297 and 306, demonstrate this without a reasonable doubt.

Again, in the matter of forming a body defense of thin metal strips interlaced or encased in fabric or in rubber, the difficulty is ever that the plates themselves are too small really to stop the course of the bullet. A narrow strip of metal would be cut in two or brushed aside and the bullet would slip along on its way. The tissue in such a defense is found in practice not sufficiently resistant to be reckoned with. One cannot deny, on the other hand, that such a type of defense has some degree of merit (all defenses have, for that matter) but as we will note under the heading of silken armor, page 293, so much material would have to enter into its making that the entire weight of the defense would hardly be less than if a single plate of good ballistic steel were employed in the beginning.

So far as armor is concerned which depends for its strength on pneumatic or vacual spaces, so far at least as we have been able to determine, its ballistic value is very slight, certainly not enough to make it of practical importance; also, to construct armor of glass seems at first sight the height of absurdity. None the less, a germ of value may be hidden in such a suggestion. Thus, it is possible that steel coated with highly resistant enamels, which of course are vitreous, might prove valuable. A statement to this effect was made by the physicist, Major Nevil Monroe Hopkins, who concludes from his experiments that "the thickness of $\frac{1}{16}$ of an inch of hard enamel or even less adds to the bullet-glancing action."

(j) LEG ARMOR

Attempts to protect the infantryman by arming his arms and legs may have seemed profitless labor. In view, nevertheless, of the statistics of wounds (cf. pages 70-72), it was suggested that at least a few simple types of defenses for these regions be tried out; for statistics indicated in 1917 that infantrymen when going over the top were subjected to heavy casualties from wounds in the leg region, especially among those soldiers in the first line which attacked.

Shin-guard

An attempt accordingly was made to provide a convenient shin-guard, or greave, which might reduce perceptibly the number of injuries. Accordingly, under instructions from H. A. E. F., a considerable lot (35,000) of these greaves was prepared and sent abroad. These defenses were fitted closely to the region of the shin (Fig. 209) and did not cause inconvenience to their wearer. They were held in place by a pair of straps, one passing above the calf and one above the ankle. The plates themselves were formed of helmet steel and lined with a band of split leather. Their weight was little—about twelve ounces each. Shipment of these was made abroad, but the authorities in France subsequently decided that the degree of protection which these defenses afforded was not sufficient to warrant an extra weight being added to the soldier's equipment. No practical trial was given them.

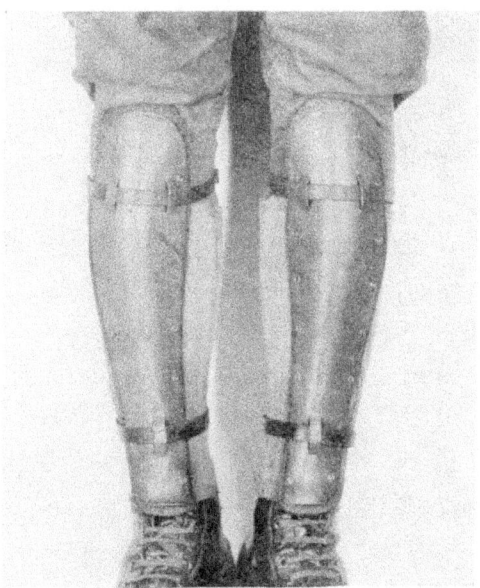

Fig. 209. Shin-guards. American experimental model, 1917

Defenses for Entire Leg

A small lot of leg armor (fifty pairs) was pressed in ballistic steel (Fig. 210) and forwarded to H. A. E. F. for trial. These defenses were fashioned after early models of well-known value, and it was found, in fact, that they could be worn with little discomfort. The upper element in these defenses was supported by a pair of straps which passed behind the thigh and by a single strap which was attached to the belt. Similar straps held the knee-plates and shin-guards in place. In view of the fact that wounds in the legs were extremely frequent, roundly 35 per cent of the number of cases treated in hospitals, there is no doubt that defenses of the present type would prevent a certain percentage of injuries—if it were found practicable to wear them under conditions of attack. When received at American Headquarters, these defenses were reported upon adversely and no further experiments were made in the direction of protecting the lower extremities. Tests made with the present ballistic models showed that they would resist a revolver bullet at ten feet. The weight of the pair of defenses for the entire leg was seven and one half pounds. They were manufactured by the Messrs. W. H. Mullins Company of Salem, Ohio.

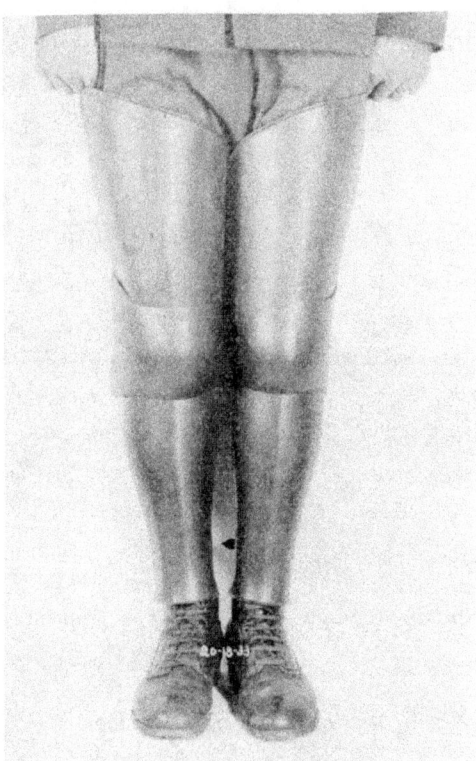

Fig. 210. Complete leg defenses. American experimental model, 1917

Statistics of casualties showed (page 71) that wounds in the upper extremities were also extremely frequent; over 30 per cent of the hospital cases, so far as figures were available (British), were found to be wounded in shoulder, arm, or hand. Hence the matter of providing arm-shields seemed worthy of attention and a few ballistic specimens were produced.

(k) ARM DEFENSES

Each arm defense (Figs. 211 and 211A) was made up of five plates, *i.e.*, for shoulder, arm, elbow, forearm and hand. These are held together by bands of leather and are attached to the arms by straps with snap catches. The weight of each arm-guard is two and one fourth pounds; this is partly supported by the soldier's shoulder strap, which, for the rest, would have to be somewhat strengthened if such a defense were generally used. The present arm-guard, we may mention, could be worn by men of different length of arm; for it may be lengthened or shortened by means of a pair

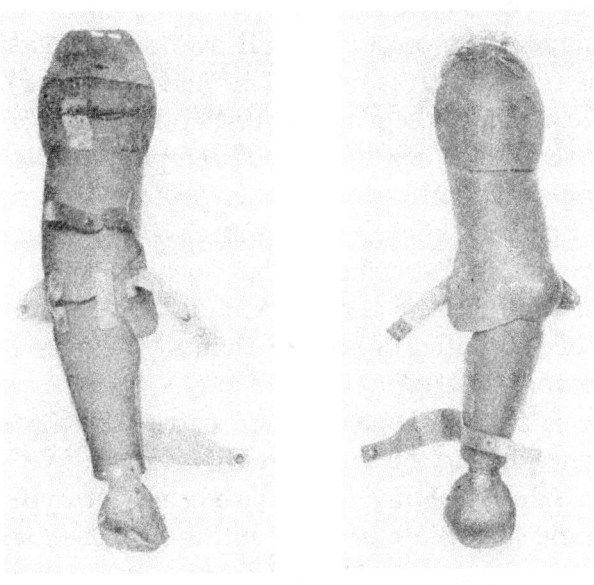

Fig. 211   Fig. 211A

Fig. 211. Arm defenses. American experimental model, 1918

of thongs which could be tied through different holes in the pieces of leather which attach the upper arm-guard to the shoulder. Tests of these arm defenses, which were made of helmet steel, showed them proof to service ammunition of the automatic revolver at ten feet. A small number (200 pairs) of these arm-shields were sent abroad for actual trial. They were not found satisfactory.

(1) AVIATOR'S ARMORED CHAIR

The problem of armoring aeroplanes touches only indirectly the theme of the present report; it belongs rather to the general subject of armor plate, *e.g.*, for shields for machine guns, cannon or ships. Nevertheless, a brief reference to the protection of aircraft may be made, since the Armor Unit of the Equipment Section was directed to prepare ballistic models of an armored chair for the aviator.

Reports from the Aircraft Service of Great Britain note that attempts have been made to armor the seats of aeroplanes; their results, however, are not known to us in detail. A statement, dated April 8, 1918, from the Armament Section of the American Expeditionary Forces (Air Service) merely states that "in the new English chasse planes the pilot seat is of steel and was shaped to protect the pilot as much as possible; also that a blue print of one type of seat is on file (in the Paris office)." And from the same source we learn that "the English Air Service is building at the present time (April, 1918), some air 'tanks.' These planes will have the motor radiator, gasoline tanks, pilot and gunner protected with 13 mm. nickel-chrome steel and 11 mm. nickel-chrome steel on the sides and on the top. Preliminary experiments have shown that such armor is a suitable protection against rifle and machine gun fire at a distance of 40 meters provided the inclination of the bullet is greater than 15 degrees to a line perpendicular to the armored plate."

The French, it further appears, were experimenting extensively with armor in aeroplanes during the early months of 1918. We learn from H. A. E. F. that "the Salmson Army Corps two seater of type LL is provided with 5 mm. chrome-steel plate beneath and is furnished with 4 mm. plates of chrome steel on the sides and on top. In this experimental plane the motor, tanks, radiator and pilot are completely protected. The pilot has but a limited vision and must peer through the slits in the armored plate. The gunner is partially protected; on the sides he is completely enclosed and below his chair he has an armored plate which may be slid aside so as to provide him with an opening through which he could shoot below him. An additional plate separates the gunner and the pilot protecting the latter when the floor plate beneath the gunner is open. This plane tested on the practice field was found safe from rifle and machine gun fire at distances greater than 400 meters." It is also to be recorded that the Italian Government has up to the present time done no more than experiment with arming the sides of an experimental plane with 7 mm. nickel-chrome steel and the top with 6 mm. As yet no tests of this machine have been made.

Accordingly, by the month of September, 1918, the Germans had been the only ones to place heavily armored aeroplanes in actual combat,

IN MODERN WARFARE

although but few of these machines appear to have been used. In certain instances they gave excellent service. In August, 1918, one of them encountered an American flying unit, destroyed several of its machines, and was responsible for the death of the American "ace," Major Lufbery. An important report dealing with the latest model German armored plane is published in the "Supplement of Aeroplane," September 11, 1918, under the heading of "Aeronautical Engineering" (Vol. 15, No. 11, pages 919-924). From this report, it is clear that the amount of armoring introduced

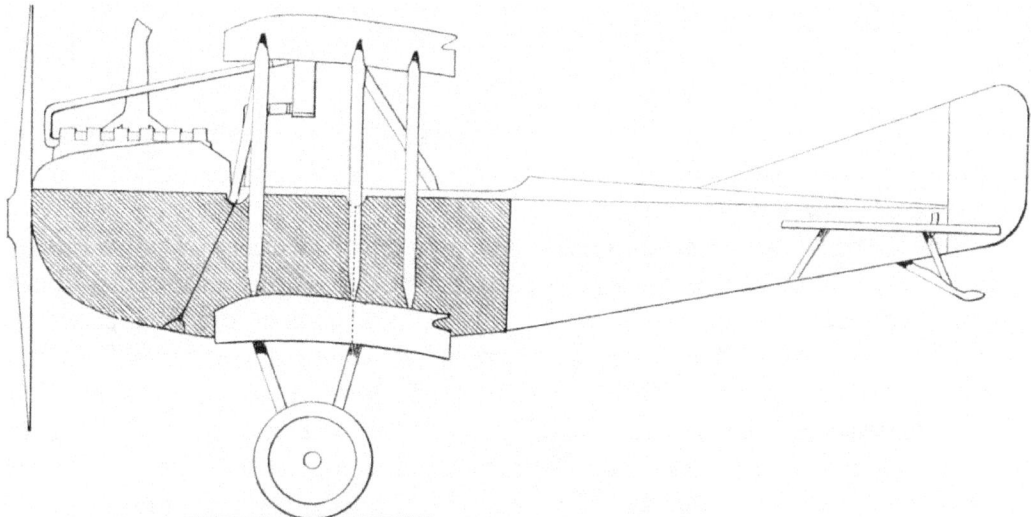

Fig. 212. Armored aeroplane. Armored areas represented by diagonal lines.
German model, 1918

by German engineers in terms of total size of the machine is quite remarkable. The machine itself, an AEG bomber, twin-engined, was not large; its fuselage measured 24 feet in length and its wings had a span of 43 feet, but its armor weighed no less than 880 pounds! The armored plates were 5.1 mm. in thickness and they covered a total area of 106 square feet. The present drawing (Fig. 212) indicates the position of the armor on each side of the plane, where it is made up of three plates. Three additional plates form the bottom of the fuselage; there is also an armored bulkhead at the back of the gunner's cockpit. Tests were made to determine the ballistic value of this armor, as shown in the following table:

Ammunition	Degrees Angle to Normal	Yards Safe Range	Yards Unsafe Range
German Armor-Piercing	0		600
	15	500	400
	30	400	300
Mark VII Armor-Piercing	0	700	600
	15	400	300
	30	300	200
German Spitze	0	150	100
	15	100	50
	30	50	
Mark VII	0	50	
	15	50	
	30	50	

From this data the plane is evidently too lightly armored to afford protection against British armor-piercing bullets fired from the ground at a lower height than 700 yards.

The German plane here described appears to have been made more or less for experimental use, since it was found that the armor formed no part of the essential framework of the fuselage. A standard plane appears to have been merely opened up and the present armored plates fitted in place by means of set screws attached to clips which in turn were clamped to the framework of the machine. In general, of course, the great weight of armor required for the protection of such a plane would so retard its movements that it would be apt to fall an easy victim to anti-aircraft guns.

The American authorities have as yet, it appears, made no definite experiments with armored planes (September 29). The suggestion to provide an armored chair for a de Haviland machine came recently to the Equipment Section of the Engineering Division through Colonel MacFarland, chief of the Aeroplane Armament Section. Such a chair was modeled at the armor workshop at the end of September, 1918 (Fig. 213). It received the comments of instructors at the Mineola school and after certain changes it was fitted in the fuselage of the de Haviland car at the Standard Aircraft Corporation works at Elizabeth, New Jersey. The model then was forwarded to the W. H. Mullins Company of Salem, Ohio (October 11) for manufacture. The plates furnished the Mullins Company were .3 inch thick; they were of a nickel-molybdenum alloy (see page 279) recommended by Dr. George W. Sargent, metallurgical consultant of the Ordnance Department.

IN MODERN WARFARE

In preparing the present chair, the effort was made to furnish the pilot of the plane the greatest degree of protection at the cost of the least weight of metal. To this end the chair fitted the back and shoulders of the pilot very much as would a steel backplate. The sides of the chair were raised so as to protect the thighs and the small of his back so far as this could be

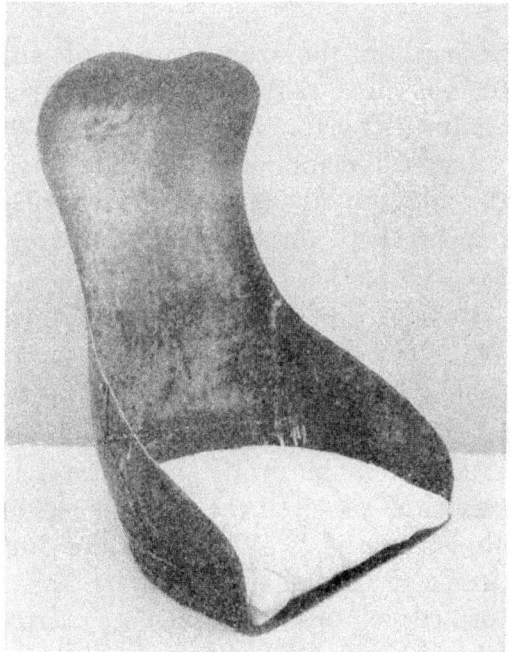

Fig. 213. Aviator's armored chair. Experimental model, American, 1918

done without interfering with the free movements of his arms in operating the plane. In view of the fact that by far the greater number of casualties is due to gunfire from below and from the back of the aviator, it is believed that such a defense would have had considerable value. Tests with this chair were expected to show it would resist the German A. P. bullet at fifty yards. The work of manufacture was completed just as the war ended.

VI

STEEL USED FOR ARMOR—CAN OTHER METAL THAN STEEL BE USED FOR THIS PURPOSE?

STEEL to be used in the manufacture of armor should be extremely hard, yet must not shatter when struck by a projectile. The latter quality is by far the more difficult to control; for if by altering its chemical components an alloy is obtained which is extraordinarily hard, and many alloys can be given this physical character, it is usually found to break to pieces when strained beyond its limit of resistance.

Early Armor Plate

It is well known that some if not much of the armor of antiquity was made of good metal and highly resistant; indeed, the armorers' "companies" laid the greatest stress, naturally, upon the ballistic value of their armor. Guilds in many cases required the armorer to "hall-mark" his work after it had been subjected to tests at or under the direction of the guildhall. In some cases tests of graded severity were prescribed for armor of "single," "double," or "triple" proof (cf. page 41). Up to the present time, however, no studies have been undertaken to show what had been accomplished in the metallurgy of armor in earlier centuries. Hence at the instance of the writer, Professor William Campbell of Columbia University examined (giving his time unstintingly in behalf of our work) some two score fragments of ancient armor with a view of obtaining hints which might be used in modern work. His studies showed that there existed a great range in the metallurgical results of the early workers, a conclusion which was not unexpected in view of the fact that the bits of armor submitted to him were made during various periods (roundly, from 1390 to 1600) and at various places, by armorers of different degrees of skill. Dr. Campbell determined, in a number of cases, that the ancient armor was made in the fashion of the best Damascus blades; the plate was forged out of a bloom, folded in two, reheated to welding point, and hammered out again. By this procedure it came about that the plate of armor was built up of thin layers of harder and softer metal interwoven. This indicated, of course, that a highly resistant material was secured which at the same time did not shatter when struck. The metallurgical explanation of the well-known virtues of the armor of Milan of the fifteenth century was also this, that the plate of metal was highly carburized at the surface, while its back remained relatively soft; the metal then would resist the entrance of a projectile but it would not shatter. How this result was obtained is another story; the high carbon content at the surface of the plate was obviously obtained by some process of cementation or case hardening, but in what way this could be brought about to the needed degree without carburizing the remainder of the plate is by no means clear. Certainly, however, the Milanese plates were tempered, as indeed the old records show, by quenching the heated plate in cold water. In a word, the experience of centuries in armor making appears to have shown that a plate should be given a hard surface—as hard as possible—and that it should be backed with soft metal.* It may be mentioned incidentally that it is the development of this system which has given rise to the blade of the Japanese sword, which practically and metallurgically considered is the best material of its kind which has ever been produced.

The great artists of the Middle Ages, we are reasonably sure, did not know that the superiority of one kind of iron over another was due to specific differences in the chemical and physical nature of the metal itself. They had no means of dividing up alloys into their component parts and ascertaining the effects of certain ingredients which would make the steel more resistant, yet which would not gravely interfere with its workable quality. They knew in practice, however, that metal from a certain mine was better than another for the use of the armorer. Thus, English iron produced armor of poor quality, but iron from Innsbruck was long famous. There can be no doubt that metal which they found best for their purpose was a natural alloy; hence it served for the making of steel just as the copper of certain mines which contained cobalt or tin was used in much earlier times for the manufacture of the best grades of bronze swords and

* Mr. William H. Taylor believes, none the less, that "Laminated plates have no advantage over solid plates" (1917).

armor. The mediaeval armorer understood clearly, on the other hand, the importance of many technical processes which seem to be quite modern. In the annealing of steel he was well posted. He had no little knowledge concerning its tempering and "drawing its temper" when brittleness was to be removed. He knew, for example, that the higher the temperature he used in his technical processes, the less brittle his material was apt to become; *i.e.*, he burned out his excess carbon. He understood practically the point in temperature when the structure of his material became again granular (from 600 to 650 degrees Centigrade). If he hammered his steel at temperatures above the critical range, he found that its grain became smaller; his work was then more difficult and his steel became stronger but not harder. When he hammered out his metal cold, and much of the earlier work appears to have been done in this way, he noted that the grains in the steel were drawn out and elongated in the direction of the working, creating a harder material, stronger, but proportionally less ductile. He observed, also, that the higher the temperature to which he brought his metal the coarser became its grain. He did not know the properties of the large polygonal grains of iron called in our modern jargon, *ferrite*. Nor did he know the properties of the mechanical mixture of iron and iron carbide, Fe_3C, which shows under a lens a pearly granulation (*pearlite*). So far as carbon was concerned he knew this only in a practical way, for he found that the iron acquired certain virtues in armor making when it had been produced by the aid of a blast from charcoal fire. He "cemented" or "case hardened" his plates by packing them in a fireproof box filled with waste scraps of leather (cyaniding) and subjected them apparently for a long time to heat of a relatively low temperature.

In a word, the maker in olden times produced in his best workshops an armor plate which, while decidedly inferior to the latest alloys, was nevertheless surprisingly good. In terms of the modern (standard English) helmet-metal, we believe that it was about 70 per cent as resistant.

Steel for Modern Armor

The metallurgist today examines with surprise plates of ancient armor produced by cementation and declares that this process is not reproduced today in a plate of this degree of thinness; for by any modern process of case hardening, the carbon would penetrate not merely the outer layer of the plate but its entire thickness. A plate, in other words, which has passed through the modern process of cementation is found of no greater ballistic value, according to the studies of Professor Howe, than a plate of steel made in open hearth or by electric furnace. Hence little encouragement can be given to him who aims to restore the physical type of metal used in ancient times for body armor. Not, of course, but that heavy plates of steel could be had in which the surface was made extremely hard by cementation or other processes; but the difficulty appears so soon as one attempts to reduce such a plate, with its brittle veneer and its back of soft steel, into dimensions of thinness. It has been suggested that the armorer may easily have cemented his plates in a heavier condition and then worked them down by hand. But this process could hardly be developed commercially today.

Alloy for Helmet and Body Armor, a New Development

The development of alloy plate has until recently been undertaken only for ship's armor, rifle shields and similar heavy defenses. When, accordingly, at the beginning of the war, a demand suddenly arose for light armor plate, the manufacturer of steel was at a loss to know precisely what type of steel should be recommended. In fact, as noted on page 80, the Adrian helmet was made of nothing more efficient than a low carbon steel. This had at least the merit of being fairly resistant; and it did not shatter when struck by a bullet. Metallurgists, however, soon realized that alloys could be obtained in thin sheets which offered far greater resistance than low carbon steel. Among them two main types were speedily developed. The first was the manganese steel adopted by the English, the Americans, and in the latest days the French. This alloy had been developed for other uses as early as 1900 by a well-known manufacturer in Sheffield, Sir Robert Hadfield. It had also been produced in the United States with certain variants by the Manganese Steel Shoe and Rail Company, under patents of Messrs. Kellogg and Aigeltinger. The second alloy is known as German silicon steel, which shortly appeared in German helmets and body armor.

The characteristics of these steels may be reviewed briefly.

Manganese steel (cf. I in the tabular analysis opposite page 274) is an open hearth basic alloy;* it is extremely tough in fiber, is not shattered when struck by a bullet but clings to it, suffering indentation. Thus a helmet .036 inch in thickness will readily resist a revolver bullet, jacketed, weighing 230 grains when traveling at the rate of 650 foot seconds; in many cases

* Cf. esp. Guillet, Réunion de membres français et belges de l'association internationale des méthodes d'essais; procès-verbal de la séance du 25 avril, 1903, pp. 71-88.

it will not be penetrated by the same bullet when traveling at 850 foot seconds. Its indentation, however, at the point of impact is often very great. In the usual test (600 foot seconds) it indents to a depth of $7/10$ to $9/10$ of an inch, measured from the original contour of the surface. In some cases the indentation will be one inch deep, or about $1\frac{1}{4}$ inches deep when struck by a similar bullet traveling at the rate of 850 foot seconds. Occasionally such a helmet will withstand a shot at the rate of 1,000 foot seconds, but its indentation then becomes hopelessly deep ($1\frac{1}{2}$ inches). When perforated the ball slips through the steel and is apt to leave behind only an irregular tear. In such cases, however, the deforming of the helmet would probably produce a fatal wound. The extraordinary feature of the present manganese alloy is that, while extremely resistant, it may be pressed into such a form as the British helmet without serious breakage—sometimes less than 2 per cent of the plates rupturing in the operation—and all this without the need of annealing or without heat treatment and "drawing" after having been pressed into a helmet. In this regard it differs from all other alloys used in modern armor. Moreover, while other alloys heated and quenched in cold water become brittle, manganese steel then acquires a condition best suited for stamping into shapes; that is, in an hydraulic press—not hammered into shape, for then it soon regains its brittleness, cracking and breaking. In fact, it is known that "the colder the water in which the manganese steel is quenched, the more perfectly it becomes annealed for the armorer's work" (Sir Robert Hadfield). It is the toughness of the manganese alloy which originally caused it to be developed in the steel industry, where it was used, for example, in the shoes of brakes where resistance to friction is of prime importance. It should be noted that this extraordinary alloy occurs in (at least) two types, one having a low degree of manganese, centering about 1 per cent, the other having a high degree, centering about 13 per cent. In the former type of manganese alloy the carbon content is about .40, and in the latter type this rises to about 1.3. Ballistically speaking, no manganese alloy is seriously to be considered in the intervening range. Elaborate experiments carried on under the auspices of the Munitions Inventions Board of London have demonstrated that while the higher manganese resists projectiles admirably in thin plates of metal, it does not give as satisfactory results in heavier plates, say from .060 inch, as some of the alloys later to be noted. While not an ideal material for use in light armor on account of its liability to deep indentation, its virtues of easy pressing and of requiring no time-consuming and delicate processes in heat treatment have caused it to be used extensively. It is especially good as a medium for resisting projectiles of low velocity.*

Silicon-Nickel Steel

The second type of alloy used largely for helmets and body armor (cf. table 3, opposite page 274) appears under two formulae: in the first of these (A) the carbon content is about one third higher and the manganese and silicon about one third lower. In the first formula the amount of nickel is about 50 per cent lower. The ballistic results given by these alloys are not widely different, though the second alloy (B), which has the higher nickel and silicon content, is somewhat the better. It is believed that the Germans developed formula A, in which the carbon content is higher, on account of the difficulty they experienced in getting nickel in sufficient quantity. The present armor alloy appears to be a combination of the regular silicon alloy which is well known in the manufacture of automobile springs, ring gears, etc., and a nickel steel which has been also largely developed in the automobile industry. In this combination an effort has been made to produce a sound steel of a high elastic limit and of great tensile strength, characteristics present in the silicon steel proper, to which are added certain advantages known in a nickel alloy. Nickel, it appears, has the effect of making the heat-treating processes less delicate to apply, for in a physical way, this element apparently dissolves in iron in various degrees, instead of merely mixing with it in a granular way. Then, too, it does not tend to segregate and produce inequalities; it has even the effect of hindering the segregation of other elements and thus keeps them from producing alloys which would be irregular in quality. The present alloy, while harder than carbon steel, has the further advantage that it can be machined and worked hot by forging; moreover, it does not require the closest attention during the processes of heat treatment so long as its nickel content does not exceed 4 per cent. It can be pressed (hot) and the Germans, judging from their product, were able to get excellent results even in a drawing operation which was a considerably deeper one than the English helmet demanded. They have, moreover, been able to get the weight of the metal well into the crown of the helmet, the thinning out in this region being rarely greater than .005 inch. Details in the annealing and heat treatment of this steel as practised by the

---

* Against shrapnel bullets 41 to the pound in plate of 18 gauge (.048 inch) it is proof at 1,100 foot seconds; 20 gauge (.036 inch) at 900 foot seconds; 22 gauge (.028 inch) at 700 to 800 foot seconds.

Germans are not known to us. Ballistic tests upon helmets and breastplates made of this steel are referred to on pages 138 and 182. It is debated whether the present alloy is better for helmet manufacturing than manganese steel. In thicker plates the silicon-nickel steel (.128 mm.) has about the same ballistic results as the American nickel-manganese-vanadium steel. It may finally be remarked that the Germans have apparently been satisfied with their steel for its present purpose and they have made large issues of it in the form of helmets and heavy breastplates.

Additional Armor Alloys

A chrome-nickel-vanadium steel whose analysis is shown in specimen No. 2 in the table opposite page 274, was early considered in the making of the American helmet. Manufacturers, however, found it extremely difficult to press into the required form, the plates rupturing in large numbers. The Columbian Enameling and Stamping Company, however, succeeded in pressing a small lot of helmets in this steel, and early in 1918, fourteen helmets were transmitted to Professor Henry M. Howe, metallurgist of the Ordnance Department, for ballistic examination. These gave results which while indecisive were encouraging, for they indicated that when the heat treatment was accurately prescribed, helmets of this alloy might be made which would stop a bullet at 1,000 foot seconds without causing severe indentation of the metal. Hence additional experiments were recommended; in November, 1918, Messrs. Budd and Company succeeded in pressing a number of helmets of this steel and the Columbian Company produced specimens in alloy having the same analysis. These will shortly be tested by Professor Howe.

A chrome-nickel steel, lacking, however, vanadium (analysis shown in No. 3, table opposite page 274), was also considered for use in the American helmet. The Columbian Enameling Company had again the distinction of producing the best dies and the best results in this work, their helmets showing none of the radial ridges or wrinkles which appeared in the experimental die-work undertaken elsewhere.* Nor was it found necessary to use

---

* In this connection, one may refer to the dies developed by the experts of the Columbian Enameling Company. As shown in Figs. 214 and 214A, the first die formed the alloy plate into the shape of a comparatively shallow saucer, its border being quite flat (Fig. 214 at I). The next die extended the crown of the helmet to its needed depth (Section II) and caused the brim of the helmet to be more inclined, producing the effect of what the manufacturer calls "a stoving die." By this means

a stoving die or drop hammer to eliminate the wrinkles from the wall of the helmet. The pressing was done in from two to three operations. Actual tests made upon these helmets did not give the best results. They failed to keep out a standard bullet at 950 foot seconds nor did they yield as good results at 850 to 900 foot seconds as the manganese helmets. These results, it must be admitted, were obtained upon a number of helmets too small to constitute a final test. Hence, 500 additional helmet shells are being pressed in this alloy at the direction of Dr. Howe, who will supervise the necessary tests upon them.

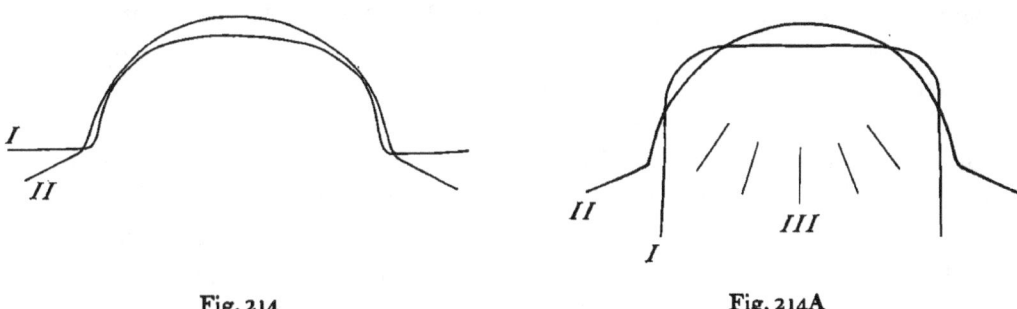

Fig. 214.   Fig. 214A

Fig. 214. Sections of dies for pressing British-American helmet model. (Faulty model shown in 214A)

The third alloy which has been employed for American helmets is the nickel-manganese steel developed by Mr. W. H. Baker of the Universal Rolling Mills Company (specimen No. 4 in table opposite page 274). This steel, again, was successfully pressed into British style helmets by the Columbian Enameling and Stamping Company and the Government accepted

wrinkling was avoided and at the same time the metal was enabled to flow inward so that the crown of the helmet was not thinned out—in fact, the Columbian Company was the only pressing concern which was able to keep the original thickness of the metal plate at the crown of the helmet. Die makers of other firms were inclined to secure the desired depth of the helmet practically by a single draw, as indicated in Fig. 214A at I. Their subsequent operation then merely gave the final contour to the helmet by rounding it out, as shown in Section II. It was in this stage of pressing that the wrinkles appeared at the points III. In this connection, it was found that the behavior of an alloy like the present one, chrome-nickel, is quite unlike the manganese. The former tends to spring away from the punch in the pressing operation, the latter clings to it.

them to the number of about one quarter of a million. For ballistic data upon this lot, we are indebted to the studies of Professor Howe, who showed that these helmets were on an average of high merit:* 90 per cent of them passed test with standard automatic ammunition (850 foot seconds) and showed a degree of indentation decidedly less than in manganese helmets. Thus, while at 800 foot seconds the latter indented to the degree of 1.25 inches, the nickel manganese indented only to the point of 1.02 inches; at 850 foot seconds the depth of indentation was as 1.33 to 1.17 inches. The only practical difficulty in producing helmets in this alloy, Professor Howe explained, lay in their heat treatment, for there always existed the possibility, e.g., that through the carelessness of an individual operator, a lot of helmets of this steel might not be given the temperature prescribed; hence they would shatter when tested. A number of instances of this kind were recorded. None appeared, however, in a lot of 200 helmets chosen from various heats and tested in the presence of the writer; the results then obtained were excellent, especially in the matter of depth of indentation. In numerous cases, the testing mark on the helmet showed hardly more than a deep thumb-print; in fact, many helmets thus tested were not rejected but finished for shipment overseas, having in the eyes of an expert an added value for having withstood the required test so successfully. It goes without saying, however, that the production of helmets in nickel-manganese steel could hardly be carried on at the same rate as in manganese steel. The former require greater care in pressing and very considerable care in heat treatment; on these accounts they would, incidentally, be more expensive to produce. In the end, it may be fairly queried whether the slightly improved results obtained with the Baker alloy compensated either the Government or the manufacturer for continuing its use in helmet making. If its ballistic value were 30 per cent better than that of manganese steel, there would of course be no question that an increased expense were warranted and a greater loss of time in manufacture.†

* At 1,000 foot seconds 80 per cent failed; at 950, 50 per cent; 900, 25 per cent; 850, 10 per cent.

† Since the foregoing paragraphs were written an admirable report has been received from Mr. W. J. Wrighton, of the Armor Committee, C. N. R., summarizing the results of his tests on various types of helmet steel entrusted him by Professor H. M. Howe, chairman of the Metallurgical Section of the Council of National Research. The tests were made upon a large series of helmets, which were pressed for the purpose by the Budd Manufacturing Company in ten kinds of alloy steel of .036 inch

A chrome-molybdenum alloy and a nickel-molybdenum alloy, both developed by Dr. G. W. Sargent, metallurgist of the Ordnance Department (specimens Nos. 7 and 8 in table opposite page 274), we believe, represent an important advance in the history of American armor plate. These have not as yet reached the stage of production but the results upon them show that they are about one third stronger than any of the preceding alloys; at a thickness of $7/16$ of an inch, they will resist an armor-piercing bullet at 2,700 foot seconds. Either material can be pressed and machined, but whether they can be successfully pressed into so deep a shape as a helmet remains undetermined. From the first experiments made by the Ordnance

thickness. Mr. Wrighton's results, which emphasize again the value of Baker's nickel-manganese steel for helmet work, are summarized as follows:

Helmet steels classified in order of their ballistic value and ease of manufacture. Cf. Table opposite p. 274 for analysis of a number of the present alloys. Others I have omitted in the present note.

Order	Ballistic Resistance	Degree of Indentation	Ease of Pressing	Range of Treatment	Ease of Securing Material	Cost of Manufacture
1	Baker's nickel-manganese	Nickel-manganese	Regular manganese	Regular manganese (requires no treatment)	Regular manganese	Regular manganese
2	Silicon-nickel A		Nickel-manganese	Nickel-manganese	Nickel-manganese	Nickel-manganese
3					Nickel-chrome 3	Nickel-chrome 3
4			Silicon-nickel A	Silicon-nickel A		
5		Nickel-chrome 3		Nickel-chrome 3		
6	Nickel-chrome 3		Chrome-nickel 3			
7		Silicon-nickel B				
8	Regular manganese	Silicon-nickel A		Silicon-nickel B		
9	Silicon-nickel B	Regular manganese	Silicon-nickel B	Regular manganese		
10	Chrome-manganese	Chrome-manganese	Chrome-manganese			

Department it seems doubtful if helmets can be produced commercially from these alloys; from nickel-molybdenum this may be accomplished but probably not from chrome-molybdenum.

Another alloy to be recorded is the zirconium steel developed by Mr. William Smith of the Ford Motor Company of Detroit. This alloy (specimen 10 in the table) has also not reached the stage of production but it has given very promising tests. Such a steel, it is claimed, will stop an armor-piercing rifle bullet at 2,750 foot seconds in a plate .375 inch in thickness at a distance of fifty yards. As yet little is known as to the degree to which this alloy may be pressed into the shape of a helmet; the only experiments in this direction made by the Ordnance Department were failures. All sheets cracked, according to the testimony of Lieutenant Kienbusch of the Armor Unit of the Ordnance.

Summarizing the situation of our work upon ballistic alloys, it is hardly too much to say that, had the war been continued another six months, our armor plate* would have improved to an appreciable degree. When the war began, the field was almost a new one in so far as armor in thin plates was concerned. To stop an armor-piercing bullet then required a thickness of an inch and a quarter of steel or about three quarters of an inch of chrome-nickel steel; in the last months of the war the same result could be had by an alloy of about three eighths of an inch in thickness. Thanks to similar advances, it might reasonably have been expected that a soldier's helmet having the same ballistic merit as the present one could have been made at least 20 per cent lighter or, if it retained its present weight, it might regularly have resisted the impact of the standard bullet at 1,200 foot seconds.

Can Alloys Other Than Steel Be Used in Armor Making?

The question remains to be answered whether any material or alloy other than steel may be used for armor. In this direction, one would naturally seek a material which shall be highly resistant, so that it will stop a missile; it must also possess the property of elongation to such a degree that it will permit the necessary shapes of armor to be pressed. The material also shall not shatter; and it should be light to carry—a feature of great

* A final steel to be mentioned is a tungsten alloy very recently developed by the experts of the Remington Typewriter Company. This, assuming that the tests are accurately reported, resists an armor-piercing bullet at a hundred yards in a plate no thicker than .20 inch. It is extremely unlikely that this alloy can be pressed into helmets; but as a material for body defenses it may well prove of great value.

importance. It must be frankly admitted at the outset that up to the present time no material for armor is forthcoming to replace alloy steel, although many combinations of likely elements have been tested. The alloy known as stellite, developed by an American chemist, Elwood Haynes, has the property of hardness to an extraordinary degree; unhappily, however, it is utterly refractory; it cannot be pressed and it shatters when struck, hence its use in armor is not for a moment to be considered. Efforts have also been made to develop aluminum compounds (*e.g.*, duralumin and others) which under some conditions are extremely hard. Thus an alloy known as navalthen was used experimentally in armor work, according to information received from an armor specialist in England, M. Félix Joubert. It was finally decided, however, that this material weight for weight did not give as promising results as steel. The Germans, also, attempted to develop an aluminum alloy, and they used this in ballistic plates which were backed with steel. This armor was given tests which it appeared to pass brilliantly. Hence efforts were made by the British Government to determine its nature and to learn the details of its manufacture. Specimens were accordingly procured, but the tests of these plates in England proved disappointing. In one case a German shield made of the new combination was found to owe its main value to the metal to which the aluminum alloy was attached. This turned out to be an extremely good tungsten steel which alone would have given an excellent test as armor plate.

The two-layered condition above noted in the German plate is but a reappearance of the ancient principle (cf. page 271) that the best armor should have an outer "skin" of extreme hardness, which prevents the entrance of a missile, while the inner substance of the plate should be tenacious and prevent the armor from shattering. This principle should again be referred to, since suggestions are constantly made by students of armor that enamels of various types might profitably be used for coating armor plates.

VII

SOFT ARMOR: ITS BEGINNING, DEVELOPMENT, AND POSSIBLE VALUE

SOFT materials made up in various ways for personal defense were unquestionably used at earlier periods than mail or plate armor, and they followed more numerous lines of development; for the principle is a primitive one which attempts to stop or deaden the effect of a blow by presenting a yielding surface. A cushion which dissipated the force of a blow was probably known even to Stone Age man, who may well have had an armor built up of numerous layers of furry hides. The underlying principle in such a type of defense was not that any of its component elements would be proof to the point of an arrow or spear, but that it would be at least sufficiently resistant to diffuse the impact over a large surface and thus by producing a constantly increasing strain upon the impinging weapon to bring it finally to a standstill.* To make this meaning clearer, let us assume that the resistance of a piece of soft armor is represented by some number, say 100, at the point A upon which a projectile impinges; by the time the projectile has produced a strain of, say, 75, the material at this point becomes pushed in and the strain upon it is relieved; the strain thereupon is carried along the soft material centrifugally to a circle of neighboring points (B-B-B-) which in turn, of course, combine to resist the impinging object. Each of these points in turn has a resistance equal, say, to the original number 100. Hence it is clear that by the time the points B respond to the need of point A, the entire resistance of the soft armor to the original impact has become much greater than the original resistance of the armor at the point A. Continuing our illustration: the strain of a projectile upon the soft material proceeds centrifugally, *i.e.*, at all points, from one circle of elements to the next, each of which in

* We here assume that the projectile is not traveling so rapidly that it perforates the soft armor before it has time to operate in the manner we have described.

IN MODERN WARFARE

turn expands the degree of resistance. So it comes about in the end that the resistance of the sum of the various points becomes greater than the force exerted upon them by the missile, which thereupon comes to a stop. Accord-

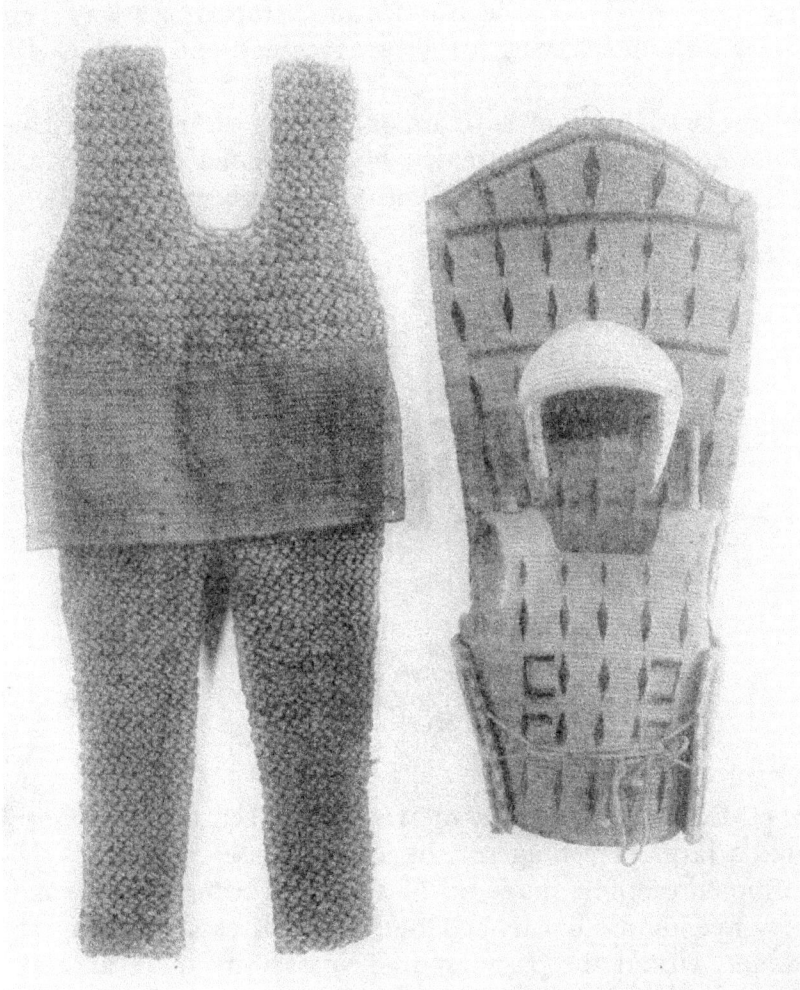

Fig. 215. Armor of cocoa fiber. Gilbert Islands, early nineteenth century.
Specimens in American Museum of Natural History

ingly, it is not the tenacity of one element, in such a piece of soft armor, which causes this defense to be strong, but rather the way in which the region which is in danger of penetration is able to draw to itself the help of another part or zone of the protecting surface. We do not mean of course to imply that in this particular principle we are dealing with physical factors which are other than those encountered in armor plate. It is merely that in the case of soft armor the processes are magnified to such a degree that we can interpret them simply. The behavior of manganese steel in which an impinging bullet produces a deep indentation forms in a way a connecting link between an armor having a rigid surface and one in which the surface is soft.

As to the actual use of soft armor: Armor of leather in the state of "raw" hide or in especially treated and hardened condition (*e.g.*, from boiling) is known from classical antiquity. It became highly developed

Fig. 216. Lining for helmet (or for chain mail hood). Swiss, fifteenth century. From Civic Armory in Lucerne. Riggs Collection, Metropolitan Museum of Art

during the Middle Ages, and in the fourteenth century, it appears to have constituted a large percentage of the armor in use.

An armored costume made up of stuff of various kinds was known at least thirty-five hundred years ago, and it is still used by savages. The Gilbert Islanders within the past hundred years wore quite an elaborate defense (Fig. 215) woven and knotted together in strands of cocoanut fiber. Even in Europe armor made of rope occurred until at a comparatively late time, often as a protective lining for metal armor. We show herewith (Fig. 216) a helmet lining made of a coil of rope which was used in Switzerland as late as the fifteenth century. In the Far East, silk was discovered to be extremely useful in a defensive costume, certainly at the beginning of the Christian era. As early as the year 600, the Chinese developed armor of padded silk and a similar type of military costume shortly appeared at other points in the Orient. Thus in Japan it is known from the seventh century. Here it was further modified; it became reinforced with steel splints, scales, or small laminae, and, in this condition, it was employed, to a certain degree at least, as late as 1870. Such armor, formed as a complex of silken braid and steel laminae, resisted admirably sword, spear, or war-arrow.

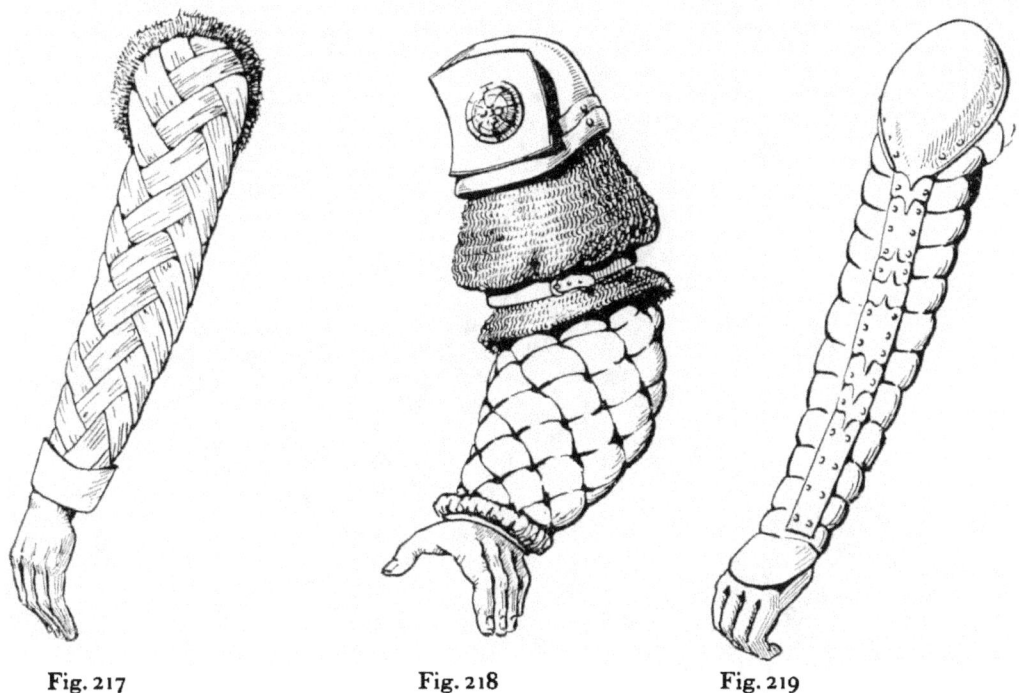

Fig. 217 Fig. 218 Fig. 219

Figs. 217 to 219. Arm defenses, woven and tufted, sixteenth century, German

Fig. 217. From altar painting in Stuttgart by Elinger
Fig. 218. From painting in Munich by Anton von Worms
Fig. 219. From sculpture by Veit Stoss, 1500, Nuremberg

Padded costumes of silk, cotton or linen appear to have been used until comparatively modern times in almost every country. In Germany quilted costumes for defense were highly developed as early as the beginning of the sixteenth century, either as stuff alone or combined with armor of plate and chain (Figs. 217, 218 and 219). Sometimes this soft armor took the form of interlaced bands of tissue which protected the wearer admirably yet gave him no little freedom of movement. In Russia a heavily quilted costume was used until the seventeenth century—and even later. Of this type of armor, shown in Fig. 220, we observe, by the way, a neck defense which resembles closely the silken necklet of the British of 1917 (Fig. 67). Silk combined with canvas and splints of steel formed the

Fig. 220. Armor of woven material, stuffed and quilted. Russian, about 1560

favorite body defense (brigandines) of southern Europe during the fourteenth, fifteenth and sixteenth centuries. In this region, too, but especially in northern Europe, various types of "jacks" were used in large numbers and during long periods, especially by infantrymen.

During the fourteenth and fifteenth centuries, a combination of buckram and silk was used extensively everywhere in Europe, and combinations of these elements covered with "leather, fustian or canvas" are referred to in documents of the time of Queen Elizabeth (1586). In England, special armorers forming a guild of "linen armorers" were well known during the thirteenth and fourteenth centuries. Curiously enough, soft armor was quite in vogue at the time of the colonization of America. In 1663 Roger North records that "an abundance of silken back and breast plates were made and sold that were pretended to be pistol proof in which any man dressed was safe as in a house, for it was impossible that any one could strike at him for laughing, so ridiculous was the figure, as they say of 'hogs in armor.'" We know, indeed, that in 1663 when the new English uniform was fixed, officers wore no armor of plate save headpiece and steel gorget. Their tufted

Figs. 221 and 222. Detail of armor (buttonhole jacks) of woven material, sixteenth century

armor, it may be remarked, was covered with an olive-drab stuff very similar to our modern khaki drill. In Connecticut we have records that our soldiers wore jackets and breeches stuffed with wool as a defense against Indian arrows. All these types of soft armor, however, the wearer found hot and uncomfortable. Hence efforts were made to secure for them better means of ventilation; eyelet doublets came into use of which the structure is shown in Figs. 221 and 222. Here the tissue of the armor was perforated at many points, and elaborate and strongly wrapped eyelets were worked into them.

With these earlier defenses in mind, the British Bureau of Munitions caused numerous experiments to be made to determine the ballistic value of soft materials in terms of modern projectiles. This investigation seemed the more desirable since "soft" armor, if it were equally resistant, would, paradoxically, be safer to wear; for in case it were penetrated it would not cause the bullet to become deformed or mushroomed—and would thus save the wearer from more dangerous injury. During these experiments, tests were made of fibers of varied types, including balata, kopak, flax, hair, cotton, sisel, hemps and silk; and the materials were studied either as raw material for padding or in the form of woven stuffs or ropes. Sometimes, also, the material was held together between layers of canvas by quilting or piping. (Figs. 223 and 224). These experimental tests demonstrated, as might have been expected, that the most resistant fiber was silk.* Hence it was that the silken necklets were devised which were described on page 111. In their manufacture the material was used both in a woven and in the

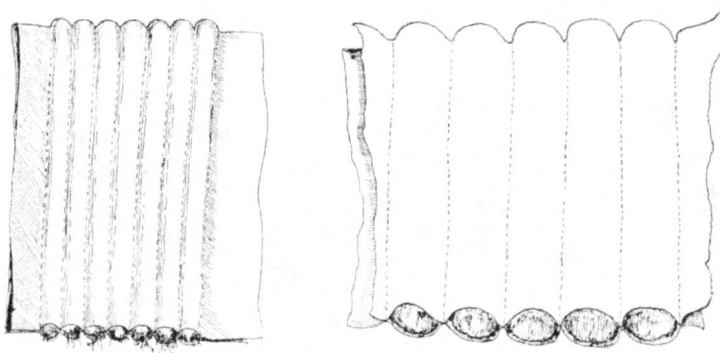

Figs. 223 and 224. Fibrous materials of various types arranged between bands of tissue for testing purposes

floss condition. Raw silk in the form of silk waste, noils from cocoons, etc., was found easier to procure and considerably less expensive. Hence an effort was made to employ it as a means of body defense by British experts; among them the governmental armor specialist, William A. Taylor,†

* The writer finds from a note furnished him by Captain Ley of the Munitions Board in London that certain of the earlier tests on the ballistic virtues of silk were quite remarkable: bombs were exploded in the "fragmentation hut" at Wembley (1915 ?); sample pads of silks were used for comparison with plates of helmet steel (Firth) of twice their weight; the silk pads were the better; they kept out 74 degrees of "medium shrapnel bullets at 600 foot seconds."

† Mr. Taylor summarizes his results as follows:
"The only material that gives materially better results than manganese steel is pure woven silk which, against shrapnel bullets up to a velocity of 900-1,000 foot seconds, has a distinct advantage, weight for weight, over steel. For example, silk

caused a doublet to be made (Fig. 225), heavily wadded with waste which would resist shrapnel at a velocity of 900 foot seconds. The best of these defenses, however, was made partly of many thicknesses of Japanese silk (60 thicknesses of 60 mommé). In general, however, it was decided that such a device was unsatisfactory in comparison with plates of alloy steel. (Cf. here, also, the results on the Chemico Body Shield, Fig. 68 and page 111.)

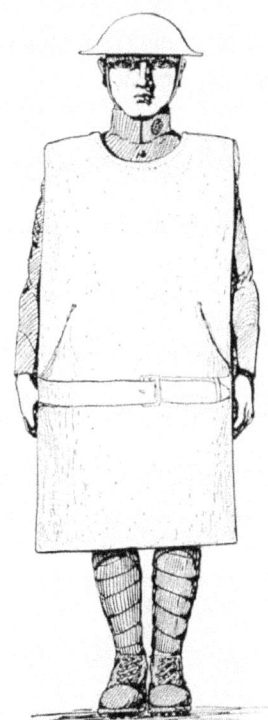

Fig. 225. Silk-lined body defense.
Taylor model, 1916-1917

It may be mentioned in this connection that earlier than the present war numerous experiments had been made in the United States in the direc-

weighing 10.8 oz. per sq. ft. is proof against shrapnel at 800 foot seconds, whereas steel to give the same resistance would weigh about 20 oz. The relative advantages and disadvantages of silk as compared with steel for body armor may be summarized as follows:—

"Silk does not give nearly the same resistance as steel against high velocity or pointed projectiles (e.g. rifle bullets or bayonet thrusts) but on the other hand it does

tion of producing a textile armor. In 1897 a Russian inventor, Casimir Zeglin, working in New York and Chicago, produced a closely woven silk cloth about one quarter inch thick (Figs. 226 and 227), and of this he prepared a waistcoat which was proof at 80 paces to a 40 caliber revolver, whose bullet was of lead and traveled at the rate of 400 foot seconds. In a plastron of this woven silk, the inventor faced a firing test successfully and since that time he has made numerous experiments in the direction of improving his bullet-proof costume. (Tests of them were made, *e.g.*, at Springfield Arsenal, 1899 and 1904.) In 1914, he directed to it the attention of our Ordnance Department but without tangible results. He also

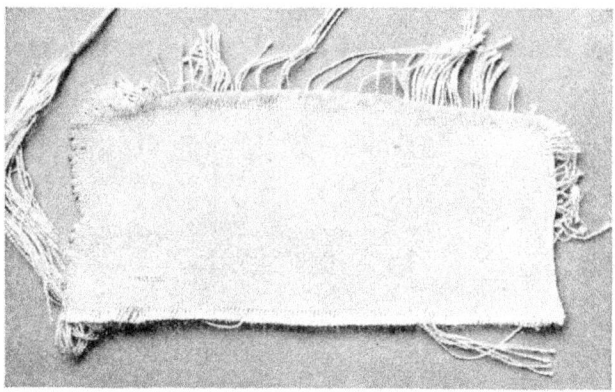

Fig. 226. Ballistic proof silken cloth or matting.
Zeglin pattern, 1917

took steps to combine his heavily woven silk fabric with a thin layer ($\frac{1}{16}$ inch) of chrome-nickel steel (Figs. 228 and 229). It was a similar type of defense, as noted on page 162, which the Russians employed during the Russo-Japanese War (1905). The Zeglin costume made of heavy silk cloth or matting one quarter inch thick covered with khaki drill, containing about

not deform a bullet when perforated. A bullet after passing through steel is deformed and would cause a very serious wound.

"Against low velocity blunt projectiles (e.g. shrapnel shell splinters, bomb fragments) up to a certain velocity silk is superior to steel, weight for weight.

"Silk sits better on the wearer than steel on account of its flexibility.

"For infantry, silk would probably be uncomfortably warm in summer and would require to be made water and vermin proof.

"Silk is more costly and difficulties of supply would be greater than with steel."

six square feet of silk, is naturally a costly defense (about $80). It weighs about six pounds and is said to be proof to shrapnel, splinters, bayonet and revolver. Tests, however, made upon the Zeglin cloth in Washington showed that it would not resist jacketed 45 automatic revolver bullets at 600 foot seconds. In point of fact, its resistance was hardly 400 foot seconds.

Fig. 227. Zeglin silken matting (bullet-proof) in process of being woven at the Crompton-Knowles loom, Cleveland, Ohio

Experiments concerning the value of soft armor were undertaken in the United States shortly after the beginning of the present war. A silk necklet of the British type had been sent to this country during the summer of 1917, and the intimation was received from abroad that our Government might be called upon to produce 10,000 or more of these defenses for experimental use at the front. The chief of the armor unit, who was then Captain A. T. Simonds, thereupon consulted the Cheney Brothers, silk manufacturers of South Manchester, Connecticut, in regard to the production of this lot of samples, but nothing came of the matter, since further advice from abroad indicated that the necklets would not be required. The Messrs. Cheney, however, became interested in the problem of producing armor of woven material, and, led to further inquiry by the promising results of their first trials, they carried on privately a series of experiments which duplicated in a way those made by the Munitions Inventions Board in London. Among the materials they considered were ramie, cotton in various states and weaves, cloths and silks of various kinds, including crêpe waste, noils and boiled-out silk waste. Their best results were obtained with loom-waste silk having a slight admixture of cotton. The latter addition, they maintain, hardly weakens the ballistic quality of the silk. In this conclusion, however, they are opposed by the results of the inventor Zeglin, who declared that for ballistic tests silk is two thirds better than cotton. It should here be explained that the Messrs. Cheney caused a large number of pads to be made and stuffed in various degrees with silk, cotton waste and other fibers, their series including pads which weighed from six to twelve pounds per square yard. These they then tested with shotgun (twelve gauge, buckshot, $3\frac{1}{2}$ grain powder), revolvers of 32, 31, and 45 caliber, and Remington rifle (35, having soft-nosed ball). The tests were at thirty feet, save in the case of the rifle, which was fired at a distance of one hundred and fifty feet. The results showed that pistol shots usually failed to penetrate any of the samples, that the shotgun tests failed in the eleven and twelve pound, usually failed in the nine and ten pound samples, sometimes penetrated the pads of seven and eight pounds, and always those of six pounds. Rifle fire presented a too severe test for even the heaviest sample. The Messrs. Cheney Brothers produced also a heavy silk cloth very much like that of Casimir Zeglin, which had apparently the same ballistic strength. This, however, proved so little better in tests than the waste silk that its use did not warrant its greater cost ($27 per yard of 24 inches as against $8 or $10).

In a general way, the studies upon soft armor made during the present war show convincingly that the ballistic value of this type of armor is not great enough to warrant its use; for when such a defense is constructed to resist not tests in "fragmentation huts" but ammunition of known velocities, it is found invariably that the weight of soft armor is so increased that there is little economy in its use. It becomes, in a word, about as heavy and as difficult to use as a defense of steel. Moreover, it is more expensive to

IN MODERN WARFARE

make, more difficult to procure, and deteriorates more rapidly in service. In this conclusion one does not of course deny that the use of silk armor would save many lives. It might even have been the means of postponing

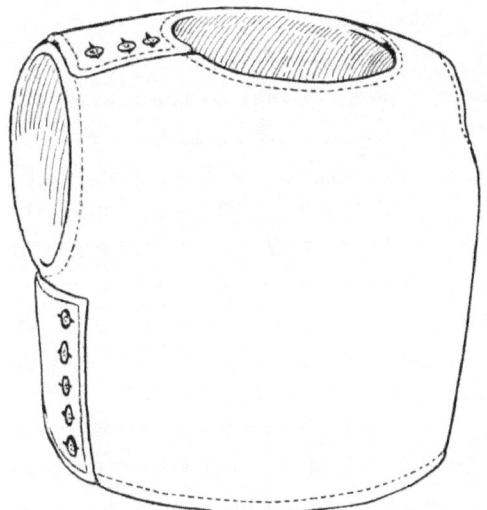

Fig. 228. Zeglin silken body defense   Fig. 229. Similar defense shown arranged with reinforcing plate of ballistic alloy

the outbreak of the present war; for it might well have saved the life of the Archduke Francis Ferdinand, who is said to have worn armor of silk on the day of the tragedy at Serajevo. Unhappily, however, the assassin shot at his head instead of his body! (The *London Daily Mail*, June 29, 1914.)

VIII
CONCERNING TESTS FOR ARMOR

THE value of armor depends upon many factors: the first and greatest of these is obviously its resistance to bullets of high impact—but even when made of the best steel in the world, no armor would be of practical value if it were too heavy or too uncomfortable to be worn. So the factors of weight, balance, ease, and security of attachment have justly to be considered. It seems, therefore, desirable to define what shall be the actual tests demanded for modern armor.

In a general way, as already noted, the total value of armor is not to be measured absolutely by its resistance to a projectile of a definite weight striking the armor at a certain rate of speed, for it is clear that the safety of the wearer would depend upon numerous, varying, and to no little degree fortuitous conditions. Among the first of these to be named is the exact way in which the projectile impinged upon the armor, *i.e.*, regarding especially its angle of approach. Also, it is clear that under certain conditions, the ball may even have perforated the armor, yet have lost its velocity to such a degree that it would not cause a fatal wound. Many instances, indeed, are cited to show that a comparatively light defense, which would have little value in an absolute test, has saved its wearer from a machine gun bullet. A helmet lately received in Washington is known to have saved the life of an infantryman who was struck in the head by such a bullet fired at a range hardly greater than 100 yards; yet the resistance of this helmet to a normal impact of a similar ball was hardly greater than 700 foot seconds while the machine gun bullet probably traveled at a rate of 2,400 foot seconds. So, too, the French helmet which resists the normal impact of a pistol ball at about 400 foot seconds is known to have deflected bullets at three times this velocity; in other cases, when it came to be pierced, it had, nevertheless, reduced the velocity of the projectile to such a degree that the wearer's skull had not been penetrated. In other cases still, such a helmet had deflected the ball slightly during the act of perforation and had caused it to inflict a scalp wound only.

In a word, it is unfair to state that a helmet or breastplate is valueless because it failed at the normal impact from service rifle ammunition at 100 yards; for it may still save its wearer from similar shots at longer range or from shots at close range which do not impinge directly. Whoever, therefore, deals with the problem of modern armor will go far astray if he does not consider on generous lines the index of probability.

By these reflections, however, one does not diminish the need of establishing a definite test by which the value of a piece of armor is to be gauged. And a diagnosis of the factors, conditions or criteria which determine its usefulness is given below. The degree to which each criterion is looked upon as essential is indicated by percentage.

Factors arranged in the order of importance, as determining the value of modern armor:

(a) Ballistic value 45%
(b) Weight 15%
(c) Comfort in wearing . . 10%
(d) Security in support . . . 10%
(e) Ease of recognition and the opposite (non-visibility) . 10%
(f) Noiselessness 3%
(g) Cleanliness 3%
(h) Durability 2%
(i) Adaptation 2%

(a) BALLISTIC VALUE

As noted in the preceding pages all armor should at a minimum test resist the impact of an automatic revolver ball weighing 230 grains, jacketed, traveling at the rate of 650 foot seconds. Most defenses mentioned in the foregoing pages were proved with standard ammunition in which the projectile traveled at the rate of 800 foot seconds. The tendency, however, in practical tests is ever to demand greater resistance. A body defense should resist 1,000 foot seconds, better still 1,200 foot seconds, though at the present time it is difficult to insure uniformity in the case of a body defense of this ballistic value which will weigh, back and front, covering a considerable portion of the trunk, less than eight pounds. One heat of metal might give an excellent practical test and the next one would fail. In order to gauge its strength, an old and reliable method was to place the armor in position on a dummy and shoot at it. In testing American helmets, however, where quick and precise results were necessary (see page 200) the shell tested was placed on a slanting board, so as to present a convenient point on its crown to the fixed line of fire of the automatic revolver; whether the helmet lay unattached to the supporting and inclined board or whether it was firmly clamped to the board made (in the writer's experience) little difference in the proof.

In testing the French helmet, earlier model, as noted on page 81, a mechanical device was sometimes employed by means of which a small punch recorded the strength of the shell in measuring a depth of indentation. For proving their helmets, the British, on the other hand, made use of "fragmentation huts" wherein the objects to be tested were arranged, *e.g.*, on sandbags, about the point (say at a distance of four feet) where a bomb was to be exploded. Under the conditions prescribed, shrapnel bullets weighing forty-one to the pound, struck the objects to be tested at a velocity of from 600 to 1,200 foot seconds. Such a test is obviously an easy one in practice but not very exact. In the same way tests were arranged in England for webbing of various kinds, waterproof covering, hide, fabrics saturated with resinous material, etc. In all instances cards are placed in front of and behind each object so as to record faithfully the number of hits and perforations. Similar methods were employed by the French, who also made numerous tests of armor in the open air, *e.g.*, in the study of the French abdominal defense, where plates were so suspended as to form a kind of screen in front of which grenades were exploded. Special loaded cartridges, however, with standard bullets which register 450 foot seconds, 600 foot seconds, 750 foot seconds, 1,000 foot seconds, etc., have been employed in various countries to great advantage. In fact, these tests are obviously the most definite of all. In conducting such experiments, however, numerous details must be considered which have been found to modify results materially. Thus, as Mr. W. A. Taylor emphasizes, it is not fair to conclude that because one plate of metal of definite thickness will resist impact at 800 foot seconds, two thicknesses, closely apposed, of the same plate, would resist 1,600 foot seconds. On the contrary, it was ascertained that the resistance of the two plates was sometimes scarcely more than the resistance of a single plate; for the part of the first plate which was "shot in" or indented appeared to strike the plate behind with almost the same force which was shown by the bullet at the time of its initial impact; obviously, therefore, the second plate was apt to behave just as though it were itself struck by the fresh projectile. This result, however, did not appear if the two plates were separated one from the other by an interval.

In studying ammunition and armor in general the British have made a great number of instructive tests. Thus, their analysis of German ammunition demonstrated its effect on armor plate of many kinds and at various distances, and the conditions which govern various cases were carefully recorded. Thus, compared to the usual service ammunition, the A. P. bullet is shown to maintain a much evener energy during its flight: the service bullet starts with a slightly greater energy (1.3 foot tons as opposed to 1.2), then it drops to about a third of its energy, in comparison with the armor-piercing bullet, at a distance of 500 yards; thereafter, however, it approaches continuously the energy of the A. P. bullet and gives similar results at about 2,500 yards. The British have also investigated in detail the effect upon armor plate of the service bullet reversed, for it was a well-known trick of the Germans in the early part of the war to remove a bullet from its cartridge and replace it back foremost; by this means, the punching effect of the bullet became much more severe than in normal tests. They studied further the mode of supporting the plate to be tested in order to determine whether or not this had any relation to the test, their results indicating that this factor was not an important one. In this series of experiments the armor plate was clamped on wood or steel either by the center of the tested plate or at the edges; they also backed it by springs. Differences, it is true, were thereupon recorded, but the results of these tests were not constant enough to warrant one's believing, *e.g.*, that a spring frame rendered a plate notably more resistant. A plate, however, clamped in position at its edges was always severely strained. In the study of the deflection of bullets, the British record material progress. They examined, also, the penetrating power of bullets of high velocity when passing through a plate at an angle.

In their studies the British analyzed their results from two points of view: from the first of these, a plate struck at an angle presents more metal to the impinging ball; from the second, a bullet which is passing through a plate changes its course to such a degree that it tears rather than drills its way through the armor. This process was further analyzed in the matter of the effect of this "tumbling" bullet upon succeeding plates; for, not striking such a plate "nose on," it cannot pierce the second plate neatly but must rotate through its substance and thus encounter greater resistance. The result of such a study led the British to experiment in the direction of attaching to the sides of their armored cars a series of outstanding plates, which, in point of fact, were found under certain conditions useful (*e.g.*, in tank armoring).

For testing its armor, each nation has naturally been led to employ the ammunition of its enemy. And a complete tabulation of results would evidently be of value for all experimental work on armor. The accompanying table deals with the question of ammunition in its broader lines.

TYPES OF AMMUNITION—RESULTS TABULATED FOR REFERENCE TO ARMOR TESTING

United States

Service rifle (1917)—weight of bullet 150 grains

Distance in yards	Velocity in foot seconds	Energy in foot pounds
0	2700	2427
100	2466	2034
200	2244	1686
300	2039	1392
400	1846	1141
500	1668	932
600	1509	762
700	1361	620
800	1238	513
900	1141	436
1000	1068	382
1200	966	312
1400	888	263
1800	765	196
2000	715	170
2500	601	121

Automatic service revolver 45 (1917)—weight of bullet 230 grains

0	802	329
25	788	317
50	773	305
75	758	294
100	744	283
125	730	272
150	717	262
175	704	253
200	691	244
225	678	235
250	666	226

U. S. Army Colt 45—weight of bullet 230 grains

        809   336

Penetration 8 in. white pine

U. S. Army Colt 45—weight of bullet 200 grains

                      368

Penetration 8 in. white pine

Under the heading of ballistic value, the matter of indentation should be considered. No helmet should pass the standard test which suffers an indentation greater than about one inch measured from the original surface-contour of the helmet. Body armor when struck by a bullet of 230 grains traveling at the rate of 700 foot seconds might safely yield a somewhat greater indentation. Thus, in plates protecting the abdomen, an indentation of this depth would not be apt to be dangerous, nor elsewhere on the body save over the breastbone. Here a cushioning should be present, preferably of sponge rubber and at least three fourths of an inch thick.

British

Shrapnel B. L. at 3,000 yards

Remaining velocity . . 819
Equivalent 100
———
919 f. s. speed of bullets contained

Add bursting charge velocity, say 600 foot seconds

Rifle Martin-Enfield (1883) 45—weight of bullet 85 grains

Range in yards	Velocity in foot seconds
0	1350

French

Service rifle D/05

0	2380
500	1639
1000	1141
1500	942

German

Mauser automatic pistol 300—weight of bullet 85 grains

Energy in foot seconds	Velocity in foot seconds
366	1394

Mauser service automatic 303 Mark VI

Range in yards	Velocity in foot seconds
0	2060
500	1281
700	1103
1000	961

Service S/05

0	2820
500	1741
1000	1086

Field Gun 3.3 inches (1906)

1525

Howitzer

Initial velocity less than 1,100 foot seconds
Krupp 75 m/m. (1908) 14.3 Shell 2 Dit.

Range in yards	Velocity in foot seconds
0	1640
1000	1140
2000	953
3000	838

Austrian

Männlicher 1895—315 steel bullet: weighing 244 grains

Velocity in foot seconds
2034

Field gun 3.01

1525

Under this heading should also be considered the question of *glancing angles* which each model of armor presents; for armor should be considered not merely as a resistant plate of alloy but as a device skilfully designed to deflect an impinging projectile. Thus, a breastplate with a flat surface obviously offers less protection than one which is well arched and modeled, for this would oftener be struck at such angles as to cause the bullets to be deflected. And the same principle is obviously true of every kind of armor: thus a helmet which presents a cylindrical curve arranged on a vertical axis would be apt to be pierced oftener by projectiles coming from a point in front of the wearer than a helmet whose axis of curvature is tilted backward at an angle of 45 degrees. The former type of curvature is shown in the forehead of the German helmet; the latter in helmet model No. 2, described on page 211. In this regard the second helmet had only to combine in its curves those of standard models of early armorers in order to obtain greater ballistic resistance without using heavier plates; a study, by the way, which few can appreciate who have not examined closely the work of master armorers. In the matter of providing deflecting surfaces, one should, of course, not lose sight of the fact that projectiles do not always impinge from the exact direction which an armor wearer might prudently have selected. But, everything considered, chances favor the armor which bears well-curved surfaces. Such surfaces, it will be seen, strengthen the plate against a projectile by bringing into play the physical principle of the arch as a resistant device. That is to say, a flat plate will resist a projectile less perfectly than a plate pressed into hemispherical form (assuming, of course, that in the process of pressing the metal be not thinned out at the height of the curve). And conversely it is known that armor gives a poor test if struck upon a surface which is concave. Thus the helmet of the British model which resists adequately a projectile impinging on its crown is apt to fail (10 to 20 per cent weaker) if struck in or near the concave zone where the rounded crown spreads outward to join the flattened rim. This strength and weakness is an obvious condition of the arch which resists a blow of a certain strength from above and fails if a similar blow be given from within.

The angle at which a projectile impinges is unquestionably an important factor in the proof of armor. In a general way, it may be stated that this angle becomes less important ballistically the greater the velocity of the impinging projectile. That is to say, a bullet which travels at the rate of 2,500 foot seconds may penetrate a plate struck at an angle of 75 or 80 degrees from the normal. A similar bullet traveling at the rate of 1,000 foot seconds would, on the other hand, probably be deflected at an angle of 40 degrees from the normal. Into these considerations, however, many factors enter which are difficult to analyze; and at the present time we are unable to establish a formula which will determine the angle of deflection for projectiles of different weights and different velocities when striking armor plates of different thicknesses and different degrees of hardness. It may be said, however, that an effort is now being made to determine such a formula; in this, when definite values can be assigned to definite elements, we may then be able to calculate what the value will be for the remaining elements. If, for example, we know the degree of hardness of a plate (H), the degree of hardness of the projectile (H'), the shape of the projectile (S), the thickness of the plate (T), the velocity of the projectile (V), and the weight of the projectile (W), we may be able to determine at what angle (A) our armor will deflect the bullet. By means of such an analysis, always checked by ballistical tests, we may learn that a projectile which perforates a plate of definite thickness on normal impact (90 degrees to the surface) will fail to penetrate a plate 75 per cent of the same thickness if impinging at an angle say of 60 degrees, or of 50 per cent if impinging at an angle of 35 degrees, or of 30 per cent if impinging at an angle of 15 degrees; all of which would indicate, of course, that armor which would be rejected by an examining board as too weak for service might nevertheless prove of considerable actual value, for it may fairly be said that of the number of projectiles which in action would be received upon a given plate only a limited percentage would impinge directly or normally. To develop the idea of glancing surfaces more clearly we refer to Figs. 230, 231 and 232, which represent three types of breastplates: the first was made about 1540 by a well-known armorer of Augsburg, the second is the new American model of heavy, or sentinel's armor (cf. page 244), the third is the similar defense of the Germans (cf. page 142). In each of these breastplates similar curvatures of the surface are indicated in similar ways (dotted lines, oblique, vertical, or transverse), these curves having been measured as angles from a series of parallel lines approaching the breastplate from directly in front. Comparison of these three models shows that a bullet which would pass through the German breastplate from directly in front (90 degrees) or from an angle of inclination of 70 degrees from this line (or normal) would be dangerous throughout the entire wide central area shown here dotted. The same projectile, however, would perforate a similar breastplate of the American model only in the narrower unshaded zone. Note, however, that it would everywhere be deflected by a similar breastplate in the ancient model. So, too, from a further arrangement of glancing surfaces, the model of the German breastplate would be penetrated more readily in the peripheral zones of its surface, assuming always that the projectile approached from the front, than would the American breastplate; while this in turn, from the same point of view, would be distinctly inferior to the breastplate of 1540. From all this, it follows that one type of body shield might be used successfully if provided with a certain curvature of its surface, while another, although made of the same thickness and of the same ballistic metal, might utterly fail in its tests. The principle which is here considered is a practical one, although it has been given but scanty notice in all work on modern armor.

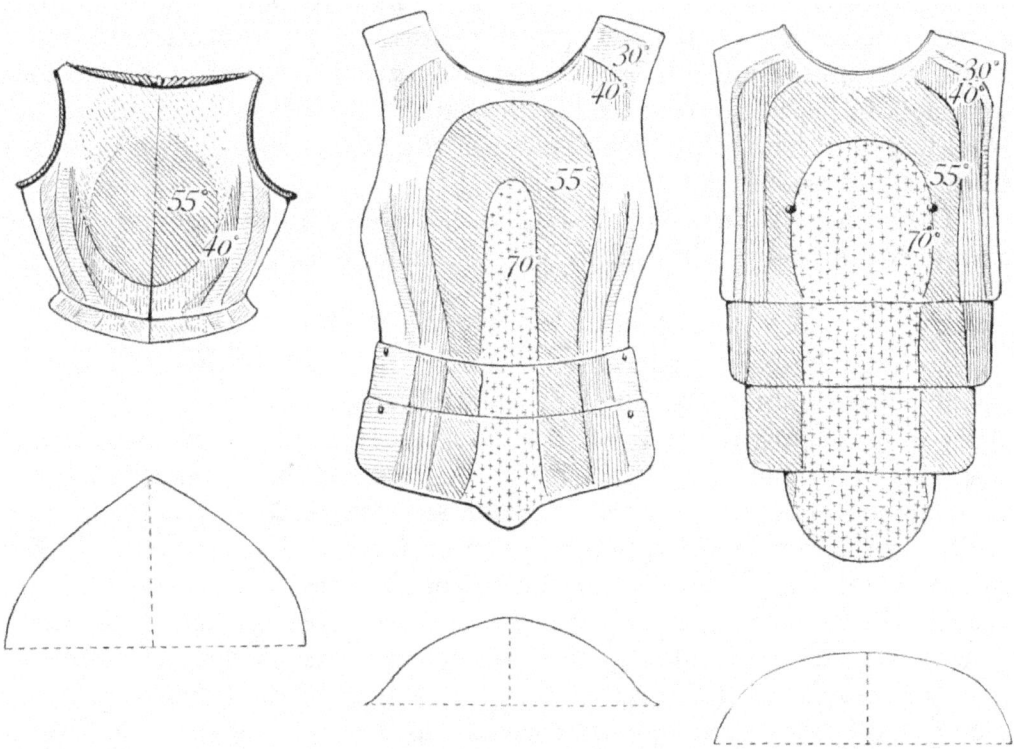

Figs. 230 to 232. Three breastplate models in which similar curvatures of surface are indicated by similar types of shading. Below each model is its transverse section

Fig. 230. Breastplate of 1540
Fig. 231. Experimental heavy breastplate for sentinel—American
Fig. 232. German heavy body armor

(b) WEIGHT

Weight is a factor of great importance in determining whether armor may be used; for without weight and, alas, in a very material degree, no complete protection can be promised,—yet with the needed weight the armor becomes unendurable. One may safely say, from the developments of the last months, that unless armor wearing should be made obligatory, there is little chance that American soldiers will consider wearing any type of body defense which is heavier than six or seven pounds. A greater weight than this the soldier would surely throw off at his first opportunity. Here we assume that he would be expected to carry his armor for considerable distances. However, should he be given his armor at the point where he is about to attack or where a defense is to be made, it is quite possible that armor of ten to twenty pounds (possibly more) might be considered—that is, for use during short intervals. This, however, even under favorable conditions, would entail considerable discomfort to the wearer and its use would by no means be probable except in the case of special men prepared to do special work.

The additional questions dealing with the weight of armor are closely akin to the present headings three (c) and four (d), *q.v.*

(c) COMFORT IN WEARING

Each headpiece or body defense should, in order to give its wearer a minimum degree of discomfort, be cushioned at the points of support. And every effort should be made to localize the weight of the armor where it will be best supported. Certain points of shoulder, neck, back, head and hips are well adapted for bearing weights. Pressure, however, upon other regions, sometimes near by, produces serious fatigue. Thus, on such a point as the temple, any degree of pressure would cause great discomfort and around the head in general means should be taken to insure abundant ventilation, for upon this depends notably the ease with which a helmet may be worn. It is for this reason, as we have seen in preceding pages, that a helmet lining was recommended which was cushioned at three points, for by this means ventilation was assured through the intervening spaces, *i.e.*, over each temple as well as over the occiput. In regions where a sudden shock or a deep indentation of metal would be dangerous, a space of about one inch should be left under the armor.

Examination of old armor shows with what care the matter of comfort in wearing was considered, and this is not to be wondered at since the soldier was then expected to wear his defense daily and often for many hours at a stretch. It should not be gathered from this, however, that even under the best conditions armor was comfortable; that it was not intolerable was the best that the wearer could expect, and in wearing "war-harness," as indeed in most details which concern physical training, great stress was ever laid on the matter of discipline. In early times, the soldier was required literally to grow up in his armor. He thus became inured to his burden, and many early references there are as to the discomfort he underwent. Shakespeare, who undoubtedly knew his theme at first hand, speaks of "armor worn in heat of day which scalds with safety." And today one does not help in the direction of reintroducing the wearing of such defenses who teaches that armor can be worn easily; one should rather make it clear that armor warrants the discomfort and annoyance of using it because of the real protection which it affords; for any soldier would be less apt to throw it off if he were convinced that by wearing it he was decreasing his chances of being injured or killed by 25 per cent—should he be hit.

As to further details in the matter of comfort in wearing armor: a plate of armor tends to distribute the shock over a considerable surface of the wearer's body. Of course, however, if a heavy object traveling at a low speed were to strike a piece of armor, a springy cushion would deaden the blow. But if so small an object as a standard bullet strike the armor with great rapidity, the cushioned support would become of small service. In the latter case, the bullet either penetrates or comes to a state of rest, sometimes deeply indenting the surface of contact, sometimes completely shattering or pulverizing the projectile itself.*

In either event, however, the effect is so sudden that the plate of metal has not the time to press back upon its supporting cushion. The fact that the body shield worn in the experiments of Dr. Brewster received a volley from a machine gun (even if the impinging bullets were not quite normal to the surface) without knocking the experimenter down, shows clearly that the shock of a series of projectiles is not actually as formidable as most of us believed. In such a case the force of the impinging bullet is distributed over

---

* Sir Robert Hadfield, discussing this matter, speaks of the critical moment in the testing of armor plate when a "conflict takes place between the projectile and the armor: if the projectile gains the mastery, the plate submits passively and is perforated: if the plate wins the test, the projectile is pulverized or deformed." In many cases a plate which fails shows apparent lamination, *i.e.*, a defect in structure, as when a bit of slag had been crushed or rolled into the plate. Such a two-layered appearance, however, may not have been caused in this way. According to Mr. W. H. Baker of Bridgeville, Pennsylvania, one of the greatest American experts in this field, the apparent layering is sometimes the result of a purely physical process; it may be neither more nor less than a zone of rupture, which appears when the plate fails; for at the critical moment in the test during the "conflict for the mastery," the projectile suddenly pushes in the one surface of the plate, while the back of the plate resists stiffly: hence in the middle of the plate, there arises a definite layer of compression and if the latter ruptures with the force of the blow, a visible lamination may result.

306   HELMETS AND BODY ARMOR

the body of the wearer and is converted instantly into other forces, mainly, perhaps, "vibratory" in nature, such as sound, heat, light and electricity. As an example of the lack of pushing force with which a rifle ball impinges upon an object, one recalls that when plates of various materials are set on

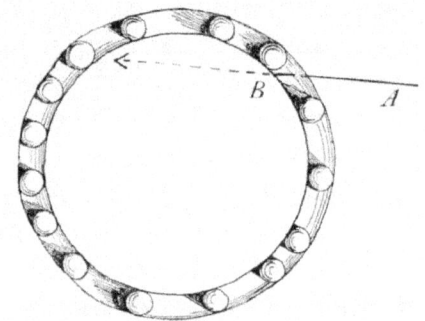

Fig. 233. Cylindrical shield (white central circle) balanced on ball bearings. The line A-B represents the course of bullet

Fig. 234

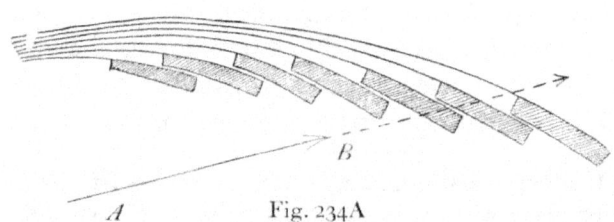

Fig. 234A

Fig. 234. A spring slip or plate to the end of which a bit of steel is fastened and a section (A) showing a series of such spring plates arranged one behind the other. The course of a bullet is shown in the line A-B

edge practically unsupported and then shot at, the ball is apt to perforate without knocking them down. Again, if a cylindrical shield supported by a ball-bearing (Fig. 233) receives the impact of a rifle ball in the direction A-B, it may be perforated before it has any "chance" to rotate upon its easily turning base. So also if spring slips bearing plates of steel at their ends (Fig. 234) be placed in the position shown in Fig. 234A, several of them may be perforated by a bullet traveling in the direction A-B before they "have time" to react and bend back upon their neighbors.* In a word, returning to modern armor, we may repeat that the question of the spring-like support of such defenses is not an extremely important part of our problem. It may be mentioned, in passing, that the matter of the spring versus the projectile is a problem in pure physics for which a definite formula may be worked out.

Fig. 235

Fig. 235. Shield formed of bent-over metallic plates. Joubert model, 1915-1916

(d) SECURITY IN SUPPORT

A helmet cannot be worn if it rests insecurely on the head. Its balance must be perfect; its center of gravity should be considered when its chin-strap is adjusted, to the end that the danger of the gradual shifting of the position of the helmet on the head may be reduced to a minimum. Even such a detail must here be considered as the balance of the chin-strap when resting on the point of the wearer's chin, instead of near the angle of his jaw-bone—for the former position is alone permissible in active service, since it insures the displacement of the helmet with the least degree of danger. A really good helmet should not wabble seriously out of place when the wearer goes through his setting-up exercise. It may be said inci-

* A breast defense or shield (Fig. 235), built up somewhat upon this plan, was recommended by the English armor expert, M. Félix Joubert, in 1915.

dentally that few of our modern helmets will stand this test! Nevertheless, it is clearly possible to support a helmet firmly without the need of drawing a chin-strap so tight as to cause serious discomfort.

Body defenses are held in place by being squarely supported on the shoulders and on the hips. In this connection, it is important to adjust the broad shoulder straps at such an angle that they shall not press upon the shoulders of the wearer save throughout their entire breadth. If properly adjusted, armor even of considerable weight can be worn with surprisingly little discomfort. Experiments with armor of the fifteenth and sixteenth centuries show how carefully this problem was considered by the armorer; his straps need not be tightened to such a degree that the wearer of the armor felt burdened* by his trappings. In modern armor the arrangement of buckles and snap-catches should be devised for special cases; in their arrangement the degree of security is to be considered and the ease with which the pieces may be put on and taken off. The strong leathern straps of old armor have now given place to bands of webbing which may be had in many widths and thicknesses. These woven straps are stronger by about 25 per cent, more durable, and more safely attached. They deteriorate less speedily from moisture and drying; and their use is a distinct war-time saving; not only are they cheaper but cotton is far easier to secure than leather, which for the rest is greatly needed elsewhere.

To be securely supported does not mean that a piece of armor need be attached rigidly. Elastic supports, *e.g.*, of sponge rubber, are on the contrary often to be recommended, for they break the jolt of the armor, especially when heavy, during the wearer's quick movements. This is aside from the question as to whether cushioning helps to resist the impact of a projectile.

(e) EASE OF RECOGNITION AND NON-VISIBILITY

The headpiece of each nation should for obvious reasons be easily recognized even at a considerable distance. It is important, therefore, that the design of a helmet should present a distinct and characteristic profile. To this end the shape of the brow or nape should be especially considered. In front view such a detail as a median ridge may become an important means in recognition, for it is apt to throw a shadow which can be seen distinctly

---

* Experiments with authentic armor have convinced the writer that it may be worn even by a novice three hours at a stretch without causing extraordinary fatigue or subsequent lameness.

at long range. The outline of the crown of the helmet can be distinguished readily whether flat, hemispherical or peaked. A straight line passing from the brow region to the nape of the helmet differentiates instantly the English from the German helmet, or a down-bent line in this region identifies the helmet as French. Every effort made to produce an American helmet which would protect the side of the head of the soldier did not meet the favor of the General Staff in France, since each model of this kind presented was held to resemble too closely the headpiece of the German.*

Fig. 236. Soldiers, one with and one without camouflaged body gear

Similarly, all body armor should bear marks of recognition. A lack of symmetry in the upper plate of a breast defense, which enables a rifle to be aimed, would be considered a favorable feature since it distinguishes this model at a considerable distance. A back defense terminating below in a point differentiates it readily from one in which the lower border is squarely cut.

Non-visibility, it must also be admitted, is similarly important as a test, for while a recognition mark in armor may deliver the wearer from his friends, it might well make him a conspicuous mark for his enemies.

* Whether such a model, by its additional degree of protection, would prevent a greater number of casualties than it would cause by its possible resemblance to the German helmet is a problem about which the General Staff gives no data.

Thus, an unusual contour may be fatal which causes a piece of armor to bring its wearer into greater prominence. To be inconspicuous, therefore, in certain phases of warfare means to be safe. Color should be neutral. The surface of plates should be slightly roughened in order to avoid reflection of light. In some cases this result may be obtained by covering a plate in cloth which, incidentally, renders it noiseless and helps to make harmless the splash of lead which follows a glancing bullet. To camouflage armor is worthy of careful attention, for it falls clearly in line with efforts made in all armies to render their men invisible to the enemy. It may here be mentioned that a study in the direction of camouflaging a breastplate was undertaken in the United States by an artist-naturalist, Mr. Dwight Franklin, whose results, however, were disappointing inasmuch as they showed that no single method could be used to make the colors of an individual merge into his background. In other words, Mr. Franklin's results indicated that for each locality and for varied conditions of lighting, widely different methods would have to be employed to gain the needed color values. Hence, it would be necessary to train each armored sniper, observer and machine gunner to become his own camouflage artist (Fig. 236). In the meanwhile his defenses could only be painted a color, *e.g.*, olive-drab, useful in as many instances as possible. This in fact was the procedure which had already been adopted in experimental work generally.

(f) NOISELESSNESS

This factor is of less importance than at first appears; for in the majority of cases where armor might be worn to advantage, any rattling sounds which, even at close distance, it would produce, would readily be drowned by gunfire. In fact, when used at close quarters, armor would be apt rather to disconcert the enemy by any sound it would cause. The Japanese, who, it may be recalled, wore armor almost within our own time, have regarded this feature as of great protective value. And in this direction they took into account not only the noise which armor produces but also the effect upon the enemy's nerves caused by grotesque steel masks—a war device in connection with armor used in close combat, which seems at first sight hardly worthy of a moment's consideration—childish, in fact—until we admit that the Japanese are among the most resourceful soldiers in the world and that their war mask as a means of inspiring an adversary with wholesome respect, if not panic, was recommended in Japanese tactics for over 600 years.

In the experimental armor of all nations efforts have been made to dampen the sounds which its plates produced in action. The English secured noiselessness by covering the plates with stuff. The German body defense is furnished with soft pads of cow-hair felt, attached between the metal parts of its apron. The American heavy armor had pads of leather inserted between the plates. In all these cases, unless a wearer moved suddenly, *e.g.*, as in falling, his armor would be apt to cause no sound which could be heard for a distance of many yards. For men on night patrol noiselessness in armor would be of especial value—were it not that armor would hardly be worn in the dark! Here quickness in movement would count and the possibility of getting out of sight if lights suddenly appeared.

(g) CLEANLINESS

Use in trenches is apt to ruin equipment speedily; any defenses which become *matériel* should not go to pieces if subjected to repeated wettings and dryings. Hence, woven materials unless very heavy are not to be recommended for covering plates of metal, for tissues are injured by rust and soon become mildewed and soften. Such stuffs, moreover, are difficult to clean; they become sodden with dirt and are apt to harbor vermin and germs of disease. Best in practical use would be armor whose surface is protected only with paint.

(h) DURABILITY

Armor cannot be used unless it is kept in good repair. Cleanliness and indestructibility go hand in hand. Leathern straps, as we have noted, are less permanent than closely woven bands of tissue which, under modern conditions of manufacture, present a surface so tightly woven that it sheds dirt and moisture in no little degree. In the matter of indestructibility, critical attention should be given to the way in which straps are riveted. Thus the rivets should be provided with washers wherever practicable. Especially where plates require a certain freedom of movement, the use of rivets having washers is always to be recommended, a practice which, by the way, has come down to us from centuries of experience.

(i) ADAPTATION

The value of a piece of armor depends in a degree upon the way in which it has been adapted to a special use. A helmet strap, for example, should be adapted for use with a gas mask so that by a separate device it may be passed immediately under the "proboscis" of a gas mask and made fast again to the helmet. So, too, a breastplate becomes of greater value if it is so laminated that the wearer can keep his position close to the ground yet push his way forward. A helmet also should not cover the ear region so completely that a telephone receiver cannot be used if needed. In this connection should be mentioned the adaptational value of a helmet of which the nape region could be used as a brow defense in case of need.

IX
SUMMARY AND CONCLUSIONS

IN the foregoing pages we have traced the development of helmets and body armor up to the present time, *i.e.*, throughout the period of the war, and have shown broadly in what lines modern armor has been successfully employed. It remains for us to consider the possibilities for its future development. In a word, we have still to attempt to answer such questions as these: (1) Whether we have attained the final development in our ballistic alloys for thin plates; (2) whether we have solved the problem of the best helmet; (3) whether it is possible still to develop a body armor which shall be willingly used.

(1) *Have we as yet solved the problem of providing the best alloy for helmets and body armor?* Many eminent metallurgists, European and American, have attacked this problem constantly and intensively during the past few years. Their results, we believe, show clearly that the end in the improvement of thin plates for ballistic uses is not yet in sight. At the present time a sheet of metal of twenty gauge (.0368) can be made in newer alloys which will resist the impact of the standard bullet (230 grains) jacketed, traveling at the rate of about 1,000 feet per second. Their result nets an advance of about 30 per cent over the conditions of a couple of years ago. It seems only a fair conclusion, therefore, that metallurgists, attacking the problem with similar industry, will be able to add an appreciable percentage to the value of armor plate during succeeding years. From all this, it follows that if the helmet of 1917-1918 was a useful defense, the helmet of 1920-1921 will be a decidedly more efficient one. The struggle, however, between bettering the armored defense on the one hand and increasing the destructive action of the missile on the other, is keener today than it was in the early history of armor. Still, judging from present data, we are convinced that recent developmental advances have favored armor rather than projectiles. Viewing the problem at closer range, we believe that an improvement in the quality of ballistic alloy may be expected even in the

course of the next months which will greatly influence all further armor work. But whether the newest alloys will be capable of being pressed into the shape of a helmet is distinctly another question. The studies of Professor Howe on helmet alloys, carried on under the direction of the Ordnance Department, have shown that it will be extremely difficult to press certain of these plates which have the highest ballistic resistance.

(2) *Have we as yet the best form of an American helmet?* We doubt gravely whether we have as yet solved the problem of the American helmet. That the "porridge-bowl" model of the British is not the best for our use, there can be but little doubt. American experts both here and abroad have agreed that this model is too shallow to protect adequately the region of the back and sides of the head, nor is it without defects in other directions. Moreover, it is fair to assume that in helmets, as in other objects of equipment, a national type should be adopted. We have noted, none the less, that the advantages of the British helmet are many; we recall especially that it is admirably suited to manufacture. On the other hand, several models were produced by the Ordnance Department in Washington and sent to American Headquarters in France which presented features superior in various directions to the British model or, possibly, to any of the others. The best proof, perhaps, that these considerations were well founded is the fact that the Swiss Government lately adopted as its national helmet a model which is precisely of the type the Ordnance Department in Washington recommended to our Chief in France nearly a year ago. It is clear, we believe, that the model which was provisionally accepted in France, known commonly as the "Liberty Bell" helmet, which is a simplified form of one of our early models, is not finally to be recommended. It does not offer a greater protection to the sides and back of the head than the British helmet, nor can it pass critical muster from the viewpoint of balance, or of general attractiveness—the latter a feature which played so important a part in insuring the success of the French helmet.

(3) *Have we as yet reached the limit of our armor wearing?* We have seen that in all armies a helmet has been accepted as part of the soldier's regular equipment. In view of this, have we reason to conclude from the preceding data that other armor defenses will ultimately come into general use? We are here dealing with a problem which presents many complicated features. It is fair to say, however, that there seems no reasonable chance that defenses for either the body or the extremities will be used, unless a different system is adopted for the transport of the equipment of the

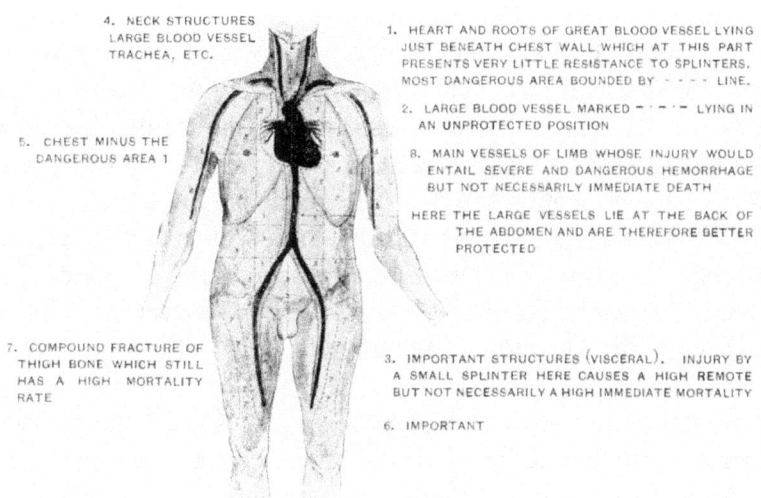

Fig. 237. Anatomical structures marked out in numbered topographical areas

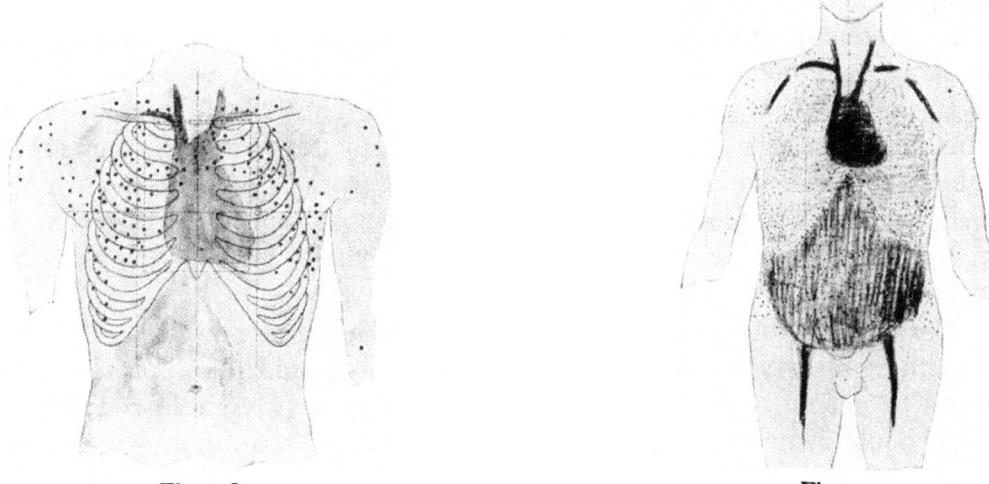

Fig. 238　　　　　　　　　　　　　　　　Fig. 239

Fig. 238. Diagram showing the anterior portion of the chest and indicating by dots entry wounds in 163 cases. Heart and roots of large vessels are here indicated.

Fig. 239. Diagram indicating by small dots entry wounds in chest and abdomen as recorded in about a thousand cases (163 thoracic, 834 abdominal). The deeper the shading, as here indicated, the greater the danger.

Figs. 237 to 239. Anatomical diagrams furnished by Trench Warfare Section, London (Captain Rose): these indicate "areas of danger" and tabulate "entry wounds" in chest and abdomen, 1918

soldier. He cannot be expected to carry his armor from point to point in addition to his regular kit, for very careful studies made on the western front have shown that even without armor the infantryman carried into actual combat as great a weight as he can be expected to bear, and that even a few extra pounds would burden him to a degree which would interfere with his effectiveness. Hence at the most he would not be apt to be given any armor which would weigh more than a couple of pounds, *e.g.*, in the form of an abdominal defense, as suggested by General Adrian, or the necklet developed by the Ordnance Department in Washington, or the gas mask container.*

In summary, the whole major problem, so far as the writer can interpret it, hinges upon the possibility of assuring adequate transport for armored defenses to regions where they are actually required. The writer is firmly convinced that if defenses of various types were kept in reserve, capable of being furnished at short notice to points where they were promptly needed for either defense or offense, the usefulness of armor would presently be admitted and many lives and much suffering could be saved. In some operations even a heavy breastplate could be worn, *e.g.*, in an advance of a few hundred yards. It seems also not beyond the limits of belief that future infantrymen might begin their attack wearing a number of body defenses which, having served their purpose, could be thrown off bit by bit. Such a procedure in our opinion would have been a means of saving many casualties during the advance of the American Army in the Argonne.

Certain it is, however, that the theory of modern defenses would have to be more clearly understood by both the officers and men before armor would be generally accepted—even under the most favorable conditions. They should come to realize that while no armor is proof, many types of it

* The writer has just received a report written by his friend, Captain I. St. C. Rose of the Trench Warfare Division, London, who has charge of the armor work in that field, which indicates that, had the war lasted, some small defense (armored gas-mask container or associated trenching tools) might have come into standard use in the British Army. Captain Rose also reconsiders the possible use of silk for a body defense for other parts of the body. Bullets would pass through the material without appreciably "setting up" (mushrooming), while shrapnel bullets would be stopped at a velocity of 800 foot seconds. In connection with his report some interesting figures appear which are here reproduced (Figs. 237, 238, 239). They show more accurately than hitherto recorded the anatomical zones of danger which the designer of armor must consider.

are useful. At the present stage of our development of armor plate no defense can be expected to render its wearer immune from a large percentage of possible injuries; nevertheless, it will serve an important function if it is able to protect its wearer from one "hit" in five—or even one in ten. The fact is that in a matter of this kind the average soldier is hard to convince. He knows that the armor is heavy and that to wear it causes him progressive annoyance. Hence he will have none of it, unless he knows that it will save him from imminent risk. Still, it is a hopeful sign that he has now reached the stage in his education in armor matters when he is willing to look with respect upon the helmet. In this particular case, he has had time to compare notes with his fellows along the line, and he has himself counted many dented headpieces which have saved their wearers from injury or death. So he may some day conclude that body armor, like his helmet, is "all right"—then he will submit to the discomfort of wearing it.

INDEX

Abadie (d'Oran), Dr., 71
Adrian, General, 8, 65, 66, 74, 80, 88, 260, 316; abdominal shield, 106; breastplate, 108; epaulets, 108; helmets, 66, substitutes for, 85, used by Belgians, 156
Aeroplanes, armored, 266-268
Agricola, Georgius, 36
Aigeltinger, 8, 273
Alloys for armor, 273-281; improvement in, 280, 313; resistance, 273, 276, 277, 278, 279, 280; tabular analysis, opp. 274
America, armor worn in, 52, 58
American armor, 242-265; in Richmond Museum, 58; *see also* Body armor
American Can Co., 195
American Car & Foundry Co., 195
American helmet, *see* Helmet, American
American Sheet & Tin Plate Co., 195
Amherst, Lord, wore armor, 52
Anatomical diagrams tabulating entry wounds, 315
Ansaldo body shield, Italian, 151-152
Archduke Francis Ferdinand at Serajevo, silk armor of, 293
Arisaka, Prof. Shozo, 176
Arm defenses, American, 264-265; French, 109; woven and tufted, 285
Armeria Reale, Turin, weight of armor in, 48-50
Armor, artistic value of ancient, 26; discomfort of wearing, 26, 46; disuse of, causes for, 26, 42, 51, 54; early forms, 27; effect of wearing, 48; importance of ancient, 34; metallurgy of ancient, 35, 43, 270-272; practical value of ancient, 27, 29; reappearance of, in Great War, 27; resistance of, 30, 52; saved by, historical instances, 30, 32-34, 52; testing of ancient, 38-45, modern, 295-300; utility, beauty of ancient, 9, 26; weight of ancient, 43, 45, 46, 48-50
Armor Committee, National Research Council, 211
Armor making, aesthetic value in, 9; ancient and modern, 36; difficulty of, 36; special tools used in, 36

Armor of proof, 25
Armored cart, Japanese, 176
Armored case for gas mask, 255
Army and Navy body defense, 123
Askew, Colonel, 8
Astori Co., Milan, 152
Austrian helmets and armor, 147
Aviator's, armored chair, 265, 266, 269; helmets, American, 228-232

Babbit, Gen. E. T., 8
Bachereau, V. R., 41
Baker, Hon. N. D., Secretary of War, 7
Baker, W. H., 8, 196, 244, 277, 305
Ballistic tests, American helmet, 196, 200-202; Belgian helmet, 159; British helmet, 130; German body armor, 144; German helmet, 138; soft materials, 287
Ballistic value of armor, 295-303; of French and British helmets compared, 80-81
Bargello, Florence, weight of armor in, 48-50
Barlow, Joel, 52
Bartel, Raymond, 8
Bassett, Lieut. Charles K., 141
Bates, Colonel, wears gorget, 55
Belgian armor, 160
Belgian helmet, *see* Helmet, Belgian
Belt and Dyer, 186-187
Benedetti, Ernest, cuirass mounted by, 63
Berkeley, John, 113, 131
Best Body Shield (folding), 120
Bethlehem Steel Co., 242
Blake, Col. Joseph A., 70
Blindness, *see* Eye wounds
Bockman, Mr., 189
Body armor, American, 242-265; Austrian, 147; Belgian, 160; British, 110-128, 131; French, 106-109, 179; German, 142-147; Italian, 151-156; Japanese, 172-177; Portuguese, 161; Slavic, 162, 186; Swiss, 163; use in World War, 67
Body armor, *see* Arm defenses, Breastplate, Epaulets, Epaulières, Face defenses, Face-

guard, Face-shields, Jazerans, Leg armor, Neck-guard, Neck and shoulder defenses, Pneumatic armor, Portable shields, Sentinel's armor, Set-shields, Shields, Silk armor, Soft armor, Visor
Boer War, armor used in, 60
Boesch, Lieut. Paul, 168
Brantôme, 33, 34, 48
Breastplate, Adrian, 108; American, 233-245; Ansaldo (Italian), 151; Daigre (French), 179; German, 142-147; Japanese, 173, 174; resistance of modern, 40; Russian, 162, 186
Brescia, Serafino di, 25
Brewster, G. O., 211, 242
Brewster body armor, 242-244, 305
British armor, 110-128, 131; see Body armor
B.E.F. (British Expeditionary Forces) shield, 120
British helmet, see Helmet, British
British Munitions Inventions Board, 111, 125, 127, 128, 138, 274
British tests of armor, 297
Brodie, Mr., 128
Budd Manufacturing Co., 138, 195, 197-199, 276, 278
Bullets, armor piercing, 45; dents of, as centers for ornament, 44; penetration dependent on, 45; shapes, 45
Bullet-proof jacket (Chiba), Japanese, 176; plastron, Japanese, 173; waistcoat, tested in New York, 62
Burgess, George K., 211
Buttin, Charles, 25, 33, 39, 41, 48, 63

Camouflaged body gear, 309
Campbell, Prof. Wm., 270
Canadians abandon heavy armor, 119
Cannelated armor, resistance of, 84
Cannelated helmet, Portuguese, 161
Capel, Sir Giles, helm of, 167
Carlson jazeran, 260
Casualties saved by use of shrapnel helmet, 68
Cellini, 45
Chain mail, efficiency of, in Crusades, 30; in Metropolitan Museum of Art, 30; Japanese, 174; modern use of, South America, Africa and the East, 58; original price of, 30; padding needed with, 31; resistance of, 30, 40; time consumed in making, 30; use of, 27; weapons used in testing, 40
Chain mail visor, British, as eye protector, 72, 133; dizziness produced in wearing, 133

Charles V as armor expert, 34; reinforcing pieces of helmet of, 34; weight of armor of, 34
Charles Emmanuel III, proof of armor of, 44
Château de la Rocca, armory of, 44
Chemico Body Shield, 111
Cheney Brothers, 291
Chiba, Chosaki, 174, 175, 176, 187
Chin-band of German helmet, 137
Chin-strap, of American helmets, 202, 215, 224, 228; of French helmet, 79
Chrome-molybdenum alloy, 279
Civil War, armor worn during, 58
Cleanliness of armor, 311
Close Body Shield, British, 127
Cocoa fiber armor, 284
Coligny, Admiral, shot with copper bullets, 45
Colombo of Brescia, 43
Columbia Steel Tank Co., 258
Columbian Enameling & Stamping Co., 196, 197, 276, 277
Combat-axe resisted by early armor, 30
Comfort in wearing armor, 304, 305
Committee on Educational Work, Metropolitan Museum, 8
Compteurs et Matériel d'Usines à Gaz, 79, 98
Condé saved by armor, 34
Corelli British bullet-proof body shield, 126
Corselet of time of Napoleon, resistance of, 56
Cost, of British body defenses, 111, 112, 114, 121; British helmet, 130; Czemcrzin waistcoat, 162; Daigre shield, 180; Zeglin defense, 291
Council of National Research, 8, 211
County Chemical Co. of Birmingham, 112
Crosby Co., 98, 194, 195
Crossbows discarded in France, 42
Crowell, Hon., Assistant Secretary of War, 7
Cruise, Captain, designer of British eye defense, 72, 133
Cuirass of XVIII-XIX centuries, protection afforded by, 56
Curtain Supply Co., 195
Cust, Mrs. Henry, 46
Czemcrzin bullet-proof waistcoat, Russian, 162

Daigre portable shield, 179
Dandelot, saved by shield, 34
Danritt, Captain, 63
David's armor, 39

Dayfield Body Shield, early British defense, 117-118
Dean, Bashford, 211
de Forest, Robert W., 8
Demetrius Polyorcetes, corselet of proof worn by, 39
Detaille, Edouard, 9, 76
Dimond, Mr., designer of mobile shield, 189
Donatello, 25
Dukes of Savoy, armory of, 36
Dunand Brothers, 96; helmet, 88, 96-102, 157, 165, 167, 210, criticism, 99; visor, 88, 96, 98, 99, 102, 210
Duncan model, American body defense, 259
Dunning, Major, 159
Dupeyron, Auguste, 79, 156
Dupuy, Dr. E., 81
Durability of armor, 311
Durand, William F., 211
Duryea's bayonet shield, American, 260

Early use of armor in Great War, 64-67
Emblem, see Symbol
E.O.B. corselet, British body defense, 125
Epaulets, General Adrian's, 108; economy in manufacture, 108
Epaulières, Italian, 156
Eye defenses, American, 234-237; British, 132-133, 233
Eye wounds, statistics, 72, 73, 102, 104, 133
Eyes, injury to the, 72-73

Face defenses, British, 131; see also Eye defenses, Visors
Face-guard (bavière), American, 237-239
Face shield, American, silk, 227; French, for sniper, 106; German, 139-141
Fariselli armored waistcoat, Italian, 152-155
Featherweight Shield, British, 119
ffoulkes, Charles, 26, 43, 44
Fiebeger, Colonel, 186
Firearms, types of, used in early times, 51
Fitting of armor, 46
Flexible Armor Guard of John Berkeley, British, 113
Florit, Don José, 171
Fluted armor, see Cannelated
Ford, Edsel, 8
Ford, Henry, 8
Ford Manufacturing Co., 204-208, 212, 216, 220
Formosa Government purchases Japanese shields, 176
Francis I, 25; saved by armor, 34

Franco-Prussian War, types of armor used, 59-60, 106
Franklin, Dwight, 310
Fraser Collapsible Breast Shield, American, 260
Frati breastplate, Italian, 155
French armor, 106-109, 179; see Body armor
French Bureau of Inventions, 88, 106
French first to accept helmet, 64, 74
French helmet, see Helmet, French

Gaya, 40, 44
General Electric Co., 138
Gerli, Paul, 228
German armor plate, resistance of, 183, 185
German armored plane, 267; ballistic test of, 268
German body armor (breastplate), see German sentinel's armor
German helmet, see Helmet, German
German sentinel's armor, 142-147
Gessler, Dr. Edward A., 167
Getty, Maj. Samuel, 68
Giants' helmets, weight of, 128
Gibbs, Miss Helen, 58-60
Glancing angles of armor, 300-303
Glass armor, value of (Szmyt), 262
Goggles, armored, 234; metal, as eye defense, 132; see also Eye defenses
Gorgeno-Collaye breastplate, Italian, 156
Gorget, 54
Gould, Charles W., 8, 27
Grayson, Mr., 245
Gun Wharf in Portsmouth, Giants' helmets in, 128

Hadfield, Sir Robert, 8, 129, 196, 273, 274, 305
Hale & Kilburn Co., 215
Harris, Thomas C., designer of eye-shield, 234
Haynes, Elwood, 281
Hazen, Nathaniel, 187
Headpiece, modern test on ancient, 41
Helmet, American, assembling, 204-208; balance of model No. 8, 224; ballistic tests, 196, 200-202; breakage allowed, 200; chinstrap, 202, 215, 224, 228; description, 196; lining, 195, 212, 215, 218, 220, 228, 233; manufacture, 194, 195, 196, 212, 216; material, 196; model, aviator's, 228-232, Liberty Bell, 232-233, No. 2, 211-213, No. 4, 213-214, No. 5, 214-217, No. 6, 217, No. 7, for

sentinel, 218-219, No. 8, 219-224, No. 9, for machine gunner, 224, No. 10, 224-225, No. 13, for tank operator, 225-228; packing, 208; painting, 204; resistance, 218, 228; table, comparison of measurements, opp. 212; visor, 210, 219-220, 228; weight, 218, 224, 228, 233
Austrian, 147
Belgian, ballistic results, 159; criticism, 160; description, 158; manufacture, 159; weight, 160; *see also* Adrian helmet
British, adopted provisionally by Americans, 193; composition, 129; cost, 130; description, 128; resistance, 129; test, 130; weight, 130, comparison with French and Dunand helmets, 81, 102
French, ballistic value, 80; chin-strap, 79; composition, 79-80; criticism, 81-83; description, 76; Dunand models, 88, 96-102; introduced in large numbers, 68; lining, 77, 79; manufacture, 78-79; morale, 82-83; newer models, 83; origin, 74-75; size, 79; symbol, 76, 78; ventilation, 78; visors, 89-99; weight, compared with British, 81, Dunand and British compared, 102
German, ballistic test, 138; chin-band, 137; composition, 138; description, 134; lining, 135-137, 142; manufacture, 138; new model, 141; reinforcing piece, siege, 139; thickness, 137; ventilation, 136; weight, 137, 139, compared with British, 134
Italian, 149-151
Portuguese, composition, description, resistance, weight, 160-161
Slavic, description, 161
Spanish, description, 171
Swiss, criticism, 167; description (experimental model), 165; lining, 166; resemblance to Dunand helmet, 165, 167; standard model, 168; symbol, 166
Helmet, *see also* Adrian, Dunand, Ladysmith, Shrapnel, Siege
Helmet making, stages and time consumed in, 36
Helmet steel, results of tests on various types of, 279
Helmets, developmental sequence, 47; ornamental metal of XVIII-XIX centuries, 57; weight of ancient, 46, 48-50
Henrion, Ernest, 157
Holbein, 25
Hopkins, Maj. Nevil Monroe, 262
Horter, Mr., plastron designed by, 258

Horwitz "Bullet-Proof Shield," 259
Howe, Prof. Henry M., 8, 211, 273, 276, 277, 278, 314
Hyslop, 52

Iron, for Japanese swords, source of, 35; sources of ancient armorers, 36
Italian armor, 151-156
Italian helmet, 149-151

Japan, armor wearing in, 58
Japanese armor, 172-177
Jazerans, American, 255-258; Franco-Prussian War, 106
Jessop Steel Co., 245
Johanneum, Dresden, weight of armor in, 48-50
Jones, Paul, wore corselet, 52
Joubert, Félix, 281, 307

Keegan pneumatic armor, 260
Kellogg, Mr., 273
Kelly, Ned, Australian bandit, armor worn by, 60-62
Keppel, Hon., Assistant Secretary of War, 7
Kienbusch, Lieutenant, 8, 280
Klein, Dresden armorer, 36
Kochi, Dr. O., 35
K. u. K. Sammlung, Vienna, weight of armor in, 48-50
Kosciuszko, wore armor, 52

Laboisière, Hospital of, statistics of eye wounds tabulated at, 102
Ladysmith, siege of, heavy helmets used, 60, 128
Lalain, Jacques de, 30
La Noue, 43, 48
La Personne, 72
Leather and steel compared, 228
Leathern armor, 28, 284; casque for aviators, 228; headpiece for sappers, 57; helmet, *see* Pickelhaube
Leatherwear Co. of America, 195
Le Blanc, Major, 190
Lee Tire Company body defense, American, 260
Leeming, Captain, 8
Leg armor, American, 262-264; French, 109
Le Maistre, Commandant, 8, 88
Leniewitch, General, 163
Leonardo, 25
Le Platenier, Charles, 167
Ley, Capt. C. H., 8, 288

Liberty Bell helmet, 232-233, 314
Lining, of American helmet, 218, 220, 221, 228; of French helmet, 77, 79; of German helmet, 135-137, 142; of Swiss helmet, 166; rope, for helmet, 284
Litchfield, Edward H., 211
Loris corselet, 62
Lorraine, Dukes of, armory of, 42
Ludendorff, signed letter on issue of armor to soldiers, 145
Lufbery, Major, 267

McCaw, Col. Walter D., 69, 70, 71
McGregor, Colonel, 8
MacFarland, Colonel, 268
MacIntosh, John, 8, 81, 157, 159, 160
Mackay, Clarence, 211
Mail of proof at Military Retrospective Exhibition of 1899 in Paris, 62
Mainzinger, Capt. H. D., 8, 215
Malta, arsenal at, Giants' helmets in, 128
Manganese steel, 129, 273; value of, in producing helmets, 129
Manganese Steel Shoe & Rail Co., 273
Martin, Dr. Walter, 69
Masamuné, Japanese sword artist, 35
Matchlocks, Japanese, improvements in, 172
Maxim, Sir Hiram, 62
Maximilian, Emperor of Austria, 25, 84
Merkert, J., 8
Metallurgy of ancient armor, 35, 270; ancient armorers' knowledge of, 43
Metropolitan Museum of Art, making of armor models in workshop of, 9, 211; weight of armor in, 48-50
Michael Angelo, 25
Miles, Gen. Nelson, 187
Military shield, British, 123
Military waistcoat, Italo-British, 156
Miller, Lieut. R., 60
Miller, V. Isabel, 8
Miller Rubber Co., 246
Missaglia, Antonio di, 25, 41
Missiles of low and middle velocity, armor as protection against, 68
Miyajima, Dr. M., 35
Mobile-fort, man-power, 190
Modern armor, factors determining value of, 295-312; instance of use of, 60-62; statistics showing usefulness, 69-73; testing of, 295-300
Montaigne, 48
Montez armor, with springs, 258
Montluc, 42

Morale, French helmet aid to, 82-83; visor handicap in, 104
Morax, V., 72, 102
Moreau, T., 72, 102
Mullins, W. H., Co., 162, 218, 244, 264, 268
Musée d'Artillerie, Paris, weight of armor in, 48-50
Musée de Ville, Geneva, weight of armor in, 48-50

Napoleon favors use of corselet and headpiece, 56
Neck and shoulder defense, American, 239-242
Neck-guard, silk, American tank operator's, 227; British, 111
Negroli, Philip de, 38
New England Enameling Co., 240
Nickel-manganese steel, 277; helmets, 278
Nickel-molybdenum alloy, 279
Noiselessness of armor, 310
North, Roger, 287

O'Callaghan, Gen. Desmond, 128
Oman, Ch., 30
Orient, armor wearing in, 58
Ornaments, see Symbol
Osborn, Col. Perry, 8

Payne-Galway, Sir Ralph, 42
Payot, Alphonse, cuirass mounted by, 63
Peck, Maj. Charles H., 69
Pedrail, see Mobile-fort
Peebles, Captain, 8
Penny plate armor, 260
Pershing, General, 8, 242
Picatinny Arsenal, experiments with armor at, 243
Pickelhaube, 64
Pistofilo, 44, 46
Pittsburgh Saw Co., 218
Plate armor, 112; increase in weight of, 45
Pneumatic armor, ballistic value of, 262
Poinçons used to certify excellence of armor, 41
Polack, Commandant, 8, 88, 100, 210; visor, 89-96, 210
Portable shields, French (Daigre), 179-180; German, 179; Japanese (Chiba), 174, 176
Portobank, British body defense, 123
Portuguese, armor, 161; helmet, 161
Prince's "Armored Belt," American, 260

Pritchett, Dr. Henry S., 8
Progressive Knitting Works, 195
Proof and half proof, see Tests
Proof armor of plate, 32
Proof of armor, 270
Puritan armor, 28
Push-shields, device for overcoming difficulty of movement, 187, 189; Spanish-American War, 186

Queen of the Belgians, assistance in helmet making offered by, 157

Raphael, 25
Real Armeria, Madrid, weight of armor in, 48-50
Recognition of armor, 308
Reinforcing piece for German helmet, 138; weight, 139
Reinforcing plates, use of, in ancient armor, 43
Remington Typewriter Co., 280
Resistance of, American helmet No. 7, 218; Belgian trench shield, 185; British E.O.B. corselet, 125; British helmet, 129; Corelli body shield, 126; Daigre portable shield, 180; Frati breastplate, 155; French helmet, 80; German armor plate, 183, 185; German siege helmet, 139; Military waistcoat, 156; Portuguese helmet, 161; Russian bullet-proof waistcoats, 163; steel alloys, 273, 276, 277, 278, 279, 280
Reynolds, Sir Joshua, 52
Rhodes, siege of, proof armor worn at, 39
Rice, Gen. J. H., 8
Richmond Museum, American armor in, 58
Riggs Benefaction, 9, 224
Ring-duelling, 30
Robins, Thomas, 211
Robinson, Edward, 8
Rochambeau, wore armor at Yorktown, 52
Rochelle, siege of, armor in, 33
Rome, siege of, Raffet's picture of, 57
"Roneo," British shield, 126-127
Rope armor, 284
Rose, Capt. I. St. C., 8, 316
Rosenwasser Bros., 185
Rowe breastplate, 62
Rushmore, David B., 211
Russian armor, 162, 186
Russo-Japanese War, bullet-proof waistcoats, 162; Japanese trench shield, 174

Rustkammer, Wartburg, Eisenach, weight of armor in, 48-50
Ryto Heart Protector, American, 260

St. Martin, Captain, saved by armor, 34
Saint-Remy, Lefevre de, 30
Sankey, Messrs., 158
Sap-roller, 128
Sargent, Dr. G. W., 8, 178, 268, 279
Saulx-Tavannes, Gaspard de, 43, 46
Saved by armor, historical instances, 32-34
Saxe, Marshal, recommends use of armor, 52
Schimelfenig, Colonel, 8
Security in support, 307
Selecta body armor, American, 258
Sentinel's armor, American, 246-247; German, 142-147
Senyard body defense, American, 259
Set-shields, 180; Belgian, 185; British, 182; German, 182; Italian (Ansaldo), 151; Russian, 186
Seusenhofer, 25
Shields, Adrian abdominal, 106-108; Belgian trench, 185; British body, 110-128; disadvantages in use of, 178; German use of, in advance through Belgium and France, 64; Italian, proof to machine guns, 156; Japanese, used in siege of Port Arthur, 60, trench, 174; Russian, 162, 186
Shields, see Portable shields, Push-shields, Set-shields
Shrapnel helmet, casualties saved, 68
Siege burganets proof to shot of large caliber, 46
Siege helmet, French, 86, 88; German, 138-141; in Riggs Collection, model for American helmet No. 9, 224
Silicon-nickel steel, 275
Silk armor, advantages and disadvantages of, 289-290, 292; ballistic tests, 288; resistance of, 292; used in Far East, Europe and America, 284-287; worn by Archduke Francis Ferdinand at Serajevo, 293; see also Neck-guard, Visor
Simonds, Capt. A. T., 8, 138, 182, 194, 211, 291
Simonds Saw Co., 194
Singer Motor Co., 189
Slavic helmet (Russian), 161
Smith, William (Ford Motor Co.), 8, 280
Società Anonima Italiana (Gio. Ansaldo et Cie.), 151
Soft armor, 110-112, 282-293; resistance of, 282

Spanish helmet, 171
Sparks-Withington Co., 195
Sprecher, Colonel, 165
Springs, value of, in deadening force of blow, 260
Standard Aircraft Corporation Works, 268
Star Body Defense, British, 123
Statistics of wounds, 68-73, 264
Steel, for modern armor, 272-280; resistance of, compared with leather, 228; see Alloys
Stellite, alloy, 281
Strozzi, saved by armor, 32
Swiss body armor, 163
Swiss helmet, see Helmet, Swiss
Swiss War Technical Division, 168
Sword blade, Japanese, analysis, hardness of, 35
Symbol, French helmet, 76, 78; Swiss helmet, 166
Szmyt glass armor, 260

Tabler, Mr., 215
Tachaux, Daniel, armorer and designer, 8, 36, 212, 213, 217
Tank, development of, 192; man-power, 188; operator's helmet, American, 225
Taylor, Wm. A., 8, 84, 138, 151, 175, 271, 288, 296
Taylor Co., 195
Taylor-Wharton Co., 195
Telley body defense, American, 259
Terron, 73
Test of British helmet, 130
Testing marks on armor, 44
Tests, ancient, 38-45; degrees of strength used in proof and half proof, 41, 42; modern, 294-300; types of ammunition used, 298-300
Tiberias, battle of, 30
Tilting armor, extraordinary weight of, 45
Tinney, Captain Roy S., 56
Tinsley, Francis X., 8
Titian, 25
Tower of London, Giants' helmets in, 128; leather headpieces in, 57; set-shields in, 180; weight of armor in, 48-50
Townshend, Marquis of, portrait in armor, 52
Tungsten alloy, 280

Universal Rolling Mills Co., 8, 144, 196, 244, 277
Use of armor in later times, 50-63

Van Allen, Mr., shield-like devices of, 258
Ventilation, French helmet, 78; German helmet, 136
Verney Family, memorial of, 44
Victor Amadeus IV, proof of armor of, 44
Visor, American helmet, 219-220, 228, 234; Dunand, 88, 96, 98, 99, 102; considered by Helmet Board, A.E.F., 210; handicap of, 104; Landret and Polack, 89; Polack, 89-96, 210; perforated, sensation produced in wearing, 100; silk, American, 228; usefulness for helmet, 72
Vulcano of Brescia, 43

Wagram, Prince of, wears corselet and casque, 57
Wearing armor, 314-317
Weckers, Prof., 157
Weight, ancient armor, 43, 45, 46, in various collections, 48-50; Ansaldo shield, 151; Belgian trench shield, 185; British E.O.B. corselet, 125; Corelli British body shield, 126; Daigre portable shield, 180; Dayfield Body Shield, 117; Fariselli armored waistcoat, 153; Frati breastplate, 156; French face-shields, 106; General Adrian's abdominal shield, 106; helmets, see under Helmets; Military waistcoat, 156; modern armor, 303-304; Russian breastplates, 162; steel for trench shields, 178; tilting armor, 45
Welch, Alexander McMillan, 8
White, Capt. Grove, 72
Whyler jazeran, 258
Wilkinson's Safety Service Jacket, 114
Williams, Gen. C. C., 8
Wilmer, Col. W. Holland, 236
Worcester Pressed Steel Co., 195
Worisbeverfeld defense, 259
Wounds, anatomical diagrams tabulating entry, 315; classification of, 71; frequency in location of, 70-71; proportion due to middle and low velocity projectiles, 69-71
Wrighton, W. J., 278

Yatsu, Dr. Naohidé, 176
Yielding armor, 110-112, 282-293
Younghusband Expedition to Thibet, 58

Zeglin, Casimir, silk armor, 62, 290
Zeughaus, Berlin, weight of armor in, 48-50
Zinsser, Col. Hans, 142
Zirconium steel (William Smith), 280

UNIFORMS & MODEL SOLDIERS

Along with re-enacting, military modelling is a booming part of the current explosion of interest in military history. Naturally interest in uniforms has always been at the forefront of the true student of conflcit and warfare. The Naval and Military Press publish a range of books on these two absorbing aspects of warfare and whether you are a modeller or a uniform buff or both, you will find books to suit your tastes here @ www.naval-military-press.com

---

HISTORY OF THE DRESS OF THE BRITISH SOLDIER
(FROM THE EARLIEST PERIOD TO THE PRESENT TIME)1852

An important and rare description of the history of the dress and uniforms of the British soldier (and the Indian Army) from Roman times until 1852. With many fine illustrations.

9781843428558

DRESS REGULATIONS FOR THE ARMY 1934
With Important 1938 Amendments

Sourced for reprinting from The Royal Military Academy Sandhurst, this is an historical document, covering the full details of British Army uniforms just prior to the outbreak of the second World War.

9781845749767

Badges of the British Army 1820-1987
An Illustrated Reference Guide For Collectors

Easy to slip into the coat pocket, it is the perfect companion to perusing market stalls in search of collectable items, providing immediate visual identification of each badge.

9781845749897

STANDARDS, GUIDONS AND COLOURS
OF THE COMMONWEALTH FORCES

The development of banners can be traced from the standards of ancient Greece and Rome. Fortescue states "Before the end of the 16th century the flags of infantry, from their diversity of hues, had gained the name of 'Colours'". In military organisations, the practice of carrying colours, standards or guidons are used both to act as a rallying point for troops or to mark the location of the commander. The Colours of the Infantry are a set of large flags, unique to each regiment, so that the ordinary soldier will be able to identify it straight away. This is invaluable information for the military student.

9781783314508

SHOULDER BELT PLATES AND BUTTONS

This is the standard work, describing and illustrating the British Army's shoulder plates and buttons. The design of buttons are covered up to 1911 with all their various changes, it is must for the serious collector and a gold mine of information for the enthusiastic

9781783310838

Richard Knötel's ARMIES OF EUROPE ILLUSTRATED (1890)

Classic descriptions complete with colour plates and vignettes by the renowned military artist and pioneer of the study of military uniform Richard Knötel, covering the armies of, THE BRITISH EMPIRE – THE GERMAN ARMY – AUSTRIA-HUNGARY – ITALY – FRANCE – RUSSIA – DENMARK SWEDEN AND NORWAY – SPAIN AND PORTUGAL – SWITZERLAND – HOLLAND AND BELGIUM – TURKEY AND THE STATES OF THE BALKAN PENINSULA. Knötel is still the most widely referenced artist in the study of military attire of the early modern era, and is still much in use as a prime reference source today.

9781783311750

GUIDE TO THE BRITISH ARMY'S LINE INFANTRY REGIMENTS 1881 TO 1914

The purpose of this book is to set out in an easily readable and well-illustrated form the structure of each line infantry regiment from 1881 up until the beginning of the First World War, an arrangement which can often be seen referred to as the 'Regimental Family'.

9781783316304

Die Uniformen der Braunhemden
£29.99 – £39.99

With 239 clear illustrations, mainly in colour, this is a contemporary source that was intended for the German population at large to recognise 'The soldiers of the Brown Army', as the foreword of this pre-war guide called the paramilitary organisation whose methods of violent intimidation played such a key role in Adolf Hitler's rise to power.

This is an encyclopaedic reference to the complicated Brown Shirts uniform system, that incorporates the major changes in SA uniforms and insignia that occurred in 1930 when Ernst Röhm was appointed as Chief of Staff of the SA.

9781474540063

REPRESENTATION OF THE CLOATHING OF HIS MAJESTY'S HOUSEHOLD 1742

The uniforms of the whole British Army of 1742 in 94 superb colour plates. Reprint of an original and rare book commissioned by the Duke of Cumberland, victor of Culloden, and presented to King George II.

9781843428305

www.ingramcontent.com/pod-product-compliance
Lightning Source LLC
Chambersburg PA
CBHW082315230426
43667CB00034B/2736